ITALY AT THE POLLS

ITALY AT THE POLLS

The Parliamentary Elections of 1976

Edited by
Howard R. Penniman

American Enterprise Institute for Public Policy Research
Washington, D.C.

ISBN 0-8447-3268-0

Library of Congress Catalog Card No. 77-90425

AEI Studies 169

Printed in the United States of America

CONTENTS

PREFACE   *Howard R. Penniman*

1 **ITALIAN ELECTIONS AS HOBSON'S CHOICE**
Joseph LaPalombara   **1**

Background to 1976   2
Prelude to Confrontation   13
Crisis, Dissolution, Elections   21
The Results of the Elections   31

2 **THE ITALIAN ELECTORAL PROCESS:**
THE ELECTIONS OF JUNE 1976   *Douglas Wertman*   **41**

Voter Participation   41
The Electoral Laws   44
Candidate Selection: An Introduction   51
Christian Democratic Candidate Selection   54
Candidate Selection in the Italian Communist Party   65
Preference Voting and the Chamber of
  Deputies Elections   74

3 **THE ITALIAN ELECTORATE IN THE MID-1970s:**
BEYOND TRADITION?   *Giacomo Sani*   **81**

The Setting   82
The Returns: How Much Change, Where, and
  for Whom?   89
Partisan Identifications, Party Images, and the Vote   98
The Correlates of the Vote   109
Political Traditions   115

4   CHRISTIAN DEMOCRACY:
THE END OF HEGEMONY?   *Giuseppe Di Palma*   **123**

From De Gasperi to the Crisis of the 1970s   126
The Years of the Crisis   131
The Campaign and the Elections   135
The Electoral Results   148
Governing through Abstentions   151

5   THE LONGEST CAMPAIGN: COMMUNIST PARTY
STRATEGY AND THE ELECTIONS OF 1976
Stephen Hellman   **155**

Background to the 1970s   157
Backlash and the Historic Compromise, 1971-1973   162
The Strategy of Tension Backfires, 1974-1976   168
The 1976 Elections   171
Conclusions   178

6   THE ITALIAN SOCIALIST PARTY: AN
IRREVERSIBLE DECLINE?   *Gianfranco Pasquino*   **183**

The "Socialist Area" and the Socialist Party   183
The Candidate-Selection Process   192
The Target Groups   196
The Campaign   200
The Elections   207
The Present and the Future   222

7   THE SMALLER PARTIES IN THE 1976
ITALIAN ELECTIONS   *Robert Leonardi*   **229**

Overview of the Elections   229
Before the Elections   233
Election Results and Future Prospects   249

8   THE MASS MEDIA IN THE ITALIAN ELECTIONS
OF 1976   *William E. Porter*   **259**

The Italian Journalist   259
The Italian Broadcasting System   261
The Press   266
The Media in the Campaign   273
After the Voting   283

9 ITALIAN FOREIGN POLICY:
THE EMERGENT CONSENSUS   *Robert D. Putnam*   **287**

    Economic Interdependence   289
    International Security and Italian Foreign Policy   295
    Public Opinion and Italian Foreign Policy   302
    Foreign Policy and Party Alliances   315
    Conclusions   320

10 THE CONSEQUENCES OF THE ELECTIONS:
AN INTERPRETATION   *Samuel H. Barnes*   **327**

    Winners and Losers   327
    Electoral Change and Regime Change   330
    The PCI and the Elections   333
    The Significance of the Elections for the Christian
      Democratic Party   341
    The Significance of the Elections for
      the Smaller Parties   345
    Epilogue   350

APPENDIX: Election Results, Italian Chamber of
Deputies, 1968, 1972, and 1976, and Senate, 1976
Compiled by *Richard M. Scammon*   **353**

CONTRIBUTORS   **373**

INDEX   **375**

ABBREVIATIONS

DC	Democrazia Christiana, Christian Democratic party
PCI	Partito Comunista Italiano, Italian Communist party
PSI	Partito Socialista Italiano, Italian Socialist party (1972 and 1976)
PSDI	Partito Socialista Democratico Italiano, Social Democratic party (1972 and 1976)
PSU	Partiti Socialisti Unificati, United Socialist party (PSI plus PSDI; 1968 only)
MSI	Movimento Sociale Italiano, Italian Social Movement
PDIUM	Partito Democratico Italiano di Unita Monarchica, Monarchist party (1968 only)
MSI-DN	Movimento Sociale Italiano - Destra Nazionale, Italian Social Movement - National Right (MSI plus PDIUM; 1972 and 1976)
PRI	Partito Repubblicano Italiano, Republican party
PLI	Partito Liberale Italiano, Liberal party
PSIUP	Partito Socialista Italiano di Unita Proletaria, Socialist party of Proletarian Unity (1968 and 1972)
DP	Democrazia Proletaria, Proletarian Democracy
PR	Partito Radicale, Radical party

PREFACE

Italy at the Polls: The Parliamentary Elections of 1976 is another in the series of studies of elections in selected democratic countries published by the American Enterprise Institute for Public Policy Research (AEI). The volumes already published or in progress examine elections in fifteen countries on four continents, and AEI plans to extend its coverage to the French parliamentary elections and the direct election of 355 representatives from nine countries to the European Parliament both scheduled for the first half of 1978.[1]

In 1976 the Italian Communist party (PCI) confirmed the pattern of electoral gains it has maintained since World War II. This time, the rise in its share of the popular vote was steeper than ever before— 7.2 percentage points, from 27.2 percent in 1972 to 34.4 percent in 1976. In fact, the 1976 increase was greater than the PCI's combined gains in all five of the national elections from 1953 to 1972. This additional popular support brought with it an even greater increase in the strength of the PCI in the Chamber of Deputies: the number of Communist seats rose from 179 to 228, or from 28.5 percent of the Chamber seats to 36.2 percent.

The largest Italian party, the Christian Democratic party (DC), maintained its share of the popular votes (38.8 percent) but saw its representation in the Chamber drop from 266 seats in the outgoing

---

[1] The *At the Polls* studies completed, in progress, or planned as of October 15, 1977 are as follows:

(1) published—Great Britain, Japan, France, Australia, Canada, Scandinavia (Denmark, Norway, Sweden), Italy, and *Britain Says Yes: The 1975 Referendum on the Common Market;*

(2) in progress—Germany, Japan, Israel, Ireland, Spain, India, and Greece; and

(3) planned—the European Parliament (1978) and France (1978).

legislature to 262 in the new one—a decline from 42.3 to 41.7 percent of the seats. The third largest party, the Socialist party (PSI), gained ever so slightly in its popular vote (up .1 percentage point to 9.7 percent), but like the DC lost four seats in the Chamber. The numerous smaller parties together garnered only 17.1 percent of the votes and 13 percent of the Chamber seats. Clearly, the largest parties gained or held their own in the popular vote at the expense of the smaller parties. Giacomo Sani's analysis in Chapter 3 of this volume shows where the votes came from and where they went. In general, the results followed the rule set down by Douglas Rae: "Electoral systems tend to award more than proportionate shares of parliamentary seats to parties with large shares of the vote, and to award less than proportionate shares of seats to parties with smaller shares of the vote." [2] Small parties are better off under Italy's proportional representation system, with its unusually small quota for winning seats, than they are in most countries, yet they still get short shrift. While a group like the Radical party, with its 1.1 percent of the vote, and four seats, fared better than it would have under most other electoral systems, it still took less than its proportionate share of the seats.

The Christian Democrats and the Communists won 73.2 percent of the total vote in 1976. As Joseph LaPalombara notes in Chapter 1, this suggests that Italy is far less a multiparty state today than it was at the time of the first national vote in 1946, when the two largest parties won only 54 percent of the total vote. Other analysts too have expressed the view that Italy is moving toward a two-party system. In this connection it is worth observing that the total vote of DC and PCI fell just 1.9 percentage points below the combined vote in 1974 of the Labour and Conservative parties in Britain, once cited as the finest example of the two-party system.

The PCI's electoral success forced important improvements in the party's position in Parliament. Pietro Ingrao was elected speaker of the Chamber of Deputies, the first PCI member to hold so high a parliamentary position. The party also received its share of committee chairmanships for the first time. More important than these formal signs of success, of course, was the vastly greater role in determining national policy that the party derived from its agreement to abstain from voting and thus allow a DC government to function. As long as that government operates on PCI sufferance it will have to consider the Communists' views.

---

[2] Douglas Rae, *The Political Consequences of Electoral Laws*, rev. Ed. (New Haven and London: Yale University Press, 1971), p. 179.

Further, as Sani shows, the PCI can look to the future with considerable optimism. Survey data suggests that 60 percent of the newly enfranchised voters—the 5,304,626 persons who cast their first ballots in national parliamentary elections in 1976—favored the parties of the left. The PCI can probably expect to win over half of that left support. Sani also stresses that the party commitments of most Italians tend to remain constant over long periods, which further reinforces the PCI's prospects.

The Communists' success, however, was not universally applauded. Sani quotes opinion survey findings to the effect that 54 percent of Italians who held views on the matter "believed that the PCI wanted to limit freedom." LaPalombara comments on the same doubts: "Those in Italy who fear the growth of the left," he says, "are doubly concerned because it is the Communist component that is growing. . . . These fears are not merely internal to Italy; they are vocalized, sometimes stridently, abroad as well," as in Secretary of State Henry Kissinger's "thinly veiled allusions to the dire consequences that might flow from the PCI's accession to power."[3]

Students of Italian politics differ about the extent to which this fear of the Communists' coming to power in Italy is justified. In Chapter 9, for example, Robert D. Putnam argues that in the sensitive area of foreign policy it is a mistake to ask, can the Communists be trusted? Instead, he says, the question should be

where do their interests lie? The penalty for transgressing the constraints traced in this chapter is not a guilty conscience, but political failure. Despite the PCI's recent celebrity, it remains a minority party in a second-rank, dependent nation. If such a party is to have any hope of success, it must adapt realistically to domestic and international constraints, both economic and political, guided by Thucydides' maxim that while the strong do what they can, the weak do what they must.

Thus, it is not surprising that many non-Communist Italian politicians find queries about the sincerity of the PCI leadership misplaced. "The impetus [for the new line] lies in reality, in the facts of economics, geography and Italian society," said one influential leader privately after the elec-

---

[3] See Henry Kissinger, *Communist Parties in Western Europe: Challenge to the West* (Washington, D.C.: American Enterprise Institute, 1977), *passim*, for a statement of his views on Western European Communist parties a year after the Italian elections.

tion. "It is in the logic of things," explained another. "Any other line would simply be stupid."

Samuel H. Barnes writes in Chapter 10,

> What the party will eventually do is almost certainly not known to anyone, including the leading actors themselves, but study after study by social scientists, repeated statements by party spokesmen, and the viewpoints of scores of important non-Communist Italian leaders all suggest that the party is very much devoted to the procedures of the Italian constitutional system. . . . It seems highly likely that the present Communist leadership and rank and file are—in principle—overwhelmingly devoted to the constitutional order and the rights and liberties it defines. That situations might arise in which there were conflicts between these and other equally valued goals—such as reform or the maintenance of power—should be acknowledged. Similar conflicts, of course, could arise for substantial portions of the Christian Democratic party.

The Socialists, who had precipitated the elections by leaving the government in which they had been a coalition partner for more than a decade, lost both seats and prestige. The PSI was psychologically damaged by opinion polls that inaccurately forecast significant Socialist gains while consistently underestimating the DC support. On the basis of inflated expectations, the party's secretary general, Francesco De Martino, publicly stated that, if the situation required, the PSI "would not evade the responsibility of providing the country with a government." As Gianfranco Pasquino notes in Chapter 6, this offer to lead a new government came from the smallest Socialist party in Western Europe. In 1972, even before the sharp rise in the Communist vote, the PSI had received only about one-third as many votes as the Communist party. The contrast between the bold picture painted by the leadership and the reality of lost seats in the Chamber forced De Martino to resign as secretary general three weeks after the elections.

One interesting and posssibly unique characteristic of Italian political analysis is great concern about the rate of candidate turnover from one election to another. Analysts of Italian politics regard a rapid turnover of candidates as good; lack of turnover or slow change they regard as bad. No other western country places so much emphasis on what sometimes seems to be change for its own sake. Americans, for example, may discuss the advantages of incumbency that accrue to a politician seeking renomination or reelection, but unless a candidate is very old, they seldom suggest that he should drop out of a race simply because he has served two, three, or even ten terms. Indeed, the incumbent campaigns in both the primary and the general election on the advantage he derives from his long experience. In Britain, where the candidate-selection process is very different from the American, there is also a respect for experience that helps the incumbent gain nomination and election. As Austin Ranney has pointed out, "almost all incumbent M.P.s who wish to stand again are readopted, usually without challenge or difficulty." In the general election of February 1974, he reported, "in 558 of Britain's 635 constituencies (88 percent), one of the candidates was an incumbent." [4] The situation is not radically different in most of the countries with proportional representation: the incumbents are usually found in safe positions near the top of the party lists.

In Italy it is said to be important to offer the voters fresh faces. For a variety of reasons, only the Communist party consistently satisfies this demand. The smaller parties have little room for maneuvers; they must depend on their few well-known leaders to retain their seats. The Christian Democrats, meanwhile, are so divided by factionalism, their method of choosing candidates is so decentralized, the strength of individual candidates is so great in some regions (often precisely because they have long held office) that rapid turnover in the DC slate is difficult to accomplish. A further deterrent to rapid turnover is the party's statutory requirement that at least 74 of the 180 members of the central committee be members of Parliament.

In 1976, the DC ran ninety-nine new candidates for the Chamber of Deputies and the Senate, far more than usual. Giuseppe Di Palma notes in Chapter 4:

> The DC is not a tight party of cadres like the PCI, which considers its members of Parliament party workers whom it can regularly reassign to other party functions. . . . Further, the [DC] members of Parliament with the longest tenure are also those that occupy the most important positions in government, in the parastate, in local politics, and in the party itself. . . . An effective renovation of this parliamentary contingent would require eliminating many of those with the longest experience of government—with seemingly grave consequences for the party.

The Communist party, by contrast, passes the candidate-changing

---

[4] Austin Ranney, "Selecting the Candidates," in Howard R. Penniman, ed., *Britain at the Polls: The Parliamentary Elections of 1974* (Washington, D.C.: American Enterprise Institute, 1975), p. 47.

test with flying colors. Party policy, as Douglas A. Wertman points out in describing candidate selection in Chapter 2, calls for a turnover of "at least one-third of its delegates and senators at each election." Only 17.5 percent of the PCI deputies elected in 1976 (40 persons), he says, had served three or more terms. Wertman suggests a number of basic reasons why the PCI is uniquely successful in this respect. In particular, he notes that "within the PCI, serving in Parliament is not seen as superior to other kinds of work for or within the party" and that the party "places a high value" on having deputies and senators who have previously served at the regional and local levels. Likewise, the party values the experience of members of Parliament as a background for holding local and regional office.

Wertman says, "Compared with the DC's relatively chaotic and well-publicized candidate-selection process, that of the PCI is efficient, well organized, and relatively hidden." The national secretariat and the organizational affairs section of the national party bureaucracy do "the major work in drawing up the PCI's candidate list." Local organizations are consulted, but the decisions are made by leading officials of the party.

> The national leadership, in particular the secretariat members directly responsible and, of course, major leaders such as Secretary General Enrico Berlinguer, Gian Carlo Pajetta, member of both the secretariat and executive committee, Giorgio Amendola, and others from the executive committee, play a central role in the selection of the "national" candidates and of the *capolista* [that is, the head of the list on the ballot] of each district (and may have strong influence over the choice of candidates for their home regions). The top national officials also play a major role in determining which candidates should be the definite winners, the possible winners, and the definite losers.

Elsewhere Wertman makes the point again, saying "the national leadership, particularly in the secretariat and the organizational affairs section, directly names a substantial number of the candidates and carefully controls the process."

If the purpose of rapid turnover is to attract voters, the case is still to be made, for it seems generally true that the long-term member who has served his region well is a better bet to draw voters than a new candidate who has built no reputation of service. In any case, Sani has persuasively argued that "electoral choice is, in the overwhelming majority of cases, a straightforward function of party identification. Parties rather than candidates or issues are the salient objects, the ingredients of the voters' decisions." He suggests a number of reasons for this judgment.

> First, the characteristics of the electoral system focus the voters' attention on parties. . . . Electoral districts are rather large, many parties contest the election, and each of them presents many candidates. . . . Second, electoral campaigns do not pivot around a single issue or a set of specific issues. The appeals made by the parties tend to be general in nature and are couched in rather abstract language. . . . Third, incumbents, even in the most visible offices . . . are typically seen as party representatives who lead a particular coalition of parties. Short tenure in office, with frequent reshuffling of cabinets . . . further decreases the personalistic elements. Last, the bulk of the electorate has been rather poorly informed about political affairs and has tended to view the protagonists of the political process in black and white terms.

If the purpose of the rapid turnover of candidates is to offer the voters a chance to choose new policy makers, then, at least in the case of the PCI, it is of limited value. The top leadership of the party, not the ordinary member of Parliament, determines policy as well as candidates, and it is precisely in the leadership positions that there is least turnover of personnel. While PCI deputies can be moved in and out of office rather like interchangeable parts, without in any way affecting the functioning of the PCI in government, the membership of the party's policy-making bodies, the secretariat and directorate, is relatively stable. Further, the PCI members of Parliament who have served three or more terms include members of the secretariat, the directorate, and other party leaders. Berlinguer himself has not served in the legislature or held other public positions for a number of years, but no one doubts that his is the strongest policy voice in the party.

Ten authors have contributed to this volume discussing the issues and events leading up to the campaign and election and analyzing the significance of the results. Joseph LaPalombara introduces the reader to the postwar politics of Italy. Douglas A. Wertman describes the candidate-selection processes of the various parties and the rules for the conduct of elections. Giacomo Sani analyzes the political attitudes of the Italian people and the vote changes since the preceding election in 1972. Giuseppe Di Palma, Stephen M. Hellman, and Gianfranco Pasquino contribute separate chapters on the Christian Democratic, the Communist, and the Socialist parties. Robert Leonardi describes the lesser parties. William Porter covers recent developments in the Italian media and analyzes their role in the elections. Robert Putnam contributes an essay on Italian foreign policy with special reference to changing Communist party attitudes on relations between Italy and the West. Samuel H. Barnes, in the concluding chapter, summarizes materials presented in earlier chapters and offers some perspectives on the future. Richard M. Scammon has provided electoral data covering the three most recent national elections.

Sani and Barnes offered much helpful advice during the planning stages of the project. Angelo Codevilla deserves special thanks for providing both advice and data as does John Lenczowski for excellent research assistance. Joseph Privitera earned high marks for his assistance in straightening out some difficult translation problems.

HOWARD R. PENNIMAN

1

ITALIAN ELECTIONS AS HOBSON'S CHOICE

Joseph LaPalombara

The Italian flair for the dramatic and the catastrophic finds its most persistent expression in politics. This seems entirely rational: historically speaking, politics has far outstripped both nature and Italy's enemies in bringing catastrophe down on the heads of hapless citizens. If people generally get the government they deserve, then this law seems to work most sardonically and grotesquely in Italy, creating some of the most Byzantine political patterns known to the Western world.

Drama and the fear of catastrophe are contagious, particularly when they tap our own uneasiness about power and power holders. They fuel our capacity to distort reality so that it seems to conform to our most disturbing nightmares. Western reactions to Italian national elections must be seen against this backdrop. Only then can we appreciate why the most dire predictions about Italian democracy —offered in Italy or abroad—have so far failed to materialize.

A clearer perspective on Italian politics is more necessary now than ever, in view of the widespread concern over the prospect of the Italian Communists coming to share power. Recent electoral results, particularly those of June 20, 1976, suggest that the voter shopping around for better government faces Hobson's Choice: whereas there are many parties among which to choose, circumstances dictate that the only real option is the Communist party. If this is so, the potentiality for genuine drama is exceedingly high.

In the preparation of this chapter, I have had the benefit of comments by Alberto Spreafico and Giuseppe Di Palma. I have also benefited by sharp-eyed editorial assistance from Howard Penniman and the staff of the American Enterprise Institute.

Not since the "Christ-or-communism" confrontation of 1948 have Italian elections elicited more international attention. In April 1948, Italian voters were preoccupied by the brutal Communist takeover in Czechoslovakia a few weeks earlier. Electoral posters depicted a menacing Stalin and asked whether voters wanted *Baffone* (the big moustache) to come to Rome, too. On that occasion the Catholic Church fielded an army of activists in the service of the Christian Democratic party (DC), making a mockery of Stalin's derisive remark about the Pope's lack of military divisions. The DC was returned to power with a parliamentary majority, there to begin almost three decades of political hegemony that many today will argue have been irresponsibly squandered.

By 1976 the fear of Stalinism had largely abated. Like Stalin, several million Italians who had voted in 1948 were no longer alive. The cold war of the Acheson and Dulles years had been replaced by Kissinger's détente. At home the Italian Communist party (PCI), in its political rhetoric at least, only faintly resembled the PCI of 1948. In recent years vast sectors of the Catholic Church itself had shown an unprecedented willingness to remain aloof from internal politics and refrain from interfering with the political dialogue that was growing up between Catholics and Communists.

There were other notable contrasts as well. The years between 1948 and 1976 were an era of unusual social and economic transformations. Early postwar efforts at economic reconstruction, shaky and problematical at first, accelerated during the period of the *miracolo economico*. During these years illiteracy was reduced to European standards, and new social welfare laws greatly mitigated Italian anxieties about living and dying. Once an overwhelmingly agricultural country, Italy was rapidly brought into the small circle of advanced industrial societies. By the early 1970s, the consumerist impulse was overpowering; an avalanche of goods and services rolled down the peninsula, leaving in its wake a standard of living that voters in 1948 would have considered an impossible dream.

How then can one account for the sense of foreboding that many in Italy and abroad expressed about the 1976 elections? We can readily identify a number of contributing factors, some of which will be treated in depth by other contributors to this volume.

Background to 1976

Economic Crisis. In 1976, Italy's economic miracle seemed buried in the past, with no one able to say how it had begun, what had stopped it, or how it might be brought back to work its wonders anew. Italy's stagflation seemed out of hand, with levels of unemployment unmatched since the early 1950s and inflation persisting at well above 20 percent. The balance of payments was so far out of kilter that the Italian *lira*, once among Europe's strongest currencies, continued to slide toward record lows, having reached record highs against the dollar only a few years earlier. Within the Organization for Economic Cooperation and Development (OECD), Italy, along with Ireland and foundering industrial countries like Great Britain, had one of the lowest rates of economic growth.

Internal production, consumption, and monetary and fiscal patterns were not reassuring to other countries and financial institutions, especially those called upon to bail Italy out of its serious debt situation. The petroleum revolution of 1973 was more than offset by the Italians' insatiable appetite for petroleum products. Even gasoline prices approaching $2.50 per gallon in 1976 failed to persuade Italians to leave their newly acquired Fiats at home. Among other things, archaic and chaotic systems of public transportation made such a prospect highly unattractive.

Italy's balance of payments was aggravated by rising costs of production fueled by wage levels that were themselves inflated by extraordinarily heavy social welfare payments and a sliding-scale, automatic wage-adjustment system that most economists consider insane. Most trade union leaders, on the other hand, consider the sliding scale to be inviolable. Industrial productivity was in serious decline, owing to strikes, the proliferation of holidays permitting long weekends (which Italians call *i ponti*, the bridges), and one of the highest labor absentee rates in the industrial world. A growing number of foreign firms responded to this situation by trying to close up their affiliates in Italy and go elsewhere.

Italian newspapers wrote alarmingly about these conditions. While the British were wondering whether their economy was really as sick as Italy's, the Italian press was asking whether Italy was really the Continent's Britain. Beyond these speculations several things seemed ominously plain to many Italians. First, the government appeared unwilling or unable to cope with the crises. Second, the trade unions, no longer the atomized weaklings that once permitted a low wage policy in industry, were unwilling to accept economic regeneration measures whose burden would fall heavily on the working class. Third, the Communist party, for all of the vague abstractness of its economic prescriptions, looked like the only major party with the will and the power to move resolutely into this economic morass.

Radicalization. Political radiation from Italy's great crisis period—the "hot autumn" of 1969—was still strong in 1976. Radical student groups continued to disrupt the universities and many of the *liceos* where most students prepare for university. The failure of governments to reform the educational system, the decline of traditional forms of discipline among both teachers and students, and the dismal employment prospects awaiting university graduates made this environment ripe for unabated agitation by the more radicalized groups. The efforts of the Communist party to harness these students to more disciplined forms of political intervention remain only partially successful. For many of them, the PCI itself is the enemy because of its apparent support for the hated system.

The events of the late 1960s radicalized the trade unions too. Radicalization went hand in hand with trade union efforts to reduce the ideological fragmentation that had earlier been their greatest weakness. It was encouraged as well by growing trade union independence from the political parties, including the PCI, that had earlier guided their behavior. In the heyday of trade union resurgence, an accommodating Parliament enacted the 1969 *Statuto dei Lavoratori*, a law whose interpretation by the courts has made labor transfers, disciplining for unwarranted absenteeism, and even dismissal for cause next to impossible.[1]

Today, one of the most perplexing unknowns in Italian politics has a double-barreled explosive potential: Can the discredited political parties bend trade union leaders to their policies? And if so, can the latter really deliver compliant behavior from their own union members? Italy's factories, like its schools, are arenas where the radicalized young are *not* inclined to follow either the DC or the PCI; both of these parties are identified as the establishment and therefore as major parts of the problem. Although this problem can be overdrawn, it is noteworthy that both the Christian Democrats and the Communist party are hard at work trying to bring their respective labor confederations under more disciplined control.

Completely alienated from the establishment are the members of the extraparliamentary left and the terrorist groups of left and right who have greatly added to Italy's political turmoil. The ter-

---

[1] One of the law's authors, acknowledging all of this, insists that he cannot be held responsible for the idiotic, ideologically motivated decisions of the courts. Nevertheless, the Workers' Law has now become a major stumbling block for any serious effort to rationalize and regenerate Italian industry. On this and related points, see Tiziano Treu, ed., *L'uso politico dello statuto dei lavoratori* [The political use of the Workers' Law] (Bologna: Il Mulino, 1975).

4

rorist groups are far from defunct, as many Italians had come to hope or believe they were. Before and following the elections of June 1976 they stepped up kidnappings, political assassinations, massive jailbreaks, and indiscriminate bombings.[2] Their message is clear: violence, not voting, is the way to achieve the kind of society they prefer.

Political Scandals. Long a staple of Italian politics, political scandals reached frightening proportions in the 1970s even by Italian standards. Scandal seemed to reach everywhere, touching the military and police establishments, the judiciary, major financial institutions, the national intelligence service, the political parties, and even former prime ministers and cabinet members. Between exposés, bombings, shoot-outs with the police, jailbreaks, rampant strikes, and impending economic disaster, there was little room for the more commonplace preelectoral events that are normally covered by the mass media.

The roll call of scandalous acts, proved or alleged, boggles the imagination and can only be sampled here. Police and judiciary were implicated in obstructing or papering over investigations into the Mafia; leading military figures were widely suspected of having plotted one or more coups d'état; key witnesses mysteriously died of poisoning or other causes while held in custody; massively corrupt municipal political bosses somehow succeeded in being reinstated as political barons; investigations in the United States pointed to millions of dollars paid to political parties or individuals, in bribes, extortions, or a combination of both.

Italians speculated before the elections about which of the Christian Democrats might be the "Antelope-Cobbler" of the multinational Lockheed scandal.[3] Some were shocked to discover that the power of money had managed to penetrate to the highest levels of govern-

---

[2] Bombings reached such a high level by December 1976 that Prime Minister Andreotti was led to call an unprecedented emergency meeting of all "constitutional" parties (from the Liberals on the right to the PCI and the Radicals on the left, see footnote 36) in order to explore what measures might be taken to quell these disturbances. On the heels of this meeting, Communist and some other political leaders insisted that the prime minister call a similar meeting regarding the country's economic crises. See, for example, the pages of *Il Corriere della Sera, La Voce Repubblicana, La Stampa, Il Messaggero, La Repubblica, Avanti!* and *L'Unità* for the period December 16-20, 1976.

[3] In Italy as elsewhere the Lockheed Corporation paid out huge sums of money to induce the sale of aircraft to governments. In Italy it is still unclear whether the "Antelope-Cobbler" (the code name used by Lockheed for one of its beneficiaries) was the president of Italy or one of two other men, both former premiers.

ment, infecting the most sensitive sectors of the nation's military, defense, and security establishments. Among the leading political parties, only the PCI could boldly state that it was untainted by these events.

As Italy's dominant political party, the DC was at the center of this storm. For example, most of the political contributions made by Esso Italiana (but made by many other firms, some of them Italian, as well) were known to have gone to that party's leaders. Most instances of rampant municipal corruption, including the extreme case of Naples, centered on local powerholders who were Christian Democratic notables. Temporizing arrangements with the Mafia in Sicily and Calabria inevitably involved some collusion by DC organizations in those places or by Christian Democrats in charge of ministries at Rome.

Under the Christian Democrats, political patronage—known as *sottogoverno*—reached remarkable levels. The party faithful have colonized an estimated 60,000 jobs, most of them extremely well paid, in a vast mosaic of public and semipublic agencies and publicly owned industrial enterprises. Much more than the DC's legislative contingent, it is the network of *sottogoverno* that provides the foundations for the Christian Democratic regime.[4]

Side by side with *sottogoverno* one finds clientelistic politics. The phrase implies a patron-client relationship where voters identify with an individual political leader or faction, support him or it uncritically in whatever policies and strategies are pursued, and expect favors in return. Clientelism, very much like the American machine politics of an earlier era, is geographically circumscribed, so that the patrons and clients differ as one moves from one area to another. Like *sottogoverno*, it is considered a major obstacle to coherent national political programs designed to effect basic changes.[5]

As June 20 approached, the evidence was strong that the intolerance of these aspects of politics expressed by the voters in the local elections of 1975 would be registered at the national level.

---

[4] On the importance of the public sector to the Christian Democrats, see Giuseppe Di Palma, *Surviving without Governing: The Italian Parties in Parliament* (Berkeley: University of California Press, 1977), esp. chap. 7; Franco Cazzola, "I pilastri del regime: gli enti pubblici di sicurezza sociale" [The regime's pillars: social security agencies], *Rivista italiana di sociologia*, vol. 17 (July-September 1976), pp. 421-447.

[5] The clientelistic system of Italian politics is nicely described by Percy Allum, *Politics and Society in Postwar Naples* (Cambridge: Cambridge University Press, 1973); Luigi Graziano, "Patron-Client Relationships in Southern Italy," *European Journal of Political Research*, vol. 1 (April 1973), pp. 3-34. See also the chapter by Giuseppe Di Palma in this volume.

Failure of Reform and Renewal. Some of Italy's most poignant jokes have to do with political reforms. From the late 1920s under fascism to the present, for example, well over twenty parliamentary committees have been appointed to reform the Italian national bureaucracy. All of them have failed, but some in more Kafkaesque fashion than others. One of them turned into a new *ministry* for bureaucratic reform and quickly became yet another center of bureaucratic patronage. Italy's bloated, arrogant, inefficient, parasitic public administration is not only a continuous drain on the economy; because it affects the citizen every day, it comes to symbolize the malaise of the Italian political system and the disdain in which political institutions are widely held.

Similarly, there have been at least a dozen proposals for the reform of Italy's educational institutions in recent years. Some of these proposals were quite sensible; all of them got bogged down in deep ideological conflict over the place of education in society. The government's solution was eventually to enact a *riforma stralcio,* which with a bit of license can be rendered as "rip-off reform." Its dubious achievement is to have ensured that Italian higher education, bloated by several thousand persons of questionable scholarly merit who automatically gained tenure, will remain mired in mediocrity for at least a generation.

If genuine bureaucratic or educational (or fiscal) reforms are rare occurrences, the so-called renewals of political parties are even greater rarities. Rather than renew themselves, Italian political parties tend to split, like amoebas, believing that strength lies in fragmentation. The postwar history of Italy's minor political parties, including the socialist parties to whom so many people looked for democratic leadership, has been one of continual fragmentation, with periodic, half-hearted efforts to put the pieces back together and start over.

Renewal—*rinovamento*—has been the unfulfilled promise of the Christian Democrats. Held together first by the cement of Catholicism and later by the attractiveness of sharing power and patronage, this party has never felt it overpoweringly necessary to renew its organization, its cadres, its basic economic and social attitudes, or its top leadership. These latter are leaders of factions, or *correnti,* political notables with clientelistic followings engaged in tenuous, uneasy, and shifting alliances with each other. Only recently have the party rules been changed to make it less attractive than in the past to form yet another faction.[6] In the light of its recent electoral decline and the real danger it faced of losing its status as Italy's leading party, the DC in 1976 promised more emphatically than ever before to undertake a general internal overhauling.

Other parties have been even less successful at renewal. The Socialist party (PSI) continues to be rent by its own factions, which persist even in the teeth of the party's ominous electoral decline. When the party's extreme-left faction could not persuade the others not to join with the DC, except on the basis of clear ideologically determined concessions from the latter, it split away in 1963 and formed the Socialist party of Proletarian Unity (PSIUP, or Proletarian Socialists). A later effort by the PSI to reunify with the Social Democratic party (PSDI, or Democratic Socialists) turned out to be abortive, falling apart after the elections of 1968 on the issue of whether, how, and when to do business with the Communists. The PSDI has long been bogged down by a factional struggle of its own and by growing evidence that several of its major leaders have been involved in corrupt behavior.

The Liberal party (PLI), once a haven for progressive civil libertarians, has been unable to adapt its economic and social ideology to the conditions of the twentieth century. Having split once in the 1950s, it remains faction-ridden despite its precipitous electoral decline. The PLI went from 7.0 percent of the vote in 1963 to 3.9 percent in 1972. Attempts in 1976 to bring in a new group of party leaders with a better sense of electoral survival seemed to come much too late to be effective. Electoral results, as we shall see, confirm this. (The Liberal party schism in the 1950s led to the creation of a short-lived Radical party. The party reemerged in the early 1970s and conducted a vigorous campaign in 1976, with surprising success.)

Factions exist within the small Republican party (PRI) as well, somewhat moderated only by the overpowering influence of Ugo La Malfa, the only effective leader the party has had for almost thirty years. As for the parties of the right, the Monarchists split in 1958, declined at the polls, and their remnants (reunited in 1972) wound up joining the neo-Fascist MSI, to form the National Right in 1976,

---

[6] There is a growing and interesting literature on the factional structure of the DC and other Italian parties. See, for example, Franco Cazzola, "Partiti, correnti, e voto di preferenza" [Parties, factions and the preferential vote], *Rivista italiana di scienza politica*, vol. 2 (December 1972), pp. 569-588, and the items by Sartori, Passigli and Zincone cited in footnote 2 of the Cazzola article. Compare R. Zariski, *Italy: The Politics of Uneven Development* (Hinsdale, Ill.: The Dryden Press, 1972); Giovanni Sartori, *Parties and Party Systems* (Cambridge: Cambridge University Press, 1976).

adding still more factions to that fissiparous organization. In 1976 the MSI suffered a new schism on the heels of its striking electoral decline. Even the tiny parties on the extreme left are faction ridden, torn by fissiparous tendencies.

For the voters, the only party that seems to have been able to renew itself (or at least to keep up with the times) without falling apart is the PCI.

Fear of Communism. A last and certainly not least important factor that made the electoral climate exceedingly tense in 1976 was the possibility that the PCI would come to power. In the previous national elections (May 1972) that prospect had seemed quite remote and the Communists had registered less than 30 percent of the vote for the lower chamber. Even with the votes of the Socialists and the Socialist party of Proletarian Unity, the left won only 38.7 percent of all the votes cast in 1972. Furthermore, those same elections gave the center-left, which had been hobbling along in coalition since the famous "opening to the left" of the early sixties, almost 60 percent of the votes and the seats in the Chamber of Deputies. The center-left, created in 1963, brought together the DC, the PSDI, the PRI, and the PSI. Great expectations at the beginning were progressively dashed by growing evidence that the Socialists' participation in government did not make all that much difference. If the center-left is now dead, the mortal blow was inflicted in early 1976 when the PSI precipitated a cabinet crisis.

The dissolution of Parliament in 1972 was the first in the Republic's history. Despite this fact, a severe recession, and the policy failures of the center-left, little happened at the polls in 1972 to suggest momentous change. On the contrary, commentaries on the electoral results centered on the surprising stability of the Italian vote.[7] The social and economic transformation of the 1960s did not seem to have affected significantly the distribution of votes among the parties.

Nevertheless, on closer observation the 1972 results seemed to confirm several interesting patterns. To begin with, in 1972 Italy's was less a multiparty system than it had been in 1946 or 1948. Although one could count more than ten parties, two of them, the DC and the PCI, gathered about two-thirds of the vote. In 1946 these

[7] For extended analyses of Italian voting behavior in 1972 and observations on the inflexibility of the party vote, see Mario Caciagli and Alberto Spreafico, *Un sistema politico alla prova* [A political system on trial] (Bologna: Il Mulino, 1975), especially the chapters by Caciagli, Spreafico, Sani, Cazzola, and Barnes in the Introduction and Part I.

two parties had accounted for only 54 percent of the active electorate. This trend was to accelerate in 1976, at the expense of all the minor parties. In that year, DC and PCI together received 73.1 percent of the vote. Thus, it is now possible to show that Italy's is as much a two-party system as Britain's, with the major protagonists being the Communists and the Christian Democrats.

The 1972 results showed the PCI continuing its slow but linear rise in electoral appeal. Far from being the party of poverty and protest many Western observers had wishfully claimed, the PCI showed a remarkable capacity to broaden its electoral following. Thirty years ago the party received only 18.9 percent of the vote, and its power base was definitely concentrated in central and northern Italy. By 1972, it had reached 27.2 percent of the electors and had achieved this in large part by becoming a genuinely *national*, as opposed to a sectional, party. Once relatively weak in the south and on the islands of Sicily and Sardinia, the PCI could now show that its electoral prowess was about as evenly spread as that of the DC. (See Table 1–1).

Thus, while the PCI made slight progress in the north and jumped ahead about 40 percent in the central "red belt," it more than doubled its electoral proportions elsewhere in the country. This Communist penetration of the areas south of Rome has been the single most important transformation in Italian electoral geography since the birth of the Republic.

Another important aspect of the 1972 elections was the apparently growing electoral gap between the PCI and the socialist parties.

Table 1–1

ITALIAN COMMUNIST PARTY PERCENTAGE OF THE VOTE FOR CHAMBER OF DEPUTIES, 1946, 1972, AND 1976, BY GEOGRAPHIC REGION

Region	PCI Vote (in percentages)			Difference, 1976 over 1946 (in percentage points)
	1946	1972	1976	
North	22.4	26.5	33.5	11.1
Central	24.7	34.4	41.4	16.7
South	10.8	24.4	32.4	21.6
Islands	10.2	22.2	29.5	19.3

Source: Alberto Spreafico, "Le elezioni politiche del 7 maggio 1972," *Rivista italiana di scienza politica*, vol. 2 (December 1972), pp. 525-568; official electoral statistics for 1976.

The latter include the Proletarian Socialists to the left of the PCI, the Socialist party itself, which remains close to the PCI even if it has joined in several DC-led coalitions since the early sixties, and the Democratic Socialists, long antagonistic toward the PCI and a mainstay of center-left and center-right postwar coalition governments. Between the last two elections the Radical party (PR) gained national prominence over the divorce referendum. It too has maintained a highly antagonistic stand toward what it considers blatant PCI collusion with the DC against civil rights.

Many Italians find disquieting the tendency of the PCI to corner larger and larger proportions of the left vote. The magnitude of this tendency through 1972, and then 1976, is displayed by Table 1–2. In the years since 1946, the left as a whole has gradually increased its proportion of the vote. But, while the PCI has improved its position among the left parties, the PSI has suffered an almost calamitous decline. The magnitude of this change can best be measured against the electoral distributions in a country like France, where the Socialists outnumber the Communists by two to one: more than the reverse is now true in Italy. Those in Italy who fear the growth of the left are doubly concerned because it is the Communist component that is growing.

Table 1–2

COMMUNIST, SOCIALIST, AND COMBINED SOCIALIST PERCENTAGES OF THE VOTE FOR THE CHAMBER OF DEPUTIES, 1946–1976

(in percentages)

Party	Election							
	1946	1948a	1953	1958	1963	1968	1972	1976
PCI	18.9	—	22.6	22.7	25.3	26.9	27.1	34.4
PSI	—	—	12.7	14.2	13.8	14.5	9.6	9.6
Total socialist voteb	20.7	—	17.2	18.7	19.9	19.0	16.6	13.0

a The PSI and the PCI ran as a single party in 1948, so no comparison is possible for that year.

b Includes the PSI plus: in 1946, the Socialist party of Proletarian Unity; in 1968, the Unitary Socialist party (PSI and PSDI) and the PSIUP; in 1972, the PSI, the PSDI, and the PSIUP; in 1976, the PSI and the PSDI.

Source: Table constructed from data contained in Mario Caciagli and Alberto Spreafico, *Un sistema politico alla prova* [A political system on trial] (Bologna: Il Mulino, 1975), pp. 66-67; official electoral statistics for 1976.

These fears are not merely internal to Italy; they are vocalized, sometimes stridently, abroad as well. In the spring of 1976 Western newspapers showed great concern about the imminent Italian elections. Some of them viewed the prospect of the PCI in power with as much alarm as they had expressed a generation earlier. Others condemned the efforts of American officials to influence Italian voters. The American secretary of state's thinly veiled allusions to the dire consequences that might flow from the PCI's accession to power were widely reported, favorably or otherwise. In some cases, the same newspaper seemed to shift its attitude depending on who happened to be writing the article or editorial. On the whole, there seemed to be agreement that outsiders should eschew attempts to influence domestic Italian politics and, moreover, that their attempts could have little effect.[8]

In Italy, overseas reactions received extensive mass media coverage, and Italians themselves understandably debated, often polemically, what might result from the PCI's winning a share in the government at Rome. At the end of May, the Communist-leaning newspaper *Paese Sera* sponsored a debate among four leading European foreign correspondents in Italy.[9] The headline read "Foreigners Judge Us." All four agreed that the forthcoming elections carried momentous historical significance. They agreed, too, that it might be healthy for Italy if the DC were taught a lesson and cut down to size. There was less agreement among them regarding what might be the necessary or sufficient conditions for bringing the Communists to power.

Among Italians verbal battles raged about the implications of a PCI victory for domestic and international politics. Domestically there were predictions that democracy would be reinforced or that the Stalinists in the PCI would take over the party and create a dictatorial regime. Debates proliferated, and are still in full swing, regarding what might be the practical meaning of the PCI's describing itself as committed to "political pluralism."[10] One major worry

---

[8] See, for example, *Corriere della Sera's* report on the *Washington Post*, April 14, 1976, pp. 1,2. Compare reports on the *Post* and the *New York Times* in *La Stampa*, October 26, 1976, p. 2. Compare *Corriere della Sera*, March 9, 1976, p. 5.

[9] May 30, 1976, p. 11. The four journalists were Brigit Kraatz (West German press), George Armstrong (*The Guardian*), Karen Dissing (Danish television), and Jacques Nobecourt (*Le Monde*).

[10] The issue of pluralism and the PCI is one of the most important in contemporary Italian politics, but it cannot be treated in this chapter. The interested reader should consult, for example, the issues of *Mondo Operaio* for the last two years; E. J. Hobsbawn, ed., *Napolitano: Intervista sul PCI* [Napolitano: an interview on the PCI] (Bari: Laterza, 1976); *La Stampa*, September 17, 1976,

is that once in power the PCI would combine with the DC to "suffocate" the democratic political system.[11]

Concern was also expressed about foreign policy. How would the PCI's sharing governmental power affect security arrangements like NATO? If the PCI were able to press its campaign for Eurocommunism, how would Northern Europe's Socialist parties react? Could the Communists be expected to lend strong Italian support to an already shaky European Economic Community? Even if the PCI did nothing to disturb Italy's constitutional institutions, was it not reasonable to suppose that the party would be more prone than a non-Communist government to follow the lead of the U.S.S.R. in foreign affairs? [12]

The worst possible outcome, some suggest, is that PCI participation in the cabinet would lead to a Chilean scenario: the flight of capital would accelerate, the government would prove unable to control wages or inflation, strikes would multiply, international financial institutions would withdraw credit, Italy might be subjected to a *cordon sanitaire* by countries hostile to the Communists, the country would collapse, and a dictatorial regime would emerge to restore order.

Prelude to Confrontation

Several major events that occurred between 1972 and 1976 go far to explain why concern about the PCI reached such fever pitch in 1976. They include Enrico Berlinguer's pronouncements about the so-called historic compromise, the referendum on divorce, the extension of the vote to eighteen-year-olds, and the regional elections of 1975.

---

pp. 1, 2; Stephen Hellman, "The PCI in Transition: The Origins of the Historic Compromise," paper delivered at the annual meeting of the American Political Science Association, Chicago, September 1976; Donald L. Blackmer and Sidney Tarrow, eds., *Communism in France and Italy* (Princeton: Princeton University Press, 1975). In any event, the PCI has not been convincing about how one can reconcile Gramsci's "working class hegemony" with "democratic pluralism."

[11] See Giovanni Sartori, "I comunisti al potere, e dopo?" [Communists in power; and then what?] *Biblioteca della libertà*, vol. 11 (July-August 1974), pp. 92-98, for a hair-raising scenario.

[12] This is not idle speculation. The PCI's claimed independence of Moscow has not been reflected in the reactions in the party press to the crises in places like Lebanon, Syria, Angola, or Rhodesia. Mr. Kissinger's efforts in Africa are consistently described as "neocolonialist imperialism"; attitudes toward the PLO follow the twists and turns established at Moscow; the interventions of China and the U.S.S.R. in Africa are judiciously ignored; Cuban troops in Angola are described as democratic liberators. See, for example, the articles by Alberto Ronchey in *Corriere della Sera*, March 3, 1976, p. 1 and September 23, 1976, p. 1.

Historic Compromise. In the fall of 1973, Berlinguer, successor to Palmiro Togliatti as leader of the PCI, startled the world and many members of his own party by announcing that the PCI was prepared to accept, indeed was determined to promote, a *compromesso storico*. Berlinguer had made this strategy known to members of the PCI central committee at its meeting in September. The bombshell was shared with a larger audience a few days later.[13] For the next several months, Berlinguer was to go to great pains to outline what the historic compromise meant and why the PCI was determined to pursue it.

Briefly, the major features of the policy are these: First, the PCI would be opposed to the left's coming to power alone even were it to receive more than 50 percent of the vote in a national election. Second, the left, even if it had an electoral majority, must seek the support of the broadest possible coalition of democratic parties of the workers, including the DC. Third, the PCI must seek to bring under this umbrella even the "new middle class" and other groups that, according to the party's analysis, are exploited in an era of monopoly capitalism.

A statement as sweeping as this required a rationale, and Berlinguer was quick to provide it. To begin with, he noted that the support of a 51 percent majority would not be sufficient to govern Italy and to bring about the renewal the country required. In particular, the left could not expect to rule alone if other parties, although a minority, recruited a good portion of their support from the lower classes. In Italy, he noted, about 90 percent of the Catholics were deeply influenced by the Catholic Church, and about 40 percent of them supported the DC. Berlinguer indicated that this DC electoral base could not be eroded. It was unrealistic, he said, to think that the left could govern Italy without the cooperation of these groups. Loyal collaboration among the masses and their representative organizations must begin at once.

Second, Berlinguer noted that Italy must finally decide what to do with a PCI that in 1972 had attracted more than 9 million voters. In local and regional governments where it shared control, the PCI had given strong evidence of its seriousness of purpose and of its respect for constitutional institutions. With emergency conditions worsening throughout the country, the PCI was perhaps the only

---

[13] See *Rinascita*, October 5, 1973. My summary is based on the reports of Berlinguer's speeches and statements in this PCI journal, in the party's daily paper, *L'Unità*, and elsewhere in the Italian press from 1973 onward.

national political force compact and disciplined enough to assume the responsibility of governing. The obvious answer was to give it a share in government through the historic compromise.

Third, Berlinguer repeatedly alluded to the unhappy events in Chile under Allende. Similar developments must be avoided at all costs in Italy, and for the left to assume power alone was not the best way to do so. In any event, Berlinguer was persuaded that both in Italy and abroad the visceral anticommunism of the cold war years was a thing of the past. He assumed that the time was therefore opportune for the PCI clearly to renounce its past statements about conquering power alone or with the left and to come forward with a new proposal, namely, the historic compromise.

Berlinguer added that the groundwork for collaboration had already been laid in the trade union sphere, where once antagonistic trade union organizations, separately representing Communists and Socialists, Catholics, and Social Democrats and Republicans, were working more and more in concert. He more than once implied that a further necessary condition had been satisfied: the PCI had demonstrated its independence from Moscow in its public statements about the "Italian road to socialism," its refusal to accept that the U.S.S.R. would guide other Communist parties, its efforts to bring the French Communists around to the PCI point of view, its support of the Socialists in Portugal, and its open criticism of infringements of liberties in the Soviet Union and certain East European Communist regimes.

Many have argued that when all of the verbiage is subjected to closer scrutiny there is little here that is really new. To some, Berlinguer in 1973 and since has been articulating an updated version of what Palmiro Togliatti had to say back in the early 1940s. For these critics, the historic compromise boils down to just another version of the well-known popular front tactic.

For others, the historic compromise represents an official recognition of tendencies that have been discernible within the PCI for some years. These involve above all what the Communists call *presenza*—that is, a presence, active participation, in the basic institutions of Italian society and politics. This presence is not designed only to avoid sectarianism and to prevent the party's being pushed to the margins of society and kept outside. *Presenza* means using the PCI, its leaders, and their undoubted skills to bring about the transformation of Italy. Not by revolution. Not even by a left majority

15

alone in government. But by a broadgauged cooperative effort in which the PCI would play the critical mediating role.[14]

The historic compromise was not universally applauded by PCI leaders. Luigi Longo, a party elder statesman, objected to the term itself, asserting that the word "compromise" might imply giving in and abandoning basic values.[15] Other party leaders, especially those from the militant red zones, were fearful lest the party's national leaders run too far ahead of its own mass followers. These militants in many cases had come to believe that *only* revolution directed by the party could possibly bring change to Italy. As recently as January 1976, Umberto Terracini, one of the PCI's founders, blasted the historic compromise and urged that the approach suggested by Berlinguer was inconsistent with the revolutionary historical mission of the PCI.[16] For many Communists the thought of collaborating with an "undemocratic" DC as opposed to coming to power with a left "historical bloc" was simply unthinkable.

Referendum on Divorce. In May 1974, the Italians went to the polls to ratify or to nullify a highly controversial law on divorce passed in 1970. The law is stringent; it makes divorce a costly, time-consuming process, and it has not been used at anything like the levels predicted or feared. Nevertheless, it offended many Italian Catholics, who worked diligently to collect the 500,000 petition signatures needed to bring the issue before the voters so they could say "yes" or "no" to the question of repealing it.

There is strong evidence that neither the Catholic hierarchy nor the PCI favored the referendum. The PCI feared that its longstanding postwar effort to avoid any head-on collision with the Church would be imperiled and that its own base might be split.[17] Neither

---

[14] For a brilliant elaboration of this view and of the probable outcome of tensions within the PCI over how to come to power and how to use power once acquired, see Hellman, "The PCI in Transition." For an additional statement that the PCI's "Italian road to socialism" is not merely a matter of tactics but a genuine historical impulse growing out of the particular circumstances of Italy, see Sidney Tarrow, "The Italian Party System between Crisis and Transition," paper delivered at the Annual Meeting of the American Political Science Association, Chicago, September 1976.

[15] *L'Unità*, November 4, 1973, p. 3.

[16] *Il Messaggero*, January 15, 1976, p. 3.

[17] PCI "understandings" with the Catholic Church abound. Thus, in 1976 accusations from Socialists, Radicals, and various lay groups that the PCI was playing the Church's game on a proposed law on abortion seemed quite well-founded. A cardinal rule of PCI behavior since 1945 has been not to fall into simple-minded, doctrinaire anticlericalism.

the Church nor the PCI wanted to force an issue that would reveal how strong (or weak) were religious and secular attitudes in the country. Even a good many DC leaders understood that a public confrontation on divorce was a loaded gun that might go off in unpredictable directions.

But die-hard Christian Democrats led by Amintore Fanfani combined with the Socialist and other lay political parties to bring the issue to a head. Once the referendum was inevitable, the PCI did indeed campaign hard and well for a "no" vote on repeal. It displayed a truly remarkable capacity to argue that the law on divorce did not in fact threaten the nuclear family, around which so many Italian Catholic emotions center.

The outcome was a chilling defeat for the DC and for the Church. Italy was showered with "no" votes as three out of five Italians voted to keep the divorce law on the books. Not only that, but a mere seven of Italy's twenty regions voted to repeal—all of them, except the Trentino-Alto Adige and the Veneto, in the south. Even there, however, most of the regions voting "yes" did so by narrow margins. In fifteen of Italy's ninety-three provinces the vote in favor of divorce exceeded 70 percent.[18] Divorce won in two-thirds of the provinces and could readily have won in a dozen more. Even the islands of Sicily and Sardinia, long viewed as Catholic strongholds, voted "no." The rank-ordered "no" vote is shown in Table 1–3.

Many consider the 1974 referendum an electoral watershed. If concrete evidence of the spread of secular values and the decline of Church influence over the Italian voter was needed, the referendum supplied it. For, clearly, there were millions of Italian Catholics, including many who might otherwise vote for the DC, who were not prepared to have the dictates of the Church or the maneuvers of the DC determine how they would respond to a basic and clearcut issue such as divorce. Moreover, fear of the PCI would not determine their response either. The referendum vote confirmed what several scholars had been arguing for some time: Italian public opinion had changed, so much so that the support of a particular view by the

---

[18] Italy's provinces are essentially administrative units of the central government. Like the French *département*, the *provincia* is under the control of a prefect. The elected provincial assemblies have had little power. Regional governments are of two kinds—constitutional and statutory—and have considerably more power and authority. The constitutional regional governments date from the beginning of the Republic; the other regional governments were created in the early 1920s. All of Italy is covered by these governments today. A number of administrative responsibilities will be devolved to them, as will greater participation in economic planning. However, *fiscal* powers of consequence have not been devolved.

Table 1–3
THE MAY 15, 1974, VOTE AGAINST REPEALING ITALY'S DIVORCE LAW, RANK ORDERED BY REGION

Rank	Region	% "No"	Rank	Region	% "No"
1	Valle d'Aosta	75.1	11	Sardegna	55.2
2	Liguria	72.6	12	Abruzzi	51.1
3	Emilia-Romagna	70.9	13	Sicilia	50.5
4	Piemonte	70.8	14	Trentino-Alto Adige	49.4
5	Toscana	69.6	15	Calabria	49.2
6	Umbria	67.4	16	Veneto	48.9
7	Friuli-Venezia Giulia	63.9	17	Campania	47.8
8	Lazio	63.4	18	Puglia	47.4
9	Lombardia	59.2	19	Basilicata	46.4
10	Marche	57.6	20	Molise	40.0

Source: *Rinascita*, May 17, 1974.

PCI and even the prospect of the PCI's sharing power were far less frightening to the electorate than they had been in the past.[19]

Following the referendum, Enrico Berlinguer did not press forward his campaign for the historic compromise. For one thing, the referendum results raised questions about one of his assumptions, namely, that the mass of Catholic voters could not be dislodged from the DC. For another, internal PCI malaise about the historic compromise and open PSI hostility to it argued for prudence. Berlinguer tried to reassure both those who might mistake the historic compromise for the PCI's short cut to power and the Socialists, who saw in it the danger of their own political extinction by a formal coalition agreement between the two electoral giants. In any event, time was required to permit more careful consideration of the domestic and international implications of what had been proposed—as well as the implications of the surprising magnitude of the referendum majority.[20]

---

[19] See, for example, Samuel H. Barnes, "Public Opinion and Political Preference in France and Italy," *Midwest Journal of Political Science*, vol. 15 (November 1971), pp. 643-660; Samuel H. Barnes, "Italy: Religion and Class in Electoral Behavior," in R. Rose, ed., *Electoral Behavior: A Comparative Handbook* (New York: Free Press, 1974), pp. 171-225.

[20] On the deliberateness that characterizes Berlinguer's behavior regarding PCI power sharing, see the article by Luigi Bianchi, "La prudenza di Berlinguer e la 'fretta' di Amendola" [Berlinguer's caution and Amendola's haste], *Corriere della Sera*, September 23, 1976, p. 2.

Regional Elections and Younger Voters. Thirteen months following the divorce referendum, Italian voters began to supply some answers themselves. Regional and municipal elections held in June 1975 involved most but not all of the peninsula.[21] Nevertheless, the electoral outcome strikingly revealed, for the first time in the Republic's history, major electoral shifts. The most noteworthy shift involved the PCI, which registered an unprecedented jump ahead of five percentage points over its regional appeal in 1970 and its national appeal in 1972. Together the left—that is, the PSI (12.1 percent), a new party of the extreme left, the DP (Proletarian Democracy), and the PCI (an outstanding 32.5 percent)—won almost 46 percent of the vote. No wonder that, with 50 percent apparently within reach, PSI leaders hostile to the historic compromise began to talk about the "Socialist alternative."

None of the public opinion polls, notoriously inaccurate about Italian elections, had predicted this change; on the other hand, the polls had predicted a much greater decline for the DC than actually occurred. That party lost less than three percentage points over its 1970 showing and slightly more compared with 1972. The right declined too, thereby helping to cover the DC's losses on its left, but this development was generally unanticipated as well.

The regional elections provided the first major voting opportunity for those between the ages of eighteen and twenty who were added to the electorate in 1975 when the minimum age for voting was lowered. These new voters numbered over 3 million. A second group—those who had turned twenty-one in 1973 and 1974—brought the total to well over 4 million. And since 1972 the electorate had also lost about 1.5 million persons who had died.

In an electorate of 40 million the loss and addition of so many voters can make a powerful difference, and attention was riveted on what this difference might be. In particular, observers wanted to see whether the results would bear out other evidence suggesting that older voters tend to be conservative and younger ones radical—so that voters' deaths will punish center and right-wing parties more

---

[21] The 1975 regional elections did not include the five regions *a statuto speciale* (created by special legislation, as foreseen in the constitution) such as Sicily, but only those fifteen *a statuto ordinario* (brought into being by general enabling legislation). In a strict sense, therefore, the regional results are not to be compared with those of the national elections of 1972, but rather with the results of the previous regional contests of 1970.

than the left, and the entry of new voters (particularly the youngest) will help the left more than the right and center.[22]

Because the vote is secret, inferences about who votes for which party or which party loses more supporters because of deaths must be based on indirect measures. One of these is the public opinion poll where people are asked how they voted in the past or which party they intend to support in an upcoming election. Because of sample and measuring error and the propensity of people not to reply to such questions or to report their behavior or intentions inaccurately, this kind of evidence must be used with caution.

In the hands of a careful analyst like Giacomo Sani, the evidence seems to say that the younger voters were a major factor in the left's unprecedented forward leap in 1975.[23] Changes in the absolute number and/or the proportion of votes any party receives in two or more elections in which it competes can be accounted for only by one or more of the following: (1) differential distribution by party of those previous electors who have died; (2) changes in the proportion of the electorate actually turning out to vote; (3) shifts in the voters' support from one party to another; and (4) the distribution among competing parties of the electoral choices of new voters.[24]

Of these four factors, the left is reported as having benefited most from the last, with almost 60 percent of the new voters supporting the left. In addition, however, the left also did better on two other counts: it lost fewer voters than the center-right through deaths and it experienced fewer defections to other parties than did those of the center-right.

If these conclusions are correct, additional inferences are in order. One is that the Italian electorate in 1975 did not become more volatile than it had been earlier. One could expect a part of the left's forward leap (that caused by the addition of over 3 million voters aged eighteen, nineteen, and twenty years) to be a one-time-only phenomenon.

---

[22] On the long-term effects of electoral generations, see the seminal work of D. Butler and D. Stokes, *Political Change in Britain: Factors Shaping Electoral Choice* (London: Macmillan, 1969); on the Italian situation, see Giacomo Sani, "Ricambio elettorale e identificazioni partitiche: verso un egemonia delle sinistre?" [Electoral exchange and party identification: toward a hegemony of the left?], *Rivista italiana di scienza politica*, vol. 5 (1975), pp. 515-544. I depend heavily on this last article for the content of the next few paragraphs.

[23] Sani, "Ricambio elettorale," pp. 522-526.

[24] There are, of course, other factors that might be added, such as the emigration of previous voters and the immigration of previous nonvoters, or the magnitude and distribution by party of ballots that are found to be blank or null and void. These were not of major import in 1975.

Another inference would be that this one-time effect will have long-term impact precisely because the Italian vote is not volatile. The left parties might therefore expect to retain the support of these voters well into the future. A third inference follows: if age peers develop long-lasting political identities and propensities, and if the public opinion data are accurate in showing younger Italians to be much more left oriented than any other part of the electorate, then it is only a matter of time before the left comes to power electorally.

One immediate upshot of the 1975 elections is that the PCI came to share governing power in several regions where it had been absent earlier as well as in many of Italy's leading municipalities. In some places the left governed alone; in others it was involved in broader coalitions. In critically important regions like Lombardy and Piedmont, and in cities like Milan and Turin, the PCI was a force to be reckoned with, not in the future but immediately in the formation of municipal and regional executives. Given the magnitude of the PCI's (and the left's) success, it seemed to many inevitable that the PCI would come to govern in Rome as well—both in the city and in the national government—when the next elections were held.

Crisis, Dissolution, Elections

In view of this highly charged background and atmosphere, few Italians—including the Socialists, who brought on the elections of June 20, 1976—really wanted another confrontation. Yet Socialist leaders were increasingly restive about the center-left, which had served the interests of the DC, promoted few policies in which the PSI could take pride, cost the Socialists a great deal in terms of their party image, and seemed to have worked out to the benefit of the PCI. Indeed, what infuriated some of the PSI leaders most was the effectiveness of the PCI in playing two roles. One of these made it appear to the general public that the only left opposition to the DC was the PCI. On the other hand, the insiders were well aware that there was considerable discussion between the DC and the PCI and that the former would really not make any major policy move without consulting the latter. The irony for the PSI was that it was left in political limbo—neither in opposition nor acting as an effective partner in the governmental coalition.

The PSI began expressing its malaise and making more stringent demands on the DC following the latter's clear defeat on the issue of the divorce referendum in 1974 and the gains registered by the left, including the PSI, in the regional elections of 1975. Things began coming to a head in the late fall of that year, as the Moro-La Malfa government tried to work out a medium-term economic policy. The Socialists suspected that the PCI was having a greater input into the content of that plan than was accorded the PSI. It seemed to them anomalous that that government should ignore the PSI, on whose benign neutrality the government itself depended, and clear its policies instead with the PCI, officially a party of the opposition. Socialist feelings were of course exacerbated by the fear that any form of cooperation between the DC and the PCI was in fact a form of collusion that would lead eventually to the historic compromise.

Tension peaked with an editorial blast issued by Francesco De Martino on New Year's Eve.[25] The PSI secretary general noted the curious behavior of the DC with respect to its allies and opponents and indicated that, in view of these under-the-table negotiations and understandings, the PSI would be withdrawing its support from the government.

The editorial was a bombshell, particularly because it came just three weeks after the PSI's directorate had voted to continue supporting the government, at least until the party congresses of the DC and the PSI scheduled for the following spring had been concluded. It is probable that De Martino made the decision to withdraw support with great reluctance. But he was under severe pressure within the PSI to harden the line with the DC as a means of extracting concessions. One of his critics replaced him as secretary following the disaster the party experienced in the elections.

The Moro government resigned in January. There followed rather frantic, highly inconsistent efforts of the PSI to salvage its plummeting reputation. Having toppled the government because of allegations that the DC was playing illicit games with the PCI, the PSI came out for an official marriage that would bring the PCI openly and immediately into the government. The tactic was blatant; the PSI really wanted to slow down DC-PCI collaboration. Moro astutely avoided giving the PSI any opportunity to recoup. The Communists were also infuriated. They charged the PSI with political immaturity, with lack of coherence in its policies and strategies, and with blatantly pushing the country toward elections.[26]

The Communists wished to avoid elections, even as they prepared for them. They had been surprised by their electoral victory of 1975. They needed time to consolidate their position, to train

---

[25] See *Avanti!*, December 31, 1975, p. 1.

[26] See the pages of *L'Unità* during the first three weeks of January 1976. In particular the editorial of January 15, 1976, p. 1.

people to assume new-found responsibilities in the governing of regions and cities. They sought an opportunity to show the country how well they could govern cities as diverse as Turin and Naples. They were also concerned that elections might precipitate, in Italy and abroad, panic over the prospect of the PCI's coming to share national power.

Socialist leaders felt they had no option in view of their estimate that Moro was moving too rapidly toward the historic compromise. Their conception of the Socialist alternative, stripped down to its essentials, meant postponing at least for some time the issue of PCI participation in the government. The Socialists were not at all reassured by the flat statement by Ugo La Malfa and other Republicans that the historic compromise was the ineluctable next step in the nation's political evolution.

Some Socialist leaders favored early elections. Although they were somewhat disappointed by the party's 1975 electoral showing, they noted that it represented a marked improvement over 1972. For some of them the prospect that they might be on the wave of a swing to the left was heady stuff; there was talk of the PSI's coming up with 15-18 percent of the vote. It was time, they felt, for Italy to consider alternation in government—the possibility that sooner or later the DC would go into opposition, leaving the left with a real opportunity, as in France, to govern under a "common program."

The upshot of the January crisis was that a Christian Democratic minority government, under Moro, was constituted in February 1976, with support from the PSI in the form of abstention on votes of confidence and investiture. Everyone understood that the government would be short-lived; implicitly elections were felt to be inevitable, timed to follow several party congresses, including those of the DC and the PSI, scheduled to occur in the spring. The more important question turned on the kind of clarifications that might emerge from the congresses, particularly those of the two major coalition parties.

The PSI convened in March. De Martino's effort to keep things flexible and moderate failed. The party officially buried the center-left, indicated no intention to rejoin the Moro government, and committed itself following elections to the search for a means of achieving the Socialist alternative. The possibility of joining an emergency government including the PCI was not ruled out.

The DC Congress was a master stroke in fence mending to avoid entering elections in a state of internal disarray. The schism between those supporting Moro and the party secretary, Benigno Zaccagnini, and others supporting more conservative groups led by

Amintore Fanfani was greatly attenuated. Moro was permitted to be the prime minister who would lead the party—and the country—to early elections. Zaccagnini, the "reformist" leader, was reconfirmed. At the same time Fanfani was named to the new position of party president. This last step greatly discouraged the Socialists, who saw in it evidence of the DC's inability to renew itself.

The PCI in the meantime was steering a studious course away from the Socialist alternative. Some Communist leaders called it sheer "fantasy," others described it as "premature."[27] The party was determined not to go to the voters with the specter of a PCI-PSI government hanging heavy in the atmosphere.

The Socialists were convinced that they were onto a magnificent strategy. On the one hand, the PCI could not simply reject the Socialist alternative. On the other hand, some DC factions would indeed see the need to be more solicitous of the PSI, less blatant than Moro in showing a preference for the PCI. Public opinion polls seemed to support the PSI's assumption that great electoral benefits lay in its having reestablished its left image.[28]

By April, the parties were maneuvering for advantage, trying to convince the public that the failure to provide a workable approach to Italy's economic emergency was the fault of others. The PSI found reasons to blast the DC for collaborating with the neo-Fascists to dilute an abortion bill. The Christian Democrats could point to PSI intransigence and lament that the parlous situation since January was largely of the PSI's making. The Republicans under La Malfa could show complete exasperation over the collapse of the DC's medium-term economic plan. In the midst of all of this the PCI could keep reiterating that it had not wanted the January crisis, did not desire early elections, and was prepared to participate in any reasonable way in a collective effort to address the major business of government—that is, coping with the emergency.

Late in April, the DC decided to raise in Parliament the question of confidence and the fate of the Moro government. On the heels of this, the PSI decided to withdraw its support, *before* a protracted Parliament could exacerbate party relations and place the PSI in a bad light. On April 30, Moro resigned. Elections were set for June 20.

The Campaign. The electoral campaign brought no great surprises on the programmatic side. The views of the political parties on many

---

[27] See, for example, *Rinascita*, February 27, 1977, pp. 1-2.

[28] Well into May and June, some opinion polls were assigning the PSI 12 to 16 percent of the vote.

pressing issues were well known, and they were reiterated, at varying levels of abstraction, in electoral manifestoes. A torrent of documents poured out of party headquarters, despite the evidence that Italians read very little, claim in large numbers not to discuss politics, and insist that they have no interest in, and do not follow, political campaigns.[29]

As in past elections, the highly disciplined PCI seemed the best prepared to launch its campaign. Party statements began to appear with predictable regularity, setting out PCI proposals on the economy, the south, the rights of women, the training and employment of the young, and a host of other topics. One false step occurred early in the campaign when the Radicals threatened to usurp the Communists' customary privilege of first place on the ballot. The upper left-hand position on the ballot goes to the party that registers its candidates with the local electoral office first, and in most places in the past this has been the PCI. In 1976, the Radicals gave the Communists some competition, waiting all night outside registration offices in order to be there the moment they opened. The PCI's handling of this irritant was summary: the Radicals were removed by force and violence. Most of the Italian press ignored or passed lightly over this interesting deviation from the PCI's often reiterated commitment to pluralism.

The most interesting campaign surprises were tactical and strategic. An effort to amalgamate the minor lay, democratic parties (the PSDI, the PRI, and the PLI) failed because the Republicans were uninterested in pursuing such a strategy. La Malfa rightly thought his PRI would do better going it alone. The Democratic Socialists were deeply tainted by scandal (particularly by the Lockheed exposé) and rent by internal squabbling; the Liberals seemed to be a party in decline with little hope that its new leadership would be able to reverse the party's fortunes so soon after its old guard had been deposed.[30] The Republicans were also interested in keeping things vague and open on the critical question whether they would partici-

---

[29] These findings are based on survey research for the 1972 elections reported by Giacomo Sani, "L'immagine dei partiti nell' elettorato" [Party images and the electorate] in Caciagli and Spreafico, *Un sistema*, pp. 87 ff. This sort of information must be handled with care. In any case, as the author well notes (p. 91), the mass media are not the only sources of political messages. Nevertheless, when tested by the survey instruments used in other countries, Italy's relative level of political information and interest is very low.

[30] Valerio Zanone, the new party secretary, had been named to that position only in December 1975. The party needed time to heal its wounds. Zanone and others, like Renato Altissimo, needed time to develop the party's new, less rigidly conservative image.

pate in a postelectoral coalition that might include the Communists. The PSDI and the PLI came out flatly against PCI participation in government. Here they were indistinguishable from the DC, a fact that probably cost them votes.

The Christian Democratic strategy was to recreate the atmosphere of 1948 by underscoring that the DC was the only force in Italy capable of dealing with the PCI. The party promised that it would renew itself, and indeed there was some evidence of this in the choice of candidates to head the DC lists. In particular, a number of younger trade unionists and several leading economists were added to party lists. The fact that the party had closed ranks, that the factions seemed united in their approach to the voters, heightened the sense of tension and drama the DC sought to orchestrate.

Greatly reinforcing DC strategy was the campaign activity of the Catholic Church. Not for many years had the Vatican hierarchy intervened so openly and insistently in a national election. On May 21, Pope Paul VI gave a widely reported speech to the Italian Episcopal Meeting. Some of his remarks La Stampa labeled "without precedent." [31] He asked Catholics to rally around the DC, which, even with its undoubted faults, remained the only guarantor of the faith. He urged people to be vigilant, united, and coherent in the Christian faith and to express this in their vote. Civic, moral, social, and religious duty, the Pope said, instructed Italians to oppose the PCI, a party that, for both ideological and historical reasons, was "radically averse to our religious conception of life." [32]

Only a very special circumstance could explain such open intervention by the Catholic pontiff, for his words could only fuel Catholic controversy over the political role of the Church and the attitude Catholics should take toward the PCI. This special circumstance was the PCI's choice of candidates: for the first time these included a number of prominent Catholics, who went to great pains to explain why they had agreed to run as independents on the PCI ticket.

The PCI's decision to draw about 10 percent of its candidates from among nonparty members was the most important innovative strategy of the campaign. The maneuver could not have been entirely well received within the PCI. If nothing else, the independents elected under the PCI banner would displace some party militants who aspired to places in Parliament. Nevertheless, the strategy was accepted and the public comments of PCI leaders expressed unbounded enthusiasm.

---

[31] La Stampa, May 22, 1976, p. 1.
[32] Ibid.

26

Those chosen to run on the PCI ticket as independents were in many cases prominent Catholics, Socialists, and others who enjoyed extensive local, national, and international reputations. They included well-known and respected economists like Luigi Spaventa and Claudio Napoleoni; Raniero La Valle, a major Catholic writer and intellectual; Giuseppe Branca, a former chief justice; the chairmen of the faculties of science at the universities of Rome and Palermo; an air force general; a former editor of the DC party newspaper, Il Popolo; and a large number of university professors, judges, doctors, journalists, and other professionals. The list also included Altiero Spinelli, an ex-Communist and former commissioner of the European Communities. Spinelli's candidacy came as a bombshell to the Italian Socialists, some of whom had hoped that he might agree to run under the PSI label.

What did this strategy mean? What could justify imposing these candidates from above? Some of the answers are self-evident. The presence on the PCI lists of prominent Catholics (whose explanations of their decision were given wide mass media coverage) helped to refute the Pope and other prelates: direct involvement with the PCI was *not* incompatible with the Catholic faith. The presence of the economists suggested that, as one of them said, "evidently one can not only talk with the Communists but also work with them."[33] The purpose of Spinelli's candidacy was specifically to reassure the voters and others in Europe that the intentions of the PCI in foreign policy were honorable.[34] To some extent, most of these candidates were designed to function as bell cows, and only the most naive among them would fail to see this.

The types of independents recruited and the selection of districts where they would run deserve more than a passing reference here. It is fascinating, for example, that the PCI ran no independents in Catholic strongholds like Como, Varese, Brescia, Bergamo, Montova, Cremona, Trento, and Bolzano or in powerful PCI constituencies like Parma, Modena, Piacenza, Reggio Emilia, Siena, Arezzo, and Grosseto. One gets the impression that some independents were run in safe districts to ensure their election, while the number of these candidates placed elsewhere was determined by some calculation of how many votes they might swing. The independents at Turin, for example, included a professor from the Catholic University, a professor of surgery, a high school teacher, and a shepherd; at Venice the group

[33] *L'Unità*, June 20, 1976, pp. 1, 4. The quotation is from Luigi Spaventa.
[34] See the comment by Giancarlo Pajetta reported in *L'Unità*, June 20, 1976. Note, too, his somewhat equivocal statement on PCI attitudes toward NATO.

included a doctor and leader of the Italian Association of Christian Workers, a lawyer, a psychiatrist, and a writer; at Naples-Caserta the group of independents included a judge and a professor of criminal law, a journalist, professors of sociology, law, Roman law, letters, and economics, and an engineer. Academics, lawyers, and judges abounded in the south. The designation of independents seemed to reflect a careful adaptation of candidates to the dominant status hierarchy in each region.

If elected, some of the independents, the party reasoned, might be available to participate in the cabinet during the transition period after the election when the presence of well-known PCI leaders might cause alarm. The risk that any of them might embarrass the PCI was relatively small, particularly in view of the PCI's insistence that these people spoke for themselves and not for the party. PCI leaders repeated throughout the campaign that the party's seriousness of purpose, its openness, and its interest in "concrete things" was to be gauged in part by who had been named as independent candidates.

With this group of independents under its wing, the PCI could argue more effectively for a government of national emergency. This seemed to be the major direction taken by the party following its unexpected electoral gains in 1975 and following the PCI's advocacy of the Left alternative. In any event, as the campaign wore on, there was clearly less emphasis on the historic compromise and more on the country's need for the broadest possible democratic front to meet the crisis. The PCI message, from Berlinguer on down, was "communism or chaos." As Berlinguer laconically put it in May, "Without us it is not possible for the country to emerge from the crisis. Rather, it will be taken to the brink of the precipice." [35]

The PSI's campaign centered on the Socialist alternative. Its leaders emphasized that the party would not again join a coalition government that excluded the Communists. They indicated a willingness to join a government of national emergency that would include all democratic and constitutional parties; [36] they stressed as well that their goal was not to encourage the historic compromise but in the long run to bring the Socialist left to power.

To some extent, the PSI's insistence on the Socialist alternative nicely served the Communists' interest by underscoring how reasonable and responsible they would remain in the teeth of such an in-

---

[35] Il Giorno, May 17, 1976, p. 1.

[36] What Italians call the "arc of constitutional parties" includes, in addition to the DC, all of the parties on the right except the neo-Fascists and the Monarchists, and, on the left, the PRI, the PSDI, the PSI, and the PCI.

vitation. The Communists were working to make credible both at home and abroad their pledge that they did not intend to come to power with the left alone or to imperil democratic institutions. In any event, PCI leaders responded that the Socialist alternative was ill advised not only because it would be badly received in Italy and elsewhere; it was ill advised because the power ratio between the PSI and the PCI was all wrong. If the PSI could change that ratio, then perhaps one might discuss a Socialist alternative. Speaking to a much broader audience than just Italy, Berlinguer emphasized that the PCI had never asked for a Communist government in Italy and had always favored a broad-based coalition in which it might play a part. In May, Berlinguer said:

> In Italy we need government of the broadest unity among diverse political forces and idealistic currents—in a pluralistic framework which is for us definitive. Each party gives and receives guarantees from the very fact of having other parties at its side, from the full respect of constitutional norms, and from the methods it follows in relating to citizens.[37]

Predicting the Outcome. Polls taken during the campaign suggested that the PCI's strategy was going to pay rich electoral dividends. Only one survey put the PCI's support below 30 percent. Others suggested that the party might garner as much as 34 percent of the vote. The forecasts for the PSI were also high, with the upper projections at almost 16 percent. Because the Liberals, Republicans, and Social Democrats were also expected to get about 11 percent combined, it seemed simple logic to anticipate a *further* decline of the DC below its 1975 vote of 35.5 percent, and considerably below its 1972 vote of 38.7 percent.[38]

These projections suggested that the PCI might accede to executive power in several different ways. To begin with, the list system of proportional representation (PR) for electing members of the lower chamber tends to favor the largest parties. This means that the largest parties can expect to win a slightly larger proportion of seats than of votes nationally.

Two mechanisms produce this deviation.[39] One is the use of

---

[37] *L'Unità*, May 20, 1976, p. 4.
[38] I have looked at data from ten public opinion polls (taken during May and June) by such organizations as Makno, Metra, Pragma, Doxa, and Demoskopea. These data were kindly made available to me by Alberto Spreafico.
[39] For a fuller discussion of the electoral system, see Chapter 2 in this volume, pp. 4-10.

plural constituencies from which from five to fifteen deputies are elected. All such plural, subnational constituency systems of PR create advantages for the largest party. The other factor is the exclusion from participation in the "national electoral college" (to which undistributed constituency seats and "remaindered" votes are referred for final distribution) of any political party, regardless of how many votes it wins nationally, that fails to elect at least one deputy in a constituency. In 1972, for example, the PSIUP, with 648,591 votes (1.9 percent), failed to elect a single deputy. In 1976, as we shall see below, the Radicals with 1.1 percent of the vote elected four deputies, and the coalition group on the extreme left, with 1.5 percent, managed to elect six.

The left-majority hypothesis was that the PCI would receive about 34 percent of the vote, the PSI between 12 and 14 percent, and the DP on the extreme left about 2 percent. These proportions were within the parameters of the pollsters' findings, albeit at the high end. The possibility that this outcome might occur and perhaps cause panic is an important reason why the PCI went to such pains to say that it sought the broadest possible coalition of democratic forces in a government of national emergency.

Even were such an electoral outcome and seat distribution to prevail in the lower chamber, it was not expected that it would be repeated in the Senate. Senators are elected either individually (if they receive at least 65 percent of the vote in single districts) or by the d'Hondt system of proportional representation from districts returning several senators. This system of PR, too, favors the largest parties for the reasons indicated earlier.

Senate races bring about unusual party alliances, designed to win seats where the separate parties would stand little chance. Also the minimum voting age for the Senate is twenty-five (as opposed to eighteen for the Chamber of Deputies). With the eighteen to twenty-four age group cut out of the electorate, it was not expected that the left would do as well. Indeed, one grim prospect was that the left would win a majority in the lower house and the center in the Senate, inviting a bicameral confrontation that would further paralyze the government.

A second possibility was that the PCI would emerge as Italy's largest party and accede to executive power. Under the Italian constitutional system the president has considerable leeway in deciding whom to call upon to form a government. Nevertheless, were the PCI to emerge with an electoral plurality and the greatest number of seats in the lower house, many would expect the president to ask the PCI leader, that is, Berlinguer, to form a government.

Were Berlinguer in such a case to decline (out of prudence) the invitation, he would nevertheless have much to say about who would become premier designate and which parties should be included in a coalition. In this situation, too, the PCI could put forward its independents as candidates for some cabinet positions.

A third possibility was that the electoral results would make it difficult, perhaps impossible, to form a government without PCI participation in one form or another. This might well occur, for example, if the PSI held to its resolution not to recreate the center-left and not to join any coalition from which the PCI were excluded.

The Results of the Elections

This last scenario—the necessity for PCI cooperation with the government—is the one that came about. In order to mitigate its more unpalatable short-term implications, Italy's dauntless political leaders invented the "non-no-confidence" formula (in which neither confidence nor no-confidence is extended to the government by the legislature), and the Andreotti government came into being.

But if there was a winner in these elections, it was clearly the DC. This faction-ridden party for thirty years had temporized with some of the country's most nagging problems. Its gerontocracy, skillful managers of Italy's sottogoverno, had successfully resisted making room for a new generation of leaders. Once greatly aided electorally by the capillary machinery of the Catholic Church, it could no longer count on these organizations for unquestioning support. Indeed some of the most politically active Catholic groups were clearly at odds with the DC and strongly disposed toward radical programs and accommodation with the PCI.

This was the party, too, that had promoted and lost one confrontation over divorce and seemed headed toward another over abortion. It had managed to antagonize the trade unions, the feminist movement, civil libertarians, intellectuals, students, and professors. It was the party around which centered growing outrage over political corruption.

Campaign fire from all quarters had concentrated on the DC; even some of its closest former allies had agreed that the DC must be taught a sobering lesson. Data on the political proclivities of the young, as we have seen, had suggested that the political-generation mechanism was also working against the party. To top all of this, the elections themselves were fought in a climate of extreme economic crisis.

And yet, the DC wound up doing as well in 1976 as it had four years earlier—and bounced back significantly from the low point reached in 1975. Compared with 1972, an additional 1.3 million voters had gone to the polls to mark DC ballots.

Analysis of the Results. Not a single polling organization anticipated the more salient aspects of the electoral outcome. For example, the growing hegemony of the PCI within the left cluster was missed, the PCI vote was underestimated, and the PSI vote systematically overestimated. Similarly, the decline of the lay parties (the PRI, the PSDI, and the PLI) as a group was missed by very wide margins.[40] Furthermore, the most striking development that the polls of May and June failed to pick up was the recuperative power of the Christian Democrats.

The electoral results for the Chamber of Deputies are summarized in Table 1–4. They reveal that the Italian left has made marked progress over 1972, but also that most of its 6.7 percentage point gain is accounted for by the PCI. The failure of the PSI to improve its relative position over 1972 and the capacity of the PCI to surprise everyone and exceed its 1975 regional showing are the most important developments on the left. It is true that both the Radicals and the Proletarian Democrats succeeded in electing a few deputies, but the proportion of the total vote won by the extreme left actually declined in the years between the two elections.

No wonder that a perceptive observer like Francesco Alberoni can write that the left actually lost in 1976. "The entire electoral campaign," he says, "was conducted against the Christian Democracy; for eight years successive waves of protest movements have crashed against the DC; after eight years the DC has succeeded in recapturing its lost votes and therefore the DC won."[41]

Italian commentators are loath to ascribe the DC's recovery to

---

[40] The magnitude of polling errors in 1976 was larger than in 1972 and, when calculated as a *percentage error* rather than a *percentage point* deviation, reaches levels that raise perplexing questions about survey research in Italy. If one predicts, for example, that the PSI will get 12.5 percent of the vote and it gets only 9.6 percent, the percentage point deviation is 2.9 but the error magnitude is 30 percent! In the case of the PSDI, the PRI, and the PLI, several polls predicted aggregate percentages of 12-13.6 percent. Since the three-party total in 1976 was 7.8 percent, the magnitude of the error was from 53 to 74 percent.
[41] Francesco Alberoni, "Ecco perche il potere resta tenace al suo posto" [This is why power remains tenaciously unchangeable], *Corriere della Sera*, June 23, 1976, p. 3.

Table 1-4

DISTRIBUTION OF VOTES AND SEATS, CHAMBER OF DEPUTIES, 1972 AND 1976, BY POLITICAL PARTY

Party	1972 Election				1976 Election			
	Votes	Percentage of total vote	Seats	Percentage of total seats	Votes	Percentage of total vote	Seats	Percentage of total seats
DP	224,313	0.7	—	—	557,025	1.5	6	0.9
PCI	9,068,961	27.1	179	28.4	12,614,650	34.4	228	36.3
PSIUP	648,591	1.9	—	—	—	—	—	—
PSI	3,208,497	9.6	61	9.7	3,540,309	9.6	57	9.1
PR	—	—	—	—	394,439	1.1	4	0.6
Other left	235,175	0.7	—	—	26,748	0.1	1	—
Total left	13,385,537	40.0	240	38.1	17,133,171	46.7	296	46.9
PSDI	1,718,142	5.1	29	4.6	1,239,492	3.4	15	2.4
PRI	954,357	2.9	15	2.4	1,135,546	3.1	14	2.2
DC	12,912,466	38.7	266	42.2	14,209,519	38.7	262	41.6
PLI	1,300,439	3.9	20	3.2	480,122	1.3	5	0.8
Other center	187,757	0.6	4	0.6	208,466	0.6	3	0.5
Total center	17,031,161	51.2	334	53.0	17,273,145	47.1	299	47.5
MSI-DN	2,894,722	8.7	56	8.9	2,238,339	6.1	35	5.6
Other	50,128	0.1	—	—	62,923	0.1	—	—
Total	33,403,548	100.0	630	100.0	36,707,578	100.0	630	100.0

Source: Officially released data, aggregated by Alberto Spreafico and kindly made available by him.

a new wave of anticommunism, but their reluctance is defensible only in a restricted sense. To be sure, little that occurred during the campaign reflected the climate of fear that was typical of 1948 or the elections of the early fifties. But fear there was, so much so that middle-class groups, particularly in the urban centers, clearly shifted to the DC as the best available defender of their interests.

The PCI succeeded in attracting elements of the *lumpenbourgeoisie* to whom it made a direct appeal. Both the major parties now have considerable interclass support, even if the DC is definitely the more conservative. Middle-class Italians were no doubt reassured by the DC's intransigence toward the PCI, by the party's talk of confrontation rather than collaboration with the Communists. However, because both major parties have interclass appeal, it would be a mistake to see the concentration of votes behind the PCI and DC as indicating an increased polarization of the Italian electorate. Empirically it seems apparent that in ideological or programmatic terms the two parties have moved closer together.[42]

The convergence of the PCI and the DC poses a mortal threat to all of the parties—Radicals, Socialists, Democratic Socialists, Republicans, and even the reformist Liberals—that have tried to find viable space between the two giants. As the electoral results attest, that space is shrinking, and the smaller parties are being squeezed. Italians who are opposed to the DC increasingly believe their opposition can best be expressed by voting for the PCI. Those who fear the extreme left turn increasingly to the DC as the most realistic and effective guarantor of the values they are trying to protect. For a variety of additional reasons the minor parties fail to recruit new voters and to hang on to them through organizational and programmatic appeals. These parties are therefore experiencing a continuing erosion of their institutional bases. The generational phenomenon suggests that the decline of these parties is irreversible.

What about the younger voters? The 1976 electoral results and the data from pre-electoral surveys make it less easy to assess their voting behavior than may have appeared earlier. One often used method for estimating how the young have voted is that of comparing lower and upper house electoral results. (The 1976 results for the Senate are depicted in Table 1–5.) Because those in the age groups eighteen to twenty-four do not participate in senatorial elec-

---

[42] On this point, see the interesting collection of articles on the 1976 party platforms in *Le promesse dei partiti* [The promises of the parties] in a special issue of *Biblioteca della Libertà*, vol. 13 (September 1976). Romano Prodi (pp. 53-57) notes that parties are far apart in the abstract, very close in concrete programs.

Table 1-5
DISTRIBUTION OF VOTES AND SEATS, SENATE, 1972 AND 1976, BY PARTY

Party	1972 Election				1976 Election			
	Votes	Percentage of total vote	Seats	Percentage of total seats	Votes	Percentage of total vote	Seats	Percentage of total seats
DP	—	—	—	—	78,170	0.2	—	—
PCI	8,312,828	27.6	91	28.9	10,637,772	33.8	116	36.9
PSI	3,225,715	10.7	33	10.5	3,208,164	10.2	29	9.1
PR	—	—	—	—	265,947	0.8	—	—
Other left	285,615	0.9	3	0.9	73,994	0.3	1	0.3
Total left	11,824,158	39.2	127	40.3	14,264,047	45.3	146	46.3
PSDI	1,613,840	5.4	11	3.5	974,940	3.1	6	1.9
PRI	918,440	3.0	5	1.6	846,425	2.7	6	1.9
DC	11,465,529	38.1	135	42.9	12,227,353	38.9	135	42.9
PLI	1,319,175	4.4	8	2.6	438,265	1.4	2	0.6
Other center	176,519	0.6	3	0.9	567,752	1.9	5	1.6
Total center	15,493,473	51.5	162	51.4	15,054,735	48.0	154	48.9
MSI-DN	2,766,986	9.2	26	8.2	2,086,430	6.6	15	4.8
Other	31,448	0.1	—	—	44,229	0.1	—	—
Total	30,116,065	100.0	315	100.0	31,149,441	100.0	315	100.0

Source: Officially released data, aggregated by Alberto Spreafico and kindly made available by him.

tions, comparing the distribution of the vote by party in each house will suggest what difference the several million younger voters made. In 1976 the PCI did slightly worse in the Senate than in the Chamber (33.8 percent versus 34.4 percent), and the DC did slightly better (38.9 percent versus 38.7 percent). For the left as a group and the center as a group the patterns are parallel.

However, as noted earlier, these comparisons tend to be spurious, for several reasons. Turnout levels in the two elections differ; some parties that compete for the Chamber do not do so for the Senate or run candidates in fewer districts; parties engage in unusual alliances for the Senate not found in the Chamber contests; some senatorial elections turn heavily on the personal appeal of candidates, and there is in the Senate an even greater tendency for votes to be concentrated in the two major parties. In any event, the mathematical proof for the unreliability of this method has been nicely provided by Mattei Dogan.[43]

Extrapolations from the findings of survey research are no less hazardous. For one thing, as Alberto Spreafico has shown in a pointed analysis,[44] the survey estimates of the proportion of young voters going to each party vary so greatly that one can in effect choose the survey that best approximates the results one is trying to demonstrate. It makes an enormous difference, for example, whether one assigns the DP 5 or 7.5 percent of the eighteen to twenty-four-year-old votes; the PCI 38 or 43 percent; the left 56 or 70 percent; the DC 15 or 30 percent. Yet these are all estimates that emerge from presumably sound survey research!

With all of these caveats in mind, Sani still claims that the 1976 results confirm what he had found earlier.[45] The parties of the center and right suffered greater attrition of supporters through death than parties of the left; the parties of the left were more successful than any others in attracting new voters; party defections were somewhat heavier from right to left than vice versa. His estimates of the 1976 results for both the Chamber and the Senate would assign about 55 percent of the youngest voters in each electoral contest to parties of the left. Nevertheless, he acknowledges that there is still

---

[43] Mattei Dogan, "Confutazione di un metodo di analisi del voto giovanile" [Rejection of one method of analyzing the vote of youth], in M. Dogan and O. M. Petracca, *Partiti e strutture sociali* (Milan: Comunità, 1968), pp. 481-489.
[44] Data made available to the author by Alberto Spreafico, in a forthcoming analysis of the 1976 electoral results.
[45] Giacomo Sani, "The Italian Elections of 1976: Continuity and Change," paper presented at the annual meeting of the American Political Science Association, Chicago, September 1976.

Table 1–6
DC AND PCI VOTE BY GEOGRAPHIC REGION, 1976
(in percentages)

Region	Christian Democracy		Italian Communist Party	
	Share of regional vote	Share of party vote	Share of regional vote	Share of party vote
North	39.1	48.7	33.5	47.0
Central	34.2	17.8	41.4	24.2
South	41.1	22.5	32.4	20.0
Islands	41.7	11.0	29.5	8.8
Italy	38.7	100.0	34.4	100.0

Source: Data provided by Alberto Spreafico.

room for doubting whether the gains of the left in 1976 stemmed primarily from defections or from the electoral choices of new voters. The only mathematical certainty is that once one raises the estimate in one of these categories, the estimate for the other must be lowered.

Like the 1975 results, the 1976 results confirm and reinforce the national character of the PCI, making it much more comparable to the DC than ever in the past. This is clearly seen in the percentage of the total vote for the Chamber each party received in the major geographic regions and in the geographic distribution of each party's total vote, depicted by Table 1–6.

Table 1–6 also suggests that the DC will face an extremely perplexing problem in the future: whereas the PCI remains extremely strong in the central regions, where about one-quarter of its vote is concentrated, its recent gains have been registered primarily in the south and the islands, which have long been the stronghold of Christian Democracy. The DC's vaunted renewal must have an impact in these areas if the DC is to remain the strongest party there.

Perhaps the most important final observation on the 1976 results is that they continue to evince a truly astounding stability in the Italian vote. As Sani notes, between 1946 and 1976 the electorate not only jumped from 28 to 40 million persons; 13 million persons who were alive in the earlier period were not around to vote in 1976. Through birth, aging, and attrition, the 1976 electorate was 25 million persons different from that of 1946. Two-thirds of those who voted in 1976 had not participated in the 1946 referendum that, by a narrow majority, changed Italy from a monarchy to a republic.[46]

---

[46] Ibid.

Despite all of these massive transformations of the electorate, the distribution of the vote among left, center, and right has not changed radically.[47] Some lament this stasis; others see it as a sign of underlying stability in Italian democracy. Within that stable framework, however, there have been political realignments. Because of them, in 1976 Italy entered a complex period of minority government and of speculation more intense than ever over the future role of the Communist party.

The months following Giulio Andreotti's investiture were characterized by continuing tension and uncertainty. With the collaboration of the PCI, the PSI, and other lay parties on the left, the government was able successfully to negotiate one loan from the International Monetary Fund, another from the European Economic Community. And at a time when the country seemed virtually ungovernable, the premier was able to impose a program of unprecedented austerity.

In the meantime the complicated game among the parties continues. On the one hand the minor parties insist that no coherent governmental program is possible without much more explicit programmatic, and even political, coordination with the PCI. On the other hand, every step the DC takes in the direction of the PCI sends tremors through the PSI and the other lay parties, for they fear the kind of agreement between the two giants that would snuff out the rest.[48]

Beyond these selfish party concerns there is deep perplexity over the impact that PCI participation in power would actually have on domestic political institutions and on foreign policy. The answer is far from clear and the PCI above all knows that it is not fully in

---

[47] On the stability of the Italian vote, see G. Galli and A. Prandi, *Political Behavior in Italy* (New Haven: Yale University Press, 1971); Giacomo Sani, "Political Traditions as Contextual Variables," *American Journal of Political Science*, vol. 20 (August 1976), pp. 375-406. For a broader comparative perspective, see R. Rose and D. Urwin, "Persistence and Change in Western Party Systems since 1945," *Political Studies*, vol. 18 (September 1970), pp. 287-319; A. Zuckerman and M. I. Lichbach, "L'elettorato dei partiti europei" [The electorates of European parties], *Rivista italiana di scienza politica*, vol. 6, no. 1 (1976), pp. 111-138.

[48] See, for example, the pains taken by the PCI and the DC to reassure the other parties that their negotiations do *not* involve sub rosa efforts to bring the historic compromise to fruition. *Corriere della Sera*, May 13, 1977, p. 2, and May 23, 1977, p. 1; *L'Unità*, May 24, 1977, p. 1; London *Times*, May 25, 1977, p. 6. For a discussion of the causes of PCI growth in Italy and the basis for consternation over its possible advent to formal power, see Joseph LaPalombara, "The Italian Communist Party and Changing Italian Society," paper presented to the Conference on Italy and Eurocommunism, American Enterprise Institute, June 7-9, 1977, Washington, D. C.

control of the conditions and events that will affect future developments.

A few months after the elections, Premier Andreotti said that those at home and abroad contemplating Italy's political situation must summon unusual patience and understanding. By mid-1977, the problem of finding an appropriate and workable role for the PCI had become so delicate, so potentially explosive, that his admonition can only be underscored.

2

THE ITALIAN ELECTORAL PROCESS: THE ELECTIONS OF JUNE 1976

Douglas Wertman

A variety of interesting features of the Italian electoral process will be discussed in this chapter. These include the very high level of voter participation, the nature of the different proportional-representation electoral systems used to allocate the seats in the Chamber of Deputies and the Senate, the candidate-selection process, the role of preference voting, and the very personalized campaigns waged by the Chamber of Deputies candidates of some parties.

Voter Participation

Of the five major Western democracies, Italy has the highest level of voter participation (see Table 2–1). In the seven Italian Chamber of Deputies elections held between 1948 and 1976, turnout ranged between 92.2 percent and 93.8 percent of eligible voters. In 1976, 93.2 percent of the eligible electors voted.[1]

The high turnout, however, is not matched by equally high rates of other types of political participation or by attitudes strongly favorable to participation. Since the early postwar period, participation in demonstrations, strikes, and movements such as those in favor of women's rights and civil rights has certainly increased—the picture of political apathy painted in *The Civic Culture* is less accurate today

---

I would like to thank Gianfranco Pasquino for his helpful suggestions on this chapter.

[1] The turnout, by geographic area, in the 1976 Chamber of Deputies elections was: 95.4 percent in the north, 95.3 percent in the center, 88.8 percent in the continental south, and 87.4 percent on the islands of Sicily and Sardinia. *Il Corriere della Sera*, June 22, 1976, p. 1.

Table 2–1

VOTER PARTICIPATION IN ITALY, WEST GERMANY, FRANCE, GREAT BRITAIN, AND THE UNITED STATES, 1955–1976

Country	Type of Election	Range of Turnout (in percentages)
Italy	Chamber of Deputies	92.9-93.8
West Germany	Bundestag	86.7-91.1
France	National Assembly (first ballot)	68.7-82.7[a]
	Presidential (first ballot)	78.2-85.0
Great Britain	House of Commons	72.0-78.7
United States	Presidential	53.3-62.8

[a] The turnout in 1962 was 68.7. If that election were excluded, the range would be 77.1-82.7.

Note: The turnout figures for Italy, West Germany, France, and Great Britain are based on registered voters, while those for the United States are based on voting-age population. Given the different registration systems, these are the most equivalent figures.

Source: Italy, for 1958-1972, *Il Messaggero*, June 21, 1976, and for 1976, *Il Corriere della Sera*, June 22, 1976. West Germany, for 1957-1972, R. E. M. Irving and W. E. Paterson, "The West German Parliamentary Election of November 1972," *Parliamentary Affairs*, vol. 26 (Spring 1973), p. 239, and for 1976, *International Herald Tribune*, October 4, 1976, p. 1. France, *Il Messaggero*, June 21, 1976, p. 2. Great Britain, Howard Penniman, ed., *Britain at the Polls* (Washington, D.C.: American Enterprise Institute, 1975), pp. 242-244. United States, *International Herald Tribune*, November 4, 1976, p. 2.

than it was in the late 1950s.[2] Nevertheless, survey data from 1972 suggest that the level of interest in and discussion of politics was, at least in the early 1970s, still quite low and that pessimism about the individual's ability to have an impact in the political process was widespread. In mid-1972, 73.8 percent of those interviewed in one survey agreed with the statement, "Politics and government sometimes seem so complicated that people like me really can't understand what is going on."[3] Moreover, another indication that the recent rise in political participation in Italy does not explain the extent of voting is the fact that voter participation has been consistently high throughout the postwar period.

---

[2] Gabriel A. Almond and Sidney Verba, *The Civic Culture: Political Attitudes and Democracy in Five Nations* (Princeton: Princeton University Press, 1963).

[3] The source is a 1972 national survey done under the direction of Giacomo Sani and Samuel Barnes and used with their permission.

One important reason for the high level of voter participation is that Italian electoral procedures greatly facilitate voting. First, there is universal registration. After a citizen reaches eighteen years of age his name is automatically entered on the voting lists in the course of the next routine updating done by the communal authorities. Second, a few weeks before an election, an electoral certificate, showing that the individual is eligible to vote and giving the date of the election, the hours the polls are open, and the location of the polling place, is delivered to each voter by a messenger from the commune, the lowest unit of government. Third, the voting takes place both on Sunday from 7 A.M. to 10 P.M. and on Monday from 7 A.M. to 2 P.M. to accommodate those for whom voting on Sunday is difficult.

Though absentee voting is not possible in Italy, a variety of measures are taken to ease and encourage voting. First, a voter can change his official residency within Italy fairly quickly and simply if he so desires. Second, special voting sections are set up in hospitals and, in 1976 for the first time, in prisons, since those not yet tried or still appealing their cases retain their voting rights. Third, military personnel and seamen may vote in the commune where they are on duty or in port. Fourth, when returning home to vote, citizens living in Italy away from their home commune are charged greatly reduced train fares and those coming from abroad are charged nothing for their entire train trip within Italy if they travel second class and only 30 percent of the normal fare if they travel first class. This practice provides a subsidized visit to family and friends, but to take advantage of it the individual may be forced to miss a week of work and to travel for as much as two days on crowded trains. Despite the problems involved, in 1976 more than 500,000 Italians, mostly coming from Switzerland and West Germany, returned from abroad by car, train, and plane in order to vote. The Italian Communist party, in particular, encourages its supporters abroad to return home to vote, reaching them through letters from friends (the PCI provides a form letter for this purpose) and from the party and through electoral propaganda in the recreational facilities provided by the PCI for Italians working throughout Western Europe.[4]

[4] The PCI has a fairly substantial organization among Italians living in other Western European countries. There are 192 party sections in Western Europe outside Italy, and in 1975 there were 131 "festivals of L'Unità," these being a major promotional and fund-raising instrument of the PCI, combining politics, food, and games. These figures come from Almanacco PCI '76 (Rome: Sezione centrale di stampa e propaganda, PCI, 1976), pp. 30-32. For a discussion of the role of the Communist festivals, see David I. Kertzer, "Politics and Ritual: The Communist Festa in Italy," Anthropological Quarterly, vol. 47 (October 1974), pp. 374-389.

Beyond all these methods of facilitating voting, at least some of which have been adopted by other democracies as well, there must be an additional explanation for the high turnout in Italy. The presence among the electorate of strong partisan commitments may be one factor, mobilization by party organizations and related political groups another. However, the most significant additional factor is probably a psychological one: voting is generally considered not only a right, but also an important civic duty. The fact that the failure to vote is recorded on an Italian's identity card for five years, though it has no practical consequences, contributes to a psychological climate that makes voting seem almost compulsory.

The Electoral Laws

Italy has a bicameral Parliament. The Chamber of Deputies and the Senate have equal legislative powers and the government needs a vote of confidence from each. Both have always been elected at the same time by two variants of the proportional-representation electoral system. Despite the different minimum voting ages for the two houses (the gap, previously four years, became seven years when the minimum voting age for the Chamber elections was lowered to eighteen in 1974), the relative strengths of the various parties have not differed substantially from one house to the other. The allocation of seats for the Senate is only marginally less proportional to the popular vote than that for the Chamber of Deputies.[5] The higher number of votes needed to win one Senate seat (there are 315 elected senators compared with 630 deputies), however, means that the smaller parties that barely win seats in the Chamber may win none in the Senate, may not run Senate candidates, or may join with other parties to run common candidates. In the 1976 parliamentary elections, the two major parties, the Christian Democrats and the Communists, together won 73.1 percent of the popular vote for the Chamber and 72.7 percent for the Senate and gained 77.8 percent and 79.6 percent of the seats respectively in the two chambers.

---

[5] The d'Hondt highest-average formula, used for the Senate elections, is most proportional when the number of seats being allocated in each district is relatively high and when there are a substantial number of parties running candidates. Both of these conditions are met reasonably well in Italy, particularly in the nine most heavily populated regions, which have between twenty and twenty-nine seats in eight cases and forty-eight in the case of Lombardy. See Douglas W. Rae, *The Political Consequences of Electoral Laws*, rev. ed. (New Haven: Yale University Press, 1971), pp. 31-33.

The Chamber of Deputies. For the election of the 630 members of the Chamber of Deputies, Italy is divided into thirty-two electoral districts. Thirty-one choose their members by proportional representation, while the region of Valle d'Aosta is a single-member district using a plurality electoral system.[6] Each of the thirty-one districts using proportional representation comprises from one to five contiguous provinces within the same region and has between four and fifty-three seats based on population size.

The largest-remainder formula, according to a study by Douglas Rae, is the most proportionate of the proportional-representation formulas; the countries using it tend to have more parties running candidates and more parties actually gaining seats in the legislature than those that use other formulae. The variant used in Italy, the *imperiali* largest-remainder system, is especially designed to help small parties gain representation in the Chamber of Deputies by lowering the "initial price" for the first seat.[7] (See Table 2–2 for an example of the operation of the *imperiali* formula.)

The process of assigning seats to parties with the *imperiali* formula begins with the determination of the *quota*, that is, the number of votes necessary to win a seat. This varies from district to district. It is determined by dividing the total number of votes cast in the district by the sum of the number of seats to be allocated in that district *plus two*. (The addition of this two in the denominator lowers the quota and thus increases the small parties' chances to gain seats in the Chamber of Deputies.) The number of votes gained by each party in each electoral district is then divided by the quota in that district to determine the number of seats and the remainders for each party in each district. Normally about 10 percent of the seats nationwide remain unallocated after the division of the vote total by the quota in each of the electoral districts.[8]

The distribution among the parties of these remaining seats is done at the national level through the *national pool*. To receive seats through the national pool, each party must meet two requirements: (1) reach the district quota in at least one district and (2) gain at least 300,000 votes nationwide. Of these requirements, the first is the major hurdle for the smaller parties. In 1976 each of the three smallest parties to qualify for seats under the national pool reached

---

[6] Valle d'Aosta was instituted as a separate region in 1946 to give special rights to its many French-speaking residents. It has only one member in the Chamber of Deputies because electoral district lines never cross regional boundaries and because its population is small.

[7] Rae, *Political Consequences*, pp. 34–36.

[8] Fifty-nine of the 630 seats remained unallocated after this initial process in 1976.

Table 2–2
OPERATION OF THE IMPERIALI LARGEST-REMAINDER FORMULA: 1976 CHAMBER ELECTION, COMO-SONDRIO-VARESE DISTRICT

Party	Popular Vote	Seats at District Level[a]	Remainders to National Pool	National Pool Seats in District[b]	Total Seats
Christian Democrats	516,128	9	29,471	0	9
Communists	308,661	5	38,296	0	5
Socialists	134,574	2	26,428	0	2
Social Democrats	42,563	0	42,563	0	0
Republicans	37,860	0	37,860	1	1
Liberals	20,040	0	20,040	0	0
Italian Social Movement	41,237	0	41,237	1	1
Proletarian Democracy	23,138	0	23,138	1	1
Radicals	11,398	0	11,398	0	0

[a] To determine the initial seats and remainders:

$$(1) \quad \text{quota} = \frac{\text{total votes cast in district}}{\text{seats plus two}}$$

$$\text{quota} = \frac{1,135,539}{19 + 2}$$

$$\text{quota} = 54,073$$

$$(2) \quad \text{seats} + \text{remainder} = \frac{\text{votes for party}}{\text{quota}}$$

For the DC,

$$\text{seats} + \text{remainder} = \frac{516,128}{54,073}$$

$$\text{seats} + \text{remainder} = 9 + 29,471$$

[b] This was the sixth of seven national-pool seats for the PRI, the fourth of eight for the MSI, and the fifth of five for the DP, based on the ratio of the remainder to the district quota.

Source: Author's computations based on electoral statistics published in *Il Corriere della Sera*, June 23, 1976.

the quota in only a single district. As Table 2–3 shows, the Radicals exceeded the quota in the Rome-Viterbo-Latina-Frosinone district by only 351 votes, and the Liberals bettered the quota in the Turin-Novara-Vercelli district by 3,356 votes. These two parties, as well as the Proletarian Democracy group and the six parties that reached the

Table 2–3

PARTIES GAINING QUOTA IN ONLY ONE DISTRICT,
1976 CHAMBER ELECTION

Party	District	Votes Received in District (V)	District Quota (Q)	Remainder (V-Q)
Radicals	Rome-Viterbo-Latina-Frosinone	57,935	57,584	351
Italian Liberal party	Turin-Novara-Vercelli	61,360	58,004	3,356
Proletarian Democracy	Milan-Pavia	80,001	57,549	22,452

Note: In the nation as a whole, the Radicals won 394,623 votes and four seats, the Liberals 478,157 votes and five seats, and Proletarian Democracy 555,980 votes and six seats.

Source: Author's computations based on electoral statistics published in *Il Corriere della Sera*, June 23, 1976.

quota in two or more districts, were then eligible for additional seats through the national pool.[9]

The national pool is made up of the *sum of all the remainders* or unused votes (including the votes gained by eligible parties in districts where they did not attain the district quota) from the entire country of all the parties eligible for further seats. The *national quota*, or number of votes necessary for each seat in the national pool, is calculated by dividing the sum of all these remainders by the number of seats not allocated at the district level. Each party's share of these seats is determined by dividing its national total of remainders by the national quota.

---

[9] The parties and groups of the "extraparliamentary left" who wanted to run candidates in the 1976 elections were worried that they would not be able to attain the district quota in any of the thirty-one multimember districts. This concern dated back to 1972 when the various parties and groups to the left of the PCI had gained nearly 1 million votes altogether, but not a single seat in the Chamber of Deputies. In 1976 three groups of the extraparliamentary left eventually joined together, after difficult discussions, to run a common list for the Chamber of Deputies under the label Proletarian Democracy, though each maintained full political autonomy within the alliance. The six seats won in the Chamber under this label are split among the three component groups. See *Corriere della Sera*, May 9, 1976, p. 7, and June 26, 1976, p. 2. On the particular problem of the quota, see Piervittorio Buffa, "Il nemico si chiama Quoziente" [The enemy called quota], *L'Espresso*, May 2, 1976, pp. 17-18.

At this point, it must be ascertained in which of the thirty-one districts each party will gain its additional seats. This is done by determining *the percentage of the individual district quota* left over for each party in each district, with the seats from the national pool being allocated on the basis of the size of the percentages for each party: each party gains its national-pool seats in the districts where the ratios of its remainders to the district quotas are largest. Because of this procedure, a district may end up with one or more seats more or less than the number to which it is entitled on the basis of its population.[10]

The final step is the determination of which candidates will win the seats allocated to each party. When an Italian votes for the Chamber of Deputies, he first chooses a party—that is, he writes an X over the party's symbol on the ballot. In each district, each party may present as many candidates as there are seats, but the order of the names on its list does not determine who will win its seats. Instead, the order in which candidates are assigned the seats won by their party is determined by the number of *preference votes* cast for each candidate.

Each voter, if he chooses to do so, may cast from one to four preference votes in districts with sixteen or more seats and from one to three preference votes in districts with fifteen seats or fewer. The preference vote may be cast only for candidates of the party the voter has selected. The voter indicates his preferences by writing, in the space provided on the ballot, the name or number on the party list of each candidate. If in marking his ballot a voter designates only a party and does not cast preference votes, it is not assumed that he supports the order on the party list; only preference votes directly cast for each candidate count in his total. In recent Chamber elections approximately 30 percent of the Italian electors have cast preference votes. As we shall see, the institution of preference voting has major implications for the style of Italian political campaigns.

The Senate. For the Senate, each of the nineteen regions having more than one senator (the twentieth region, Valle d'Aosta, has only one senator) is divided into a number of districts, with each party nominating one candidate per district. There are fewer senatorial districts

---

[10] Another discussion of the electoral system used for the Chamber of Deputies and the Senate may be found in: John Clarke Adams and Paolo Barile, *The Government of Republican Italy*, 3d ed. (Boston: Houghton Mifflin Company, 1972), pp. 173-178. For the text of the electoral laws, see the official booklet published by the Ministry of the Interior, *Le Leggi Elettorali* [Electoral laws] (Rome: Istituto Poligrafico dello Stato, 1976).

than there are Senate seats to be filled in each region; therefore, more than one senator, though from different parties, may be elected from the same senatorial district. The voter's choice of a party is automatically a vote for his party's one candidate (and, therefore, the whole question of preference votes does not arise). Any candidate who receives 65 percent or more of the votes in his district is immediately declared elected—but this occurs very infrequently (only in 5 districts out of 241 in 1972 and in 2 districts in 1976). Candidates who receive less than 65 percent of the district vote must pool their votes with all the votes cast for their party in their region. The seats are then allocated among the parties within each region using the d'Hondt highest-average proportional-representation formula.

This process, illustrated in Table 2–4, proceeds as follows: (1) Each party's *average* at each step is calculated by dividing its total popular vote in the region by the sum of the number of seats it has thus far been allocated *plus one*. (2) Thus, each party begins with a denominator of one when it has no seats, and, as each seat is assigned, the party gaining the seat has its denominator increased by one, thereby *decreasing its average*. (3) The first seat is assigned to the party with the largest number of votes, that is, the highest average, and, after this seat or any successive seat is assigned, the new average is calculated for the party winning the seat at that stage; the *averages* of all the parties are then again inspected and the party with the highest average at this stage is the winner of the next seat. (4) This process of calculating the new average and determining which party wins the next seat continues *one seat at a time* until all the Senate seats in the region have been allocated.[11]

After the number of Senate seats for each party in each region has been determined, the final stage is to allocate the seats to the individual candidates of each party within each region. First, the *proportion* of the popular vote won by each party's candidate in each senatorial district is calculated. Then the seats won by each party are assigned to the candidates from that party with the highest percentages of the votes won in their districts *compared with the percentages won by other candidates of the same party* in other districts of the same region.

One result of this procedure is that the two large parties have a substantial number of safe districts, while the smaller parties, even the Italian Socialist party with 10 percent of the national popular vote, cannot count on many safe seats. In other words, based on the

---

[11] Adams and Barile, *Republican Italy*, pp. 176-177.

Table 2–4
OPERATION OF THE D'HONDT HIGHEST-AVERAGE FORMULA: 1976 SENATE ELECTION IN THE REGION OF LIGURIA

Step One: Allocation of the Seats among the Parties

Party Winning Seat (its total seats at that point)	Party Average at Each Stage					
	DC	PCI	PSI	Lay Alliance	MSI	Radicals
PCI (1)	406,266	464,440	149,076	103,382	54,894	16,180
DC (1)	406,266	232,220	149,076	103,362	54,894	16,180
PCI (2)	203,133	232,220	149,076	103,362	54,894	16,180
DC (2)	203,133	154,813	149,076	103,362	54,894	16,180
PCI (3)	135,422	154,813	149,076	103,362	54,894	16,180
PSI (1)	135,422	116,110	149,076	103,362	54,894	16,180
DC (3)	135,422	116,110	74,538	103,362	54,894	16,180
PCI (4)	101,567	116,110	74,538	103,362	54,894	16,180
Lay Alliance (1)	101,567	92,888	74,538	103,362	54,894	16,180
DC (4)	101,567	92,888	74,538	51,676	54,894	16,180

All ten seats in Liguria allocated to parties

Step Two: Allocation of the Seats Among the Candidates in Each Party

Senatorial District	Proportion of the District Vote of Parties Winning Seats				Senator(s) Elected
	DC	PCI	PSI	Lay Alliance	
Imperia	40.0	32.9	11.0	9.1	DC-second
Savona	34.9	40.4	12.8	7.1	DC-fourth
Genova I	27.2	49.3	13.2	5.8	PCI-first
Genova II	28.2	48.5	13.2	5.0	PCI-second
Genova III	29.7	42.4	14.5	7.0	PCI-fourth; PSI
Genova IV	37.2	23.3	10.7	19.5	DC-third; lay group
Chiavari	42.4	29.3	11.9	9.9	DC-first
La Spezia	32.8	43.0	12.3	7.2	PCI-third

Source: Author's computations based on electoral statistics published in *Il Popolo*, June 22 and June 23, 1976.

party's past performance in each district and the estimate of the party's performance in the coming election in terms of the proportion in each district and the number of Senate seats it will win in each region, the DC and the PCI in particular can put candidates that they definitely want in the Senate in their party's safe senatorial districts.

One distinction between the electoral systems used for the Chamber and the Senate must be emphasized. For the Chamber of Deputies in the case of most parties (though *not* the PCI), because of the use of preference voting, the final choice of which candidate will win the party's seats is made at the stage of popular voting and the candidate must be able to attract enough preference votes to gain one of his party's seats in the district where he runs. For the Senate, the voter, in casting his ballot in his district, chooses a party which has already selected its one candidate for that district. (Of course, a small party may improve its chances for a Senate seat by nominating a prestigious individual who can bring additional votes to the party.) Therefore, in the case of the Senate, the important stage for determining which individuals will win many of the Senate seats (especially in the case of the DC and the PCI) is that of intraparty candidate selection. This distinction between the Chamber of Deputies and Senate electoral procedures is particularly important for the formation of candidate lists within the DC.

Candidate Selection: An Introduction

In the 1976 electoral campaign the formation of candidate lists was especially important for the DC and the PCI. Both parties were concerned about their public image. The Christian Democrats were attempting to revitalize their parliamentary delegation by creating a meaningful turnover and bringing new faces into the DC lists, while the Communists sought to recruit a number of independent candidates as part of their effort to further the PCI's legitimization as a political force committed to pluralist democracy. After briefly discussing a few general points about candidate selection and its importance for the Italian Socialist party and the three small lay parties in the center and center-right of the Italian political spectrum, this chapter will focus primarily on the candidate-selection process in the Christian Democratic and Communist parties.

Though there are no residency requirements for candidates, a large number of the candidates are residents of the areas where they run. This is especially true of candidates for the Chamber of Deputies, whose election depends on their ability to attract preference votes.[12] The same candidate may run for the Chamber of Deputies

---

[12] The exception is the PCI, which is generally able to direct the preference votes of its highly disciplined supporters very effectively, regardless of whether the candidates are local figures or outsiders. See the discussion of Communist candidate selection, pp. 65-74.

Candidate Selection in the Small Lay Parties. Like the other small parties, the three small lay parties in the center and center-right of the Italian political spectrum—the Italian Liberal party, the Italian Social Democratic party, and the Italian Republican party—generally win only a few seats, none of which can be considered safe. Thus, there is relatively little competition for the nominations of these parties. They cannot afford to exclude any incumbents who might bring votes to the party, and in 1976 they renominated nearly all of them—thirty-eight out of forty-one (92.9 percent) for the PSDI, nineteen out of twenty (95 percent) for the PRI, and twenty-five out of thirty (83.3 percent) for the PLI.[18]

Each of these parties, of course, had its own problems. The PLI, which had slipped from 3.9 percent of the vote in the 1972 Chamber of Deputies elections to 2.5 percent in the 1975 regional elections, feared a substantial decline in its parliamentary representation. The explicit goal of the PSDI was merely the reelection of its incumbent members.[19] The PRI, meanwhile, which had gained slightly in 1975 compared with 1972 and was expected to increase its parliamentary representation in 1976, tried to include several prestige candidates who would help the party cultivate an image of competence and responsibility. Such figures as Gianni Agnelli, president of Fiat, and Guido Carli, ex-director of the Bank of Italy, however, eventually declined its offers.[20] The PLI tried to reach a broad electoral agreement with the PRI and the PSDI for the Senate elections, but the PRI in particular, which considered its own prospects good and was wary of a political alliance with the PLI, resisted. In the end the three parties reached a "technical" agreement to present common Senate candidates in six regions where none of the three parties was likely to win a seat by itself.

Christian Democratic Candidate Selection

By 1976 the Christian Democratic party had been the dominant party in the Italian government for slightly more than thirty years. Each of the thirty-three governments between December 10, 1945, and June 1976 was led by a Christian Democratic prime minister. But by 1976 many people in Italy believed that the DC had failed both

---

[18] *Corriere della Sera*, May 21, 1976, p. 2.

[19] The official in the PSDI responsible for organizational affairs, Michele Di Giesi, stated, "Our only objective is to support the incumbent members of Parliament and ensure that they are reelected," *Panorama*, May 18, 1976, p. 48.

[20] *Corriere della Sera*, May 9, 1976.

to initiate necessary economic and social reforms and at the same time to revitalize and reform itself. Not only had the same leadership group dominated the party for more than two decades, but the DC parliamentary group had changed less over the past ten or fifteen years than any other. In fact, 48.5 percent of the DC deputies and senators serving at the time of the elections in 1976 had been members of Parliament for three terms or more, that is, thirteen years or more.[21] The issue of candidate selection by the DC in May 1976, therefore, took on particular importance as part of the general question of whether the DC could reform itself as well as Italian society.

After a discussion lasting two days, the DC's national executive committee published the formal rules for the designation of parliamentary candidates. The executive committee, which is elected by the DC national council, includes representatives of all eight or nine factions as well as all the major DC leaders among its forty-three members. It meets frequently and is the major policy-making body of the DC.[22] In the discussions preceding the publication of the party rules for candidate selection, the executive committee focused on the question of revitalizing the DC parliamentary delegation.

Among the specific proposals considered by the executive committee as criteria to recommend to the provincial electoral commissions were: (1) to exclude anyone who had served four terms or more in Parliament (in 1976, this meant 34.5 percent of the incumbent DC deputies), (2) to exclude deputies older than sixty-five years of age (who could then run for the Senate) and senators older than seventy, and (3) to exclude deputies with poor records in Parliament based on their attendance at committee and full Chamber sessions, the number of speeches they had given in Parliament, and the number of bills they had introduced.[23] In this connection it was proposed that the leadership of the DC in the Senate and the Chamber of Deputies

[21] Gianfranco Pasquino, "Crisi della DC e evoluzione del sistema politico" [The crisis of the DC and the evolution of the political system], *Rivista italiana di scienza politica*, vol. 5 (December 1975), p. 462.

[22] The DC national council is composed of slightly more than 200 members, 120 of whom are chosen on the basis of the relative strength of the factions at the DC National Congress, while the other 80 or 90 members include 12 elected by the Chamber of Deputies delegation of the DC, 12 elected by the DC Senate group, the 20 regional secretaries, 20 representatives of local governments, and all past DC national secretaries and prime ministers.

[23] The largest number of absences for any single DC deputy was 278 out of 400 sessions. Maurizio Pensa, who held this record, was a surgeon and director of a clinic in Turin. He was elected for the first time in 1972 and not renominated in 1976. Ultimately, out of the eighteen with the most absences (all more than 200), six were not renominated, two became Senate candidates, and the others were again Chamber candidates.

should send an evaluation of each incumbent to the appropriate provincial electoral commission.[24]

None of these three proposals was adopted. One objection apparently expressed by members of the DC executive committee—apart from the fact that excluding those with four terms or more in Parliament would have meant excluding many of themselves—was that the removal of some long-serving local notables might cost the DC votes. The rules on candidate selection ultimately issued by the executive committee suggested in a general way that the quality and length of parliamentary service should be taken into account by the provincial electoral commissions.[25] The executive committee also intended to try, informally, to encourage veteran incumbents to retire voluntarily. However, beyond these general policies and the expression of a desire to include many new candidates in the DC lists, the executive committee left the initiative for revitalizing the party lists to the provincial electoral commissions.

The voting members of the DC provincial electoral commissions include the provincial DC secretary as presiding officer, eight members chosen on a proportional-representation basis by the provincial party committee, and the provincial delegates of the youth movement and the women's movement of the DC. Generally the composition of the commissions proportionately reflects the strength of the various DC factions within the province. These commissions nominate candidates for the Chamber of Deputies (the number each commission selects is decided by the national executive committee) and the Senate. The executive committee reserves a number of senatorial districts for itself to allocate and decides which provincial electoral commission should choose the senatorial candidate when two or more provinces each include 25 percent or more of the electorate of the senatorial district. The electoral commissions for the electoral district in the case of the Chamber of Deputies and for the region in the case of the Senate are chaired by the regional party secretary and contain three members from each of the provincial electoral commissions in the relevant area as well as the regional delegates of the DC's youth and women's movements. The electoral district commissions play a role in determining the order of candidates, though it is the national executive committee that makes the final decision, while the regional commission puts together the list of Senate candidates on the basis of the decisions of the various provincial electoral commissions. The

---

[24] *Corriere della Sera*, May 4-7, 1976.

[25] The candidate-selection rules were printed in *Il Popolo*, the Christian Democratic party newspaper, on May 6, 1976, p. 2.

regional commission may also make suggestions concerning the senatorial districts in which the executive committee has reserved the right to nominate the party's candidates.[26]

Since the provincial electoral commissions contain representatives from all the factions important in the provincial DC and since the factional struggle for seats in the Chamber of Deputies takes place particularly in the battle for preference votes during the electoral campaign, the drawing up of lists by these commissions is not in most cases used to prevent the candidacy of individuals from any factions that are strong in the province.[27] This kind of reciprocity probably occurs throughout the country, for two reasons: (1) different factions are dominant or in a minority in different provinces, and (2) the national executive committee, where all factions are represented but where a locally dominant faction may be weak, can put candidates excluded at the provincial level in the final lists. In some cases personal or factional feuds in a province, or the incentive to exclude strong opponents and thereby reduce the competition for preference votes, leads the local intraparty majority to exclude candidates of certain factions. Usually, however, the factional struggle in the candidate-selection phase within the DC locally and nationally is concentrated on the battle for safe Senate seats and for the role of *capolista*, the first name on the party's list of Chamber of Deputies candidates in each electoral district. It should be added that the formation of the lists by the provincial electoral commissions also involves consultation with organizations related to the party, the most important being the Confederation of Small Farmers (Coltivatori Diretti).

The provincial electoral commissions (along with the provincial and regional party organizations, particularly their secretaries) play an important role in the candidate-selection process, but the national executive committee has many powers that allow it also to play a major part in the selection of parliamentary candidates. First, the national executive committee keeps one position for itself to fill in the Chamber candidate list in each of the districts where there are twenty seats or fewer and two places where there are more than twenty seats, giving it a total of forty-three places to fill directly; of course, because of the competition for preference votes, the com-

---

[26] According to the party rules, the members of the provincial, district, and regional electoral commissions may not be candidates for Parliament.

[27] Gianfranco Pasquino, "Le radici del frazionismo e il voto di preferenza" [The roots of factionalism and the preference vote], in Giovanni Sartori, ed., *Correnti frazioni e fazioni nei partiti politici italiani* [Currents, fractions, and factions in Italian political parties] (Bologna: II Mulino, 1973), pp. 88-89.

mittee normally chooses a candidate who is well known in the area where he runs. Second, it reserves a number of very safe senatorial districts whose candidates it chooses directly (in 1976 it reserved at least twenty-three). Third, it decides the final order of all the Chamber district lists, including the name of the *capolista*, though this often involves negotiation and discussion with the local party officials and factions.

Fourth, incumbents excluded from the candidate lists at the local level can appeal to the national executive committee and may be reinstated or put in a senatorial seat in that region or another region, particularly if they have significant influence at the national level or have a "godfather" among the top leaders on the executive committee. In 1976 some veteran incumbents, including several who had actually been reinstated at the national level, retired because of local pressure. However, there were also a number of cases of incumbents excluded at the provincial level who appealed to the executive committee and were put back in the candidate lists. Finally, in a general sense, according to the candidate-selection rules issued by the national executive committee, the committee "approves in a definitive way, with possible modifications, the lists of candidates proposed by each of the [district or regional] commissions." [28]

In sum, the national leadership has the ultimate right, which it sometimes uses, to make changes in the lists proposed at the provincial and regional level. However, the provincial and regional party officials and factional leaders also have a significant input in the candidate-selection process and play a direct role through their influence on the provincial electoral commissions. The finalization of the lists often involves negotiation among national, regional, and provincial party leaders, but the final authority of the national executive committee is only occasionally challenged at the local level. Local resistance to the final lists violates the party rules and often leads to the resignation of local officials.

The national executive committee or components of it met nearly continuously in 1976 for the period from May 14 until the afternoon of May 19, just a few hours before the deadline for the presentation of candidate lists. It handled numerous difficult problems directly and assigned others to subcommittees or individual negotiators.[29]

---

[28] *Il Popolo*, May 6, 1976, p. 2.

[29] The provincial and regional party officials (and particularly the secretaries) remain involved while the national executive committee is finalizing the lists, and sometimes even go to Rome to discuss the lists with executive committee members.

The most controversial issues were discussed by a special subcommittee chaired by Party Secretary Benigno Zaccagnini and including Amintore Fanfani, who is an ex-party secretary and ex-prime minister and was at that time president of the DC national council, as well as the chiefs of all the factions.[30]

To illustrate the problems involved in DC candidate selection in 1976, the following section of this chapter will focus on three cases: (1) the Umberto Agnelli candidacy; (2) the efforts of the Emilia-Romagna DC to create a substantial turnover in its parliamentary delegation; and (3) the revolt of the party organization in Lombardy and several of its provinces against decisions made by the national executive committee.[31]

The Candidacy of Umberto Agnelli. Many DC leaders placed great importance on their party's nominating Umberto Agnelli, one of Italy's most prominent industrialists, particularly at a time when the PRI was trying to persuade Umberto's even more famous brother Gianni to run on its ticket. Significant from the point of view of party strategy, the Agnelli candidacy is also interesting as an illustration of the personal and factional conflict that often besets the DC's policy-making process.

The Piedmontese DC offered Umberto Agnelli, one of the top executives of the Fiat corporation, the very safe senatorial district of Cuneo and suggested that an alternative possibility might be a senatorial district in the city of Turin.[32] Agnelli was receptive to the idea of becoming a DC candidate, but he preferred to run for the Chamber of Deputies in Turin rather than for the Senate in the largely agricultural district of Cuneo. This was immediately opposed by some party leaders in Turin, in part because Agnelli's well-known name and financial means would allow him to amass a large number of preference votes and thereby damage the chances of other DC candidates in the district. Particularly strong opposition came from Carlo Donat Cattin, the top national leader of the left-wing *Forze Nuove* faction, a deputy from Turin since 1958, a long-time member of the national executive committee, and a minister in seven of the

---

[30] *Corriere della Sera*, May 14-22, 1976.

[31] There are a number of other particularly interesting cases, including the battle over whether Antonio Gava would be *capolista* at Naples, the imposition of a candidate by the national executive committee in the senatorial college of Cagliari despite strong local protests, the choice of Giorgio La Pira as *capolista* in Florence, and the revolt in Molise against the imposition of a senatorial candidate.

[32] The Agnelli case was covered extensively by the Italian newspapers, including *Corriere della Sera*, from May 13 through May 22, 1976.

nine governments since July 1969. Donat Cattin argued that the industrialist's candidacy for either the Chamber or the Senate in Piedmont would change the "popular" nature of the DC there. Donat Cattin may also have feared competition from Agnelli if the latter were placed on the Chamber list in Turin (in fact, Donat Cattin eventually finished only fifth among DC candidates in the district despite being *capolista*).

The Agnelli case, therefore, almost immediately became one that could be decided only by the national executive committee. While Donat Cattin continued to oppose Agnelli's candidacy, arguing that he did not want the DC to become a "party of industrialists," Fanfani suggested that Agnelli would be valuable to the DC in helping to attract the votes of the middle class and the industrialists.[33] During the May 14-18 period, while the special subcommittee chaired by Benigno Zaccagnini was dealing with the most controversial issues, including the Agnelli case, Donat Cattin and Guido Bodrato (another *Forze Nuove* member of the executive committee, also from Piedmont) threatened to withdraw their candidacies if Agnelli were given a senatorial district in Piedmont. The executive committee, on May 18, voted to offer Agnelli the choice among five different safe senatorial districts, including Cuneo in Piedmont, Chieti in Abruzzo, and three in Rome. Donat Cattin was the only member of the executive committee to vote against this proposal (Bodrato being absent at the time). Almost immediately, however, Donat Cattin and Bodrato again threatened not to run if Agnelli were a candidate in Cuneo.

Agnelli finally told the executive committee on the morning of May 19 that he would be willing to run in Cuneo. After further talks that morning with Donat Cattin and then with Fanfani and the DC leaders in the Senate and Chamber, Zaccagnini, extremely fatigued and pressured from all sides on the Agnelli issue, apparently said that if Agnelli took the Cuneo district instead of one in Rome he would be forced to resign as DC party secretary. Giulio Andreotti, himself a Roman, then appealed to Agnelli, for the sake of party unity, to accept a senatorial district in Rome, which Agnelli finally did at 3 P.M. on May 19, five hours before the closing of the presentation of lists.

Problems in Emilia-Romagna. The case of Emilia-Romagna is particularly important because it relates directly to the issue of revitalizing the DC parliamentary delegation. At the regional congress of the Emilia-Romagna DC in March 1976, a resolution, supported by the

---

[33] *Corriere della Sera*, May 15, 1976, pp. 1-2.

relatively new regional secretary Leonardo Melandri and the regional executive committee, was unanimously approved: it recommended that incumbents who had been in Parliament for three terms or more not be renominated and suggested that this should be the national policy of the DC. The Emilia-Romagna DC, therefore, proposed a relatively drastic step which, it argued, was necessary if the DC wanted to bring about a substantial turnover in its parliamentary delegation.[34]

The Emilia-Romagna DC did, in fact, very carefully follow this policy in candidate selection, except in renominating Benigno Zaccagnini, a deputy from Ravenna since 1948, who was national secretary of the DC and had come to symbolize the reform movement within the party. None of the other three senators and five deputies who had served three terms or more was renominated by the provincial electoral commissions in Emilia-Romagna. Several of them accepted their fate, including veteran Senator Giuseppe Medici and Deputy Giovanni Elkan. Angelo Salizzoni, a deputy since 1948, in May 1976 undersecretary in the office of then Prime Minister Aldo Moro and a long-time associate of Moro, was reinstated in the candidate lists because of the efforts of Moro within the national executive committee; however, as local pressure continued, Salizzoni finally decided to give up his candidacy.

Several others appealed to the national executive committee to have their names returned to the DC candidate lists. The DC regional secretary, Melandri, went to Rome while the executive committee was working on these cases to fight the reinsertion in the lists of these incumbents excluded at the provincial level; afterward he publicly criticized the executive committee's actions.[35] Out of the eight excluded by the provincial and regional DC in Emilia-Romagna, three were put back in the candidate lists by the national executive committee, which had created a special subcommittee to consider the Emilia-Romagna issue. Several members of the executive committee objected to the adoption of any rule that automatically excluded certain incumbents.

---

[34] An article written by one of the major proponents of the three-term limitation within the Emilia-Romagna DC appeared in *Corriere della Sera* on May 1, 1976: Ermano Gorrieri, "La DC emiliana: solo tre volte in Parlamento" [The Emilian DC: only three times in Parliament], p. 6.

[35] In addition to returning several candidates to the lists, the national executive committee further angered the Emilia-Romagna DC by replacing a newly nominated woman, Wilma Preti, who had been chosen for an ultra-safe senatorial college and is from the left of the party, with a small businessman who is a member of Fanfani's faction. *Corriere della Sera*, May 18, 1976, p. 2.

Giovanni Bersani, a deputy from Emilia-Romagna since 1948 and the national president of the *Movimento Cristiano Lavoratori*, was given the very safe senatorial district of Cuneo in Piedmont. Carlo Buzzi, a deputy since 1953, was also renominated. The fact that he was national president of the Italian Catholic Teachers' Association was important, according to Melandri, in Buzzi's ability to have himself renominated through pressure from the executive committee after his exclusion at the provincial level. Negotiations between the regional DC and the national executive committee ended in Buzzi's being allowed to run in two senatorial districts in Emilia-Romagna, at least one of which was moderately safe.[36] Alberto Spigaroli, three-term senator from one of the DC's two ultra-safe senatorial districts in Emilia-Romagna and undersecretary for culture in the Moro government in May 1976, was also unwilling to accept his removal from Parliament. After a series of discussions involving the national executive committee, the DC regional officials, and the provincial party officials in Piacenza, it was agreed that Spigaroli would be *capolista* for the DC in the Chamber district of Parma-Modena-Piacenza-Reggio Emilia.[37]

In summary, the extent of the DC's revitalization was greater in Emilia-Romagna than elsewhere in Italy, but three of the eight incumbents removed at the provincial level were still able to secure renomination through the intervention of the national executive committee.

The Revolt in the Lombardy DC. The case of Lombardy is an example of local defiance of the national executive committee in direct contravention of the party rules. It raises the issue of the rights and powers of the provincial electoral commissions and the local party in general versus those of the national party leadership.

In Lombardy, particularly in the provinces of Sondrio, Bergamo, and Varese, there was substantial dissatisfaction over the decision of the national executive committee to change several of the senatorial designations made at the local level, all in safe senatorial districts. In Sondrio the provincial electoral commission had unanimously de-

---

[36] Ibid., May 15, 1976, p. 1 and May 18, 1976, p. 2.

[37] Spigaroli, in a real rarity for a DC *capolista*, did not obtain enough preference votes to win election to the Chamber of Deputies, in part because, having always held a very safe Senate seat, he was not prepared to run the kind of campaign necessary to gain preference votes. Shortly after the election, it seemed as though Spigaroli had won; however, eventually the PCI gained a seat and the DC lost one, so Spigaroli was the first of those not elected nationwide among all the DC candidates. *Corriere della Sera*, July 26, 1976, p. 3.

cided to replace veteran Senator and ex-Finance Minister Athos Valsecchi with a two-term deputy, Eugenio Tarabini. The strong opposition to Valsecchi within the local DC was due to allegations of his involvement in the oil company scandal. But the national executive committee decided to renominate him as the senatorial candidate in his old district despite the local decision. This led to the resignation of the entire provincial DC committee in protest and its opening of an independent headquarters in a new office. There were also numerous threats of resignation from DC provincial councillors, communal councillors, and mayors in the province of Sondrio.[38]

In Bergamo, the provincial electoral commission had nominated for senator Angelo Castelli, incumbent deputy and chairman of the joint Senate-Chamber of Deputies committee investigating the Lockheed scandal. (As a senator, Castelli would be able to continue as chairman of the committee since the chairmanship was due to pass to the Senate in the new Parliament.) The incumbent senator, Giovanbattista Scaglia, had been in Parliament since 1948. The commission also chose Vincenzo Bombardieri, the provincial secretary of the Italian Confederation of Workers' Unions (CISL) in Bergamo since 1969 and a native of Bergamo, as candidate in the senatorial district of Treviglio. Both these decisions were reversed by the national executive committee, which returned Scaglia to the Senate and Castelli to the Chamber and replaced Bombardieri with Senator Vittorio Pozzar, a native of Friuli Venezia-Giulia who had previously been elected in the senatorial district of Monza in Lombardy.

On May 17, 1976, the DC provincial committee in Bergamo announced (after a vote of twenty-nine in favor of the resolution, four against, and two abstaining) that it would resign if the candidate lists were not finalized in the form originally proposed by the provincial electoral commission.[39] The national executive committee eventually accepted the Senate candidacy of Castelli, offering Scaglia the position of DC *capolista* for the Chamber of Deputies in the Bergamo-Brescia electoral district. (Scaglia, however, decided to retire rather than accept this Chamber candidacy because he did not want to compete for preference votes.)

The DC provincial electoral commission in Varese had nominated a local deputy, Aristide Marchetti, for the senatorial college of Varese, but the national executive committee instead chose Gino Colombo, an important DC leader from Milan who had been communal party secretary in Milan for eight years and president of the

[38] Ibid., May 18, 1976, p. 2.
[39] Ibid.

regional council in Lombardy for five years. Marchetti then threatened to resign from the DC, as did a Lombardian regional councillor from Varese.[40]

In sum, in the safe senatorial districts of Sondrio, Treviglio (in the province of Bergamo), and Varese, the national executive committee had replaced natives chosen by the respective provincial electoral commissions with one local incumbent and two nominees from outside the province concerned. The outcome was that the regional executive committee of the DC in Lombardy presented the Senate candidates chosen by the provincial electoral commissions in these three cases and one other instance, in direct contradiction to the decisions of the national executive committee. Tarabini, Bombardieri, and Marchetti, the local choices, were all nominated and ultimately elected to the Senate in Sondrio, Treviglio, and Varese respectively. For the Chamber of Deputies it presented essentially the list for the Milan-Pavia district that had been approved by the national executive committee. These actions led to many recriminations among the various factions in Lombardy, the resignation of the DC regional secretary, and the appointment by Zaccagnini of a commissioner to run the party in Lombardy and examine the problems there while decisions were made about what further actions to take.[41]

The DC candidate-selection process, which is relatively chaotic (particularly in the last several days when the national executive committee is finalizing the lists), is complicated by factional conflict, negotiations among the provincial, regional, and national leaders, and the importance of a parliamentary career for access to power within the DC. Though the national executive committee did not approve any specific criteria for maximizing turnover in the DC parliamentary delegation, the attempt at revitalization was partially successful, with 18.4 percent of the Chamber incumbents and 40.7 percent of the Senate incumbents not renominated for either of the two houses.[42] Among the ninety-two incumbent deputies who had served four terms or more by May 1976, fifty-three (57.6 percent) were renominated (and forty were reelected), fourteen (15.2 percent) became Senate candidates, one ran for both the Chamber and the Senate,

---

[40] Ibid., May 20, 1976, p. 2.

[41] Ibid., May 22-25, 1976.

[42] Altogether, therefore, 74.5 percent of the DC incumbents were renominated in one of the houses. The figures for the other parties are: 69.2 percent, PCI; 88.7 percent, PSI; 92.9 percent, PSDI; 83.3 percent, PLI; 95.0 percent, PRI; and 93.9 percent, MSI.

and twenty-four (26.5 percent) were not renominated.[43] In comparison, 14.4 percent of those who had served one to three terms were not renominated. Finally, there were some new faces, though generally these were people who were already identified with the Catholic subculture and/or the Christian Democratic political world.

Candidate Selection in the Italian Communist Party

For the Italian Communist party in 1976, the major issue in candidate selection was not the question of revitalizing the parliamentary delegation. The PCI has always ensured that there would be a turnover of at least one-third of its delegates and senators at each election. In the past its policy had been not to allow any but the most important leaders to serve more than two terms. This was relaxed slightly in 1976 to allow the party to retain certain specialists who would be useful to the PCI in Parliament, but even so only 17.5 percent of the PCI deputies elected in 1976 have been elected three or more times (compared with 45.4 percent of the DC deputies and 50.8 percent of the Socialist deputies).[44]

This relatively high rate of turnover in PCI parliamentary delegations can be explained by several characteristics of the party. First, the PCI is not fraught with factionalism, as are the DC and the PSI, and factionalism tends to prolong parliamentary careers. In addition, within the PCI, serving in Parliament is not seen as superior to other kinds of work for or within the party. Finally, a local-national interchange is useful for the party and for its elite. The PCI places a high value on having members of Parliament who have worked in communal, provincial, and regional governments and understand their problems, as well as on having former members of Parliament with a detailed understanding of the national political process serving in the subnational governments.

In putting together its candidate lists in 1976, the PCI sought, above all, to bring a number of independent candidates into its lists, as it had done to a degree in past elections. Ultimately, the independents on the PCI lists included a variety of people from all sectors of Italian society who had not previously been identified with the Communist party. Among these were a number of dissident, though

---

[43] These statistics are based on information from a number of issues of *Corriere della Sera* in May and June 1976.

[44] The policy of limiting most members of Parliament to two terms has clearly not changed very much: after the 1972 election 16.7 percent of the PCI deputies had been elected to three terms or more (compared with 17.5 percent in 1976).

practicing, Catholics; Altiero Spinelli, a member of the EEC Commission at the time of his nomination; Nino Pasti, a former air force general and NATO deputy supreme commander, as well as several other ex-military officials; Giuseppe Branca, ex-president of the Constitutional Court; Luigi Spaventa, an economist at the University of Rome and columnist for the Milan daily *Il Corriere della Sera*—for the Chamber and Senate, a total of forty. These independents were given safe Senate seats or assured election to the Chamber.

The importance attached to the participation of independents by the PCI leadership was reflected in the inch-high headline in *L'Unità*, the PCI daily newspaper, on May 16, 1976, the first day of presentation of the candidate lists: "Other Independent Personalities Enter the Communist Lists." Their function was to further the image of the party as one committed to pluralism and parliamentary democracy, to help legitimize the PCI as a democratic political force. These independents were not expected to become PCI members or to join the PCI party groups in the Chamber of Deputies or the Senate. Instead, those who were elected were generally encouraged to join the "mixed group" in the Chamber or the "independents of the left" in the Senate and have not been bound by party discipline in parliamentary votes, though they almost always have voted with the PCI on important issues.

In naming independent candidates the PCI also sought to elect a substantial number of experts or specialists, including those with experience in communal, provincial, and regional governments and competent in various fields.[45] This was particularly important since the party expected to be playing a larger role in policy making than ever before (as it turned out, the PCI held a number of committee chairmanships for the first time) and might even have a role in the government. The PCI also wanted to increase the number of women among its candidates and members of Parliament.

The PCI has a substantial number of safe senatorial seats, and, because of the relative discipline of the PCI electorate and the lack of an intraparty battle over preference votes, it also has positions on the Chamber of Deputies lists through which it can ensure that a specific individual will be elected. In fact, the PCI leadership is able to make a relatively accurate calculation, normally within two or three percentage points and based in part on past performance,

---

[45] For example, Guido Fanti, elected to the Chamber of Deputies, was an executive committee member and had been president of the region of Emilia-Romagna. Fanti became chairman of the joint Senate-Chamber of Deputies Committee on Regional Affairs in the new Parliament.

of the proportion of the popular vote it will obtain nationwide, in each region, in each Chamber electoral district, and in each senatorial district. Thus, it can predict the number of Senate seats the party will win in each region, in which senatorial districts in each region it will win its seats, and the number of Chamber seats it will win in each electoral district. As a result, the PCI, in effect, has three groups of candidates: those it definitely wants to elect to Parliament, the possible winners who will obtain seats if the most optimistic party estimates of the vote are borne out, and those who will represent the party as candidates but lose.

Compared with the DC's relatively chaotic and well-publicized candidate-selection process, that of the PCI is efficient, well organized, and relatively hidden. While the DC is usually the last to turn in its candidate lists throughout the country (sometimes only hours before the deadline) the PCI for thirty years has almost always been the first to turn in its candidate lists, at the beginning of the presentation period.[46] The government electoral offices, which accept the lists, opened at 8 A.M. on May 16, 1976; in most of the cities where lists were to be handed in, hundreds of PCI members or sympathizers waited outside the building the entire night before to be ready literally to run into the building and up to the electoral office to present the Communist lists when the door opened. In 1976 the PCI, almost for the first time, had some competition. There were some scuffles between Radicals and Communists during the all-night waits in several cities, but the Communists, with their larger number of supporters, were usually able to secure the first spot on the ballot by winning the race to the electoral office.

The major work in drawing up the PCI's candidate lists is done by the national secretariat and in particular by the organizational affairs section of the national party bureaucracy. The PCI's national executive committee, composed of more than thirty members and containing the major party leaders, meets approximately once every three weeks (compared with the central committee, which usually has 175–200 members and meets three to six times a year). The executive committee makes major policy decisions, while the secretariat, which normally has seven or eight members, meets at least weekly and directly supervises the party bureaucracy. The executive committee meets early in the candidate-selection process and makes

---

[46] One reason that the PCI always tries to put its lists in first is to ensure that it will have the upper lefthand position on the ballot, making it easier to explain clearly to PCI voters how to vote for the party. Confusion sometimes arises because several parties have symbols similar to that of the PCI, incorporating in some form the hammer and sickle.

general policy decisions, determining the criteria that should be followed in selecting candidates.

The first and most important stage of candidate selection, apart from the determination of the general criteria by the executive committee, is an informal process, not officially included in the party rules. First, there is a technical evaluation of each incumbent member of Parliament by the PCI leadership in the Chamber of Deputies and the Senate, and a judgment is made as to which members are essential and which are nonessential for the effective functioning of the PCI in Parliament. The evaluation is based on attendance, committee work, and special expertise. Second, the regional party organizations, and in particular the regional party secretaries, suggest names of candidates from the local areas throughout the country, since it is electorally useful and representationally proper to present some candidates who are well known at the local level for their activities within the party and/or the communal, provincial, or regional government.

The regional secretaries have real political weight within the PCI; usually a number of them are members of the national executive committee, and they are an important source of recruitment for promotions to the national secretariat.[47] The regional party officials base their suggestions on discussions and negotiations with the provincial party organizations, particularly the provincial secretaries. The importance of the local candidates from the party organization and the communal and regional governments can be illustrated by a list of the previous jobs of some of the new PCI members of Parliament in 1976 from the province of Bologna: immediately before their election in June 1976, five of the new members were, respectively, president of the regional government, party secretary for the province, party secretary for the city of Bologna, mayor of Imola (a city of more than 50,000 near Bologna), and city councilman (since 1960) in Bologna.[48]

In addition to the candidates prominent in local politics, a substantial number of national figures are nominated. These are individuals whom the national party leadership, particularly the secretariat, specifically wants nominated and elected because of their national reputation or their expertise in particular fields. Some of them work at the national party headquarters; the independents also

---

[47] There are currently five regional secretaries sitting on the national executive committee, and the two newest members of the Secretariat, added in October 1976, both came from regional secretary jobs. *L'Unità*, October 21, 1976, p. 1.

[48] *Il Resto del Carlino*, June 23, 1976, p. 4.

fit into this category. Many of these "national" candidates run for Parliament in their home areas (and, of course, the national party officials, apart from the suggestions of the regional and provincial party officials, may directly choose some people from the local party organizations or the local governments). Others are slated in districts or regions either where enough PCI members are normally elected to allow space for some "national" candidates in addition to the local ones or where their expertise may be particularly useful in building contacts with locally prominent social groups.[49] Either because they are nominated in safe senatorial districts or because the party mobilizes sufficient preference votes to elect them to the Chamber of Deputies, these "national" candidates almost always win.

The input for choosing candidates, in sum, comes from the general criteria laid down by the national executive committee, from the technical evaluation of each of the incumbents by the leaders of the PCI parliamentary groups, from the suggestions of the regional and/or provincial party officials, and the selection of the "national" candidates by the national party officials. This informal, though most important, process of drawing up the lists is coordinated through the organizational affairs section of the national party bureaucracy, with the members of the secretariat playing a major role.

When the candidates were being chosen for the 1976 elections, the organizational affairs section was headed by Ugo Pecchioli who was then a member of both the secretariat and the executive committee; since October 20, 1976, it has been headed by Giovanni Cervetti, already a member of the secretariat, but also named a member of the executive committee at the time he received the responsibility for organizational affairs. This position, considered very crucial within the PCI, is important in candidate selection because the PCI lists include many officials from the communal, provincial, and regional party organizations, whose appointments are handled through this section. One or two members of the secretariat or executive committee may be responsible for dealing with the candidacies of a particular region and participating in the discussions with the regional and provincial officials from that area. The national leadership, in particular the secretariat members directly responsible and, of course, major leaders such as Secretary-General Enrico Berlinguer, Giancarlo Pajetta, member of both the secretariat and executive committee, Giorgio Amendola, and others from the executive committee, play a central role in the selection of the "national" candidates and of the

---

[49] See the Peggio case, pp. 73-74.

capolista of each district (and may have strong influence over the choice of candidates for their home regions).[50] The top national officials also play a major role in determining which candidates should be the definite winners, the possible winners, and the definite losers.

Once they have been drawn up, the proposed lists are referred to the provincial party officials, though *officially*, apart from the determination of general criteria by the national executive committee, the candidate-selection process begins at the provincial level. The provincial secretariat, which is usually in constant contact with the national and regional secretariats over the composition of the lists, proposes the list for its province to the provincial executive committee, which in turn proposes it to the provincial party committee. After this committee, which may have as many as 160 members, approves it, the list is forwarded to all the party sections throughout the province. The sections, which are the basic units of the PCI, then hold meetings to discuss the candidates. Often there is one meeting or set of meetings for party members and another for the general public. After the discussions, the party members vote on the candidate lists, and the results of the discussions and votes in all the sections are forwarded to the provincial party committee, which gives its final approval to the list from the province and sends it to the national party headquarters.

The entire process at the provincial level, which may take anywhere from ten to twenty-five days depending on whether it is an early or regular election, does not usually alter the candidate lists, though it is a way for the party to learn whether there is strong opposition to any of the candidates. The process is a means of consultation with the base of the party, though its result is basically the ratification of the lists put together behind the scenes at the national level in the manner described above.

At this point, the lists are finalized and ratified by the secretariat and an ad hoc commission of the central committee set up for this purpose. They are then approved by the full central committee a few days before the opening date for their presentation. The national leadership, however, sometimes makes changes up to the last minute and did so in 1976, with the addition on May 15 of Altiero Spinelli as Chamber candidate in Rome and Milan.

The PCI's candidate-selection process is efficient and well organized. There is important input from the provincial and regional

---

[50] P.A. Allum makes this point with relation to Giorgio Amendola and his native city of Naples. P.A. Allum, *Politics and Society in Post-War Naples* (Cambridge: Cambridge University Press, 1973), pp. 180-181.

party officials, whose suggestions are quite often accepted, in part because of the political power wielded within the party by the regional and provincial secretaries. But the national leadership, particularly in the secretariat and the organizational affairs section, directly names a substantial number of the candidates and carefully controls the process. At the beginning of the candidate selection process in 1976, for example, the PCI leadership decided that the number of women candidates should be doubled. Officially, it announced that female representation in the lists should be increased, without citing any quota. As a result, 145 women candidates were presented by the PCI compared with 72 in 1972; of these, 48 were elected, compared with 21 in 1972.

Two Cases of Communist Candidate Selection. The PCI's effort to recruit independents from the Catholic subculture was one of the most publicized aspects of the PCI candidate-selection process. In the middle of April, the PCI national leadership decided that it would attempt to place about twenty Catholics on its lists. These candidates were to be chosen from among: (1) the dissident, though practicing, Catholics who opposed, for example, the antidivorce efforts of the Catholic hierarchy and the Christian Democratic party; (2) officials of the CISL, which is basically a Christian Democratic trade union confederation, though it no longer has the collateral ties with the DC that existed in the 1950s and 1960s; and (3) officials of the Christian Association of Italian Workers (ACLI), an organization for Catholic workers, whose ties to the DC also loosened in the 1970s.[51] Once this decision was made, the local party leaders throughout the country were told to make exploratory contacts in their areas.

The attempt to nominate Catholics as PCI candidates was intended to further the legitimization of the PCI as a party supporting pluralist democracy, to blunt an anti-Communist offensive within the Catholic community, and to help the PCI make inroads into the Catholic subculture. Giancarlo Pajetta said of the Catholic candidates:

> Certainly, we do not ask any form of discipline from them. Once they are elected, they may join the Communist group or the mixed group, or, in the Senate, that of the independents of the left. We want to give them the opportunity to conduct their political battle and testify to the openness of

---

[51] See Douglas A. Wertman, *Perspectives on the Italian Christian Democratic Party*, manuscript, The Johns Hopkins University School of Advanced International Studies, Bologna, Italy, June 1976.

the Communists toward unifying processes. This is at a time when some parties point toward confrontation.[52]

In a postelection analysis published in the party weekly *Rinascita*, the PCI pointed again to the overall importance of the Catholic candidates for image building. Though the article admitted that the candidates individually did not appear to have brought much extra support to the PCI in their separate electoral districts or senatorial colleges, it contended that the results of including the Catholics in the PCI lists should not be seen as "negligible." Rather, the *Rinascita* article argued, "These men were and are the evidence of a process that seems unstoppable—the coming together of and understanding between workers and intellectuals of Socialist and Catholic inspiration—which is the key to all civil, political, and social progress."[53]

In late April the PCI offered candidacies to a number of well-known Catholic dissidents as well as continuing its efforts to attract some CISL and ACLI officials throughout the country. This project was directed and coordinated by Ugo Pecchioli, then head of the organizational affairs section of the PCI.[54] Pecchioli offered Raniero La Valle, former editor of the Catholic newspaper *L'Avvenire*, a Senate candidacy. However, La Valle and many of the others approached decided that they should discuss the proposition among themselves before agreeing to be candidates.[55]

Approximately twenty dissident Catholics, some of whom had been offered candidacies, met secretly in Florence for a day-long discussion of the PCI proposal. In the end, there was no formal vote. Several of those present opposed the PCI initiative, some on the grounds that the operation was being conducted by a small group in the party leadership and did not reflect the will of the base of the party; others favored joining with the PCI. The meeting left the decision up to the individuals, and, eventually, after further PCI assurances that anyone elected under the PCI banner would have complete autonomy—and mainly because of their opposition to the

---

[52] Quoted in Filippo Ceccarelli and Pasquale Nonno, "Croce e martello" [Cross and hammer], *Panorama*, May 25, 1976, p. 43. Author's translation.

[53] Celso Ghini, "Dentro il voto" [Inside the vote], *Rinascita*, vol. 33 (July 2, 1976), p. 7. Author's translation.

[54] Ceccarelli and Nonno, "Croce e martello," p. 42.

[55] Fabrizio De Santis, "Il retroscena dell'operazione cattolici-PCI" [The background of the Catholic-PCI operation], *Corriere della Sera*, May 15, 1976, p. 9.

Christian Democrats [56]—a total of eleven people identified with the Catholic world became PCI candidates. This was fewer than the PCI had hoped to run. Among them were only one ACLI official, Giovanni Carlassara, ACLI president in the Veneto region, and one CISL official, Carlo Ramella, secretary of the CISL metalworkers union in Verona. Raniero La Valle explained his participation saying: "I believe in what the Communists would do if they got into the government because what they have done in Italy in recent years has enriched our country, but I also hope that my gesture will help to avoid further polarization of political forces in Italy tomorrow." [57] The inclusion of Catholics in the PCI lists was clearly a decision of the top party leadership in the secretariat and the executive committee and was coordinated and carried out through the organizational affairs section of the PCI national headquarters.

A second case history of PCI candidate selection is that of Eugenio Peggio, one of the "national" candidates chosen by the central party leadership who became, after the election, chairman of the Public Works Committee in the Chamber of Deputies.[58] Peggio had begun working in the economic section of the national PCI headquarters in 1952, when he was twenty-three years old. Later he became one of the top economic experts of the party and head of the economic section. In early 1966 this was transformed into the Centro Studi di Politica Economica (CESPE), of which Giorgio Amendola was president and Peggio director.[59] From 1966 to 1969, CESPE published the *Bolletino CESPE*, which in 1970 became a monthly journal called *Politica ed Economica*, widely distributed throughout the business and academic world. CESPE also sponsored a number of conferences in the 1970s on a variety of economic problems, and in these Peggio played an important role. Thus, aside from being a party bureaucrat and a central committee member, Peggio was a well-known figure in the Italian business community.

In 1972 Peggio, considered to be an economic expert who would be useful to the party in Parliament, was proposed by the national

---

[56] Mario Gozzini, a Florentine lay theologian who has worked for the Italian Bishops' Conference and who ran as a PCI Senate candidate in a very safe college in Florence, stated in mid-May, "It is sad to admit it, but above all, in my view, it must be recognized that the DC is today the major cause of atheism." Quoted in Ceccarelli and Nonno, "Croce e martello," p. 45.

[57] *Newsweek*, June 7, 1976, p. 21.

[58] Some of the information about Eugenio Peggio comes from an interview with the author, which took place on November 20, 1976, in Bologna, Italy.

[59] Davide Lajolo, *Finestre aperte a Botteghe Oscure* (Milan: Rizzoli, 1975), pp. 182-183.

party leadership as a candidate for the Chamber of Deputies in the Bologna-Ferrara-Ravenna-Forli electoral district and was elected. Peggio was nominated to run in this district largely because the PCI wins a substantial number of Chamber seats there and can afford to run some "national" candidates on the district list. Though Peggio had consulted with the Communists in Emilia-Romagna (where the district is located) on regional problems, he was certainly not widely known within the party there, and in 1976 the party leadership judged that he could be more useful to them elsewhere. Thus, in 1976 Peggio was nominated to run in Milan, the headquarters in Italy of many banks and corporations. According to Peggio, the choice reflected the party's concern to promote PCI contacts with industrialists and managerial executives through his familiarity with business and economic circles in Milan.[60] Like most candidates nominated by the national leadership, Peggio was, in due course, elected.

Preference Voting and the Chamber of Deputies Elections

Under the voting system used for the Chamber of Deputies, the number of preference votes received by each candidate determines who will win each party's Chamber seats. Thus, Chamber of Deputies candidates of the same party are running against each other for the preference votes of their party's supporters, as well as campaigning against the other parties. As a result, all but the Communist candidates tend to conduct highly personalized campaigns, and the most intense intraparty conflict for the Chamber of Deputies elections occurs within most parties during the election campaign rather than during the candidate-selection phase.

The choice of the *capolista* in each district is usually the only aspect of the drawing up of the Chamber of Deputies lists which prompts intraparty conflict as lively as that which arises during the campaign itself.[61] The position of *capolista* carries extra prestige, and, of course, in the case of the DC, the *capolista* rarely loses his seat. Sometimes the names of well-known candidates follow that of

---

[60] One of the CESPE conferences, which was on the topic, "Small and Medium Industry in the Italian Economic Crisis," was held in Milan in November 1974. Peggio was one of the important PCI participants at the conference; among the other participants were a number of people from other parties, including the DC, the PSI, and the PRI, as well as some business executives. See Lajolo, *Finestre aperte*, p. 183.

[61] Giovanna Zincone, "Accesso autonomo alle risorse: le determinanti del frazionismo" [Independent access to resources: The determinants of factionalism], in Sartori, ed., *Correnti frazioni e fazioni*, pp. 65-66.

the *capolista,* but usually most of the names on the list are simply in alphabetical order.

The level of preference voting for the entire nation has been approximately 30 percent in the last several parliamentary elections. However, the percentage of electors casting preference votes varies widely from region to region and from party to party. In many of the provinces in northern and central Italy, only 10 to 20 percent of the electors cast preference votes, while in some of the provinces of the continental south and on the islands of Sicily and Sardinia the figure is sometimes more than 50 percent. The high incidence of preference votes in the south usually is explained by the more clientelistic, personalistic style of politics there, particularly, though not only, among the Christian Democrats.[62] In several southern provinces, more than 60 percent of the DC voters have cast preference votes in the past several parliamentary elections, while the figure was as low as 20 percent in some northern and central provinces. Nationwide, nearly 40 percent of DC voters have cast preference votes in the past four Chamber elections, more than in any other party.[63]

For the PCI nearly everything is decided during the candidate-selection phase and then is, in effect, implemented in the election. The PCI's selection of Chamber candidates also includes the decision as to which nominees will win, which might win if the PCI does very well, and which will lose. The provincial party organizations distribute cards to party members and known Communist voters, showing them the party's choices for preference votes. Since those receiving these cards normally follow the party's wishes, the Communist leaders in the province usually have a very accurate idea of the number of preference votes each candidate will receive, according to the number of cards distributed bearing the various types of instructions. It is very rare for an incumbent Communist deputy or a candidate chosen by the party leadership as a sure winner to lose. Similarly, there is often a significant gap between the last elected

---

[62] Samuel H. Barnes and Giacomo Sani, "Mediterranean Political Culture and Italian Politics: An Interpretation," *British Journal of Political Science,* vol. 4 (July 1974), pp. 289-303.

[63] On preference voting before 1976, see: L. D'Amato, *Il voto di preferenza in Italia (1946-1963)* [The preference vote in Italy, 1946-1963] (Milan: Giuffrè, 1964); and Franco Cazzola, "Partiti, correnti, e voto di preferenza" [Parties, factions, and the preference vote] in Mario Caciagli and Alberto Spreafico, eds., *Un sistema politico alla prova* [A political system on trial] (Bologna: Il Mulino, 1975). The information on preference voting in the 1976 elections comes from the author's computations based on electoral statistics provided by the Provincial Electoral Office in Bologna, Italy.

candidate and the first of those not elected. This is particularly true in certain districts located in the north and center. In the Parma-Modena-Piacenza-Reggio Emilia district, for example, where the PCI elected ten deputies, the *capolista* received 55,282 preference votes, the second candidate to win a seat got 24,953 preference votes, and the last winner, who placed tenth, got 19,987, while the first loser received only 9,964 preference votes. Though this great a gap occurs only in some districts, it is indicative of the effectiveness of the PCI's efforts to direct the preference votes of its supporters.

Campaigning for Preference Votes in the DC. If the PCI candidates have least reason to conduct highly personalized campaigns for the Chamber of Deputies, the Christian Democratic candidates are most prone to do so. Indeed, few Christian Democrats win seats without running personalized campaigns that are both extensive and costly. Many place advertisements in newspapers, distribute door-to-door pamphlets containing personal biographies, or have small cards handed out that can be carried into the voting booth and show the voter how to cast a preference vote for the candidate. In competing for preference votes each candidate mobilizes whatever support he can from factions within the party (each of which seeks to maximize its representation in Parliament and thus its weight within the DC nationally) and from organizations related to the Christian Democratic party or the Catholic subculture, as well as his personal support base. Well-known national leaders, such as Moro, Andreotti, or Zaccagnini, of course, have an advantage in the widespread public awareness of them as well as in their extensive personal contacts. Most candidates attempt to build up the bulk of their preference votes in their native province.

The factional apparatus is very important in mobilizing support for individual candidates for the Chamber of Deputies. Each of the DC factions maintains its own office in Rome (and sometimes elsewhere) and holds a number of conferences each year. In addition, many publish newspapers or journals and have their own press agencies or officers. They also support a number of study centers or cultural associations, of which there are more than fifty related to DC factions in Rome alone. All of these become electoral instruments during campaigns.

All of these activities of the factions, as well as those of the parties as a whole, require substantial amounts of money. The issue of party and factional financing is a particularly difficult one to study since there are no effective means of public control over party finances. The parties apparently often do not report their real income (or its sources); in addition, the direct financing of factions from sources external to the party complicates the picture.[64] Little, in fact, is known about the sources of factional funds. The explanation accepted by most observers (though, except in a few cases, not proven) is that much of the money comes from both private industry and public corporations, the control of which has always been an important point of competition among the DC factions.[65]

In May 1974 a law was enacted providing public funds for Italian political parties.[66] This law, first, provides 45 billion lire annually to be divided among the parties represented in Parliament.[67] It also provides, during a year of parliamentary elections, 15 billion lire to pay for the campaign expenses of all the parties which: (1) present candidate lists under the same symbol in at least two-thirds of the Chamber districts; and (2) gain at least 300,000 votes nationwide plus the district quota in at least one electoral district.[68] In addition, the law requires that each party publish an annual budget showing its revenues, the source of these funds, and its expenditures. The law does not provide any effective means for examining or challenging a party's report, but it stipulates that private corporations must publicly report all contributions they make to parties and forbids public corporations from making political contributions.

---

[64] See, for example: Stefano Passigli, "Italy," *The Journal of Politics*, vol. 25 (November 1963), pp. 718-736; and Giovanna Zincone, "Finanziare con giudizio" [Finance with judgment], *Biblioteca della Libertà*, vol. 12 (May-June 1975), pp. 59-72.

[65] Antonio Padellaro, "Chi paga le correnti della DC?" [Who pays the factions of the DC?], *Corriere della Sera*, November 12, 1976, p. 2.

[66] Though of the parties represented in Parliament in 1974 only the Liberals opposed the public financing bill, since its passage there have been several attempts made to force a referendum on the question of repealing the law.

[67] Of this 45 billion lire, one-third goes to the Senate and two-thirds go to the Chamber of Deputies for division among the parties. In each chamber the money is allocated on the following basis: 2 percent is divided equally among all national parties, 23 percent is divided equally among all the national and regional parties, and 75 percent is divided among the parties on the basis of their vote in the previous election. See Donald Sassoon, "The Funding of Political Parties in Italy," *Political Quarterly*, vol. 46 (January-March 1975), pp. 94-98.

[68] There are also special provisions which state that if a party does not meet these conditions it can still gain a share of the public funds if it has won at least 2 percent of the vote in the election or if it reaches the district quota "in at least one region in which the special statute provides particular rights for linguistic minorities." This second provision was largely designed to ensure part of the funds to the Südtiroler Volkspartei (SVP). Ernesto Bettinelli, "La legge sul finanziamento pubblico dei partiti" [The law on public financing of parties], *Il Politico*, vol. 39 (December 1974), p. 658.

This law appeared to have some impact in the 1976 election—in particular through its effect on faction funding, particularly within the DC. Each DC faction receives a proportionate share of the funds allocated to the party under the public financing law. These funds now replace at least some of the money the factions once received from private corporations. The corporations in turn are reticent to make political contributions that they must publicly report. However, it must again be emphasized that the mechanics of party and faction financing in Italy are still not fully known.

Another source of support for DC candidates in the battle for preference votes is the influence of organizations tied to the DC or active within the Catholic subculture.[69] These organizations include Catholic Action, the main lay arm of the Church; labor groups such as CISL and ACLI (though their commitment to the DC is declining); Comunione e Liberazione, a strongly religious Catholic group whose leader in Milan was elected in 1976 with the second highest number of preference votes of any DC candidate in the district; and the Confederation of Small Farmers. The Confederation of Small Farmers, an important, if slowly declining, force in rural Italy, works particularly actively to turn out preference votes for its members and supporters, who in recent elections have won as many as 15 percent of the DC's seats in Parliament.

The power of the Confederation of Small Farmers was illustrated by the support it mobilized for Giuseppe Zeuch in the 1976 election. Zeuch, who was thirty-two years old at the time of the election and comes from the rural area north of the city of Vicenza, was called an "obscure farmer" by La Stampa.[70] Nevertheless, supported by the Confederation of Small Farmers, Zeuch gained more preference votes than Mariano Rumor in Rumor's home province of Vicenza (56,251 compared with 45,128). Rumor, a five-time prime minister, ex-secretary of the DC, and foreign minister at the time of the election, won more preference votes in the entire electoral district of Verona-Padova-Vicenza-Rovigo than Zeuch (73,729 compared with 67,235), but his total represented a precipitous decline from the 266,710 preference votes he had polled in the 1972 election. This decline was largely due to the allegations of Rumor's involvement in the Lockheed scandal, but it also owed something to the confederation's ability to mobilize preference votes for Zeuch.[71]

[69] In the past, the endorsement of a particular DC candidate by the Catholic clergy of the electoral district was also considered very useful.
[70] La Stampa, June 23, 1976, p. 5.
[71] At the district level, Rumor was beaten by Antonio Bisaglia, one of the major leaders of the dorotei faction, the minister of state participation, and once a

Personal wealth, personal campaign organizations, and clientelistic ties with voters are further sources of support. Particularly wealthy or well-financed individuals can afford intensive campaign publicity, and some maintain private organizations that shift into high gear during elections. Antonio Bisaglia, for example, maintains a private secretariat in the Veneto.[72] The clientelistic ties of individuals like Emilio Colombo in Basilicata, Ciriaco De Mita in Avellino, Giulio Andreotti in Lazio, and Aldo Moro in Puglia ensure them a significant base of supporters to help build their preference vote totals. This personalistic politics is most pervasive in southern Italy, but even in the north a figure like Bisaglia maintains an important clientelistic network.

In summary, within the Christian Democratic party there is significant competition among the individual candidates and factions for the party's seats in the Chamber of Deputies. For the Senate, the factional competition takes place in the candidate-selection phase; for the Chamber of Deputies, the real factional competition, apart from that over the choice of *capolista*, occurs during the campaign. For the Italian Communist party, the choices made through the candidate-selection process are implemented in the elections; the discipline of the Communist electorate allows the party leadership not only to determine who will run, but also to predict with confidence who will win.

---

protégé, now an intraparty rival, of Rumor. Bisaglia had been second to Rumor in preference votes in the electoral district in 1968 and 1972. In 1976 Bisaglia won 103,819 preference votes (compared with 138,241 in 1972).

[72] Giampaolo Pansa, *Bisaglia Una Carriera Democristiana* [Bisaglia: a Christian Democratic career] (Milan: Sugar Editore, 1975), pp. 222-223.

3

THE ITALIAN ELECTORATE IN THE MID-1970s: BEYOND TRADITION?

Giacomo Sani

Hindsight and trend analysis are marvelous instruments for identifying major political realignments, the significant turning points at which changes in mass political orientations crystallize. Deprived of these tools the analyst of contemporary political phenomena is often in a quandary, torn between the tendency to stress evidence that confirms the pattern of the past and the fear of missing the significance of novel symptoms that might anticipate future developments. When is a departure from the previous record an indication of a temporary swing, and when is it the beginning of a more permanent state of affairs?

Contemporary students of Italian politics are faced with a set of questions of this sort. For the first twenty-five years of the postwar period the distribution of the vote among the parties has remained reasonably stable.[1] To be sure, some political forces have improved their position and others have declined, but on the whole continuities have prevailed over change. All parties, with the significant exception of the Communists, have experienced occasional gains and losses; their strength has oscillated over time. But the elections of the mid-1970s have introduced considerable novelties. The returns of the regional elections that were held nationwide in June

This chapter was written in the fall of 1976 when the author, holding a Guggenheim Fellowship for the academic year 1976-1977, was visiting scholar in the Department of Political Science of the University of California at Berkeley. I am grateful to my colleagues Samuel Barnes, Alberto Marradi, and Giovanni Sartori for sharing with me data from their surveys of the Italian electorate in 1968 and 1975 respectively. Giuseppe Di Palma provided useful advice for the preparation of the manuscript. The assistance of the Polimetrics Laboratory and the Computer Center of the Ohio State University is gratefully acknowledged.
[1] For an overall view of electoral trends in Italy since 1968, see the statistical appendix in this volume.

1975 and those of the parliamentary election that took place a year later were out of line, in some respects, with past trends. Some observers were more sanguine than others about the magnitude of the changes, but few, if any, doubted the existence of novel elements.[2] To all, the returns pose a number of questions: What lies behind this discontinuity? Should the results be interpreted as a symptom of further changes in the same direction? What are the implications of the changes that have already occurred for the strategies of the parties? What are the prospects for a restructuring of the party system?

Some of these questions, and others implicit in them, will be explored in this chapter. After a brief examination of the setting in which the 1976 election occurred and a summary analysis of the results, attention is focused on partisan identifications and issues, the correlates of the vote, and the influence of political traditions.

The Setting

The number of Italian voters called to the polls in June 1976 was the highest ever. A record 40.4 million people were asked to cast their ballots to choose the 630 members of the House. Almost 35 million of these voters, being twenty-five years of age or older, were also eligible to vote for the Senate.[3]

In 1976 the number of electors qualified to vote for the two assemblies was considerably higher than in the preceding parliamentary election of 1972. But whereas the increase in the electorate eligible to vote for the Senate reflected only population trends, in the case of the House the figure reflected also the lowering of the voting age to eighteen years. Because of this extension of the suffrage, the expansion of the electorate in 1976 was considerably greater than in previous elections. From 1946 to 1972 the mean increase in the size of the electorate between two consecutive elections had been 4.8 percent; between 1972 and 1976 the figure was 9.2 percent.

I have attempted to show elsewhere that this expansion was a significant factor in the 1976 election. The ballots cast by the new voters, together with the passing away of some older cohorts of

---

[2] An interpretation that emphasizes the magnitude of the changes that occurred in 1975 is to be found in the volume by Celso Ghini, *Il terremoto del 15 giugno* [The earthquake of June 15] (Milan: Feltrinelli, 1976).

[3] Electoral laws and registration procedures are discussed in this volume in the chapter by Douglas Wertman.

electors, had a significant impact on the distribution of the vote.[4] The differences in the political orientations of the generations will be discussed later. At this point it is important to note that the expression "new voters" used throughout this chapter is not entirely accurate. In 1976 many young people voted for the first time in a parliamentary election, but they had already made their entry into political life in the regional and local elections of the year before and a number of them had cast their first ballot in the May 1974 referendum on the divorce issue.[5]

Electoral participation in Italy, as in other European countries, has traditionally been very high. In 1976 the rate of participation was fully in line with the turnout levels of previous elections: 93.1 percent of the registered voters went to the polls. A number of institutional factors account for this: the automatic nature of registration procedures, the home delivery of voting certificates, subsidized travel to the commune of residence, the scheduling of elections over a day and a half, and the legal definition of the act of voting both as a right and as a duty. In addition, parties usually engage in door-to-door canvassing to induce participation, and the overwhelming majority of the citizens appear to have internalized a conception of the voting act as something that one ought to do, a primary political obligation.[6] As a result of these internal and external forces impinging upon the electors, the turnout rate has been consistently above 90 percent, reaching 92.0 in 1948 and a high

---

[4] Giacomo Sani, "Ricambio elettorale e identificazioni partitiche: verso una egemonia delle sinistre?" [Electoral change and party identifications: Towards a hegemony of the left?] *Rivista italiana di scienza politica*, vol. 5, no. 3 (1975), pp. 516-544; Giacomo Sani, "Le elezioni degli anni settanta: terremoto o evoluzione?" *Rivista italiana di scienza politica*, vol. 6, no. 2 (1976), pp. 261-288.

[5] The law extending the suffrage was passed in March 1975. It became effective for the communal, provincial, and regional elections of June 15, 1975. In 1974 two cohorts of new electors (approximately 1.5 million) had been added to the electoral registry since 1972 and became eligible to vote for the first time in the referendum over the divorce issue.

[6] For a review of factors involved in the high rate of participation see, among others, Giorgio Galli et al., *Il comportamento elettorale in Italia* [Electoral behavior in Italy] (Bologna: Il Mulino, 1968); Samuel H. Barnes, "Religion and Class in Electoral Behavior," in Richard Rose, ed., *Electoral Behavior: A Comparative Handbook* (New York: The Free Press, 1974). On voting as the only, or at least primary, component of the "obligation to participate," see Gabriel Almond and Sidney Verba, *The Civic Culture* (Princeton: Princeton University Press, 1963), and Guido Martinotti, "Le caratteristiche dell'apatia" [The characteristics of political apathy], in *Quaderni di Sociologia*, 1966, pp. 3-4. Joseph La Palombara, "Italy: Fragmentation, Isolation, Alienation," in Lucian W. Pye and Sidney Verba, eds., *Political Culture and Political Development* (Princeton: Princeton University Press, 1965).

of 94.0 percent in 1958. These figures actually underestimate the true level of participation since they are computed on the basis of the total number of registered electors which includes a fair number of people who are permanent emigrants. If the computation took into account only people who resided in the nation or in nearby countries, the percentage of electors who went to the polls would be even higher than these figures indicate.

As noted before, the participation rate for 1976 was well within the range of values obtaining during the postwar period. And, as in other elections, turnout levels tended to vary somewhat in different parts of the country. In general, relatively fewer people voted in the south than in the north. However, even in the southern regions participation was substantial. The lowest turnout figure was posted by the region of Calabria with 85.4 percent. Furthermore, there are reasons to think that the lower rates in the south do not reflect lower levels of interest but are due, rather, to an uneven distribution in the national territory of workers who migrate more or less permanently. The southern provinces have traditionally been a labor reservoir and it seems likely that a contingent of these workers did not return to their places of residence in order to vote from the northern regions of Italy, Germany, France, Belgium, and other countries.[7]

Participation remains massive even when one takes into account the phenomenon of "nonvalid votes." Not all of the electors who go to the polls vote properly. Some place blank ballots *(schede bianche)* in the urn, others render their vote invalid *(schede nulle)* by marking the symbol of more than one party, writing inappropriate (sometimes obscene) sentences on it, or leaving on the ballot marks that in principle could be used to identify the voter. In 1976, 2.6 percent of those who went to the polls failed to cast valid ballots. Thus the rate of *effective* participation (valid votes/registered voters) was 90.8 percent for the House and approximately the same for the Senate. Because of these high levels and because there is no indication that rates of participation vary systematically in different segments of the electorate, turnout does not appear to be a major factor in the outcome of Italian elections as it is, for example, in the United States or in Great Britain.[8]

---

[7] On the political consequences of migrations, see Stefano Passigli, *Emigrazione e comportamento politico* [Emigrations and political behavior] (Bologna: Il Mulino, 1969) and the literature cited in this volume.

[8] Since the southern regions are also characterized by greater electoral instability than others, it is possible that turnout levels are responsible in part for this phenomenon. The point is explored later in this chapter.

As in preceding elections, in 1976 Italian voters had a rather wide choice of parties and candidates. The election was contested by over 100 political groups. However, only a much smaller number entered lists in all of the thirty-two multimember districts in the country. Nine parties contested the election for the House in all of the national territory, and they were identified on the ballots by their official symbols. The list, from left to right, included: Proletarian Democracy (DP), a coalition of groups of the radical left; the Italian Communist party (PCI); the Italian Socialist party (PSI); the Radical party (PR); the Social Democratic party (PSDI); the Republican party (PRI); the Christian Democratic party (DC); the Liberal party (PLI); and the Social Movement-National Right (MSI-DN), which is commonly referred to as the neo-Fascist party. With the exception of the region of Trentino-Alto Adige where there are strong local groups, the parties just listed were the protagonists of the election: together they polled 99.2 percent of all valid votes.[9] In the case of the Senate the situation was similar, the most notable difference being the absence on this ballot of two of the smallest groups, the DP and the PR.[10]

The positions taken by the parties during the campaign and the themes of the political debate covered by the mass media are discussed in detail in other chapters in this volume. For the purposes of this essay the major issues can be identified and summarized as follows.

Many of the arguments advanced during the campaign dealt with the worrisome state of the economy. All of the parties addressed themselves to the problems of high inflation and unemployment, the low rate of investment, the flight of private capital abroad, and the growing national debt. Unfair distribution of the burden of taxation and the question of tax evasion were also rather prominent in the debate.

A second theme that surfaced during the campaign was crime and political violence. Outbreaks of political violence shortly before the election inflamed the controversy over the causes of such dis-

---

[9] In the province of Bolzano the Südtiroler Volkspartei (SVP) polled over 60 percent of the vote corresponding to 0.5 percent of the national vote. Other lists polled 0.3 percent and the remaining 99.2 percent went to the nine parties listed in the text. The SVP, an ethnic regional party, attracts the vote of most German-speaking inhabitants of the province of Bolzano.

[10] The decision by leaders of the DP and the PR not to compete for the Senate can be understood in light of the characteristics of the electoral system used for the upper house, which make it difficult for very small parties to obtain representation. See the chapter in this volume by Douglas Wertman.

order and its possible remedies. In many ways this was a continuation of arguments that had been at the core of the 1972 campaign and which had flared up on and off in the interelection period.

Charges of corruption on the part of leading political figures and consequent rebuttals and denials were also important issues in the campaign. The Lockheed scandal had surfaced earlier in 1976, but the accusations and suspicions, involving primarily politicians of the DC and of the PSDI, became more salient during the campaign. In the weeks preceding the election the attentive segment of public opinion was often focused on the actions of a parliamentary committee in charge of investigating this and other episodes of corruption allegedly involving high governmental figures.

Some parties also raised issues related to the clerical-secular continuum. The question of abortion had not been resolved by the previous Parliament, and, in fact, the inability of the parties to find a solution to this problem was one of the factors leading to an early election. The abortion issue was stressed especially by the Socialists and the Radicals. These and other forces brought to the attention of public opinion the need for a revision of the 1929 Concordat between the state and the Church.*

In the campaign there were also a fair number of references to what Italian commentators call "reforms," that is, solutions, already delayed for many years, to a set of problems in the fields of health, education, welfare, transportation, housing, and so on.

The last and most important issue was not, strictly speaking, a substantive issue in a given field, but rather it dealt with the question of future political alignments. The issue that dominated the campaign concerned the role that the Communist party might play in the political system after the election. "Historic compromise," "left alternative," and "emergency coalition" were the terms on which the debate among the parties turned.[11]

The 1976 election was called a year ahead of schedule and came twelve months after a set of nationwide regional and local elections. Since, in terms of the distribution of the vote, subnational elections

---

* Editor's Note: The Concordat and Lateran Treaties of 1929 brought about a reconciliation between the Vatican and Mussolini's Fascist state. Their most important provisions granted official status to the Roman Catholic Church in Italy and made religious education compulsory, opening the way for the penetration of the teaching profession by Catholics and allowing the lay organization Catholic Action to survive under fascism. The PCI voted with the DC to incorporate the Concordat in the constitution of 1948; it can be modified only by mutual consent of the original signatories or by constitutional amendment.

[11] For a review of this issue, see Giacomo Sani, "Italian Communism on the Threshold," *Problems of Communism*, December 1976.

in Italy do not differ greatly from parliamentary ones, it was natural for observers and politicians to take the 1975 returns as a baseline for their comments and forecasts.[12] The most common questions raised by commentators were: Would the strength of the Christian Democrats be further eroded and by how much? Would the Communist party register further gains, and would it outstrip the DC to become the largest party? Would the Socialists consolidate the positions acquired in 1975 and improve them further? Would the Radicals receive enough votes to obtain parliamentary representation? Finally, how likely was it that the parties of the left might obtain a majority of the seats in the new Parliament?

Answers to these questions varied from observer to observer, largely as a function of their political sympathies. A number of public opinion polls were taken during the campaign. Several were released to the press and used by commentators and analysts in their predictions.[13] Comparison of these polls suggests a number of observations (see Table 3–1). First, all of the polls tended to systematically overestimate the strength of the Socialists, a fact that might account for the optimism of observers sympathetic to the PSI and for the disappointment that ensued.[14] Second, all five polls underestimated the vote for the DC—in one case by eleven percentage points.

Third, there was only a slight underestimation of the strength of the Communist party. This fact represents a significant departure from past polls. In earlier periods surveys tended to underestimate significantly the Communist vote.[15] Pollsters and commentators have advanced the supposition that in recent years Communist sympathizers have become less reluctant to expose their political views, since they feel more accepted, or at least less deviant, than in the

---

[12] Communal, provincial, and regional elections are similar to parliamentary elections in several respects: turnout levels are consistently high; the elections are contested usually by the same national parties; issues are often not local but national in scope; a proportional-representation list system similar to the one used in national elections is used. Because of this, politicians and observers attribute national significance to the results of local elections, which are often considered a significant test.

[13] For interesting observations on the polls, see Arturo Parisi and Gianfranco Pasquino, "20 giugno: struttura politica e comportamenti elettorali" [June 20: political structure and electoral behavior], Il Mulino, vol. 25 (1976), pp. 342-386.

[14] For an example of these feelings of disappointment and frustration, see L'Espresso, July 4, 1976.

[15] For a comparison of several surveys from the 1950s and 1960s which underrepresented the strength of the PCI, see Giacomo Sani, "Mass Level Response to Party Strategy: The Italian Electorate and the Communist Party," in Donald Blackmer and Sidney Tarrow, eds., Communism in Italy and France (Princeton: Princeton University Press, 1975), especially Table 4.

Table 3-1

COMPARISON OF PRE-ELECTION POLLS AND RETURNS, 1976 ELECTION

(in percentages)

Parties	Forecasts						(G) Election Returns	(H) Difference (F-G)
	(A) Demoskopea	(B) Doxa	(C) Makno	(D) Pragma	(E) Metra	(F) Average of all polls		
DP-PR[a]	3.0	2.5	2.5	3.9	3.0	3.0	2.6	+0.4
PCI	32.9	34.0	33.2	34.5	29.5	32.8	34.4	−1.6
PSI	12.5	12.5	12.3	15.7	15.0	13.6	9.6	+4.0
PSDI	4.5	—	4.3	3.7	3.5	4.0	3.4	+0.9
PRI	5.0	11.0[b]	4.7	3.8	3.5	4.3	3.1	+0.9
PLI	2.0	—	2.0	2.3	1.5	2.0	1.3	+0.7
DC	34.0	33.5	35.2	27.6	37.0	33.5	38.7	−5.2
MSI	6.1	6.5	5.8	8.5	7.0	6.8	6.1	+0.7
Others	—	—	—	—	—	—	0.8	−0.8

[a] The Radicals (PR) and the Democratic Proletarians (DP) ran separately but were considered together by some pollsters.

[b] Poll B, carried out by Doxa of Milan, estimated the potential votes for the PSDI, the PRI, and the PLI together. This was in part justified by the fact that in some districts these parties ran together in the election for the Senate.

Source: *Il Mondo,* June 30, 1976, p. 18. Polls appeared in the press as follows: A, *La Repubblica;* B, *La Stampa;* C, *Il Mondo;* D, *L'Espresso;* E, *Il Giornal.* Respondents who were undecided or refused to reveal their partisan preference were distributed among the parties by the polling institutes on the basis of different criteria.

past. According to this interpretation, in the mid-1970s it is the centrist or the right-wing voter who feels uneasy about disclosing his partisan preference. And this might explain the underestimation of the votes for the Christian Democrats.[16]

Last, some polls were closer than others to the results for a particular party or group of parties, but none of them succeeded in approximating the *pattern* that emerged from the returns, that is, a higher concentration of the vote in favor of the two major parties and a corresponding depletion of the strength of the intermediate forces. The DC and the PCI received together 73.1 percent of the popular vote; the polls had predicted that the combined strength of these two parties would have ranged from a minimum of 62.2 percent to a maximum of 67.5 percent.

The Returns: How Much Change, Where, and for Whom?

As the contours of the outcome emerged in the night of June 21, there were mixed reactions, as one might have expected. There was considerable disappointment among the radical left and the Socialists and near panic among leaders of the PSDI and the PLI. The Christian Democrats were visibly relieved by the outcome and more euphoric than the Communists, even though by any objective standards the latter had most reason to celebrate.[17] These reactions become more meaningful to the reader unfamiliar with Italian politics when the 1976 returns are compared with the results of the preceding parliamentary elections of 1972 and the regional elections of 1975 (see Table 3–2).[18]

Clearly, the feelings of satisfaction or disappointment were rooted in expectations which took as a key point of reference regional elections held a year before rather than the preceding parliamentary elections of 1972. The Christian Democrats and the Socialists maintained their strength unaltered between 1972 and 1976, but what mattered most in the eyes of politicians and commentators were the changes that had occurred with respect to 1975. The only political party that could claim victory without having to make reference to any specific baseline was the PCI. In 1976 the Communists con-

---

[16] On this point, see Parisi and Pasquino, "20 giugno."

[17] The DC official daily, *Il Popolo*, proclaimed victory with a huge headline that took up most of the paper's first page.

[18] Since the regional, communal, and provincial elections were held only in ninety-two of the ninety-five provinces, some caution is required in comparing these returns with those of the parliamentary elections of 1972 and 1976.

Table 3-2
RESULTS OF THE PARLIAMENTARY ELECTIONS OF 1972
AND 1976 AND OF THE REGIONAL ELECTION OF 1975

Party	Parliamentary Election, 1972	Regional Election, 1975[a]	Parliamentary Election,1976
Extreme Left[b]	2.9	1.3	1.5
PCI	27.2	32.4	34.4
PSI	9.6	12.1	9.7
PR	—	—	1.1
PSDI	5.2	5.6	3.4
PRI	2.9	3.3	3.1
DC	38.7	35.6	38.7
PLI	3.9	2.5	1.3
MSI-DN	8.7	6.9	6.1
Others	0.9	0.3	0.7

[a] Figures for 1975 refer to the ninety-two provinces in which regional or provincial elections were held. Figures for 1972 and 1976 refer to all ninety-five provinces.

[b] Parties of the extreme left include in 1972 the PSIUP, *Manifesto*, and the Marxist-Leninist group; in 1975, the PDUP; and in 1976, the DP.

Source: Official returns, Ministry of the Interior.

firmed a record of uninterrupted gains since 1946 and, what was more, the party's growth in the two elections of the mid-1970s had proceeded at an unprecedented rate.[19]

In the aftermath of the election, commentators and politicians addressed themselves to several questions bearing on the interpretation of the results. Not unexpectedly, the most important of these queries dealt with the sources of the gains and losses of votes of different parties. Before examining and evaluating some of these interpretations, it is useful to look at the returns in somewhat greater detail. The discussion that follows is based on an analysis of data aggregated at the provincial or at the regional level.[20] In some respects these levels of aggregation are not entirely satisfactory, and a further breakdown of the electoral statistics is necessary for the an-

---

[19] For an overall view of electoral trends in the postwar period, see Celso Ghini, *Il voto degli Italiani* [Italians at the polls] (Rome: Editori Riuniti, 1975).

[20] Pending release of official statistics I have used figures published by the press. Percentages of the vote received by the parties in the provinces were cross-checked in two dailies: *Il Corriere della Sera* and *L'Unità*. It is possible that official statistics differ slightly from the ones used here, but the differences are unlikely to affect the substance of the analysis.

alysis of specific topics. Nevertheless, these data are adequate for a general overview of the geographical distribution of the vote and for the analysis of the major changes since 1972.[21]

How much electoral change occurred in 1976? Was the pattern of change diffused or localized? How much continuity was there in the distribution of the vote for the several parties?

Data useful for answering these questions are displayed below and in Tables 3–3 and 3–4. One crude measure of change is the absolute sum of the differences between the percentage of the vote received by each party in two consecutive elections. For each of the seven pairs of consecutive elections since the war, this figure is as follows:[22]

Elections	Electoral Change
1946–48	44.8
1948–53	25.4
1953–58	8.8
1958–63	16.0
1963–68	15.2
1968–72	9.6
1972–76	17.0

As one can see, the value for the 1972–1976 period is considerably higher than the figure for 1968–1972. However, the amount of change occurring in 1976, while the highest recorded since 1953, is barely above the levels of change that occurred in 1963 and in 1968. In short, the returns of 1976 do not stand out, at least in terms of this particular measure, as setting a record for change. How does one reconcile this finding with the notion widely held by politicians and commentators that 1976 was a turning point in Italian politics?

The most likely explanation seems to be that observers were not

---

[21] One province, Aosta, has not been included in the analysis. Because of the characteristics of the electoral system used in this autonomous region, parties do not contest the election separately but form electoral groups. The votes cast in the province account for 0.2 percent of the national vote. In 1976, 50,940 valid votes were cast in Aosta. The leftist group, including Communists, Socialists, and left-wing Socialists, polled 52.5 percent of the vote. The omission of this province does not affect appreciably the analysis of overall national trends.

[22] Obviously this measure is not sensitive to the direction of change and is affected by changes in the number of parties contesting the elections resulting from splits, unification attempts, and the like. Data for the 1946-1972 period are drawn from Alberto Spreafico, "Risultati elettorali ed evoluzione del sistema partitico," in Mario Caciagli and Alberto Spreafico, eds., *Un sistema politico alla prova* (Bologna: Il Mulino, 1975).

Table 3-3

VARIATIONS IN THE STRENGTH OF THE PARTIES BY REGION, 1972–76

(in percentage points)

Region	PCI	PSI	PSDI	PRI	DC	PLI	MSI
Piemonte	+ 9.2	−1.1	−2.2	+0.6	−1.0	−4.6	−1.0
Lombardia	+ 7.8	+0.4	−2.0	+0.3	+0.1	−3.8	−2.0
Trentino-A. A.	+ 5.6	+0.8	−2.5	+0.8	−6.5	−1.9	−1.1
Friuli-V. G.	+ 6.4	+0.5	−3.0	+0.8	−0.8	−2.9	−2.0
Veneto	+ 6.4	+0.8	−2.0	+0.9	−1.7	−2.5	−1.1
Liguria	+ 7.5	−0.3	−2.4	+0.3	+0.9	−4.1	−1.8
Emilia-Romagna	+ 4.6	+0.7	−2.2	+0.4	+1.6	−2.6	−1.0
Toscana	+ 5.4	+0.9	−2.3	+0.2	+0.4	−1.7	−1.8
Umbria	+ 5.6	+1.8	−2.2	+0.1	−0.1	−1.3	−1.5
Marche	+ 7.1	+0.4	−1.5	−0.3	−0.5	−1.8	−1.2
Lazio	+ 8.8	—	−2.2	−0.2	+1.1	−2.8	−5.1
Abruzzo	+ 7.9	+0.9	−1.4	+0.2	−4.0	−1.4	−1.3
Molise	+ 8.6	+1.6	−3.6	+0.6	−4.4	−1.0	−1.2
Campania	+ 9.6	+0.4	−1.3	−0.1	+0.3	−1.4	−5.8
Basilicata	+ 8.4	+0.5	−2.4	+0.1	−4.6	−0.7	−0.8
Puglia	+ 6.0	−0.9	−0.6	—	+0.1	−1.3	−2.8
Calabria	+ 7.1	−0.9	−0.7	+0.1	+0.3	−0.9	−3.5
Sicilia	+ 6.3	+0.4	−0.4	—	+2.5	−1.8	−4.9
Sardegna	+10.3	+1.2	−1.3	−0.5	−1.0	−2.2	−4.1
ITALY	+ 7.2	—	−1.8	+0.2	—	−2.6	−2.6

Source: Author's computations based on official returns.

Table 3–4

CONTINUITY IN THE DISTRIBUTION OF THE VOTE FOR
THE PARTIES IN NINETY-FOUR PROVINCES,
1972–76 AND 1975–76

(correlation coefficients)

Party	1972–76 Elections	1975–76 Elections
PCI	.986	.981
PSI	.886	.847
PSDI	.839	.800
PRI	.946	.876
DC	.976	.970
PLI	.856	.874
MSI	.977	.981

Note: Figures are coefficients of linear correlation between the percentage of the vote for each party in the ninty-four provinces for the two pairs of elections 1972–76 and 1975–76.

Source: Author's computations based on official returns.

interested in the absolute magnitude of change per se, but were impressed, rather, by the direction of the changes, and by their political implications. And from this vantage point the picture did present a number of novel elements. The Communist party jumped from 27.2 percent to 34.4 percent of the popular vote and closed the gap with the DC; there was a sizable decline of the groups of the right (the PLI and the MSI) and a weakening of the Social Democrats; finally, there was an increase in the rate of concentration of the vote in favor of the two largest parties. As a consequence the balance of forces in the 1976 Parliament had changed: center-right and centrist coalitions were no longer numerically viable; conversely, the role of the Communist party was enhanced. In short, one could say that the political implications of the returns were out of proportion to the amount of change in the strength of the parties.[23]

Table 3–3 supplies some evidence pertinent to the second query. It appears that changes in the parties' strength tended to be generally distributed rather than being concentrated in specific geographical areas. One party, the PCI, won in all nineteen regions considered here. Three parties (the PSDI, the PLI, and the MSI) declined in all

---

[23] One factor that enhanced the position of the PCI was the negative attitude of the Socialists toward another center-left coalition. Although numerically feasible, this coalition had become politically unviable given the position taken by the PSI.

parts of the country. The gains by the Communists were distributed fairly equally in the north (+6.6 percentage points) and in the south (+8.1 percentage points). The Social Democrats and the Liberals suffered somewhat higher losses in the north than in the south, while the opposite obtained in the case of the neo-Fascist party. But the differences are small, and little can be made of them. Similar observations apply to the three parties whose positions did not change between 1972 and 1976 (the PSI, the DC, and the PRI). Analysis of these changes at a lower level of aggregation confirms the findings obtained at the regional level. One can conclude that the variations in the parties' strength that occurred in 1976 were diffused rather than localized.

On the third point—the continuity in the distribution of the vote for the several parties over time—the data indicate that the changes that occurred in 1976 did not appreciably alter the pattern that had obtained in the past. The correlations between the percentage of the vote received by each party in 1972 and the percentage received four years later in the ninety-four provinces are very high (see Table 3–4). This indicates the existence of considerable continuity over time, a phenomenon that is particularly marked in the case of the Communist party ($r = .986$) and of the Christian Democratic party ($r = .976$). The coefficients for the PSI, the PSDI, and the PLI are lower but still substantial. It seems plausible to think that this somewhat greater discontinuity reflects a greater propensity for voters who favor the smaller parties to float from one to another. In this connection it is important to note that the variations in the vote for the minor parties acquire considerable significance when one looks at them in terms of the groups' limited size. For example, the losses suffered nationally by the PLI from 1972 to 1976 amounted to 2.6 percentage points; but since the Liberals had only 3.9 percent to begin with, this figure means that in four years they lost two-thirds of their support. Similarly, the negative variations for the PSDI and the MSI (−1.8 percentage points and −2.6 percentage points respectively) correspond to the loss of about one-third of their 1972 support base.

We can now return to the question on which politicians and commentators focused their attention in the aftermath of the election: Who had gained from whom? In spite of its apparent simplicity, this is really a complicated question. The task of mapping the flow of voters to and from the different parties is a difficult one, for a variety of reasons. In the first place, we are dealing with three points in time rather than with two, and the shifts that occurred in

1972–1975 need not be similar—in direction and magnitude—to those of 1975–1976. Second, switches in voting behavior were only one of the components of electoral change in the mid-1970s. Electoral turnover was also a considerable factor, especially in the 1972–1975 period. Third, the survey data needed to map these flows of voters are not available and one must resort to inferences made on the basis of ecological correlations. Given these constraints, the observations that follow should be considered tentative propositions rather than firm conclusions.

At the core of the interpretations of the results advanced by politicians and observers were two points: the sizable gains made by the PCI both in 1975 and in 1976, and the relative success of the Christian Democrats, that is, the ability of this party to recover the losses it had suffered in 1975. The first phenomenon was attributed, in part, to the predominantly leftist orientations of the new generations of voters and, in part, to the ability of the PCI to attract dissatisfied moderate voters and disillusioned Socialist electors. The second phenomenon was generally interpreted as follows: the DC was able to hold its own because it managed to attract rightist and centrist voters, that is, people who previously had voted for the MSI, the PLI, and the PSDI. In short, the DC lost to its left but compensated for these losses with gains from the right. In a recent work, I have examined the tenability of these interpretations in the light of alternative explanations, and I have attempted to estimate the size of the flow of votes involved in these hypotheses.[24] On the basis of survey evidence relative to 1975 and changes in the composition of the electorate I arrived at the figures displayed in Table 3–5, which seemed to be the most realistic estimates of the different components involved in the overall change between 1972 and 1976.

More recent analysis of electoral statistics aggregated at the provincial level appears to confirm these explanations. The rationale underlying the analysis is simple: if the gains by the DC in 1976 have taken place at the expense of the MSI, the PLI, and the PSDI, one should find a negative correlation between the variations in the percentage of the vote for the DC and the percentage of the vote for the neo-Fascists, the Liberals, and the Social Democrats. Similarly for the other hypothesis: the gains by the PCI should have been greater in the provinces where the losses by the Socialists were more pronounced, yielding again a negative correlation. The results of this correlation analysis are summarized in Figure 3–1. The chart refers to the transition between 1975 and 1976, rather than to the

---

[24] Sani, "Le elezioni degli anni settanta."

Table 3–5

ESTIMATES OF THE COMPONENTS OF CHANGE, 1972–76

(in millions of votes)

	MSI, PLI, PSDI, PRI	DC	Total
Center-right			
1972 votes	7.0	13.0	20.0
Turnover	+0.3	+ 0.5	+ 0.8
Defections to parties of the left	−0.5	− 0.9	− 1.4
Defections to the DC	−1.6	+ 1.6	
1976 votes	5.2	14.2	19.4

	PSI, PR, PSIUP, DP	PCI	Total
Left			
1972 votes	4.3	9.1	13.4
Turnover	+0.7	+ 1.6	+ 2.3
Defections from parties of center-right	+0.5	+ 0.9	+ 1.4
Shifts to the PCI	−1.0	+ 1.0	
1976 votes	4.5	12.6	17.1

Source: Giacomo Sani, "Le elezioni degli anni settanta: terremoto o evoluzione?" *Rivista italiana di scienza politica*, vol. 6, no. 2 (August 1976), pp. 282–283.

entire 1972–1976 period, because the shorter interval between the last two elections minimizes the impact of other factors such as the turnover. The values associated with each arrow in the chart are the zero-order correlation coefficients between the variations in the strength of the parties in the ninety-four provinces. As one can see, the correlations corresponding to the shifts predicated on the interpretations cited above are indeed negative and fairly high.

On the other hand, the dotted lines in the diagram—that is, the flows that should not have existed according to the interpretations advanced above—are associated with low correlations or with positive correlations as shown at the bottom of the figure. In principle, the electoral results of 1976 could be explained by a number of different combinations of shifts in voting behavior: direct and indirect

Figure 3-1

SHIFTS IN ELECTORAL CHOICE, 1975-76

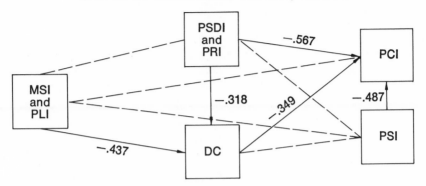

The coefficients corresponding to the
dotted lines are as follows:

MSI-PLI/PSDI-PRI = +.008
MSI-PLI/PCI = +.165
MSI-PLI/PSI = −.005
DC/PSI = −.164
PSDI-PRI/PSI = +.247

Note: Figures are zero-order correlation coefficients between variations of the percentages of the vote received by the different parties or groups of parties. For explanation and discussion, see text, pp. 95-97.

Source: Author's calculations based on official provincial level returns.

flows, two-way exchanges, and the like. These findings appear to indicate that some flow channels were not operative or were considerably less important than others. For example, there is little evidence of shifts of neo-Fascist or Liberal voters directly to the PCI; the same holds for shifts involving the DC and the PSI. As students of electoral behavior well know, ecological correlations must be used with great care, for they can lead to erroneous inferences on the behavior of individual voters. In this particular case the risk involved in accepting the findings is minor since the results of this analysis tend to corroborate conclusions reached on the basis of other types of analysis.

One explanation that is not supported by this ecological analysis is the one that attributes part of the losses of the Socialists to the emergence in 1976 of the Radical party. Socialist spokesmen and commentators have argued that the half million or so votes received by the Radicals came from the ranks of Socialist voters. This interpretation is not supported by provincial data. The correlation between changes in the percentage of the vote for the PSI and the percentage received by the PR is practically zero. While in itself this finding does not exclude the possibility of a flow of votes from the PSI to the Radicals, it certainly indicates that the proposition commonly accepted by observers and politicians needs to be carefully reevaluated. Survey data, if available, and ecological analysis at a smaller level of aggregation would throw considerably more light on this point.[25]

Partisan Identifications, Party Images, and the Vote

Partisan identifications, the durable attachments of different groups of electors to different parties, play an important role in shaping mass political behavior in Italy. Electoral choice is, in the overwhelming majority of cases, a straightforward function of party identification. Parties rather than candidates or issues are the salient political objects, the ingredients of the voters' decisions.

A number of factors account for this phenomenon. First, the characteristics of the electoral system focus the voters' attention on parties. Electoral districts are rather large, many parties contest the election, and each of them presents many candidates. Except in the cases of a few well-known politicians with national reputations, candidate visibility is rather low. As a consequence the personal traits of the candidates tend not to be a significant factor in the voter's choice of party. Second, electoral campaigns do not pivot around a single issue or a set of specific issues. The appeals made by the parties tend to be general in nature and are couched in rather abstract language. Furthermore, when clear issues have emerged they have usually been procedural (or instrumental) rather than substantive; that is, they have dealt with coalition formulas, with the question of who should rule rather than what is to be done in a particular policy area. Third, incumbents, even in the most visible offices such as that of prime minister or mayor, are typically seen as party representatives who lead a particular coalition of parties. Short tenure in office, with frequent reshuffling of cabinets or *giunta* in

---

[25] It is possible that the lack of a correlation between the changes in the PSI vote and the PR vote is due to the fact that the electorate of the latter is concentrated primarily in the large urban centers. Since the correlations were computed on the basis of data aggregated at the provincial level, this might account for the discrepancy between the finding and the common explanation advanced by observers.

local government, further decreases the personalistic elements. Last, the bulk of the electorate has traditionally been rather poorly informed about political affairs and has tended to view the protagonists of the political process in black and white terms. In the oversimplified maps of the political world that these electors use to make sense of politics, parties are by far the best-defined and best-known components.

Given these characteristics of the political context, the analytical distinction between partisan identification and electoral behavior is practically nonexistent empirically. The association between partisan identification and reported vote is extremely high. Indeed it is so high as to make the analyst believe he has used two different measures of the same variable. And public opinion institutes occasionally attempt to predict electoral results on the basis of answers to questions designed to measure the proximity of the voters to the different parties. It might very well be that Italian voters rationalize their electoral choices by bringing their partisan identification in line with their last electoral decision. This too would be congruent with the characteristics of the system in which they operate. If the pull of candidates and/or issues is minimal, one either votes for the party he identifies with or switches his vote *and* his partisan identification to another party. In short, the phenomenon of crossing party lines at a given election while retaining one's original identification does not occur often in Italy because the conditions under which mass political actors operate render this form of behavior meaningless.

The propensity of some segments of the electorate to float might seem to contradict the model just sketched. After all, are not partisan identifications supposed to be relatively durable? If they are, how could floating occur? I believe the objection can be disposed of when one reflects that partisan identifications go together, for most electors, with a spatial ordering of the political parties. Indeed it seems likely that one's self-location in political space proceeds, or at least is coterminous with, partisan identification. Now, if floating occurred mostly among parties that were perceived as being contiguous on the political spectrum, it would imply minimal change in the voter's spatial identification. On the other hand, drastic changes in voting behavior, say from the PLI to the PCI, would entail not only a shift in partisan identification but a change in what might be called "camp" identification. The voter moves out of a political family, so to speak, and joins a different one. What we know about voting behavior in Italy suggests that changes of camp are rather dramatic events that imply a reevaluation of the political world. Moreover, they appear to have been rather infrequent. Floating among contiguous political groups, on the other hand, does not imply the acquisition of a new political identity. As far as we know, this type of shift has constituted the bulk of movements across party lines at least until very recently.

These observations become more understandable when we consider the relationship between party identification and the location of political objects in the political space. The terminology of left, center, and right not only is used by political elites and the attentive public but also is part of the discourse of a significant portion of the electorate. Research on this topic has shown that the mass public sees the parties as being located on a spectrum, and the aggregate view of these locations provides a picture that coincides with the judgment of informed observers.[26] In addition, many voters view themselves as belonging somewhere on the same continuum. When we examine these self-locations, we find that they are generally congruent with partisan preferences.

Data on the self-location of different subgroups of Italian electors collected in 1968, 1972, and late 1975 are shown in Table 3–6. Several points emerge from the evidence. First and foremost, the ordering of the different subgroups of partisans has remained unchanged. The data go back only to 1968, but there are reasons to suspect that the order would not have changed even with respect to earlier times. Indeed it seems likely that the mean locations of parties, as reflected in the views of identifiers, have remained unchanged throughout the postwar period.

Second, the figures are not likely to surprise knowledgeable observers of Italian politics; indeed the location of partisans coincides with the distribution of the seats in Parliament. Third, the existence of political families is clearly reflected in the data. The neo-Fascists are clearly isolated on the far right; the centrist parties (the DC, the PRI, and the PSDI) are relatively close to each other and they appropriately cluster around the center portion of the space.

Last, focusing on changes that have occurred over time, it might at first glance seem strange that almost all groups of partisans have in 1975 a mean location which is somewhat more to the right than in 1972. In terms of spatial locations we have a slight move to the right—yet in the elections of 1975 the Communists and the Socialists

---

[26] Samuel H. Barnes, "Left, Right and the Italian Voter," *Comparative Political Studies*, vol. 4 (July 1971), pp. 157-176; Giacomo Sani, "A Test of the Least Distance Model of Voting Choice," *Comparative Political Studies*, vol. 7 (1974), pp. 193-208.

Table 3–6
MEAN SELF-LOCATION OF DIFFERENT GROUPS
OF ITALIAN PARTISANS ON THE LEFT-RIGHT
CONTINUUM, 1968, 1972, AND 1975

Partisan Preference of Respondent	Year of Survey		
	1968	1972	1975
Extreme Left[a]	—	9	5
PCI	17	20	25
PSI[b]	33	36	37
PSDI[b]	33	47	47
PRI	45	53	48
DC	56	55	59
PLI	72	58	67
MSI	80	80	87

a This refers to the *Il Manifesto* group in 1972 and to the PDUP in 1975.

b In 1968 the PSI and the PSDI were united in the PSU. The figure in the table refers to this latter party.

Note: In the first two surveys respondents were asked to place themselves on a scale ranging from 0 (left) to 100; in the third survey the scale ranged from 1 to 10. For purposes of comparison the latter scale has been converted to a 0 to 100 scale.

Source: Unpublished national surveys of the electorate by Samuel Barnes (1968), Samuel Barnes and Giacomo Sani (1972), and Giovanni Sartori and Alberto Marradi (1975).

increased their strength. The paradox is easily resolved: the change in the mean location of Communist partisans makes sense if we assume that the party has grown at the expense of moderate voters. Perhaps even Communist voters have become less extreme, but the more centrist mean location of PCI voters in 1975 could simply be explained by the addition to the electorate of this party of a combination of Socialist and moderate voters.

Similarly, in the case of the DC, the mean location of identifiers was slightly more to the right in 1975 than four years before. This too makes sense if we assume that the contingent of voters who left the DC came from the ranks of its most progressive electors. Perhaps the shift is too small to be substantively significant. But in any event, it is certainly not out of line with trends in electoral behavior.

In Italian political life the left-right continuum is much more than a cognitive device, a map used by political actors to locate salient, important political objects. Underlying the continuum there is a strong affective component. Right and left are the poles of an evaluative dimension—they have a positive or a negative charge depending on the actor's own location. Partisan literature and the opinions expressed in conversations provide abundant evidence for this. In a world structured by a spatial dimension we would expect the pattern of antagonisms to run along the left-right continuum.

As the figures of Table 3–7 indicate, this appears to be the case. If we attempt to measure, however crudely, the feelings of different segments of the electorate toward the parties, we find the ordering of parties on the left-right continuum and the location of the respondents to be systematically associated. Mean sympathy scores displayed in the table are extremely orderly: positive feelings for the PCI decrease systematically as one moves from one group of respondents to another and they reach the lowest point in responses of right-wing partisans; similarly for the MSI. In fact the scores for this party are generally low and demonstrate the fundamental isolation of this political force in Italian life.

Also of some interest is the symmetry of the pattern. For example, Communists and Christian Democrats are negatively oriented toward each other, roughly at the same level (scores of 25 and 31); the same obtains for other pairs: DC and PSI, PSDI and PSI, PSI and PCI, and so on. This dimension of affect also clearly emphasizes the presence of what have been referred to above as political families.

Table 3–7
SYMPATHY TOWARD FIVE ITALIAN PARTIES, BY PARTISAN PREFERENCE

Party Evaluated	Partisan Preference							
	PDUP	PCI	PSI	PSDI	PRI	DC	PLI	MSI
Communist party	70	83	59	41	41	31	25	24
Socialist party	59	55	76	55	54	44	38	28
Social Democratic party	17	31	46	64	43	46	43	30
Christian- Democratic party	12	25	40	49	40	73	46	34
Neo-Fascist party	2	10	13	17	17	25	35	77

Note: Figures are mean "sympathy" scores for each group of partisans. Respondents were asked to express their positive or negative feelings toward the parties using a scale ranging from 0 to 100.

Source: Sartori and Marradi survey, 1975.

Scores easily identify clusters of homogeneous forces. Finally, it should be noted that the more central the position of a party, the less likely it is to receive a highly negative or positive mark. This is clearly a result of the spatial distribution of political forces. If feelings are a function of distance, the more peripheral parties are likely to be penalized, being the target of both the center and the opposite extreme.

Since political discourse often involves groups and institutions other than parties, one might wonder whether and to what extent the feelings toward these other political objects are also correlated with partisanship and with the evaluation of parties. Given the fact that some social groups or institutions are more explicitly associated with partisan politics than others—in Italy, the Church or the unions, for example—we would expect partisan preference to be more closely correlated to feelings about these groups than others. Analysis of the structure of orientations of a sample of Italian voters provides an overall view of what might be called the pattern of antagonism existing in Italian politics at the mass level in the mid-1970s.

The positions of sixteen politically relevant groups in a two-dimensional space generated through factor analysis is displayed in Figure 3–2. Two major clusters of objects emerge. The first includes parties and groups normally associated with the center-right portion of the political spectrum (the DC, the clergy, industrialists, the police, and so on). The second cluster is composed of parties or groups that have come to be associated with the other part of the spectrum (the PCI, the PSI, the unions, the women's liberation movement, and so on). Sandwiched between the two clusters one finds objects that are less salient in a partisan sense or that do not elicit strong negative or positive evaluations. Similar findings were reported on the basis of data collected in 1972.[27] And this suggests that the configuration of political cleavages remains in the mid-1970s reasonably similar to the pattern that existed in the past.

This finding might surprise the observers who believe that considerable changes have taken place in Italian politics in recent times. In part this continuity may be due to a misalignment between what goes on at the mass level and the dynamics of politics at the elite level. Developments on the latter cannot be assumed to be automatically reflected in the former. Indeed the data just analyzed might throw light on the phenomenon of mass resistance to initiatives taken at the elite level. If the distance between the DC and the PCI in the

---

[27] Sani, "Mass Level Response to Party Strategy," figure 6.

Figure 3-2

CONFIGURATION OF POINTS REPRESENTING
THE EVALUATIONS BY A SAMPLE OF ITALIAN VOTERS
OF SIXTEEN POLITICAL OBJECTS, 1975

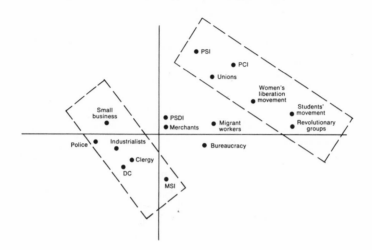

Note: The axes represent the first two factors of factor analysis. The points show the relative position of each variable (group) in the space generated by the two factors, orthogonally rotated.

Source: Sartori and Marradi survey, 1975.

minds of the electorate is truly reflected in Figure 3–2, it comes as no surprise to learn that sizable segments of the Christian Democratic and Communist electorates are unhappy about the experiment of the current DC cabinet openly supported by the PCI. What the elites are doing is not congruent with the affective map of the political world that many voters use to orient themselves. Perhaps in time mass orientations will change, partly as a consequence of changed elite behavior and the influence of channels of political communication. For the moment, however, the cleavages persist.

I have argued in the preceding pages that electoral choices in Italy are closely related to partisan (and spatial) identifications and that these attachments are deeply embedded in the structure of antagonisms that characterizes the voters' view of the political world. If this is the case, it should follow that shifts in partisan preference and voting behavior, especially across camps, are likely to be associated with changes in the electors' image of the parties. Thus one is led to investigate the extent and the direction of modifications of the voters' view of the different political forces. Not all the data that would be required to carry out this kind of analysis are available. We do, however, have some evidence that corroborates the general proposition linking the popular images of the parties to voting behavior.

The Doxa public opinion institute has recently published a summary of findings from four surveys conducted between 1967 and 1976. Respondents were asked questions dealing with traits or qualities that the parties might or might not have, such as competence or honesty.[28] Re-analysis of these data provides some insights into the success of the Communist party in the recent election. The figures, reported in Table 3–8, indicate variations in the popular images of seven parties from 1967 to 1976, in terms of nine traits. More precisely, the figures are increases or decreases in the percentages of the voters sampled who agreed with the survey statements.

The trends emerging from Table 3–8 are unmistakable: there is a general and sizable improvement in the image of the PCI and, conversely, a systematic and severe deterioration in the popular view of the DC. The Communist party was given better marks by the electorate, particularly on modernity, youthfulness, opposition to violence, and the soundness of its ideas. On the other hand, many voters were skeptical about the positive traits of the DC. Of all the DC's negative ratings, its score for honesty stands out most clearly. The finding is totally understandable in the light of recent and widely publicized disclosures of scandals involving DC leaders who had had important responsibilities in governmental posts in past years.

As the pattern of plus and minus signs indicates, the voters' evaluations of the other parties were mixed. In general it seems that the center-left parties (the PSI-PSDI and the PRI) fared somewhat better than the Liberals and the neo-Fascists. It should also be noted that the variations relative to these groups are somewhat less reliable than those concerning the DC and the PCI. Minor parties are not well known by many electors and there is a high frequency of inconclusive answers (uncertain, do not know, and so on) to questions about them, which limits the usefulness of the findings. In any event, the general impression one gathers from these data about the changes in the parties' images seems to be well in line with the electoral results of the mid-1970s. The electoral progress of the PCI is clearly related to positive changes in the popular view of this party.

At this point the reader might ask: (1) if the image of the Com-

---

[28] *Bollettino Doxa*, September 1, 1976.

Table 3-8

CHANGING IMAGES OF ITALIAN PARTIES, 1967–76

(in percentage points)

Survey Statement	Political Parties Evaluated						
	PCI	PSI	PSDI	PRI	DC	PLI	MSI
The party has many good ideas.	+30.6	−27.4	−16.4	+ 5.4	−23.0	− 1.5	− 4.5
The party is honest.	+10.7	−42.4	−26.4	−17.5	−42.4	+ 1.5	−25.1
The party is simpatico.	+20.7	−22.5	−17.3	−11.6	−33.9	−13.1	− 8.2
The party is against violence.	+30.8	+ 5.1	+ 2.5	+ 2.1	−25.3	− 1.5	− 0.8
The party is united.[a]	+ 8.0	− 2.4	− 3.1	− 0.7	−27.4	−29.2	+ 6.2
The party is competent.[b]	+ 8.2	−12.6	−11.2	− 2.6	−14.9	−12.0	+ 8.3
The party is young (youthful).[a]	+27.3	+ 6.0	− 0.3	−12.1	−15.1	− 0.9	+ 3.8
The party is modern.[a]	+32.9	− 4.0	+ 9.8	−14.1	−25.2	−21.7	− 1.7
The party defends the interests of people like us.[a]	+26.1	+ 7.2	− 4.3	+37.9	−19.4	−14.1	− 8.1

[a] Comparison between surveys carried out in 1967 and 1975. For the PSDI comparison limited to 1974-75.
[b] Comparison between surveys carried out in 1974 and 1976.

Note: Figures are the differences between the percentages of respondents agreeing with each statement in 1967 and in 1976.

Source: Reelaboration of data published in Bollettino Doxa, vol. 30, September 1, 1976.

munist party has improved so dramatically, why has the party not gained more than it has, and (2) how did the Christian Democratic party manage to hold its own in the presence of increased public distrust and disapproval? These questions bring to attention a very important aspect of electoral politics in Italy.

A discussion of this point should begin with the observation that until 1972 the electoral growth of the Communist party had been slow and gradual. It has been argued elsewhere that the major impediment in the path of expansion was the diffuse and rather strong anticommunism existing in large segments of the electorate. One of the key components of this negative image of the PCI had to do with the question of the democratic nature of the party. The arguments advanced by other political forces cast doubts on the loyalty of the Communists to the democratic system and on the depth of the party's commitment to preserving a pluralist society. The solidarity between the PCI and the international Communist movement—especially the party's ties with the U.S.S.R.—were seen as proof that the PCI was fundamentally an antisystem party. Anti-Communist arguments stressing this point were used at one time or another by all of the other parties. To be sure, the arguments advanced by the Socialists were far less negative than those put forth by right-wing parties; nevertheless, anti-Communist appeals were widely used. Doubts about the democratic legitimacy of the PCI were repeatedly expressed by the DC, and it was this party that reaped most of the fruits of the anti-Communist campaign. The Christian Democrats could persuasively argue that only a mass party could block Communist advances. Only the DC could provide an effective "anti-Communist dike." In the crucial election of 1948 the argument carried the day, and in later elections the same appeal managed to slow down Communist growth.

For the PCI the acquisition of democratic legitimacy—that is, full acceptance from other members of the political system—became a major goal. Developments within the party in the last few years have pushed the PCI closer to that goal. Party leaders have explicitly stated their acceptance of democratic institutions and fundamental rights; they have been critical of other Communist regimes; they have asserted their autonomy and their right to define an Italian road to socialism. At the same time the longstanding rejection of the PCI by members of the non-Communist elite has softened. The role of the mass media too has changed; anti-Communist bias has been replaced by a more neutral orientation and in some cases by sympathetic interest. In part as a consequence of these developments, the doubts

107

in the people's minds about the democratic nature of the PCI appear to have declined. At the same time, the positive characteristics of the party have contributed to the overall improvement of its image.

We now come to the crucial point. If doubts about the PCI are less widespread than they were, they certainly have not evaporated. Considerable segments of the electorate have maintained their suspicions. In 1975 a sizable percentage of non-Communist voters still believed that the PCI was nondemocratic. These feelings were more common, as one might expect in the light of our previous discussion, in the center and right wing of the spectrum than among Socialist sympathizers. But even among these latter, acceptance of the PCI as a fully democratic partner was by no means unanimous. Similar findings apply to the revolutionary nature of the PCI. In short, the residues of one of the central components of the earlier image of the PCI were still very much in evidence in the mid-1970s.

Data collected shortly before the election seem to me to explain why the PCI did not do better and why the DC managed to hold on to its strength at the expense of other moderate parties. As the figures in Table 3–9 indicate, 45 percent of the voters queried by Doxa in 1976 believed that the PCI wanted to limit freedom; the percentage becomes 54 when we exclude from the computation those who did not know or were uncertain. Only the neo-Fascists were thought of as less democratic. On the other hand, the Socialists and

Table 3–9
VOTERS' OPINIONS OF PARTIES' STANDS ON FREEDOM, 1976
(in percentages)

Survey Statement	Parties Judged							
	PCI		PSI		DC		MSI	
	I	II	I	II	I	II	I	II
The party wants to defend freedom.	39.0	46.0	62.0	77.5	60.0	70.6	12.0	15.4
The party wants to limit freedom.	45.0	54.0	18.0	22.5	25.0	29.4	66.0	84.6
Uncertain, does not know, no answer.	16.0	—	20.0	—	15.0	—	22.0	—
Total	100	100	100	100	100	100	100	100

Note: Columns labeled I include undecided respondents, columns labeled II exclude them.

Source: Partial reelaboration of data published in *Bollettino Doxa*, vol. 30, September 1, 1976.

the Christian Democrats were viewed mostly as being endowed with democratic legitimacy. The DC and the PSI might be seen as factionalized, scandal-ridden, and responsible for the economic situation, but what were the alternatives open to a moderate voter whose mind was not made up?

In conclusion, the success of the PCI and the relative success of the DC seem to pivot, or be predicated, on the same point: the power of anti-Communist appeals to carry the day. The erosion of the anti-Communist barrier continued to progress in 1976, and the DC resisted mostly at the expense of other forces of the anti-Communist camp. It was hardly a victory, especially since the reservoir of moderate and right-wing voters appears to be gradually shrinking.

The Correlates of the Vote

What is the relationship between partisan identification and the social characteristics of the voter? Is there a definite alignment between political cleavages and social divisions? Many students of Italian politics have attempted to find systematic linkages between the voters' social traits and their political behavior.[29] The most common focus of these analyses has been social stratification or class. But attention has also been paid to other variables such as sex, age, education, and religious practice. Multivariate models attempting to determine the combined influence of several social correlates of the vote and to ascertain the relative contribution of each of them have also been discussed.

The findings vary somewhat from study to study, partly as a function of the time of the investigations and the data used. But one general proposition appears to hold: the position an individual occupies in the society is related to his electoral choice, but the relationship is not strong. Other variables more proximate to the realm of politics are much more significantly related to the direction of the vote. A cultural component intervenes between the purely structural variables and voting behavior, amplifying or depressing the influence of the former on the latter. Evidence for this argument is to be found in studies of electoral behavior in Italy during most of the

---

[29] For example, Gianfranco Poggi, *Le preferenze politiche degli Italiani* [Political preferences of the Italians] (Bologna: Il Mulino, 1968); Galli et al., *Il comportamento elettorale in Italia*; Mattei Dogan, "La stratificazione sociale dei suffragi" [The social breakdown of the vote] in Alberto Spreafico and Joseph LaPalombara, eds., *Elezioni e comportamento politico in Italia* [Elections and political behavior in Italy] (Milan: Comunità, 1963); Barnes, "Religion and Class."

postwar period. We shall now see that the proposition appears to be applicable to the mid-1970s.

The information displayed in Table 3–10 provides a summary social profile of different groups of Italian partisans. The data, drawn from a survey conducted in the fall of 1975, pertain to six social characteristics of Italian voters. Clearly, no two groups of identifiers are alike in all respects. Even the profiles of sets of partisans that are similar to each other present some difference with respect to at least one of the traits. Thus, social traits appear to discriminate between or among parties. But it is also immediately clear that the differences in social characteristics do not parallel the left-right ordering of the parties.

Unbalanced sex ratios can be found on both extremes of the spectrum. Respondents from lower strata represent over two-thirds of the PCI's following, but the figure for the Christian Democratic party is not much lower. Similarly, the mean level of education of the different groups of partisans varies in a manner which is largely independent of the main political dimension of the Italian system.

The variable that appears to be most in line with the left-right ordering is church attendance. This is interesting, for this variable is the least "structural" of the six, that is, it can be properly seen as an indicator of being part of the Catholic subculture, of being enmeshed in the network of political communication of which the Church represents a significant component. The same can be said for union membership, which also happens to be a highly discriminating variable as far as the direction of the vote is concerned. Similarly, the political tradition of the family, which is clearly a cultural variable, plays an important mediating role between the objective position of the individual and his political orientation.

The interplay between these last two variables and their connection with partisan preference emerge from Figure 3–3. The data reported are the results of a simplified version of "tree-analysis." We can see that the percentage of respondents favoring parties of the left (the PCI, the PSI, or the PDUP)—54.0 percent in the sample analyzed—varies considerably in different subgroups of electors, as the process of subsetting proceeds. The first split (manual versus nonmanual occupation) does produce a differentiation along the lines that one would expect. The propensity of the lower strata to prefer parties of the left is summarized in the difference between the two groups of manuals and nonmanuals (6.8 percentage points).

It is clear, however, that the breakdowns that follow discriminate considerably more than the first variable. Affiliation with the

110

Table 3–10
SOCIAL CHARACTERISTICS OF ITALIAN PARTISANS, 1975
(in percentages)

Social Characteristics	Left[a]	Party Preference								Total Sample
		PCI	PSI	PSDI	PRI	DC	PLI	MSI	None[b]	
Male	64.1	50.5	53.0	62.5	67.4	38.6	56.7	61.4	48.4	48.6
Manual occupation [c]	27.0	67.4	53.7	35.6	30.4	62.9	25.9	48.4	55.7	58.8
Rural residence [d]	20.7	30.7	28.7	56.2	8.7	48.2	10.0	23.9	30.3	34.2
Elementary education	15.4	47.6	45.6	34.8	28.9	61.9	13.8	37.3	53.4	50.5
Age 45 years or older	10.3	20.8	35.9	31.6	36.1	44.8	32.4	22.6	33.7	32.4
Regular church attendance [e]	5.1	13.4	25.7	36.2	20.0	65.5	43.3	19.4	35.4	36.6

a Includes identifiers with PDUP and other groups.

b Respondent did not indicate a party preference.

c Based on the profession of the respondent or head of the household.

d People living in communes with less than 10,000 inhabitants.

e Attending church "weekly" or "often."

Source: Sartori and Marradi survey, 1975.

Figure 3-3

CORRELATES OF PARTISAN PREFERENCE:
OCCUPATIONAL STATUS, UNION TIES, AND POLITICAL
TRADITION OF THE FAMILY, 1975

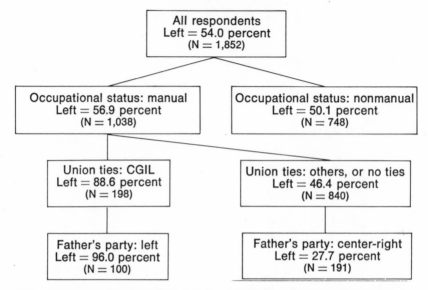

Note: Percentage for the left includes respondents whose partisan preference went to PDUP, PCI, or PSI. Occupational status is based on the profession of the respondent or the head of the household.

Source: Sartori and Marradi survey, 1975.

union that traditionally has organized Communist and Socialist workers (CGIL, the General Confederation of Italian Labor) or with Catholic or independent unions does make a difference. Finally, when we add information on the political background of the respondent, measured by the partisan leanings of his father, our ability to isolate subgroups of respondents with sharply divergent party preferences increases further. The difference between the percentages of leftist voters in the last two subsets of the figure is considerable, and yet both groups are composed of people who come from the same lower-class background. In conclusion, it is clear that one's position in the system of social stratification has a minor impact compared to union identification and family background.

Somewhat similar observations can be made for the other social traits. Sex, rural versus urban residence, and education are dimensions useful for identifying differences among the parties, but the connection between these variables and the direction of partisanship is not particularly pronounced. In some cases these social divisions overlap and their relationship with partisan preference becomes stronger. In other cases, these dimensions appear to be cross-cutting, and when one combines them the original relationship is considerably modified.

To illustrate: among DC voters, women and rural people are markedly overrepresented. We have also seen that two-thirds of Christian Democratic electors are regular churchgoers. This immediately suggests that the relationship between the urban or rural context in which the voter lives, or his/her sex, and his/her party preference might in reality be an artifact, the result of a different distribution of religious practice in different segments of the population. Joint analysis of these variables makes it possible to disentangle the relationships and to clarify, to some extent, the issue.

In the particular case of the sex variable, the data reported in Figure 3–4 indicate that, if controls for religious practice are established, the propensity of women to vote for the Christian Democratic party is only slightly higher than that of men. The direct influence of sex not mediated through religiosity is really very modest. The latter variable is considerably more potent in isolating Christian Democratic voters within both male and female subsets of respondents. The average difference in DC identification traceable to the religious factor, controlling for sex, is about forty percentage points. The inescapable conclusion is that at least some of the bivariate relationships presented in Table 3–10 might in fact conceal more than they show and might lead to erroneous deductions.

The thrust of the argument advanced so far is that social background characteristics are not, in the Italian case, very significant correlates of partisan preference. There is, however, one rather important exception: evidence collected in the last few years indicates that the distribution of party identification in different age cohorts of electors varies considerably. This fact and the expansion of the electorate that has taken place since 1972 were among the reasons given by some observers for the electoral growth of the left in the mid-1970s. Basically it was argued that the impact of electoral turnover favored the left, and particularly the Communist party. As the younger generations of voters replaced the older cohorts of more conservative electors, the overall balance shifted somewhat in favor of the left. This thesis has been discussed at length elsewhere and

113

Figure 3-4

SEX, RELIGIOSITY, AND PREFERENCE FOR THE DC, 1975

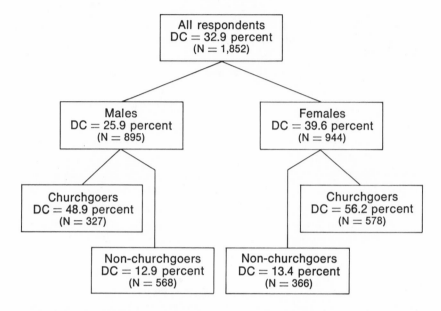

Note: Church attendance, originally measured on a five-point scale, was dichotomized. Churchgoers are defined as respondents attending church weekly or often.

Source: Sartori and Marradi survey, 1975.

little need be added here.[30] But the significance of age-related differences in the direction of partisanship goes beyond the results of the last election, and a brief examination of the phenomenon appears to be useful at this point.

A certain imbalance in the distribution of party identification of young and old voters was reported by Barnes on the basis of data collected after the parliamentary elections of 1968.[31] A survey conducted four years later confirmed the finding: the proportion of Communist and Socialist voters was higher among the younger cohorts of electors. More marked differences were unveiled by a survey carried out by the Doxa Institute in 1974 and even more dramatic findings emerged from the Sartori-Marradi survey of 1975. An inter-

---

[30] Sani, "Le elezioni degli anni settanta."

[31] Barnes, "Religion and Class."

mediate estimate based on the latter two studies gave to the parties of the left (Communists, Socialists, and other groups) 60 percent of the potential vote of the newly enfranchised electors. Other estimates arrived at by political commentators were only slightly lower.[32] The critical question raised by this evidence has to do with the nature of these differences. Are these truly generational differences, or are they, at least to some extent, phenomena related to the life cycle? In other words, do the preferences of the younger voters indicate a major and lasting discontinuity between generations, or are the predominantly leftist orientations of the new cohorts of electors imputable to a temporary radicalization of Italian youth?

Only longitudinal studies could provide a fairly definitive answer to these questions. Lacking appropriate data, the analyst can advance only tentative propositions. The hypothesis that seems most plausible to this writer is that the phenomenon reflects both components but that the generational factor is considerably more important than the impact of causes related to the life cycle. This supposition rests, in large measure, on arguments and evidence pertaining to changes in the pattern of political socialization. It is part of the larger theme of cultural change and political traditions to which we now turn.[33]

Political Traditions

Political traditions have been stressed by many students of Italian politics.[34] Expressions such as red belt, white areas, and industrial triangle have been used to designate unusual concentrations of the strength of certain parties or blocs of parties in specific areas of the country. In a narrower sense, the term tradition refers to the presence within all or most territorial units of segments of the population sharing political beliefs and partisan preferences, that is, having a distinct political subculture.

The continuity of political traditions, their persistence over time, has been well documented. At the macro level, it has been shown that the traditions existing prior to the advent of fascism resurfaced

---

[32] Sani, "Le elezioni degli anni settanta," p. 270, notes 8 and 9, and "Ricambio elettorale."

[33] Additional reasons that render the generational interpretation more plausible are presented in my paper, "Generations and Politics in Italy," delivered at the Convegno sulla Crisi Italiana, Turin, March 24-27, 1977.

[34] The importance of traditions and their reemergence after fascism are well documented in Galli et al., Comportamento elettorale in Italia.

when democracy was reinstated and that they have lasted without major modifications for most of the postwar period. Analysis of data at the micro level shows the existence of a high level of continuity in partisan preference across generations among members of the same family.[35]

The two major political subcultures in Italy are often identified by the labels Catholic and Socialist. Of course, there are other clusters of orientations, but they appear to be far less cohesive and influential. It has been argued that the persistence of these two major traditions has been made possible by an organizational apparatus which performed the function of socializing the young and reinforcing the beliefs of the older generations. These organizational structures, together with primary groups, acted as channels of political communication and influence. They harnessed mass support, especially for the large, popularly based parties. A major difference between the two subcultures was that, while the Catholic tradition could rely heavily on the organizational structure of the Church and related organizations, the Socialist subculture was organizationally autonomous. Its backbone was the Communist party and a number of associations that paralleled the party. This proved to be an initial disadvantage from the point of view of the expansion of the Socialist culture. While the Catholics could count on the impressive Church-related network and later on could use the spoils made available by the control of the state machinery, the survival of the Socialist subculture rested mostly on the capacity of the leftist parties (and especially the PCI) to build an organizational network through which popular support could be first consolidated and eventually expanded. However, the initial advantage for the DC—its reliance on a reservoir of Catholic voters mobilized by the Church—had a number of drawbacks. First, the presence of an outside structure reduced the incentives for the party to build its own autonomous organization. Second, the confessional nature of this support base made it difficult for the party to become a moderate, secular force, that is, a mass conservative party. Third, a possible decline of religiosity could prove very costly, for it would automatically weaken the party's electoral strength. Last, the party's dependence on the Church was risky, for if the institution withdrew its support or simply took a more neutral posture toward the various political forces this would have a definite negative impact on the party's strength.

---

[35] These points are discussed in my essay, "Political Traditions as Contextual Variables: Partisanship in Italy," *American Journal of Political Science*, vol. 20, no. 3 (August 1976), pp. 365-406.

It is my contention that the changes in the distribution of partisan preference that occurred in the mid-1970s can be seen, at least in part, as the result of a process of secularization which has gradually altered Italian society and eroded the Catholic tradition. There are several indicators of this secularization.[36] There has been a decline in religious practice; the mass of practicing Catholics has shrunk and, insofar as Church attendance acted as a channel of politically significant communication, the implications of the phenomenon are evident. In addition there appears to have been a decline of clericalism; even among practicing people the willingness to follow the precepts of the Church in political matters has diminished. In this respect perhaps the most striking development has been the emergence of a movement of dissenting Catholics who in the campaigns of 1974, 1975, and 1976 asserted their right to make an autonomous electoral choice and who in many cases supported parties of the left. The fact that a number of well-known Catholic intellectuals ran as independents on the Communist ticket was a striking demonstration of this departure from the pattern of the past. Furthermore, there appears to have been a marked decay of the once powerful organizational network sponsored by the Church which in the past had been very effective in channelling popular support toward the DC. Last, public opinion data gathered at the time of the 1974 referendum indicate that the clergy was less active and less effective in that campaign than in earlier ones.[37] It is true that in recent years a new Catholic youth movement has sprung to life (Comunione e liberazione), but as far as one can tell this revival has had only limited impact. In the mid-1970s the reach and effectiveness of the Catholic network are a far cry from what they were at the time of the *Comitati Civici*.[38]

This process of secularization is clearly reflected in the attitudes of the different generations of Italian voters. The data displayed in Table 3–11 show that, irrespective of the specific indicator used, the younger cohorts socialized in the late 1960s and early 1970s differ systematically from the older cohorts socialized, or resocialized, in the immediate postwar period. Whether we take the percentage of people considering themselves Catholic or rates of church attend-

---

[36] On the crisis of the "Catholic world," see the essay by Arturo Parisi, "Questione cattolica e referendum: l'inizio di una fine" [The Catholic question and the referendum: the beginning of the end], Bologna, 1974.

[37] Sani, "Ricambio elettorale."

[38] The *Comitati Civici*, local committees working for the DC, were especially significant in the election of 1948.

Table 3–11
ATTITUDES TOWARD RELIGION IN DIFFERENT
AGE GROUPS, 1975
(in percentages, real figures in parentheses)

Indicators of Religiosity	Young Voters	Intermediate Cohorts	Older Cohorts
Do not consider themselves Catholic.	23.3 (939)	11.4 (481)	6.2 (869)
Never attend church.	27.2 (995)	18.9 (492)	11.0 (876)
Attend church in 1975 less often than five years before.	51.2 (989)	30.6 (485)	25.1 (879)
Consider themselves not religious.	43.7 (979)	33.8 (483)	21.9 (874)

Note: "Young voters" include respondents who obtained the right to vote in 1972 or in 1976; "older cohorts" include voters who voted for the first time in 1946, 1948, or 1953. Other respondents were included in the "intermediate cohorts."

Source: Sartori and Marradi survey, 1975.

ance or decreases in the frequency of church attendance or religious feelings, we come to the same conclusion. And insofar as these different indicators of religiosity can be taken as a measure of the size of the reservoir of Catholic voters, the implication is clear: there seems to be little doubt that the pool from which in the past came a considerable proportion of DC votes is getting smaller.

Further analysis of the same data shows the existence of another phenomenon (see Table 3–12). Among the younger cohorts high levels of religious practice are no longer associated with a strong tendency to vote for a party of the center-right, and especially the DC, as was the case in the past. Among the older cohorts only 25 percent or so of those who go to church regularly prefer a party of the left; among the younger cohorts the corresponding figure is 44 percent. This suggests that as far as the younger generations are concerned the objection to parties of the left on religious grounds has lost much of its effectiveness.

In conclusion, then, the impact of secularization is twofold. First, secularization tends to reduce the size of the mass of voters positively oriented toward religious institutions; second, it acts as a solvent, as it were, eroding the bond that tended to exist in the past between religious feelings and behavior and electoral choice. The net

118

Table 3–12

**SYMPATHY FOR THE LEFT, BY AGE AND LEVEL OF
RELIGIOUS PRACTICE, 1975**

(in percentages; real figures in parentheses)

Age	Religious Practice	
	Low	High
Young voters	80.0 (439)	43.8 (313)
Intermediate cohorts	67.9 (209)	27.7 (166)
Older cohorts	66.4 (253)	26.6 (384)

Note: The figures indicate the portion of each subgroup favoring parties of the left.

Source: Sartori and Marradi survey, 1975.

result is to undermine the recruitment base of some political groups. The distribution of preferences for the two major parties in the different age cohorts bears witness to the pervasiveness of the secularization process. We have seen before that once the religious factor is taken into account, the differences between male and female respondents practically vanish (Figure 3–4). Figure 3–5 shows a sharp contrast between the younger and the older cohorts. Among the latter, women, traditionally more clerical than men, are predominantly in favor of the DC and considerably more so than their male counterparts. On the other hand, among the younger generations the discriminating power of the sex variable is very limited indeed. And this is precisely the result one would expect to flow from a general process of cultural change such as secularization.

Additional factors are involved in the weakening of the Catholic tradition. The occupational structure of the country has changed considerably in the second part of the postwar period: the percentage of the work force employed in industry, especially in the service industries, has grown at the expense of the agricultural sector.[39] This has been accompanied by considerable internal migrations from the agricultural areas to the industrial ones and from the countryside to the cities. But perhaps the most significant aspect of social change has been the expansion of the educational system, due in part to relative affluence and even more to a series of reforms enacted from

---

[39] For a discussion of these changes see, among others, Paolo Sylos Labini, *Saggio sulle classi sociali* [Essay on social classes] (Bari: Laterza, 1974); Corrado Barberis, *La società italiana* [Italian society] (Milan: Angeli, 1976).

Figure 3-5

PERCENTAGES OF DC AND PCI VOTERS
IN DIFFERENT AGE GROUPS, BY SEX, 1975

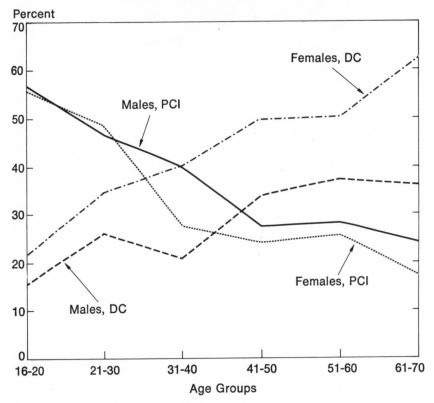

Source: Sartori and Marradi survey, 1975.

the early 1960s on. The extension of compulsory education to four-teen years of age and the expanded access to secondary education and to the universities have had a dramatic impact on the level of education of the younger generations. Since older people did not benefit from these changes in the educational sphere, the contrast between the older cohorts and the younger ones is now very sharp. Over half of the young voters have gone beyond the compulsory eight years of instruction. On the other hand, 70 percent of the older voters never went beyond the five years of schooling that was the minimum required in their time. Comparable differences can be found with respect to secondary and university education.[40]

120

Table 3–13
PARTY PREFERENCE OF RESPONDENT AND
RESPONDENT'S FATHER, BY AGE GROUPS, 1975
(in percentages)

Party Preference of Father	Party Preference of Respondent		
	Left (PCI, PSI, others)	Center-right (PSDI, PRI, DC, PLI, MSI)	N
Young Voters			
Left	90.8	9.2	(217)
Center-right	44.2	55.8	(208)
Intermediate and Older Cohorts			
Left	74.2	25.8	(248)
Center-right	25.1	74.9	(275)

Note: See note to Table 3–12.
Source: Sartori and Marradi survey, 1975.

The relationship between these dimensions of social change and the distribution of partisan preferences in the country has been discussed at length elsewhere. It has been shown that the propensity to favor a party of the left is greatest within those segments of the population whose lives have been most significantly affected by the modern dynamics of Italian society: the young, the urban, the better educated.[41] That these are some of the groups in which secularization has made the greatest inroads does not come as a surprise. One could argue that the integrity of the Catholic subculture rested as much on tradition as it did on pure religiosity and that the winds of social change have been eroding this tradition.

The traces of this erosion are quite visible from the analysis of what might be called the pattern of political mobility across generations (see Table 3–13). Traditionally there has been a strong correlation between the partisan leanings of people and the partisan preferences of their fathers. Inspection of recent data indicates that, while the correlation still holds for the older generations, in the case of the younger cohorts there is a tendency for people coming from moderate or conservative backgrounds to move toward the left. This suggests that in the presence of forces put into motion by significant

---

[40] Sani, "Generations and Politics," table 24.
[41] Ibid., table 35.

social change, the effectiveness of politically moderate families in shaping and reinforcing political orientations has decreased, while the influence of age, homogeneous primary groups, and the mass media has correspondingly increased. If we add to this the contrast between the images of the leftist parties and of the moderate and conservative forces analyzed earlier, the recent electoral trends are not difficult to understand.

In this brief discussion of political traditions I have emphasized change rather than continuity. But if the electoral returns of the mid-1970s can be seen as a consequence of the erosion of one of the two major political traditions of the country, this does not mean that political subcultures have become irrelevant in Italian politics. The Catholic tradition, though eroded, has not collapsed, and there is no indication of decline within the Socialist subculture. The balance of forces has shifted and the once dominant tradition has lost its primacy. Indeed, it seems very likely to be replaced by its antagonist. But its demise does not appear to be imminent.

4

CHRISTIAN DEMOCRACY: THE END OF HEGEMONY?

Giuseppe Di Palma

Vilfredo Pareto once wrote: "The declining elite becomes softer, milder, more humane and less apt to defend its own power. . . . On the other hand, it does not lose its rapacity and greed for the goods of others, but rather tends as much as possible to increase its unlawful appropriations and to indulge in major usurpations of the national patrimony."[1] With due allowance for Pareto's literary emphasis and sweeping sense of drama, his words nevertheless capture something of the fate of Christian Democracy from the elections of 1948, the first parliamentary elections under Italy's new republican constitution, to those of 1976.

In 1948 the Christian Democratic party was on a rapid-expansion course. The 1946 elections for the constituent assembly had already made it the first party in the country. Two years later, the cold war, the geopolitical support of the United States, the split in the Socialist party over the alliance with the Communists, and the ouster of the Socialists and Communists from the national coalition government were all factors working in its favor. Even more important in the long run were the undivided support of the Church and its lay associations—the only cultural and organizational network to survive almost unscathed under fascism—and the confidence of the business and professional communities in the DC's leadership of postwar reconstruction.

In 1976 the DC is an old and proven party, internally divided, and apparently on a declining course. After the local elections of

---

This chapter was written in the fall of 1976, while the author was holding a Guggenheim Fellowship.
[1] Vilfredo Pareto, *The Rise and Fall of Elites* (Totowa, N.J.: Bedminster Press, 1968), p. 59.

June 1975, its undisputed place as the first party is in question. Thirty years of improvident and corrupt government have eroded the confidence of the business community. Even the Church, the lay Catholic organizations, and Catholic labor have progressively moved away from the DC, in part as a result of the secularization of society, in part because of resentment at the inefficiency and corruption of the party. It is, on the contrary, the Communist party that is on the upswing. Détente, the progressive acceptance by the party of pluralist principles, its claims to independence from the Soviet Union, the rapid secularization of society—signally among the young—are all factors that help the PCI. So are its record of honesty in local government, especially when compared with the record of the DC, and the vast network of partisan and community organizations through which the PCI has doggedly pursued its politics of participation and exchange in society.

The difference between the elections of 1948 and 1976 is reflected in the campaign strategies of the DC. In 1948 the party, solidly united under Alcide De Gasperi's leadership, adopted a simple and unequivocal strategy of ideological confrontation with national and international communism, to conquer as much political space as possible. Its objective was nothing less than an absolute majority of the votes and the undivided control of future governments. The anti-Communist crusade and the appeal to religious sentiments paid off: without quite conquering an absolute majority of the electorate, the DC conquered more than half of the contested seats in Parliament. Palmiro Togliatti himself cheered his fellow Communists, chagrined at the extent of their defeat, by suggesting that they could have done worse.

In 1976, despite efforts at recreating unanimity behind Benigno Zaccagnini's new leadership, lingering party factionalism hampered the DC's capacity to wage an effective campaign. There were, moreover, serious questions about the political feasibility and the prospective payoffs of the various strategies at hand. In view of the impressive Communist successes and of the DC's tarnished record, any hope for a new and undivided mandate—like that of 1948—seemed out of the question. The very factors that supported the Communist drive suggested that, despite lingering fears of Communism in significant sectors of the electorate, a campaign banking exclusively on anti-Communism might no longer pay.[2] The crisis of the alliance

---

[2] On changing attitudes toward Italian communism see Giacomo Sani's chapter in this volume, with references to other works of his.

between the DC and Catholic organizations may be too advanced to be effectively arrested and may cost the party a substantial number of Catholic votes, especially among the young and the workers. Besides, given the advancing secularization of society, revealed most dramatically by the divorce referendum of 1974, a campaign excessively focused on traditional religious appeals might backfire. The *rifondazione* or reform of the party, undertaken in earnest under Zaccagnini especially through the retirement of old parliamentary and organizational cadres, seems to have been a case of too-little-too-late and clashed with established leadership and factional interests. Finally, there was little question of running on the party's legislative accomplishments. Yet, to its own surprise and contrary to all opinion polls, on June 20 the DC conquered all the lost ground and, with close to 39 percent of the votes, maintained the same strength it had had through the sixties and early seventies.

Just as the mass media and the political pundits had hastened to announce the demise of Christian Democracy and of organized Catholicism, so they now were quick to read the electoral results as yet another proof that Christian Democracy is solidly embedded—culturally and organizationally—in Italian society. It is, however, questionable whether the success of the party signifies more than a temporary holding action.[3] Furthermore, the success of the DC carried a heavy cost, not only for the DC but also for the Italian party system as we have known it for thirty years. Every postwar election, including 1948, has shown that Christian Democracy expands or regains ground never at the expense of the PCI, always at the expense of the smaller parties of the center and right. And since on June 20 the PCI took a giant leap, the result has been a substantial weakening of those center parties that have offered support to Christian Democratic governments and a continuous if uncertain and expensive buffer between Christian Democracy and communism. Though the elections do not spell the decline of the DC as a party, they probably spell the end of its hegemony. The Communist leadership points out that the present DC government—which for the first time since 1947 must count on the abstention of the PCI to survive—is not just a transitional government but the government of transition.

---

[3] For an acute analysis along this line and an intelligent critique of mass media predictions and interpretations of the DC vote, see Arturo Parisi and Gianfranco Pasquino, "20 giugno: struttura politica e comportamenti elettorali" [June 20: political structure and electoral behavior], *Il Mulino*, no. 244 (May-June 1976), pp. 342-386.

From De Gasperi to the Crisis of the 1970s

To understand the DC's predicament and the party's response to it during the campaign, a brief overview of the party and its evolving place in the Italian party and government system is necessary.[4] Alcide De Gasperi's design in the few years after the war was to forge Christian Democracy into a dominant center party that would secure, in a context of deep ideological divisions, a relatively smooth transition from a Fascist authoritarian regime to a competitive one. Memories of the failure of liberal governments in the first transition (after World War I) suggested that there was no room after World War II for parties that were strictly conservative and middle class. Rather, to revive democracy required a party that was popular, inter-class, moderate, and Christian but not confessional.

Much emphasis has been placed on the Catholic roots of De Gasperi's interclassism, but it had other historical roots that deserve equal emphasis. In a political society that, from the time of its formal unification, has never been able to tolerate a system of straight competition and alternation between left and right, inclusive parties capable of attracting toward the center as many interests as possible have always been in the best position to control and steady political regimes. Fascism itself was an authoritarian version of this formula. De Gasperi pursued his version by relying amply on the organizational support of the Church and its secular organizations, and also by adopting policies of determined but orderly reconstruction designed to attract not only the entrepreneurial, professional, and bureaucratic classes but also larger popular strata that had been ravaged by the war.

De Gasperi's formula of aggregation toward the political center, legitimized by the support of the smaller secular parties, has remained in its broad lines the DC strategy to the present, but with some extremely significant variations to be described below. One crucial factor in these variations is the fact that De Gasperi was not entirely successful in eroding the two extremes of the party system. The contingent explanations are many. The significant one from the viewpoint of the evolution of the party and of its government formula is the fact that under De Gasperi the party was still dependent for its organization and financing on the Church and on business and

---

[4] A more exhaustive treatment of this subject is found in Giuseppe Di Palma, *Surviving without Governing: The Italian Parties in Parliament* (Berkeley and Los Angeles: University of California Press, 1977), chapters 3 and 6.

agrarian interests.[5] Both sets of forces pressured the DC from a conservative position and advocated an opening of the governing coalitions to the right. These pressures left space to the left while increasing the potential for a recovery of the previously discredited right. In 1953, the party lost its absolute majority in Parliament, never to regain it, while both the right and the left expanded. The elections confirmed and brought home the fact that Italy's is an extreme multiparty system, whose governing center is constantly attacked by the far left and the far right. They also confirmed that the main antagonist of moderate Catholicism was the Communist party.

To understand the evolution of the DC until 1953 is to understand, if not to predict, much of what happened to it in the two decades that followed. In the second part of the fifties, the task of the party, now under the leadership of Amintore Fanfani—De Gasperi's most outstanding successor—was to regain its image as a popular party and to build the autonomy from private and religious interests which had escaped De Gasperi. In other words, Fanfani's task was to complete and perfect De Gasperi's design. Yet the party that emerged at the end of the fifties was in many ways not on a par with the one envisioned by De Gasperi's enlightened skepticism.[6] The fact is that the conditions for creating a coalition of moderate reformism, led by an autonomous and organized mass party capable of regaining a competitive edge over left and right, appeared limited.

Despite Fanfani's undeniable success in building a new party apparatus at the local and national level, the channels of cadre and membership recruitment remained heavily those of the Church and its lay organizations. And the Church was firm in its visceral cold-war anticommunism. Nor were business interests, for reasons that cannot be discussed here, ready to legitimize policies of aggregate reform, even those designed to create a modern competitive economy. Yet their support seemed crucial to a party that intended to remain in power. Fanfani's answer to this problem—that is, the expansion of the public sector of the economy under party supervision [7]—proved quickly to be a further impediment to any coalition of reformism.

The expansion of the public sector was facilitated by the very

---

[5] See, most recently, Gianfranco Pasquino, "Crisi della DC e evoluzione del sistema politico" [The crisis of the DC and the evolution of the political system], *Rivista italiana di scienza politica*, vol. 5 (December 1975), pp. 443-472.

[6] For an analysis by a Catholic of the party's original identity, see Gianni Baget-Bozzo, *Il partito cristiano al potere* [The Christian party in power] (Firenze: Vallecchi, 1974).

[7] Pasquino, "Crisi della DC," pp. 450-453.

size of the public sector under fascism. For example, the Institute for Industrial Reconstruction, one of the largest European holdings today, had been originally created in the thirties to rescue bankrupt private firms. The expansion was also facilitated by the relative autonomy of the public sector from the more cumbersome ministerial bureaucracy, by the country's objective needs for reconstruction, and by the considerable public resources made available to the dominant party by the collapse of the Fascist regime. Expansion of the public sector offered the DC an opportunity to make itself independent of the financial support of business. In principle, it could also constitute a channel through which the party might pursue reform policies in relative independence from Parliament and from the ministerial bureaucracy, the former stalemated by the presence of a strong delegitimizing opposition and the latter historically incapable of pursuing a modernizing plan. But the expansion of the public sector failed to produce a reform coalition. On the contrary, whether intentionally or not, it became a powerful incentive to the fragmentation and clientelization of the state apparatus by the Christian Democratic party, increasingly bent on a policy of spoils to cement its power.[8]

In part, this degeneration was facilitated by the strong factionalism of the DC. In the emerging internecine fight for the control of public resources, factionalism expanded and increasingly became what Giovanni Sartori has called interest factionalism.[9] In part, the degeneration can be explained by the fact that a politics of spoils and narrow benefits seemed the easiest way to consolidate power for a government party that felt no danger of being voted down by the electorate and yet was unable—because of the ideological disparities manifest in extreme multipartism—to pursue a majority plan. In part, also, the use of the public sector for clientelistic purposes served to keep business interests dependent on the state and the party and to buy their support. Policies of reform would, on the other hand, alienate business.

In short, the idea of a coalition for aggregate if moderate reforms under the leadership of the DC degenerated in the fifties into the reality of state clientelism, tying private interests to the DC via

---

[8] On why the DC has not been able to hold together a reform coalition, see also Sidney Tarrow, "The Italian Party System between Crisis and Transition," paper delivered to the Panel on the "Italian Party System in Transition," Conference Group on Italian Politics, American Political Science Association Annual Meeting, Chicago, Ill., September 2-5, 1976.

[9] Giovanni Sartori, "Proporzionalismo, frazionismo e crisi dei partiti" [Proportionality, factions and crisis of the parties], Rivista italiana di scienza politica, vol. 1 (August 1971), pp. 629-655.

the distribution of narrow, noncompetitive benefits. The balkanization of the public sector by DC factions had an equivalent in the parliamentary committees, which used their constitutional right to enact legislation without reporting it to the floor to pass a stream of detailed legislation benefiting all sorts of potential government supporters. Though the strategy succeeded in attracting toward the DC and the governing center a wide array of constituencies, including popular ones, the political edge it gave the DC over right and left took its toll in improvidence, financial irresponsibility, and the progressive loss of government efficiency and effective decision making. The mechanism of decay was built-in.

As for the party, the occupation of power eroded its image as a social Christian party, and endemic factionalism eroded Fanfani's new party apparatus. In a way, the interpenetration of factions and public and semipublic interests ended up by making Fanfani's party less cohesive and autonomous than De Gasperi's. Party factions became institutionalized—with their own leaders, headquarters, budgets, and mass media. Their expanding number was not justified by ideological disagreement but by the need to organize in order to control expanding resources. Fanfani himself lost the leadership at the end of the fifties. From then on, no single figure would dominate a heavily feudalized party.

Having said this much about the consolidation of the DC as an entrenched governing party in the fifties, one can understand the evolution and beginning crisis of the party in the following decade. The international events of the mid-1950s demonstrated, contrary to expectations, that the Communist party was perfectly capable of coping critically with the embarrassments of Stalinism and repression in Eastern Europe and of preserving unscathed its electoral strength and expanding apparatus. In the Italian multiparty system the main challenge to the DC and its governing center comes unquestionably from the Communists. The replacement of the old governing alliances between the DC and the smaller moderate parties (the Social Democrats, the Republicans, and the Liberals) by the center-left alliance between the DC and the Socialist party in 1963 was the response of the DC and the clientelized public sector to the challenge. It was made possible by the rift between Communists and Socialists over the events in the international Communist movement and was impelled by the unprecedented modernization of Italian society in the very early sixties—expanding production, intense social mobility, increasing mass consumption, and secularization under the pontificate of John XXIII.

But the decade of the center-left, far from propelling the DC on the reformist course it proclaimed, sealed state clientelism as a practice of government and a party coalition strategy. Once again the DC failed to form and dominate a coalition of reform. Because of the presence of the Socialists, the center-left represented a greater ideological spread than the old governments, and therefore a lesser capacity for internal accommodation and legislative planning. Socialists and Christian Democrats did not give their program of "structural reforms" the same meaning. Some DC leaders either opposed the new alliance or agreed to go along with it instrumentally in the hope of stretching their influence and isolating communism. There was no unified party leadership interested in, or capable of, reorienting the public sector from clientelism to planned reforms. The interpenetration of the public sector and the DC factions prevented it. Though the various public enterprises unquestionably had a role in crucial aspects of modernization, each was determined to preserve its autonomy and corporate interests. In sum, as far as Christian Democracy was concerned, the center-left proved to be a reactive and difficult formula, imposed on the governing party by the predicament of a stalemated party system in a suddenly changing society. The formula survived because it was politically the only one available—but it lost momentum in the second part of the decade.

The most significant sign of its decay was not the fact that the Communists made their first important gains precisely in the decade of the center-left. After all, the DC—with an electorate slightly below the 40 percent mark—still maintained in 1963, 1968, and 1972 almost the same strength as in the 1950s. Nor was the continuing instability under the center-left (nine cabinets from 1963 to 1972, compared with twelve post-De Gasperi cabinets from 1953 to 1963) the most significant indication of the DC's decay. Instead it was the accentuation of the state-party interpenetration and interest factionalism already apparent in the previous decade. The years of the center-left could be called the golden years of state clientelization and party factionalism. These developments were promoted by the increasing importance ostensibly given the public sector by the platform of the coalition and by the centrality of growth issues during the sixties. Then, too, the Socialists—unwilling to remain a junior partner in government—readily embraced the logic of the occupation of power and developed concomitantly their own brand of interest factionalism. But the root cause, as in the past, remained the fact that a coalition devoted to aggregate reform was impossible.

The rapid social and economic changes of the 1960s, however, proved the undoing of state-party clientelism and spelled in turn the crisis of the party. The presence of the Socialists in the government and the productive growth of the public and private sectors compelled the DC to accommodate the growing and often conflicting demands of new constituencies—the industrial working class, but also the spreading service sector and the very bureaucratic middle class created by the proliferation of the parastate. Because, however, the public structures remained unchanged—cumbersome in the ministerial bureaucracy, fragmented and personalized in the public enterprises, costly in all cases—clientelism "writ large" quite literally went bankrupt. That is, the DC was able to operate a politics of special benefits without immediately excessive costs as long as social change was slow and the constituencies were limited in number and restrained in their demands. But in a context of rapid change, the DC formula revealed its inflationary potential.[10] The problem was worsened by the economic crisis of the early seventies—by far the most serious since the war—which was only partially imported from abroad. Indeed, the rapid growth of the early sixties—a case of "repressive development"[11] based on the exploitation of cheap and abundant labor in a context of traditional labor-intensive industrial structures heavily protected by the state—led eventually to the *autunno caldo*, the hot autumn, of 1969. And skyrocketing labor costs, for which industrial structures were unprepared, contributed heavily to the stagflation of the following years.

All of these developments increased the dependence of the private industrial sector on the state-party apparatus, already overburdened by the new union militancy demanding the protection of labor salaries *and* job security. Typically, governments, unable to impose a rationalization of industrial and labor structures, ended up by placing the social costs of their improvidence on the entire community. As profits fell, Christian Democracy began to lose hold of its constituencies, and the delicate postwar equilibrium around the governing center seemed for the first time in serious jeopardy.

The Years of the Crisis

In 1972, for the first time in the history of the Italian republic, Parliament was dissolved before the expiration of its constitutional man-

---

10 For the inflationary potentials of clientelism, see James Scott, "Corruption, Machine Politics and Political Change," *American Political Science Review*, vol. 63 (December 1969), pp. 1142-1158.

11 Michele Salvati, "L'origine della crisi in corso" [Origins of the present crisis], *Quaderni Piacentini*, vol. 11 (March 1972), pp. 2-30.

date. In the May elections both the PCI and the neo-Fascist *Movimento Sociale* (MSI) strengthened their positions. The history and the political climate of the following four years, leading to the elections of June 20, are well documented in Joseph LaPalombara's introductory essay in this volume. But a few points of direct relevance to Christian Democracy are worth recalling.

The crisis of the regime compelled the party to begin a search for a new internal equilibrium and new leadership and to curb internal factionalism. The old equilibrium, theorized and practiced as a "permanent mediation" among factions, had not satisfied the factions; instead it had whetted their appetites. When applied to government, it had also failed to bring together the coalition parties and to produce consensual government policies. The leadership could not fall to the Dorotei, the sprawling faction of government and party notables that had controlled the center of the party since the end of Fanfani's leadership in 1959. Nor could it fall on Aldo Moro—the most subtle practitioner of "permanent mediation" and the main DC figure behind the alliance with the Socialists. He preferred to sit the transition out. Leadership fell for the first two years to Fanfani who, undaunted after losing a bid for the presidency of the Republic in December 1971, was again ready to pursue his design of a strong party for a strong government.

But the unanimous support for the so-called Palazzo Giustiniani pact, with which the DC factions reinstated Fanfani in the leadership of the party in June 1973, contributed little to solving the DC's internal and external problems. The sudden deterioration of the economy, triggered in the second part of the year by the oil crisis, and the revelation of a wave of government scandals and authoritarian conspiracies at the beginning of 1974 left Fanfani little time and space to maneuver. Matters were further complicated by the popularly initiated referendum to repeal the divorce law, which only a parliamentary agreement to reform the law could prevent. But, for reasons that probably went beyond Fanfani's firm opposition to divorce, no agreement was reached. Whether by choice or by necessity, the new secretary and the whole party decided eventually to support the referendum. Fanfani threw all his resources into the head-on confrontation. The results of the referendum in May 1974 revealed, beyond all expectations, the advanced secularization of society. Opposition to repealing the law was quite strong, if not majoritarian, even in "white" regions like Veneto and the traditional peasant cultures of the south.

Perhaps more important, the head-on confrontation over the

132

issue dealt a final blow to the revamping of the center-left—the only government formula still conceivable short of an opening to the Communists. In the fall, the Socialist party—itself seduced by the possibility of a confrontation with the DC—definitively left the government, which it had rejoined with great hesitation the year before. Partial local elections in the following months indicated a decline in the electoral strength of the DC even in traditional party bailiwicks such as Trentino. Though the neo-Fascist drive of the early seventies lost electoral momentum, right-wing terrorism and new revelations of scandals and plots—often involving high military and government officials—threw further shadows on the resolve and credibility of the governing class. If the new Moro-La Malfa cabinet formed after the exit of the Socialists managed to last almost until the parliamentary elections, this was largely and overtly due to the "responsible opposition" of the PCI, which embarked on its *compromesso storico* strategy after the events in Chile in 1973. The Communist party, now under the leadership of Enrico Berlinguer, appeared to more and more electors to be the only steady element in the crazy-quilt panorama of these years. They rewarded it, in the local and regional elections of June 1975, with its most significant victory since the war. In those elections Christian Democracy reached its lowest ebb, barely ahead of the PCI.

In July the national council of the DC ousted Fanfani and appointed Benigno Zaccagnini secretary of the party. The national council of July revealed that underneath Fanfani's failure to hold the party factions together lay the most serious crisis of the DC, a crisis that went well beyond that of the previous months, and one under which the party still labors. The first aspect of the crisis grew out of the realization by many *(but not all)* sectors of the DC that Fanfani's head-on confrontation policy for the referendum might not be sufficient to rescue a party stained by the arrogance of power. The second, newer, and most important aspect, which radically simplified the internal setup of the party, was the sudden fall of interest factionalism. Briefly, the local and regional elections triggered a process that would ultimately deprive the DC of its control of *all* the major city governments (Rome, Milan, Naples, Turin, Genoa, Florence, Venice)[12] and of six of the twenty regional governments. A dominant party that suffers such losses, implying as they do the loss of innumerable public and semipublic local centers of power, can no

---

[12] Though city elections were not held in Rome until one year later, local returns for the regional elections indicated correctly that the capital would also be lost.

longer afford to be divided by interest factionalism. The incentives are no longer at hand. For the first time since they had appeared, the interest factions became empty shells, and new internal alliances emerged as part of new strategies to save the party and refurbish its tarnished image.[13]

Zaccagnini's election reflected this turning point in the history of the party. The new secretary, himself a member of Moro's faction and president of the party's national council until his promotion, was generally recognized as a man of absolute integrity and decency, above the wheeling and dealing of state patronage. His good will and dedication to the party were not in question. His past as a resistance fighter and his identification with the popular tradition of the Catholic movement were also assets of importance at this juncture in the history of the party. There was, finally, no question that Zaccagnini—perceived originally as a fallback transitional figure—established in the months following his election a firmer grip on the party than expected. Elected with many reservations by a heterogeneous coalition of left-wing groups and followers of Fanfani, the new secretary drew strength from the dispersion of the party factions. After gaining the unanimous endorsement of the party directorate in the fall, Zaccagnini aspired to break the pattern of factional alignments, an endeavor that found an enthusiastic echo in many sectors of the party—especially among backbenchers and local party cadres, increasingly resentful of the monopoly of the established leadership. The party congress of March 1976, acclaimed as the congress of the *rifondazione del partito*, scored a personal success for Zaccagnini. For the first time a national secretary was directly elected "presidential style" by the congress rather than through outside deals among the factions.

But Zaccagnini's personal successes were not enough to provide the DC with the capacity to find constructive unity and to carve a new and stable place for itself in the changing political panorama. "Undoubtedly," wrote the Communist *L'Unità* of March 21, "by far the worst treated party at the Christian Democratic congress is the DC." Though the attacks on the old leadership from the floor, at times rowdy and merciless, might speak well for the vitality of the party, the DC emerged from the congress with no firm agreement on the strategies for its reconstitution. Zaccagnini was reelected with a narrow margin over Arnaldo Forlani, former party secretary and Fanfani's most gifted protégé. Fanfani himself was elected president of the national council. And the support of Prime Minister Moro—

[13] Alberto Sensini, *Corriere della Sera*, September 28, 1976.

the other big leader of the party and Fanfani's main antagonist—was essential to Zaccagnini's survival. Though the party executive intended to make good on its promises of internal renewal by effecting a turnover in the older parliamentary and ministerial personnel at the next election, there were questions about the credibility and the payoffs of such moves, as well as about the wisdom of thus squandering years of accumulated governing experience—such as it was. Also, there was obvious resistance from those who had attached themselves to the seats of power. Finally and more important, though every leader was ready to recognize, more or less defensively, that the party could not survive through the strategy of patronage and the cultivation of parasitic interests, the constraints of early elections—only three months after the congress—further undermined the search for new space in the evolving party system.

The Campaign and the Elections

The main constraint stemmed from the fact that the DC was not willing to occupy that conservative pole of the party spectrum toward which it was pushed by the increasing importance of the major parties and the unavailability of the Socialists for a new coalition. If one does not understand this, one cannot understand the predicament of the DC as it faced the June elections. The crux of the matter was that in order to occupy the center and to make good its aspirations as a moderate-reformist party—at a time when the center was eroded, when the party seemed to be losing influence over Catholic workers and the modern middle classes, and the Socialists had demanded that the government be open to the Communists—the DC was forced to deal directly with the PCI and its proposal for an inclusive coalition. But could the DC eat at the devil's table with a long enough spoon? Could it embrace Moro's "strategy of attention" to the PCI without losing its identity? Could it balance this with Fanfani's anticommunism without risk of isolation? And was fear of communism sufficient to retain for the DC an electorate apparently more disturbed by DC corruption than by Communist growth? [14] What electorate did the party finally need in order to save itself?

The outcome of these difficulties was a juggling act: the DC insisted on a new alliance with the Socialists as the best way to avoid Communist blackmail, but could not definitively close any door. Fanfani's spirit of crusade was balanced by the pliability and the emerg-

---

[14] See Sani's chapter in this volume.

ing statesmanship of Forlani. Nor did Fanfani's appeals find complete support from the old Dorotei notables, now split by the defection of Mariano Rumor, leader of the faction and long-time prime minister. The "strategy of attention" to the PCI, advocated by Moro and the left-wing Base faction and legitimized by Zaccagnini, contrasted, on the other hand, with the sudden anti-Communist outbursts of Carlo Donat Cattin, the leader of Forze Nuove—traditionally the most leftist of the DC factions. The argument of many DC leaders to the effect that a new rapport with the PCI did not and should not alter the essential democratic distinction between majority and opposition sounded cryptic and unconvincing. The last two governments before the elections had survived for seventeen months thanks to the tolerance and indeed the legislative support of the PCI. Though the months leading to the elections were replete with *rifondazione* meetings of various ad hoc party groupings (factions, union leaders, representatives of regional governments, intellectuals, economic experts), none of these groupings coalesced around a clear political plan that went beyond the available strategies.[15]

At the end of April, the DC was compelled by the increasing disaffection of the Socialist party toward Moro's *monocolore* (one-party) government and by the government's plummeting credibility (what with the Lockheed scandal, the collapse of the *lira*, the abortion law, and mounting terrorism) to choose between the Communist proposal of a broad national emergency coalition and early elections. It opted finally for the second. But the parliamentary debate leading to Moro's resignation had a novel and subtle twist worth recording. In order to save his party and the country the trauma of new elections, Moro suggested a government without the Communists but based on a program acceptable to the PCI. The Communists, and the Socialists, rejected the offer.

In principle, there were several avenues that the DC could pursue in the seven weeks until the elections in order to regain its lost ground, loosen the PCI embrace, and reassert itself as the dominant center of Italian politics. First, it could address itself squarely to the issues of economic decay and political violence. Second, it could essay a renovation of its parliamentary cadres, in keeping with the spirit of the March congress. Third, it could try to recover the organized Catholic vote partially lost by the end of the alliance between

---

[15] There was nothing comparable, for instance, to the Club phenomenon in France during the restructuring of the radical and Socialist left in the second part of the sixties. The Clubs—associations of leftist intellectuals and political figures often organized around prestigious journals—played an important role in the rebirth of the French Socialist movement.

DC and Catholic lay organizations. Fourth, it could try to amend its image as a party with a traditional and parasitic social base by making special appeals to the modern productive strata. Fifth, it could tackle directly the issue of the Communists in government and of government coalitions in general. In reality, it was the last issue area that tended to monopolize the DC campaign. The other areas received more guarded attention, either because the payoff seemed dubious or because they proved difficult to tackle.

Economic Decay and Political Violence. Because the DC was the governing party, the issues of economic decay and political violence became issues of government ineffectiveness and irresponsibility. The best strategy open to the DC—which was united on this point—was not so much to argue the merits of the issues but rather to dump responsibility on other parties and social forces and to suggest that the solution was a further strengthening of the DC and the political center. In so doing, the party ended up by transforming the problems of economic decay and political violence into problems of governing coalitions. This is staple strategy in Italian elections, and it was facilitated by the climate of emergency. The economic crisis, the DC leaders argued throughout the campaign, might well stem from the fact that the country had lived beyond its productive means, but the responsibility did not fall exclusively on the government and its much maligned clientelism. It fell also, as Moro remarked in a speech in Foggia at the beginning of June, on a fragmented Parliament in which even the Communists consistently pushed for expenditures designed to please sectional interests. Beyond this, it fell on a volatile party system and on political allies which the DC was objectively not always in a position to control. It fell also on the excessive militancy of the unions, often legitimized by the Socialists and the Communists, which had already made the cost of labor skyrocket and, by insisting on job security, now prevented a restructuring and rationalization of the industrial sector. The diagnosis suggested the treatment: a stronger DC and therefore a more effective government capable of negotiating with a more responsible Parliament and more responsible unions.

Similarly, the DC pointed to political violence to argue that the continuing threat of right and left extremism required a stronger center. Two events gave new credibility to the DC line: the killing of a prominent judge in Genoa by the tupamaros-style Brigate Rosse on June 8, and that of a young Communist at a neo-Fascist rally near Rome on May 29. The latter episode involved Sandro Saccucci, a

137

neo-Fascist deputy and candidate already under prosecution for alleged terrorism and conspiratorial activities. There were, however, two interesting elements in the position of the DC vis-à-vis political violence. First, while it accused the neo-Fascist party of direct responsibility for violence, it neither could nor wanted to extend the same treatment to the PCI. Political violence offered the DC an opportunity to reassert its firm anti-Fascist credentials, somewhat tarnished by recent revelations of right-wing conspiracies in high places. Second, aside from Fanfani's calls for a curb on the abuses of freedom, the DC was very guarded in its response to demands for restrictive and emergency measures to fight violence. For one thing, such measures would most probably be attacked by other parties as undercutting civil rights.

The Renewal of the Parliamentary Cadres. The selection of the parliamentary candidates engaged more directly the organization of the party and caused considerable internal tension between the national headquarters and local federations of the party. On May 2, Zaccagnini invited young voters to cast preference votes in the parliamentary elections that would free the DC of corrupt and stale elements. But there was skepticism in many quarters about the ability of the DC to effect a drastic purge of its parliamentary contingent. The DC is not a tight party of cadres like the PCI, which considers its members of Parliament party workers whom it can regularly reassign to other party functions. Within the DC, members of Parliament occupy a strategic position, both because of the party's factionalism and because of its long practice of government. By party statute, 74 of the 180 or so members of the national council must be drawn from Parliament. Further, the members of Parliament with the longest tenure are also those that occupy the most important positions in government, in the parastate, in local politics, and in the party itself. At the dissolution of Parliament, 33 percent of DC senators and 36 percent of DC deputies had been in Parliament for at least four terms, or a minimum of twenty years. An effective renovation of this parliamentary contingent would require eliminating many of those with the longest experience of government—with seemingly grave consequences for the party. Otherwise it would amount to mere cosmetics.

Ultimately, however, the renewal went further than the skeptics expected. The party's national directorate, meeting at the beginning of May, rejected as too rigid Zaccagnini's proposal that the local federations be urged to drop all incumbents with at least four terms who were not ministers or members of the directorate. But the party asked the chairmen of the parliamentary groups in the Senate and Chamber of Deputies to issue a report on each DC member, based on his attendance record and his participation in legislative activities including sponsorship of bills, speeches, and committee work. The reports would assist the local federations in selecting which members should run again. National headquarters reserved for itself the allocation of one Chamber seat per electoral district and twenty-three Senate seats. All controversial cases were to be referred to Rome.

The new element in this complex procedure was the autonomy asked by and accorded to the periphery. In past elections candidate selection had been, at least formally, located in Rome. By and large, the DC periphery seized upon its new powers to retire a good number of its parliamentary representatives. In the ensuing tug-of-war it was Rome that put on the brakes. According to a report in the *Corriere della Sera* of May 7, only some 20 of the 266 DC members of the Chamber of Deputies—by and large, obscure backbenchers—had been given negative reports by the party whip. But in Emilia-Romagna the regional organization of the party decided to heed Zaccagnini's more stringent proposal and to drop nine incumbents with more than three terms. Rome stepped in, and four of the nine were finally allowed to run. Open and publicized conflict between Rome and the periphery occurred in Sardinia, Piedmont, Lombardy, and Molise. The most significant politician to fall victim to these conflicts was Athos Valsecchi, former minister of finance under investigation for oil price fixing. Overruling Rome's verdict, the Sondrio federation (Lombardy) replaced Valsecchi with another local member of Parliament.[16]

When the lists were finally filed, in a last flurry of patching up, 99 of the 401 DC deputies and senators were no longer in the running. The turnover was much greater in the Senate (41 percent) than in the Chamber of Deputies (17 percent). But even the figure for the Chamber of Deputies was on the average almost twice as large as that of previous parliamentary elections.[17] To be sure, among the dozen or so prominent figures who retired or were retired, some were affected by a combination of age and political superannuation.[18] Also, with the exception of Valsecchi and possibly Silvio Gava, the recent

---

[16] *La Stampa*, May 20, 1976.

[17] Data on previous elections are reported in Maurizio Cotta, "Classe politica e istituzionalizzazione del parlamento: 1946-1972" [The political class and the institutionalization of Parliament: 1946-1972], *Rivista italiana di scienza politica*, vol. 6 (April 1976), p. 93. The data are limited to the Chamber of Deputies.

[18] Giuseppe Spataro, Silvio Gava, Giuseppe Pella, Gennaro Cassiani, and Giuseppe Togni were among these.

wave of scandals and corruption had no significant victims. But it was unquestionable that, along with many obscure backbenchers, a good number of intermediate notables with power in the periphery and the parastate were also purged. Fifty-eight percent of the deputies who were not renominated had been in Parliament for at least four terms. Throughout the campaign, Zaccagnini and his colleagues pointed to the parliamentary ticket as evidence of the rejuvenation of the party.

Recovering the Catholic Vote. Another set of reasons, beyond the party's parliamentary and governmental stakes, helped to make the circulation of parliamentary personnel controversial. Traditionally, the DC had recruited most of its party and parliamentary cadres from the lay organizations of the Church (the Christian Association of Italian Workers—ACLI—and Catholic Action and its member organizations), as well as from the Catholic unions (CISL). Though this practice had been amply and correctly criticized by many for narrowing the avenues of party recruitment and socialization, it was nevertheless unquestionable that it also offered the DC a vast and fresh pool from which to draw from generation to generation. But the crisis of *collateralismo*—that is, the end of the close relations between DC and Catholic organizations—had progressively closed the pool. The expansion of state-party clientelism, in turn, had attracted to the party ambitious power-oriented individuals more difficult to displace. Though some analysts asserted that the renovation of party lists during the campaign had allowed new candidates from Catholic organizations to enter the DC lists, the extent of the phenomenon is difficult to verify with the data at our disposal. And a note of skepticism is temporarily justified in view of the fact that practically none of the Catholic organizations engaged in the campaign side by side with the DC.

The only exception was Comunione e Liberazione, an interesting and unique association born of the student movement of the late sixties and particularly strong among the young and in the universities, especially in the north. It had become a powerful competitor of leftist campus organizations, combining a strong social consciousness with a religious commitment emphasizing rededication, Catholic orthodoxy, and charismatic communion. Well received by the Church, the movement supported the DC and ran candidates on the DC ticket in the areas where it was strong.

But aside from Comunione e Liberazione, whose appeal was special and limited, there was no longer space for a new *collateralismo*. There was only space for individual commitment. Typical in this

140

regard was the choice of Marino Carboni, who resigned on May 15 from the presidency of the ACLI to run as a DC candidate, so as not to compromise—as he said—the political autonomy of his movement. The same day, the executive committee of ACLI—some of whose members were known sympathizers of the left—declared that the organization would neither endorse parties nor lend its apparatus to the campaign of any candidate, but would respect the freedom of choice of its members. A similar statement was issued jointly on May 11 by the three general labor confederations. Bruno Storti, general secretary of the Catholic CISL, commented that involving labor in the elections would violate the right of workers to make their choices in perfect freedom. The lists of DC candidates contained only one prominent leader of CISL (Vito Scalia) and seven local and national officials of lesser status. But one provincial leader of the metalworkers (Verona's Carlo Ramella) chose to run as an independent candidate with the PCI.

All of this touches directly on the third potential issue area of the DC campaign: the recovery of the organized Catholic vote. What has been said above indicates the limits of the recovery, given the neutrality of lateral organizations and the attraction of the Catholic vote by the left—especially in urban and industrial areas. But there was another side to the story. The DC itself was by and large very wary of pushing the issue. In part this was because the Catholic organizations wanted to stay neutral. But in part it was also because the party feared that a Catholic appeal might degenerate into a confessional crusade that would not fit with the DC's projected image.

Most revealing in this connection was the reaction of the DC leaders to the intervention of the Italian Episcopal Conference (CEI) and of Paul VI in the campaign in the middle of May. This was the first time since the death of Pius XII that the Church had stepped into an electoral campaign. Unprecedented though it was, the Church leaders' intervention is explained by the exceptional stakes of the elections. It was precipitated by the much publicized decision of six "dissenting Catholics" prominent in the Italian Catholic world to run as independent candidates with the PCI. Also, the Church of Pope Paul VI behaved more guardedly than that of Pius XII and spoke on the issue in muted tones. Though the conference condemned the six dissenters for placing themselves "outside the Church community," there was apparently disagreement among the bishops about the appropriateness of the condemnation. Nor were there, in any document of the conference or in any other Church statement, references to sanctions against the six. In fact, the plaintive tone with which the conference addressed itself to the dissenters suggested more a paternal reprimand than a fiery excommunication. Pope Paul himself, speaking to the conference on May 21, struck a pastoral rather than a political note. And though he referred to the elections as "decisive for our future for what concerns many religious, pastoral, doctrinal, ethical and social questions," his call for a DC vote was obscure and circumlocuted to the point of defying English translation.[19] Father De Rosa, a columnist for the Jesuit *Civiltà Cattolica*, contended the day after that the Pope's speech contained "neither threats nor references to canon law. It is only an appeal to Christian conscience; an appeal to which the Pope is entitled." Further, though the CEI invited Italy's parish priests to communicate and discuss the Church's message, press reports indicated that the invitation often fell on deaf ears.

More important from our viewpoint, the DC leadership—including Fanfani—remained uncommitted. They responded to the accusations made by many leaders of other parties that Pope Paul had improperly meddled in Italian affairs not on the merits of the Pope's message but exclusively on his right, as bishop of Rome, to speak to his followers and to exercise internal discipline. And though DC leaders personally expressed their political disagreement with the choice of the six dissenters running for the Communists, they purposely underplayed the event. Giovanni Galloni, vice-secretary of the party, went so far as to declare in an interview published in the *Corriere della Sera* of May 27, "The DC has neither negative nor positive reactions [to the Pope's speech]. As far as we are concerned, Catholics may well run with the PCI. This fact, which does not disturb the DC, disturbs the Church." *Il Popolo*, the DC daily, at first gave limited attention to the speech and only four days later published a comment by De Rosa arguing mainly that the Church had been compelled to step in. The DC showed similar detachment toward Comunione e Liberazione, whose support the party accepted without much publicity and fanfare.

Modernizing the Party's Image. If the DC did not want to embark on a campaign to recover Catholic votes, an alternative strategy, in keeping with the desire of the new sectors of the party to modernize

---

19 "It is not appropriate to avoid the electoral duty," thus goes Paul VI's call, "when this is connected with a profession of faithfulness to nonrenounceable values and principles, even though their perfect representation may be questioned in some instances and regards." The first part of the sentence is supposed to refer to the DC (representing basic principles and values) and the need to support it. The second part is supposed to contain a mild criticism of the DC.

and secularize, was to appeal to the productive strata of society—in industry and in the middle classes—by attracting candidates from their ranks. But here, too, the party tended to fall between two stools. There was considerable talk at the beginning of May about a new political commitment among industrialists, managers, and economic experts disturbed by the political and economic crisis. Many (foremost among them, Fiat's Gianni Agnelli and the Bank of Italy's former governor Guido Carli) were allegedly planning to run for Parliament. Political commentators were beginning to speak of an incipient technocratization of Italian politics, capable of breaking up stale alignments. Soon, however, the balloon was deflated. While parties like the Republicans and Liberals had always attracted and continued to attract a good number of managerial candidates, very few private industrialists became candidates for the other parties. One reason was that the powerful partisan logic dominating Italian politics tends to frustrate independent contributions to party renovation.

But in the case of the DC, another and more significant factor was at play, which revealed the DC's uncertainty and confusion about its modernization. Anticapitalist populism was dying hard within the party and there were still sectors of the DC that considered it inappropriate for a popular party to run an industrialist as a candidate. Thus, on one side the secularization of society, the dispersion of the Catholic vote, and the costs of clientelism advised the party to turn its attention to the new middle classes and to those groups in private business that had grown increasingly restless under state dependency. This seemed to be a way of removing the parasitic incrustations on the party and of building that moderate-reformist coalition which always escaped the DC leaders. On the other side, populist sectors of the party believed that such a strategy would set the DC on a dangerous conservative-technocratic path reminiscent of Gaullism and Giscardism.

The most telling illustration of the DC's internal divisions on the matter came from the much publicized events surrounding the candidacy of Umberto Agnelli, the only prominent industrialist on the DC ticket. Umberto, Gianni Agnelli's younger brother and vice-president of Fiat, indicated at the beginning of May that he was available for a Chamber seat in Turin, Fiat's headquarters. On May 11 the Agnelli candidacy became a national affair. Turin's Donat Cattin, former minister of labor and of industry and leader of the left-wing Forze Nuove faction, opposed publicly the inclusion of Agnelli's name on the city's ticket. Agnelli's candidacy, Donat Cattin declared, "would obliterate the DC in its relations with the regional and city administration and would replace it with the interests of Fiat, which are always inclined to compromises and are at any rate profoundly different from those of a great popular party." [20] The twist in this statement is that the city administration of Turin and the regional government of Piedmont happened to be Communist. Donat Cattin's fear that Fiat would establish a special rapport with an ever-pragmatic PCI oddly contrasted with his distaste at the idea of sharing the ticket with a prominent capitalist. Yet Donat Cattin's populistic resentment at both Communists and capitalists has a long tradition in the party, even, and perhaps especially, among its left-wing syndicalist sectors. Agnelli's case was referred to Rome. But when Agnelli insisted on a seat in Piedmont if not in Turin, Donat Cattin, joined by Guido Bodrato, another Forze Nuove leader, threatened to withdraw from the ticket. Agnelli seemed ready to abandon the campaign, but a few hours before the party lists were filled he accepted a senatorial seat in Rome.

There was another side to the Agnelli affair, which confirmed the difficulties the DC had in dispelling its historical image—namely, the public reaction to Agnelli's candidacy. Agnelli's explanation for choosing the DC over one of the smaller secular parties was that the DC is the party that counts. Once within the DC, he intended to join the fight to renovate the party along modern lines. But many commentators, noticing that the expected wave of new managerial candidates had shrunk to a trickle, doubted that Agnelli's modernization could succeed. Others even argued that the DC's lingering ambivalence toward competitive capitalism and its longstanding practice of state-party patronage belied Agnelli's true intentions. Productive and parasitic interests could not be easily distinguished within the party, especially in times of rampant stagflation. Agnelli's decision to run for Parliament, as Massimo Riva commented in the *Corriere della Sera* of May 16, was probably motivated by a desire to get the maximum out of this "neoprotectionist" reality.

The Problem of Coalitions. In sum, the *rifondazione* of the DC during the campaign had muted effects. To be sure, the party ticket was substantially purged. Also, many economic experts and political advisers traditionally close to the DC had become DC candidates.[21] However, there is no clear evidence that either the organized Catholic

---

[20] *Corriere della Sera,* May 11, 1976.
[21] These included Nino Andreatta, Gaetano Stammati, Francesco Paolo Bonifacio, Siro Lombardini, Antonio Faedo, and Leopoldo Elia.

vote (labor in particular) or the productive middle strata and business were looking at the party with increased confidence. The moderate-reformist coalition remained an aspiration yet to be tested. The political emergency induced the party to throw most of its resources into the last issue area: the definition of the future governing coalition.

Like the leaders of the other parties, the DC leaders filled their speeches and declarations with references to the issue of who should govern after the elections. At its core, the position of the DC leaders remained strictly unchanged: there would be no government with the Communists. The DC needed more votes. Only a stronger DC could reconstitute a solid alliance with the smaller constitutional parties, necessary to take the country out of its present crisis. Though the party was ready to become a responsible opposition in case of defeat, there was no telling what internal and international consequences a PCI victory might have for the country.

Yet a few doors were left cautiously ajar. For one thing, the presence of parties to the left and right of the DC suggested a strategy of appeals on two fronts. For another thing, the defensive position in which the party found itself, and the political climate favorable to the left, prompted some leaders to adopt a carrot-and-stick strategy, especially toward the left. The DC leaders divided their roles: Fanfani covered the right wing, especially in the more traditional south, while Moro and Zaccagnini worked the other side.

Despite the general leftist trends, Fanfani had the easier job. He threw himself with abandon into a whirlwind of political campaigning, the central theme of which was extremely simple and clear: The Communists cannot be trusted and the Socialists are playing the Communists' game. The DC needs the electoral support of right-wing voters. A vote for the neo-Fascist MSI is a wasted protest vote. On communism the analysis was consistently of cold-war vintage. Communism is by nature always red. Fanfani declared in an interview with *Die Welt*, "There is no such thing as 'white communism,' different from and less dangerous than 'red communism.' "[22] Because he also believed that few votes could be recaptured from the left, Fanfani said in an interview with the weekly *Tempo* at the beginning of June: ". . . the electorate of the extreme right must reflect and decide to move to the DC. . . . There are no barriers against them from our side." To clinch his appeal, the DC president insisted more than any other leader on the strength of the PCI. The situation, he said, was "largely favorable to the left." He stated in another

---

[22] Reported in *La Stampa*, May 27, 1976.

interview, with the weekly *Gente*, "The Communists and the Socialists are superior to us. They have more money, more means, an impressive propaganda machine." "The future of Italian democracy," he added, "is played on a razor's edge." [23]

It would be wrong, however, to believe that Fanfani was pursuing a reactionary design. Though he appealed to its electorate, his condemnation of the MSI as a party of violence outside the constitution was consistent and explicit. Rather, Fanfani's strategy was to recover votes on the right so as to make possible a new centrist government and to push the Socialists to the ropes, either with the DC or with the PCI in opposition. The strategy stemmed from Fanfani's belief that the Socialists were practically lost to the government and that friendly persuasion would not do. But one interesting point about Fanfani's campaign is that he never discussed the issue of a future alliance with the Socialists, either to advocate it *or to reject it*. Even Fanfani left this door ajar. After all, he had not been disinclined to seek the support of the left in his personal bids for the presidency of the Republic.

Moro, Zaccagnini, but also many of the Dorotei notables, on the other hand, led a more complex and more open campaign. The difference was that behind the core rejection of any government that included the PCI were both a recurrent appeal to the Socialists to reenter the coalition and the recognition that the PCI had substantially, if not persuasively, changed over the last few years. Therefore, the DC intended to establish a *confronto* with the Communists, that is, a constructive dialogue in Parliament and in local government. In an editorial of May 15 inspired by Zaccagnini in response to Berlinguer's renewed proposal for a long-term emergency government, the DC's *Il Popolo* rejected the proposal by pointing to the historical differences that divided the PCI from the DC and to the incomplete and uncertain conversion of the PCI.

At the National Council of May 20, Zaccagnini himself appealed to the Socialists, as he put it, "with a respect that may seem even excessive, given their ungenerous and hard behavior toward us, because we don't want to deteriorate the mutual relations we must resume after the elections." He continued by warning the Socialists of their risk of being crushed by the more powerful Communists and concluded by saying: "We believe sincerely in the possibility of resuming our collaboration with the Socialists." But the *Il Popolo* article already cited also offered some revealing subsidiary reasons for rejecting Berlinguer's proposal: it would eliminate any "intermediate

---

[23] Interview quoted in *Corriere della Sera*, June 6, 1976.

hypothesis" such as "external support of the PCI for an emergency government" or "a caretaker government." And in a passage reminiscent of Moro's counterproposal during the parliamentary debate preceding the dissolution of Parliament, the article asked, "Why, as it is done in other countries, can't the economic emergency be dealt with through an armistice between majority and opposition on issues of common interests?"

The theme of the *confronto* was sounded again by an appeal from Paolo Baffi, governor of the Bank of Italy. In his annual report, which was given wide publicity, Baffi called for an "expansion of the area of consensus" in the government to face the economic emergency. Commenting on Baffi's call in a newspaper interview, former Prime Minister Giulio Andreotti offered a foretaste of his future conduct: ". . . leaving aside formulae and confusions on the structure of governments, I believe we must pursue with energy the parliamentary path. Did you see the new bill on the South? We worked hard on it, first with the regions and then in Parliament. It turned out a very good bill, almost unanimously approved." [24] A few days later, Zaccagnini closed the campaign by arguing that the elections were not a referendum on a DC versus a PCI government and that the real issues about which people were worried concerned the economy, public order, and the expansion of the democratic system. In his view, these were issues on which, after the elections, all political forces should be able to come together with good will. [25]

It would be wrong, however, to read into Moro and Zaccagnini's overtures to the left a greater trust in the reasonableness of the Socialists or a lesser fear of communism than Fanfani had shown. The two leaders probably had few illusions on these matters. This was especially true, for reasons of temperament, of Moro. When the Socialists exploited the neo-Fascist Saccucci's escape abroad to avoid arrest, using it to subject the prime minister to repeated personal attacks for his alleged negligence in prosecuting terrorists, Moro was not averse to escalating the ominous tone of the campaign. The theme of a necessary alliance with the Socialists remained unchanged, but for the remainder of the campaign counterattacks on the left dominated Moro's speeches. His hard-nosed tack was that the Socialists were taking irresponsible and dramatic risks and that without a stronger DC, democracy in Italy was in jeopardy. This view implied no special confidence in the left. On the contrary, the tone of Moro and Zaccagnini's campaign probably stemmed from a greater

---

[24] Interview in ibid.
[25] Interview in ibid., June 18, 1976.

pessimism than Fanfani had about the capacity of the DC to recreate the old centrist equilibrium and from an equal, perhaps even greater, feeling that the day belonged to the left. Hence Fanfani's frontal attacks might, in their view, recover the votes but worsen the overall prospects. Fear of isolation compelled the DC to come to terms with the left. The division of campaign roles among DC leaders was neither a cynical ploy nor proof of greater or lesser appreciation for the left. It simply revealed different readings of how far the crisis had traveled and what it would take for the DC to survive.

The Electoral Results

On June 22 the computers of the Ministry of the Interior showed that the DC had obtained 38.7 percent of the votes for the Chamber of Deputies and 38.9 percent for the Senate. The percentages were essentially the same as those obtained by the party in the three previous parliamentary elections (1963, 1968, and 1972). To understand how the DC managed to hold its ground and recover the votes it had lost the year before, one must keep in mind that the election also produced a significant expansion of the PCI and an equally significant loss among the smaller parties of the center and right. The PCI gained approximately 2.5 points over its 1975 results and 7.3 points over 1972. The smaller center parties (at least the Liberals and Social Democrats) and the MSI lost more than 4 percentage points with respect to 1975 and close to 7 points with respect to 1972.

The most widely accepted and probably accurate interpretation of these realignments is that, as in previous cases of Communist and left expansion, Communist gains at the expense of the whole center-right went together with an internal realignment within the center-right itself that favored the already dominant DC.[26] That is, both the DC and the smaller parties lost votes to the Communists, but the DC in turn compensated for its losses at the expense of the smaller parties. The alternative interpretation—that the DC retained its 1972 electorate and received a proportionate share of first-time voters—seems implausible. For one thing, it would imply that PCI

---

[26] I am not considering here the other important source of PCI growth since 1972, which is the disproportionate support of young voters (eighteen-year-old persons could not vote before 1975). See Sani's chapter, as well as Sani, "Ricambio elettorale e identificazioni partitiche: verso una egemonia delle sinistre?" [Electoral change and party identifications: toward a hegemony of the left?], *Rivista italiana di scienza politica*, vol. 5 (December 1975), pp. 515-544; "Le elezioni degli anni settanta: terremoto o evoluzione?" [The elections of the seventies: earthquake or evolution?], *Rivista italiana di scienza politica*, vol. 6 (August 1976), pp. 261-288.

148

gains among 1972 voters had come only from the smaller parties. This does not fit with the estimates presented by Giacomo Sani in this volume. The growing attractiveness of the PCI in the early seventies is a phenomenon generalized among center-right voters. In fact, in view of the strong popular social base of the DC, it seems improbable that its voters would be more impervious to PCI appeals than the voters of more clearly middle-class, conservative, or even downright anti-Communist parties like the Republicans (the only small party, in fact, that retained its strength), the Liberals, or the MSI.

To prove unequivocally which interpretation is correct is beyond the power of aggregate data analysis. Internal realignments escape detection, especially in view of the fact that in 1972 realignments were rather evenly distributed at the provincial and district level. However, some evidence compatible with the first interpretation is offered by Sani in this volume and in other essays.[27] For instance, the 1972–1976 variations in the vote for the smaller center-right parties in the ninety-four provinces are negatively correlated with those of the DC (−.487).[28] More specifically, in none of the provinces in which the DC increased its vote is the increase higher than the combined losses of the smaller parties. This, too, is compatible with the notion that it was the smaller parties that paid for the DC recovery. In fact, the latter data also bear on another point: if anyone has any doubts, there is no apparent sign that the DC obtained votes from those who had voted Communist in 1972. There are, to be sure, regions where DC gains *over the local elections of 1975* surpass the losses of the small parties and may in fact stem from DC inroads in the Communist camp. But, as Arturo Parisi and Gianfranco Pasquino show, these regions are largely PCI showcases in north central Italy, where the Communists control local government and where moderate voters, though not disinclined to vote PCI at local elections, return to the moderate fold at parliamentary elections.[29]

In sum, the DC has probably suffered losses, if marginal ones, among its traditional electorate. A reasonable estimate, based on extrapolations from Sani's survey and demographic data, is that the

---

[27] Sani, "Le elezioni degli anni settanta."

[28] Also, even assuming that the DC had kept its 1972 electorate and a proportionate share of the new voters, estimates from electoral results and demographic turnover data made available by Sani show that *at least* 600,000 out of 14.2 million DC votes must have come from the smaller parties. This means that the smaller parties must have lost to the DC *at least* 9 percent of their 1972 electorate still voting in 1976.

[29] Parisi and Pasquino, "20 giugno," pp. 369-370.

DC has lost to the left approximately 7.5 percent of its old voters. Has the DC made inroads in the new middle classes and the managerial strata? Traditionally, these have supported the smaller center parties, whose strength has now been eroded by the DC. Can we therefore assume an increase in the "modern" DC electorate? Aggregate analysis cannot speak directly to the point of motivations and to the way voters perceive party appeals. Its results are moot. The DC made no disproportionate gains in highly industrial and urban areas, in which the modern vote should be concentrated. Rather, as shown by the fact that provincial correlations between elections are close to 1.0 (.976 for 1976–1972 and .970 for 1976–1975), DC variations are rather evenly distributed over the national territory. Further, the correlations are even stronger in the industrial north (.988 and .989 respectively) than in the south (.908 and .851). The question therefore remains open to analysis. The least we can suggest, however, is that the events surrounding the Agnelli candidacy should make us wary of judging the new DC votes as modernizing in intent.

It is fair to conclude that the recovery of the DC is no definite sign of a successful *rifondazione*. Rather, what we are probably witnessing is a holding action. Very simply, the new votes reflected largely the unwillingness of some strata to risk a Communist experiment. Though these strata may not traditionally belong to the DC, they chose to support it as the strongest party. Fanfani's strategy paid off. Even the youth vote does not alter this interpretation. Comparatively speaking, this is the brightest aspect of the DC recovery. Everything tended to suggest a disproportionately heavy loss of youthful votes to the PCI. Instead the DC seems to have held almost as well among the young as among the older cohorts. A comparison between the DC vote in the Chamber of Deputies and in the Senate (where only persons aged at least twenty-five can vote), though in several ways unwarranted, suggests that the DC received 37.6 percent of the votes among those aged less than twenty-five, or just 2.3 percentage points less than among the older cohorts. The loss is minor. Yet it is also true, as Parisi and Pasquino show, that—except for 1953—this is the first time since 1948 that the DC has done less well among the young than among older voters. Despite the personal success of Comunione e Liberazione candidates in Rome and Milan, the youth vote for the DC in the areas where this movement was present remained lower than elsewhere and declining.[30] And Sani's data confirm that young voters are mainly attracted by the PCI. If

---

[30] Ibid., p. 367.

this is indeed a generational trend, the holding capacity of the DC is still in question.

More important than the analysis of the actual sources of the DC recovery, which is still admittedly sketchy, is the way the DC reads the results. And the fact is that, after the first elation and public declarations of victory, the DC was much less than sanguine about interpreting its votes as a significant reversal of trends. "The PCI's progress has been tremendous," Arnaldo Forlani declared, "and it has taken place, whatever we say, on our ground." "There has been great emphasis on the DC recovery," Forlani added, "but this has amounted to collecting voters among forces essential to democratic equilibrium and to a gradual and constructive *confronto* with the PCI. The DC has . . . devoured its children." [31]

More important still, as Forlani recognized, the DC recovery, coupled with the Communists' leap forward, has created a political vacuum between the DC and the left. The smaller parties of the center have been reduced to a mere 7.8 percent in the Chamber of Deputies and represent a largely older electorate. Aside from this numerical weakness, they are politically uncertain about resurrecting centrist coalitions. Such coalitions, in any case, would need the votes of the Socialists, who, despite their poor showing, are adamant in their opposition. However the DC may interpret its recovery, the urgent matter at hand is governing. And the erosion of the center has aggravated it. Fanfani's strategy may have brought in votes, but Moro and Zaccagnini's strategy awaits its test.

Governing through Abstentions

One can accuse the Italian governing class of anything except a lack of imagination and of a fine sense for tactical equilibria when the times require them. In the months following the elections, Italy's political leaders managed to wiggle out of the most serious impasse since the war. The feat was chiefly accomplished by Giulio Andreotti, De Gasperi's keenest pupil in the years immediately after the war and probably the Catholic politician with the best knowledge of the state and parliamentary apparatus. His subtle negotiating skills and his longstanding care to keep his options open within his party made him generally acceptable as the appropriate person to form a new government. At the beginning of August, Andreotti put together a minority DC cabinet with a program of economic emergency meas-

---

[31] Both quoted in *Rinascita*, July 2, 1976.

ures and a series of strict deadlines for a number of social and institutional reforms. He won the votes of his party and the abstention of the PCI and all the other parties except the extreme right.

But the DC paid a clear price for the relative celerity and smoothness of the operation. Andreotti met individually with each of the parliamentary parties except the extreme right. Though he insisted that the meetings did not involve negotiations, he nevertheless made it very clear that the government would implement its program in close collaboration with Parliament. A new, closer relationship with Parliament was in fact Andreotti's chief strategy for insuring the survival of the minority cabinet. But to speak of a special relationship with Parliament is to speak chiefly, though euphemistically, of a special relationship with the PCI. Andreotti's subtle characterization of abstention as a vote of *non-sfiducia*—literally, "non-no-confidence" —has the same meaning. But euphemisms cannot hide reality. They can simply (and perhaps significantly) make it more palatable and reduce the potential for polarization built into the electoral results. The reality includes the fact that the Seventh Parliament is also the first one in which the Communists have occupied important leadership positions. In recognition of its strength, the PCI obtained, with the support of the DC and the abstention parties, the chairmanship of seven out of twenty-five standing committees (including the Finance Committee in the Chamber of Deputies) as well as the presidency of the Chamber.

Aside from these concessions, two things explain Andreotti's success. The first is the weak position in which the two winning parties find themselves on the issue of who shall govern. Neither can govern alone. Neither, on the other hand, has an interest in leaving the country ungoverned. Second, both parties have popular and inclusive aspirations. The DC has manifested them for thirty years through its strategy of centrism. The PCI has exposed them recently through the *compromesso storico*. And now the simplification of the party spectrum pushes the two adversaries toward each other. At any rate, the Andreotti government seems to mark the end of Christian Democratic monopoly over Italian governments. In October 1976, when emergency measures were approved by the cabinet, the government was pressed into a flurry of tough overt negotiations with the PCI, the unions, and the left in general over their demands. At the same time, the DC's national council legitimized the changes by appointing Moro as its president. Moro and Zaccagnini, the main exponents of the "strategy of attention to the PCI," now occupy the two top offices in the party. They are, to be sure, by no means sold on the idea of a government with the Communists. Their design remains a new coalition with the Socialists. But can they stop the PCI at the threshold of the "creeping compromise"?

Their main hope is the *rifondazione* of the DC, to make possible that moderate-reformist coalition which the party has never quite achieved. But, as a modernization of the social bases of the party, the *rifondazione* seems to have failed. To be sure, there has been a renewal of the party's parliamentary contingent. Only 24 percent of the DC deputies in the new Chamber, compared with 36 percent in the old one, have been in Parliament for four or more terms; and 36 percent sit in the Chamber for the first time, compared with 24 percent in the old Chamber. But the presence of new deputies, including Agnelli and the new technocrats, does little to clarify the party's new vocation. Under the constraints of the lingering emergency, the internal party debate after the elections produced little that was firm beyond the available external strategies. As Arturo Parisi commented before the election, Zaccagnini's most significant achievement is still . . . Zaccagnini's election to the leadership of the party.[32] The *rifondazione* remains a never-never land.

In the somewhat longer range, three scenarios can be envisioned: (1) the government will be compelled to make more room for the PCI; (2) the Socialists, finally disgruntled with expanding Communist influence, will reenter the coalition (while the PCI remains an effective and influential semi-opposition force); (3) ungovernability will become such that new elections are needed.[33] In all cases the evolution leaves space for the PCI, especially if it manages to move with careful determination. Does this mean that the PCI will eventually be able to replace the DC at the core of future coalitions? This is a question which I address elsewhere.[34]

---

[32] Arturo Parisi, "Ancora su rifondazione, rifondatori e compromessi," *Il Mulino*, vol. 25 (January-February 1976), pp. 113-133.

[33] For the three scenarios see Giacomo Sani, "The PCI on the Threshold," *Problems of Communism* (November 1976), pp. 27-51.

[34] Giuseppe Di Palma, "Italy: Transitions," paper delivered at the annual meeting of the American Political Science Association, Washington, D.C., September 1-4, 1977.

5

THE LONGEST CAMPAIGN: COMMUNIST PARTY STRATEGY AND THE ELECTIONS OF 1976

Stephen Hellman

Events may yet demonstrate that there was no real winner of the Italian elections of 1976, but the Italian Communist party certainly attracted the greatest attention during the campaign and emerged from the voting as the party that had gained the most. Already the largest Communist party in the west prior to the election, the PCI appeared to have a good chance of becoming Italy's largest political party. This did not occur, but the Communists' rise to 34.4 percent of the vote, along with the left's advance to 47 percent, changed the political arithmetic of Italy.

For years the PCI had been arguing that no solution to Italy's problems was possible without Communist participation in the fundamental decisions facing the country. The June 1976 elections did not force the ruling Christian Democratic party to accept the PCI as a coalition partner, but it did force the DC to come to terms with the PCI in ways that would have been unthinkable without so strong a showing at the polls. From 1947 on, the PCI had systematically been excluded from what the DC and its allies called "the constitutional area"; in 1976 the barriers began to crumble. In many instances, what the PCI obtained had been due to it all along as Italy's second party: the presidency of one of Parliament's two chambers, a proportional number of chairmanships of parliamentary committees, and the right to sit on the interparty committee that assigns these positions. For the first time, the Christian Democrats were forced to make certain political concessions to the Communists—to consult them prior to the formation of a DC cabinet and to solicit PCI abstention on the vote that permitted the government to take office. Both the Communist vote and these formal and informal gains greatly strengthened the PCI's claim to recognition as a legitimate constitutional party. They also forced the DC to renege on its campaign promise to reject any rapprochement with the PCI, any relationship smacking of the "historic compromise" that was the central plank in the Communist platform.

What sort of Communist party is it that runs a campaign that places the blame for Italy's ills at the feet of the DC but simultaneously refuses to propose an alternative that would incite the electorate to turn the rascals out? The PCI conducted a masterful campaign, but the large Communist vote cannot be interpreted as merely a payoff for shrewd electoral tactics. Nor can we attribute the PCI's success to a generic protest vote, for this simply is not consistent with Italian voting patterns.[1] The PCI has steadily increased its share of the total vote for three decades. Moreover, the 1976 election was largely a referendum on whether the Communists should enter the Italian government; under the circumstances, it is most unlikely that anyone would have cast a vote for the Communists lightly. In short, however much the PCI may have benefited from the events that surrounded the elections of 1976, a satisfactory explanation of the evolution of the party's strategy and of its electoral success requires a context far broader than that of a single campaign.

In this chapter I will attempt to provide such a context, considering the 1976 vote as the culmination of a political process that began at the very start of the decade. The first stage of this process threw the PCI and the left in general onto the defensive and saw the PCI leadership enunciate the strategy of the historic compromise. The second stage witnessed the PCI's resurgence and steady advance, which have brought us to the present stand-off between the Communists and the Christian Democrats. How long this stand-off is likely to last and where the PCI and the Italian political system may go from here are questions we can address in the conclusions to this chapter.

---

[1] Italian voting patterns have been remarkably stable since the end of World War II, with nothing like the volatility that a protest-vote hypothesis would require. The regional, subcultural, organizational, and sociological correlates of the vote have been ably discussed in numerous works. For some of the best recent studies, see: Giorgio Galli and Alfonso Prandi, *Patterns of Political Participation in Italy* (New Haven: Yale University Press, 1970), pp. 42-71; Samuel H. Barnes, "Italy: Religion and Class in Electoral Behavior," in Richard Rose, ed., *Electoral Behavior: A Comparative Handbook* (New York: The Free Press, 1974), pp. 213-220; in addition to Giacomo Sani's contribution to this volume, see his analysis in Donald L. M. Blackmer and Sidney Tarrow, eds., *Communism in Italy and France* (Princeton: Princeton University Press, 1975), chap. 12.

Background to the 1970s

The Italian Road to Socialism. The most important reason for the new direction in PCI strategy has undoubtedly been the party's response to the crisis in Italy, which has grown increasingly serious since the late 1960s. Superficially, the crisis would seem to have favored the PCI at every turn. It has weakened the influence of the Vatican and undermined the Christian Democrats' hegemony over Italian society and politics. It has led to increased trade-union militance and unity. And it has seen the system's pivotal party, the Socialists, come to insist on Communist participation in government. In reality, however, both the development of the crisis and the PCI's response to it have been tortuous and uneven.

The PCI's reaction must be understood in the light of the party's entire postwar posture, most specifically its famous strategy for an "Italian road to socialism" (*via italiana al socialismo*). For, in spite of the attention that has been given to "Eurocommunism" recently, there has been great continuity in the PCI's strategy since the end of the Second World War, and especially since 1956.[2] Moreover, important similarities between the PCI's strategy and that of other Western European Communist parties (especially the French) should not obscure the fact that many differences exist and that the basic tenets of the *via italiana* are not new.[3] The *via italiana* stressed four points: (1) the PCI must be a large *mass* party with an active presence in every part of Italian society; (2) the PCI and the working class will need a broad system of alliances in order to transform Italy; (3) this transformation can—and should—take place within the framework of democratic rules and institutions; and (4) the U.S.S.R. provides neither the ideal model of socialism for the West nor the uncontested leadership of any presumed world revolutionary movement. Each country must discover the road to socialism for itself, without external interference.

The author of this strategy was Palmiro Togliatti, who led the party out of the postwar period and who, along with his collaborators, forced these principles on an often reluctant party until his death in 1964. Togliatti's efforts and those of his successor, Luigi Longo, made clear that the *via italiana al socialismo* was extremely

---

[2] Donald L. Blackmer, *Unity in Diversity: Italian Communism and the Communist World* (Cambridge, Mass.: M.I.T. Press, 1968); see also chaps. 1 (by Blackmer) and 15 (by Tarrow) in Blackmer and Tarrow, *Communism in Italy and France.*

[3] For a profoundly insightful comparison of the PCI and PCF, see Blackmer and Tarrow, *Communism in Italy and France,* chap. 15.

well suited for some purposes, but less so for others. It freed the PCI from the stultification of Stalinism more rapidly and thoroughly than any other Western Communist party. By the late 1950s, Togliatti and the "renovators" around him had divested the party of its most sectarian attitudes and practices.

But these very points of strength also represented some of the most chronic weaknesses of the *via italiana*, which was more clear about what it was not than about what it proposed for Italy's future. Nor should this surprise us: the postwar party, with its emphasis on an activist mass base, broad alliances, and the defense of republican institutions, remembered the traumatic defeat of the PCI by the Fascists in the 1920s. Indeed, one senses a certain nostalgia for the broad anti-Fascist unity of the immediate postwar period. One also gets the impression that despite the relatively bold break with Stalinism, the PCI's strategy is fundamentally incomplete. Italian Communists have criticized the Soviet Union, but they have been extremely slow to develop a systematic analysis of its shortcomings. A "reform strategy" has been discussed for two decades, but an explicit and coherent alternative PCI program for the transformation of Italy has not come forward. The importance of broad alliances has been stressed constantly, but defined in so vague a way that nearly all groups in Italian society would appear to qualify as potential allies of the working class. And while the PCI has consistently defended democratic institutions, it was reticent for a long time to spell out whether, should it arrive in power, it would long tolerate the existence of other parties or would step down after an electoral defeat.

Clearly the PCI has been groping for answers to questions that have always plagued radical parties of the left. But many of the ambiguities in the party strategy also reflect Togliatti's special style of leadership. Because they correctly identified the major imperative facing the PCI as the need to break with Stalinism and sectarianism, Togliatti and then Longo seemed content to leave other aspects of the party line quite flexible. When the leadership did intervene forcefully in internal party debates (notably in 1957, 1959–1960, 1965–1966, and 1969), its purpose was less to impose definitive clarifications than to establish what the acceptable boundaries of interpretation might be.

These debates became increasingly frequent and lively in the 1960s. Destalinization opened up long-stifled issues just when developments in Italy were challenging the PCI's comfortable orthodoxies. Most disturbing was the decision of the Communists' old ally, the PSI, to join the Christian Democrats in a center-left coalition in 1963; simultaneously, the PCI had to come to grips with Italy's so-called economic miracle.

These developments, apparent at the very start of the 1960s, frightened the Communists and threw them onto the defensive. Relations with the PSI had been strained for some time, but the PCI had taken cooperation with the Socialists—and Communist hegemony over the organized working class—largely for granted. Now the Socialists were prepared to disrupt their relationship with the Communists, provide the DC with the stable majority it had been seeking since 1953, and directly contest the PCI's predominance among workers. The PSI believed that if a center-left coalition could provide the reforms Italy so desperately needed, voters would switch their ballots from Communist to Socialist; this was an explicit threat, and it promised perpetual isolation for the PCI. Most threatening of all was the Socialists' pledge to reform the country. The dynamism of Italian capitalism in the 1960s took the PCI very much by surprise. Locked into unexamined assumptions about the inability of the Italian system to provide any basic reforms, the Communists did not know how to react to the claim that, with the Socialists in power as spokesmen for the working class and the downtrodden, the system would be made to deliver the goods.

This combined political and economic threat brought the tensions inherent in the *via italiana* to the surface, and extensive debates took place within the party throughout the first half of the 1960s.[4] The debates demonstrated the PCI's willingness to tolerate serious disagreements between its top leaders, even when these disagreements became public. They also revealed the party's readiness to jettison old formulas and to focus its attention on areas largely ignored in earlier years. But the debates did not resolve the ambiguities in the party strategy and even raised new questions concerning both the economic system and the major political forces in the country. Could, for instance, radical reforms be realized without the PCI in power? Were the Communists totally opposed to the center-left, or did they believe cooperation possible or desirable if genuine reforms were proposed? Were the Communists wooing the DC's working-class

---

[4] The substance and context of the debates are discussed in Stephen Hellman, "PCI Strategy and the Problem of Revolution in the West," in Shlomo Avineri, ed., *Varieties of Marxism* (Berkeley: Sage Publications, 1976). For a discussion by an ex-PCI member, see Lucio Magri, "Italian Communism in the Sixties," *New Left Review*, vol. 66 (March-April 1971), esp. pp. 41-44.

electorate? Were they trying to split the DC so that its most left-leaning elements could join a broad coalition of the left, or did they feel that the DC itself could move to the left, losing only marginal support in the process? Such questions arose out of broad strategic disagreements as well as around narrow tactical issues.

The Crisis of the Late 1960s. The PCI leadership did not have to make the difficult choices these questions implied. A respite came when the center-left failed to live up to its wildly optimistic promises and the economic miracle foundered. The Socialists had proven incapable of eliciting serious reforms from the Christian Democrats, and the PSI had itself become entangled in a system of power based on clientelism, patronage, and pork-barreling. Through its persistent opposition to the center-left coalition the PCI had increased both its electoral strength and its hegemony over the working class by the end of the 1960s.

By then the crisis in Italy's entire power system and economy was growing. The governing majority's failure to develop a coherent economic policy, to realize meaningful reforms, and to head off the feudalization of state and local power by party factions had exacted a serious toll. The DC showed itself to be not only unwilling, but also structurally unable, to formulate or effect rational policies. The social disruptions of the late 1960s were all the more intense in that reforms had been put off for so long. Every new issue which arose—from the student movement to simple demands for civic modernization to labor militancy—was of unusual intensity and duration and became, almost automatically, a serious *political* issue. This phenomenon of radicalization is nowhere more evident than in the case of the labor movement which, during the "hot autumn" of 1969, spilled out of the factories into the political and social spheres. The unions became political protagonists and played a direct role in the struggle for pension, housing, transportation, educational, and other reforms.

Increased demands for higher wages and broader social reforms generated growing pressure for united action, and ultimately for the organizational reunification of Italy's major trade-union confederations. Divided and antagonistic since the cold war, trade unionists of all political persuasions now found themselves allied in common agitations. Especially significant was the growing collaboration of the more militant Catholic unionists with Communists and others of the left. This was accompanied by a loosening of ties between the

160

DC and the Catholic union confederation, the CISL (Confederazione italiana di sindacati liberi, Italian Confederation of Workers' Unions). The Communist party was the primary beneficiary of these developments, but it certainly did not instigate them. Indeed, the PCI often had to rush to keep up with the most militant sectors of the labor movement. But the Communists were sensitive to what was happening, and the Twelfth National Congress, held early in 1969, marked a more militant turn in the *via italiana*. Enrico Berlinguer had become the leader-designate of the party in 1968, and his first appearance in this role seemed to vindicate that part of the party which had pressed for a more radical interpretation of party strategy. In his closing remarks to the Congress, Berlinguer played down the purely institutional and political dimensions of change in favor of greater reliance on the action of radical social forces.[5]

This period also saw the PCI assume an increasingly critical stance toward the Soviet Union in the aftermath of the invasion of Czechoslovakia in 1968. The PCI reaffirmed its criticism of the invasion at the congress and, significantly, did so again later that year in Moscow at an international conference of Communist parties.[6] Although the Italian Communist critique of the U.S.S.R. created some internal problems, especially among many rank-and-file members who had remained intensely loyal to Moscow, the unity of the national and provincial party leadership enabled the PCI to weather the storm of Czechoslovakia better than many other Communist parties. Thus, on the international front as well as domestically, the PCI appeared to have at least begun to resolve many of its traditional strategic and ideological ambiguities.

A closer examination of the Communists' behavior even in this most militant period reveals, however, that they were hardly prepared to press matters too far on either front. The party frequently acted to slow the process of union unification when it feared that some sectors of organized labor would take too radical a stance. And while it paid lip service to the independence and autonomy of the student movement and promised to support its own youth federation (FGCI), it stood by and watched the FGCI collapse at the

---

5 *XII Congresso del PCI: Atti e risoluzioni* [Twelfth Congress of the PCI: acts and resolutions] (Rome: Editori Riuniti, 1969), pp. 768-770. For comments by a contemporary observer, see Luigi Covatta, "Appunti sul XII Congresso del PCI" [Notes on the PCI's twelfth congress], *Quaderni di azione sociale*, vol. 20 (February 1969), pp. 222-248.

6 *XII Congresso*, pp. 750-754. For the PCI's position at the 1969 Conference of Communist Parties at Moscow, see Luigi Longo and Enrico Berlinguer, *La Conferenza di Mosca* [The Moscow conference] (Rome: Editori Riuniti, 1969).

end of the 1960s.[7] Perhaps most indicative of all is the case of *Il Manifesto*, a left-wing group within the PCI, which demonstrated that the party would tolerate only so much radical rhetoric and action both domestically and internationally. When the group, called to heel by the party leadership, continued to publish and press its views, its leaders were expelled in the midst of the autumn crises in 1969, and many followers either resigned from or were rooted out of the PCI shortly thereafter.[8]

There are two reasons for dwelling on the 1968–1970 period. One is to indicate the rather severe limits the PCI set on its own behavior and, to a lesser degree, on its rhetoric. The second is that the PCI's own interpretation of the events of this period largely explains the abrupt turn the party would make in the 1970s. What appears to an outside observer to have been a rather cautious testing of the radical waters has already gone down in official PCI history as a dangerous period of flirtation with extremist, irresponsible positions. The haste with which Berlinguer has criticized the party's behavior and rhetoric—and by extension his own earlier leadership—is remarkable. In the immediate aftermath of events, the PCI engaged in a kind of self-criticism that usually comes much later, if at all, in Communist parties. This criticism and the PCI's determined commitment to the historic compromise, to entering a government with the DC, began in earnest in 1971.

Backlash and the Historic Compromise, 1971–1973

Enrico Berlinguer's career prior to and immediately after his rise to the top of the party suggested that he would be very much in the Togliattian tradition, acting above all as a mediator. Even a case so contentious as that of *Il Manifesto* seemed to confirm a continuity

---

[7] In 1967, the year the student movement erupted, the FGCI had 135,000 members. By 1970, the figure had fallen to below 67,000. There has since been a strong recuperation, with the 1974 figure at 120,000. This reconstructed FGCI has much closer ties to the parent party. Figures from PCI, *Dati sulla organizzazione del Partito* [Data on party organization], official party statistics provided to delegates at national congresses for 1968, p. 7; 1972, p. 46; and 1975, p. 51.

[8] This affair is discussed at some length in Hellman, "PCI Strategy." For a record of the debate in the PCI central committee and the eventual expulsion motion, see PCI, *La questione del "Manifesto": Democrazia e unità nel PCI* [The question of "The Manifesto": democracy and unity in the PCI] (Rome: Editori Riuniti, 1969).

of leadership style.[9] But since 1971 Berlinguer has left little doubt about where he intends to take the PCI. Singleness of purpose has emerged as his characteristic trait.

Berlinguer's choices for the top party leadership in the 1970s were telling. In the past, the highest ranks of the PCI had tended to represent the various shadings of opinion in the party. Under Berlinguer, in contrast, these top positions have gone almost exclusively to people of the secretary's own generation or from among the party's rising stars who essentially share his outlook. Furthermore, while some top leaders have gone to considerable lengths to explain the historic compromise whenever necessary, Berlinguer himself has often seemed singularly uninterested in finding a synthesis between different positions.[10] This is not to say that internal debate is being suffocated, but any extensive discussion of strategic goals since the enunciation of the compromise strategy has been notable for its absence. Most discussion tends to be directed to the pros and cons of specific initiatives, not general rationales or alternatives.

Why did party strategy take the definitive turn it did in 1971? The answer lies in the extent and severity of the social agitation that erupted in 1969 and in the reaction it provoked. For the autumn of 1969 was not simply a period of disruption: in its wake came a good deal of reform legislation. Much of this addressed the plight of the urban worker, but many of the legislative victories of the left benefited other strata as well. And aside from new reform laws, several key pieces of progressive legislation—notably the divorce law, reforms of both urban and agricultural rent practices, and measures granting a significant degree of autonomy to Italy's regions—were enacted after long delays.

Militant unions and a resurgent left, inroads into entrenched privileges, a highly polarized and unstable social situation, and a deepening recession had combined to produce a severe backlash by

[9] Although he has been the de facto party leader since 1969, Berlinguer was vice-secretary during the period between the twelfth and thirteenth party congresses (1969-1972) and was formally elected secretary at the latter, succeeding the aging and ailing Longo. His mediating skills were apparent much earlier, however. See his measured intervention at the very heated Eleventh National Congress of 1966, in *XI Congresso del PCI: Atti e risoluzioni* [Eleventh Congress of the PCI: acts and resolutions] (Rome: Editori Riuniti, 1966), pp. 584-595.

[10] For example, see his closing speech to the December 1974 central committee meeting which prepared the Fourteenth National Congress, now reprinted in Enrico Berlinguer, *La "questione comunista"* [The Communist question] (Rome: Editori Riuniti, 1975), vol. II, pp. 964-965; see also his closing speech to the congress in *XIV Congresso del PCI: Atti e risoluzioni* (Rome: Editori Riuniti, 1975), pp. 634-635.

the end of the sixties. The ugliest aspect of the backlash had begun to appear with scattered acts of terrorism late in 1969, and these have continued intermittently throughout the seventies. The PCI has been quick to condemn unequivocally all such acts, but they have not been decisive in its view of the crisis. What truly frightened the PCI—with so much of its strategy and support rooted in opposition to fascism—were the mass dimensions that the backlash assumed late in 1970 and in 1971.[11]

These were most dramatic in the south, underscoring, once again, how this region had been left behind in the sixties. The neo-Fascist Italian Social Movement manipulated widespread popular discontent and occasional outright rebellions to great advantage, and in many of the largest southern cities it doubled and on occasion tripled its vote in the local elections of 1970 and 1971. Some of these advances came at the expense of the PCI, which had always been considerably weaker in the south than in Italy as a whole. And even in the north, fierce middle-class resentment of some reforms and of working-class militance in general was capitalized on by the extreme right and by the most conservative elements within the DC. The Christian Democrats, in fact, were forced to move sharply to the right to recuperate their losses to the MSI. Although a few of the less conservative groups within the ruling party were embarrassed by this turn of events, the party as a whole went along with and benefited from the exacerbated climate of polarization, aptly dubbed "the strategy of tension."

The center-left had been moribund for some time, and the conservative wing of the DC now began to speak openly of excluding the Socialists from power. The backlash climate offered the DC the chance to recoup its losses, head off further reform demands, and hold onto power. It used the opportunity to attempt to drive the left, and particularly the PCI, into a corner. When the 1972 general elections, the first premature elections in Italy's postwar history, found the center parties reinforced, the DC exhumed the "centrist" (that is, center-right) formula of the 1950s, admitting the conservative Liberal party to the government. From 1971 through most of 1973, the conservative strategy seemed to be paying handsome dividends.

---

[11] Concern over the mass right-wing backlash and over the responsibility the PCI bore for not having been alert enough to the fears of the middle class is evident in all major party pronouncements and publications from early 1971 onward. See especially the weekly party journal, *Rinascita, passim*, for this period. For more specific and reflective citations, see footnote 12.

The Emergence of the Historic Compromise. It was when the left's fortunes were at their nadir, between 1971 and 1973, that the contours of the *compromesso storico* came into focus. By the time of the PCI's Thirteenth National Congress in 1972, they were clear.[12] The argument that Berlinguer put forward can be summarized as follows:

(1) Although the hot autumn and subsequent struggles had made an important contribution to reforms in Italy, the PCI and the unions had restricted their attention excessively to problems concerning the factories and the urban working class.

(2) This narrowness of vision had exposed the party's flanks in both a geographical sense and a sociological sense, as events in the south and among the middle strata proved.

(3) It was therefore necessary to change directions radically and propose far-reaching reforms that would incorporate the neglected regions and social strata.

(4) It would only be possible to realize such profound changes in a time of worsening crisis by demanding sacrifices of *all* groups in society, including the working class and other "popular strata." [13] Such sacrifices and changes could only be achieved under existing conditions in Italy if the three great components of Italian politics—the Communists, the Socialists, and the Catholics—would collaborate.

This program was fully enunciated by early 1972, and the next year saw the appearance of its controversial label, historic compromise, in an article written by Berlinguer about the right-wing coup that

---

[12] See Berlinguer's address and conclusions, *XIII Congresso del PCI: Atti e risoluzioni* (Rome: Editori Riuniti, 1972), pp. 15-16 and 475-489. An extremely important document, which reflects the anxieties of the party leadership during the backlash period, is the special supplement to the PCI's bimonthly theoretical journal, *Critica marxista*, in honor of the PCI's fiftieth anniversary: *Storia politica organizzazione nella lotta dei comunisti italiani per un nuovo blocco storico* [History, politics, and organization in the struggle of the Italian Communists for a new historic bloc], *Critica marxista*, Special Supplement no. 5 (1972), *passim*. Particularly useful are the contributions of Emilio Sereni, Gerardo Chiaromonte, and Luciano Barca.

[13] There is no exact English translation for the Italian adjective *popolare*, which figures prominently in the Communist lexicon. The connotation for the PCI is highly positive; technically the popular strata include all the "common people" with whom the PCI would like to forge alliances. Precisely because the PCI projects alliances which are extremely broad, not to say all-embracing, it tends to leave the meaning of this term vague.

crushed the Unidad Popular movement in Chile.[14] But even the most publicized argument from Berlinguer's articles on Chile—that the Communists would not want to govern with a 51 percent majority if that meant governing in the face of open hostility from 49 percent of the nation—was on the record months before the Chilean events.[15] Chile only served to confirm a shift that had been underway for two years.

With hindsight, the timing and dimensions of changes in strategy emerge more clearly than they do at the time they occur. Because of the PCI's penchant for portraying all its positions as fully within party tradition, there was a good deal of uncertainty at first as to how new Berlinguer's proposals really were. And when the term historic compromise proved controversial, Berlinguer was almost apologetic.[16] But two aspects of his proposal came to be seen as significant clarifications of long-obscure elements in PCI strategy. One key issue was the question of alliances: as we have seen, in the past the party had always been reticent to indicate just which social groups it wanted on its side. More to the point, it had been hesitant to spell out whom it expected to find irreconcilably opposed to it. Now it emerged that the PCI wanted to form a bloc that included *all* the groups in Italian society save the most hopelessly corrupt and reactionary. Berlinguer clearly stated that if a proposed reform should come into conflict with the maintenance of the broadest possible alliance front, priority should be given to the alliance rather than the reform.[17]

The second longstanding ambiguity in the *via italiana* which Berlinguer's formula clarified concerned the Christian Democratic party. The PCI had in the past always left open the question whether its proposed *political* allies would by definition exclude the DC. The "Catholic component" sometimes seemed to mean a coalition of ex-DC and independent radical Catholics; on other occasions it appeared to include the bulk of the DC. Berlinguer now made an explicit

---

[14] Berlinguer's reflections on Chile were featured in three consecutive articles in the PCI weekly journal, *Rinascita*. The first two appeared in the issues of September 28 and October 5, 1973. The third, in which the term historic compromise appears, is "Alleanze sociali e schieramenti politici" [Social alliances and political alignments], *Rinascita*, October 12, 1973, pp. 3-5.

[15] Gerardo Chiaromonte, "I conti con la DC" [Taking account of the DC], *Rinascita*, May 25, 1973, p. 14. But the general argument had been used by the PCI for years, if in less explicit form.

[16] See, for example, his comment in *La "questione comunista,"* II, p. 652.

[17] See Berlinguer's address to the November 1971 central committee, *ibid.*, I, p. 383; also passages on the December 1974 central committee, *ibid.*, II, p. 919 and pp. 929-930.

assumption and drew an equally explicit conclusion: the assumption was that the DC had an electoral base that was both popular and quite stable; the conclusion, that the PCI would abandon any attempt to split off the presumably healthy parts of the DC and would hereafter act to make Christian Democracy *as a whole* accept the necessity of governing with the Communist party.[18]

This partnership was not proposed as an immediate goal, or one that would be easy to achieve, but the seriousness of the crisis and the disasters that might occur if polarization continued made it absolutely necessary. Berlinguer would argue subsequently that his choice of the term historic compromise had been intentionally provocative, but it could not have been more exact.

The formula underscores the wariness of the PCI. It presents the new strategy as the only way for the Communists to enter a national government without provoking a major crisis in the Italian political system—which does not permit the alternation of majority and opposition in power precisely because the major opposition is a *Communist* party. The compromise formula also recognizes the very special nature of the Christian Democratic party in the Italian power structure. To an extent unique in Western democracies, the ruling party in Italy embodies what Marxists refer to as state power. Indeed, the degree of interpenetration between party and state structures makes it difficult to say where one ends and the other begins. The special nature of this party's power would make it exceedingly difficult—and destabilizing—to dislodge it suddenly from its position in society and the state. Since the PCI was not prepared to launch a head-on attack on the DC and on state power in Italy, it had to find another approach.

The backlash of the early 1970s convinced the PCI that an aggressive approach to the DC, based on constant confrontation and polarization of the kind that had occurred during the hot autumn, might well result in the isolation that has been the PCI's special nightmare since the Fascist period. In fact, the DC's acquiescence in the strategy of tension left little doubt that it would happily exploit a polarized climate of opinion to the detriment of the left. Always uncomfortable with an aggressive posture that sharpens class alignments, and poignantly reminded by the events in Chile of how high the stakes in the game could be, the Communists were convinced

---

[18] Berlinguer, speech in the Chamber of Deputies (July 5, 1972), ibid., I, p. 469 and p. 473. See also ibid., II, p. 657, for a similar statement in November 1973; for 1975 see Berlinguer's concluding remarks, *XIV Congresso*, p. 635.

that the worsening Italian crisis made overtures to the DC unavoidable.

If the PCI's proposal was motivated by defensive self-interest or even by outright fear, it had the effect of focusing attention on the DC's shortcomings. By putting themselves on the line and demonstrating their willingness to compromise in order to pull the country out of a crisis, the Communists shrewdly put the ball in the DC's court. What will the ruling party do to demonstrate its willingness to save the country from impending economic collapse, they seemed to ask. The PCI put itself on record as approving all but minimal extensions of the already sizable public sector of the economy. It singled out three critical areas to be attacked—unemployment, the south, and Italy's woeful social services—and around which it would be willing to discuss concrete proposals, with the understanding that it would moderate its stand on many other issues (notably, its support of escalating wage demands).[19] But the PCI demanded that the DC, too, indicate in concrete terms the measures it was willing to take and the interests it was prepared to attack. It is an indication of both Communist intelligence and the seriousness of the Italian crisis that so fundamentally moderate a set of demands could have a broad impact.

There is increasing evidence of both the intelligence and the irony of the Communists' position. The new strategy was spelled out at a time when the fortunes of the left seemed unrelentingly bleak and the DC could ignore the PCI entirely. But the political tide began to turn late in 1973 and did so with increasing force in 1974. The PCI firmly held to the compromise strategy, and, as Communist fortunes improved and the crisis worsened, the party's plea for responsibility and some evidence of a commitment to action had an increasingly powerful effect.

The Strategy of Tension Backfires, 1974–1976

Hindsight once again enables us to identify a turning point: support for the PCI and for the left in general began to rise late in 1973 and early in 1974. Partial local elections held that winter showed impor-

---

[19] The Communist party's specific proposals and the order of its priorities have fluctuated, but the emphasis noted above has been consistent throughout the 1970s. See the PCI's "Political Program" in *XIII Congresso*, p. 555ff. For specific (and sometimes exhaustive) details as well as a useful overview of PCI economic policy, see Luciano Barca et al., *I comunisti e l'economia italiana 1944-1974* [The Communists and the Italian economy, 1944-1974] (Bari: De Donato, 1975), Introduction and p. 373ff.

tant losses for the DC in some of its traditional strongholds. But the decisive and unmistakable signal that the electorate was losing patience with the DC's substitution of political maneuvers for serious action came in May 1974. The referendum to repeal the 1970 divorce law, which the DC's right wing attempted to turn into an anti-Communist crusade, dealt the ruling party its most humiliating defeat since the war.

A referendum on an emotionally charged national issue was precisely the kind of polarizing showdown the Communists desperately wanted to avoid. In 1972, they had gone along with the early dissolution of Parliament in order to postpone the referendum, but by 1974 there was no longer anything to prevent it.[20] The PCI indicated that it was quite willing to water down the already very restrictive divorce law to this end, but the DC, riding the backlash and hoping for a crushing victory, refused this overture. Fearing the worst, the Communists threw themselves into the campaign. In contrast to the strident DC, the PCI projected an image of civic and political responsibility.

This campaign was the first of several that found the country's two major parties radically opposed to one another in style as well as in substance. The Communists hammered away at the DC's unwillingness to make hard choices and act, while underscoring their own desire to attack specific problems reasonably, responsibly, and in a spirit of cooperation. The DC in turn warned against impending disaster, presenting itself as the last beachhead of Western civilization against the Communist hordes. During the referendum campaign the zeal and irrationality of the antidivorce forces threw this contrast into especially sharp relief. Many DC leaders were intensely embarrassed by the entire affair and did all they could to stay out of the fray. Those Christian Democrats who did campaign were themselves embarrassed by the fact that the only other antidivorce party was the MSI.

Thus, when the prodivorce forces won a 60-40 victory, the humiliation of the Church and of Christian Democracy was profound. No longer could they claim to speak, as they had for so long, for the beliefs of a great majority of the Italian people. The total antidivorce vote was in fact barely higher than the DC's electoral percentage in the 1972 general election (38.7 percent).

---

[20] Under the Italian constitution a referendum may only be called to abrogate a specific law. Had the old divorce law been rewritten, it no longer would have been the law formally designated by number in the petition gathered by referendum supporters. Hence a new campaign would have been required to gather the half-million signatures necessary to call a new abrogative referendum.

The obverse of the DC's humiliation was the vindication of the PCI. The importance of this cannot be overstated. For the first time since the 1946 referendum that abolished the monarchy, the PCI was clearly aligned with a majority of the country. And for the first time *ever* it was the largest party in a majority bloc—for in 1946 the Socialists had polled more votes than the Communists.

The referendum seemed to open the floodgates. A year later, regularly scheduled local elections saw the DC vote fall below 35 percent, dipping to its lowest level in postwar Italian history. The same elections, which the PCI fought on the slogan "Our Hands Are Clean," produced a jump of six percentage points in the Communist vote to just under 33 percent. The psychological impact of what seemed to be the equalization of the country's two major parties was enormous. Furthermore, the PCI's unprecedented advances meant that the PCI would soon be a formal coalition partner in six of the country's twenty regional governments, almost all the governments of Italy's major cities, and nearly 900 additional municipal governments.[21]

It is significant that even in the midst of this dramatic turn in their fortunes, the Communists remained exceedingly cautious. They had clearly been surprised (along with everyone else) at the magnitude of the divorce victory, and they continued for some time after the referendum to warn their followers not to overestimate the shift in the country's mood. Still chary of the backlash, Berlinguer warned his party that whenever the forces of progress advanced, they could expect a conservative counteroffensive not long afterward.[22] He also left no doubt of his willingness to commit the party to the compromise strategy, for even with the Christian Democrats in serious trouble, he insisted that the DC as a whole had to be forced to come to an agreement with the Communists.[23] The *compromesso storico* had been formulated during a difficult moment for the PCI, but it clearly was not going to be abandoned when that moment passed.

---

[21] Prior to the 1975 elections, the PCI directly participated in the governing *giunte*, or cabinets, of just over 1,600 of Italy's approximately 8,000 towns and cities. After the elections, this total rose to just under 2,500. Figures reported in *L'Espresso*, July 20, 1975, p. 9.

[22] Address to the June 1974 central committee, La *"questione comunista,"* II, pp. 758-759.

[23] Berlinguer, *Governo di unità democratica e compromesso storico: discorsi 1969-1976* [Government of democratic unity and historic compromise: speeches, 1969-1976] (Rome: Sarmi, 1976), p. 184 and pp. 164-165.

The 1976 Elections

The 1976 dissolution of Parliament was the second consecutive instance of the calling of early elections in Italy. The Parliament that sat from 1972 to 1976 had been elected during the backlash and had a centrist majority, yet the PCI was adamantly opposed to its dissolution. The DC, meanwhile, though reeling from two successive defeats, did nothing to avoid it. Why?

Even beyond the Communists' extreme caution and the Christian Democrats' lack of the same, there were compelling reasons for the two parties to take these paradoxical stands. First, these were *national* elections with the government of Italy at stake; both sides questioned whether votes would be cast as readily for the PCI or against the DC as they had been in the previous year's local elections. Second, Amintore Fanfani's leadership of the DC had been in serious trouble ever since his miscalculation on the referendum, and the PCI was looking with intense interest on what it saw as internal shifts that promised a more flexible DC. The few percentage points they might gain in an election were less important to the Communists than a change in DC leaders, especially since regularly scheduled elections were only a year off. Fanfani, the party leader whose position was in jeopardy, naturally hoped to hold onto power a little longer before attempting to redeem himself at the polls. Third, the 1976 elections would be the third major, highly contested national poll in three years, the fourth in five years. The Communists correctly argued that frequent campaigns diverted funds and attention from the deepening crisis; they also viewed this new sign of institutional instability with some alarm. Delicate compromises need to be worked out in the antechambers of power, they claimed, not in the polarized atmosphere of campaigns. The Communists, moreover, were already on the record as opposing frequent summonses to the polls, as their proposals to make referenda more difficult demonstrate.[24]

The Campaign. As soon as the elections were called, Berlinguer quickly moved to head off speculation that the PCI might reverse the compromise strategy in the light of its recent gains and the DC's losses. There was some pressure from within the party, as well as

[24] Berlinguer, address to the December 1974 central committee meeting, *La "questione comunista,"* II, p. 901. The major changes the PCI would like to see in the referendum law involve an increase in the number of signatures needed to call a referendum, a several years' trial period before a referendum petition could be circulated, and a limitation on the kinds of laws that may be abrogated.

171

from parts of the PSI and the extraparliamentary left, for the PCI to step forward as the leader of a "left alternative" government that would relegate the DC to the opposition. But Berlinguer instead announced that the Communists would fight this campaign on a platform calling for a "government of national unity," that is, a coalition of all the democratic parties in Italy, as the only formula capable of pulling the country out of the crisis. Although some effort was expended to convince the party faithful that this really was the same as the historic compromise, it was in fact more limited. It recognized that, at least for a number of years, the DC would not undergo the far-reaching changes that the more ambitious *compromesso storico* required.[25]

The unity proposal indicated that the Communist leadership was prepared to push the party's position to its logical conclusion. Even with their fortunes on the upswing, the Communists signalled their willingness to moderate their demands still further by joining an emergency coalition of all parties. This indicated the seriousness with which the PCI viewed the crisis. It might be the easiest way for the PCI to enter an Italian government, but it also would restrict the PCI's freedom of action once in power more drastically than any other course. This was perhaps the most deft of the Communists' recent tactical strokes, for it made the PCI the focal point of the entire electoral campaign, and not just as the target of the nonleft parties. The party's increasing strength and credibility permitted it to influence the setting of the political agenda in Italy, and it showed itself more than equal to the task. Once again the PCI campaigned as the voice of reason, moderation, and responsibility, challenging the scandal-ridden DC, in effect, to spell out *any* constructive proposal upon which it was prepared to act.

The PCI could not conduct the campaign entirely as it pleased, however. Now that it was in the spotlight, the party had to dispel, or at least play down, the many fears Italian voters still nurtured about its intentions. The DC constantly stressed the PCI's "Moscow connection," calling into doubt both the Communists' desire and their ability to maintain a truly independent position should they one day find themselves in power. In response, the PCI could confidently outline the history of its criticisms of the Soviet Union and the Warsaw Pact countries. But its position on NATO was far less clear. On record as opposing the existence of any military pacts in Europe, the

---

[25] Address to the Central Committee meeting of May 1976, in Gustavo Tomisch, ed., *La grande avanzata comunista* [The great Communist advance] (Rome: Sarmi, 1976), pp. 10 and 15.

Communists had, through the sixties, denounced NATO as nothing more than the arm of American imperialism. They had bitterly decried the PSI's acceptance of NATO during the center-left period, and the overall PCI position had been, for a long time, summed up in the slogan "Italy out of NATO and NATO out of Italy." But things had begun to change in the 1970s, subtly at first. The Communists began to use the phrase Atlantic pact rather than NATO, and by 1972 they were on record as no longer totally opposed to Italian membership in the alliance.[26] Nonetheless, many observers were surprised to hear Berlinguer say, in an interview during the campaign, that he felt an independent socialism could be achieved more easily outside the Warsaw Pact (and the reach of the Soviet Union) than inside it. Even more startling, he went on to suggest that the Atlantic alliance offered a certain degree of security against those who might feel they knew the one true path to socialism.[27]

The PCI was also repeatedly challenged on its democratic credentials during the campaign. The proposal for a government of national unity was a far cry from a Socialist program, but the PCI knew that, by claiming that it deserved a formal governing role in the country, it opened itself up to questions about how democratic it could be expected to be once in power. Here again it was able to fall back on longstanding pronouncements about its vision of a pluralistic society that would provide ample room for small private enterprise and full respect for democratic institutions.[28] While its affirmations added nothing of substance to the Communist position, they forced the party to reiterate unambiguously its stands in certain sensitive areas.

The PCI's tone in the 1976 campaign, then, was as respectable, as responsible, and as reassuring as the party could possibly make it. Its most persistent theme was that Italy simply could not emerge from the crises at hand without the participation of the PCI in the crucial choices ahead. As if to underscore the party's broad appeal and respectability, an extremely varied and impressive group of

---

[26] Compare the evolution of the terminology in the following citations. Berlinguer's concluding remarks, XII Congresso, p. 760: ". . . belong to no military pact, hence Italy must leave NATO and NATO must leave Italy"; Berlinguer's address, XIII Congresso, p. 27: ". . . overcoming the subordination which ties our country to NATO does not boil down to a simple pronouncement for or against the military pact"; and finally his address to the XIV Congresso, p. 31: "We do not raise the question of Italy's departure from the Atlantic pact, since this eventuality, and any other unilateral exit from one or the other bloc . . . would result in an obstruction or even a reversal of international détente. . . ."
[27] Interview reprinted in Tomisch, ed., La grande avanzata comunista, p. 134.
[28] Succinct synthetic statements by Berlinguer can be found in ibid., pp. 131-133.

public figures spoke out in the party's favor, announced that they would support the Communists, and in some cases even ran for office as independents affiliated with the Communist lists. This had long been a favored electoral tactic of the PCI, but never before had it been used so extensively or to such effect. Throughout the campaign, leading cultural and intellectual figures announced their support; a surprising number of leading Catholic personalities did the same, and several stood for Parliament and were elected. In all, thirteen deputies and twenty senators were elected as PCI-affiliated independents. Among the most impressive of the new faces were Altiero Spinelli, a former leader of the Italian delegation to the European Economic Community, and Nino Pasti, a retired army general and a former vice-commandant of NATO.

Results of the Vote. The PCI's unexpectedly strong showing at the polls in 1976 surpassed by nearly two percentage points its previous all-time high in the 1975 local elections. The Communists had special cause to be pleased with their successes in the south, which saw them surge nearly five percentage points in one year, moving from 26.6 percent in 1975 to 31.4 percent in 1976. The PCI's southern vote had long lagged far behind gains in the rest of the country, and the Communists had even lost some ground early in the seventies in the wake of neo-Fascist advances. The 1976 vote saw the MSI on the wane almost everywhere, and the PCI in the south within three percentage points of its national showing, developments which did not escape the attention of Communist observers.[29]

If the PCI's strong showing represented a pleasant surprise for many of its own supporters, the DC's ability to maintain its 1972 level of 38.7 percent undoubtedly constituted the Communists' greatest disappointment in the voting results. The PCI had been counting on Christian Democratic losses to force the DC to undertake the initiatives and house cleaning it clearly was not prepared to do voluntarily. Preelection polls, combined with over-optimistic predictions from numerous politicians and pundits, had reinforced the expectation that the DC would in fact be lucky if it held its losses to the 1975 nadir. In the wake of the 1976 vote, numerous Communist leaders confessed that the PCI had come to expect a poor DC showing and that,

---

[29] Rosario Villari, "Non si tratta di vento del Nord" [It is not a wind from the north], *Rinascita*, July 7, 1976, pp. 4-5; Giorgio Amendola, "Il nuovo balzo del Mezzogiorno" [The new leap ahead in the South], *Rinascita*, July 16, 1976, pp. 7-8.

when this had not materialized, disillusionment had swept over the party, especially its lower ranks.[30]

Yet the DC's was, at best, a mixed victory. The DC remained the strongest vote-getter in the country, and there was no question of its being reduced to a state of abject dependence on the left. At the same time, the DC had been able to retain its 1972 percentage only by "raiding" Liberal, Social Democratic, and to some extent MSI support. The center bloc in fact lost its absolute majority and fell from 50.6 percent to 46.5 percent: this would severely restrict DC freedom to maneuver in the future.

The 1976 electoral results did not merely confound the short-run expectations of many Communists. They also raised serious questions about the party's long-run analysis. We must avoid attributing greater shifts to the Italian electorate than in all probability occurred, but certain tendencies are apparent.[31]

We have already noted the DC's decimation of its former coalition partners. This has implications for the ruling party's social bases of support as well as for the arithmetic of coalition forming. A party that, despite its name and origins, has always had a very large non-Catholic vote, the DC now is less Catholic than ever. Its social base is also more conservative than ever in certain important respects. DC gains appear to have come predominantly from the urban middle classes, who flocked to the banners of the country's largest party because they saw in it the most effective roadblock to Communist advances.[32] But this recently acquired support may well

[30] This account of the opinions expressed after the election by PCI leaders is based on the author's extended (if unsystematic) conversations with provincial and regional elites in July 1976. He visited four regions in north-central Italy in the immediate aftermath of the elections. For an article written in the same period by a leading Communist which addresses the general disillusionment in the party over the DC's strong showing, see Giuseppe Vacca, "Perché stupirsi per il voto DC?" [Why the surprise over the DC vote?], Rinascita, July 16, 1976, pp. 10-11.

[31] Giacomo Sani's important analyses of voting shifts suggest that fully half the left's gains can be attributed to generational turnover in the special conditions of the 1976 general elections, in which eighteen-year-olds voted for the first time. See his "The Italian Elections of 1976: Continuity and Change" (mimeograph, 1976) and his contribution to this volume.

[32] There are as yet no systematic studies of the shifting class basis of the 1976 vote, but the marked transfer of urban middle-class votes to the DC has been noted by all journalistic and scholarly observers. The best recent general analysis is found in Arturo Parisi and Gianfranco Pasquino, "20 giugno: struttura politica e comportamenti elettorali" [June 20: political structure and electoral behavior], Il Mulino (May-June 1976). For 1975, when the DC's absorption of urban middle-class voters was much less pronounced, see Celso Ghini, Il terremoto del 15 giugno [The earthquake of June 15] (Milan: Feltrinelli, 1976), p. 148ff.

175

prove to be "soft," in that it comes from relatively well-educated and well-organized strata. Many of these new DC voters opted in the past for the secular parties of the center and right, and they could well do so again.[33]

These shifts may not bode well for the DC, but they cannot be altogether reassuring to the PCI, since they seem to undermine some of the basic assumptions behind the historic compromise. These are that a rapprochement with the DC is both desirable and necessary in the light of Italy's largest party's unique ability to speak for (1) the bulk of the Catholic component of Italian politics and (2) social strata which, although linked to the DC, are fundamentally progressive in outlook and origin. But the DC now appears to be both less Catholic and less potentially progressive than ever.

Nor does the evidence of an increased social polarization in the 1976 vote—with all the problematic implications for the PCI's analysis that entails—stop here. We must remember that although the DC gained votes, especially from the urban right and center, its overall percentage remained stationary. Where, then, did it lose support? The best estimates suggest that DC losses were greatest among the urban lower and working classes; many of these voters appear to have shifted their support directly to the PCI.[34]

The PCI, in turn, appears to have increased its support among all strata of Italian society (including youth and the middle classes), but its greatest gains—pending much-needed further analysis—seem to have come in working-class areas.[35] Some of the rare systematic evidence available at the time of writing comes from a quintessentially working-class city, Turin, and the data fully confirm our supposition. Between 1972 and 1976, the PCI gained nearly 13.5 percentage points in the heavily populated working-class districts. In the same areas, the DC lost nearly 6 percentage points. Christian Democratic electoral stability was gained in Turin largely at the expense of the Liberals in the city's most middle-class and upper-class districts: in these less populous areas, the DC increased its vote by over 16 percentage points during the same period. Turin's high degree of

---

[33] This point is made by Aniello Coppola, "Il nuovo Parlamento é alla prova" [The new Parliament must prove itself], *Rinascita*, July 7, 1976, p. 3.

[34] Parisi and Pasquino, "20 giugno," esp. p. 356.

[35] Figures for Turin were kindly provided by the PCI Provincial Federation of Turin. For important examples of very large PCI gains in highly concentrated working-class residency areas, see Celso Ghini, "Dentro il voto" [Inside the vote], *Rinascita*, July 2, 1976, p. 2. See also Parisi and Pasquino, "20 giugno."

industrialization may exaggerate the general nationwide trends, but alterations of this magnitude were unheard of in northern Italy prior to 1975.[36]

Ironically, it may be that at least part of the PCI's traditional analysis of the DC was vindicated shortly after the PCI turned away from it. Before adopting the compromise strategy, the Communists had long argued that the DC's immobility would eventually undermine its interclass nature and drive away significant parts of its "popular" or "healthy" mass base; a schism in the DC was considered likely. Under the *compromesso storico*, the Communist analysis shifted to accommodate the DC's presumed ability to hold onto this mass base indefinitely. Hence the PCI now argued that the DC would have to move to the left to hold onto its support. The eventuality of a mass base which retained its previous dimensions but was sociologically altered was apparently given much less attention, and this is precisely what occurred. The issue here is not whether the Communists make good or bad prophets, but how they plan to come to terms with a DC that is less likely than ever to have much freedom to move to its left.

The Communists' reaction to the more unsettling implications of the 1976 vote has largely been to ignore them. This is most evident with respect to the apparent class-based shifts in the balloting, but it can even be seen in relation to the irrefutable evidence of an electoral polarization around Italy's two largest parties. The Communists' lack of penetrating attention to these issues is not a result of analytic incapacities or of indifference. It is, rather, a reflection of their political concerns and goals. The PCI's increased hegemony over the left is a source of satisfaction to party leaders, but it also makes them uncomfortable. The concentration of votes around the PCI on the left and around the DC on the center-right makes many people leery of what the historic compromise ultimately will mean. And the PCI is highly sensitive to the suggestion that it really means an eventual deal between Communists and Christian Democrats at everyone else's expense rather than a broad understanding between all parties. That charge was immediately made by almost all the smaller parties following the elections, and the Communists resorted to tortured and

---

[36] For 1975 figures from Milan and Bologna, see Ghini, *Il terremoto* and "Dentro il voto." For the PCI stronghold of Emilia-Romagna in the same elections, consult Robert Leonardi and Gianfranco Pasquino, "Le elezioni in Emilia-Romagna" [The elections in Emilia-Romagna], *Il Mulino*, July-August 1975, esp. pp. 578-581.

sometimes curious logic to deny that there had been a polarization or to downplay its importance.[37]

Conclusions

The PCI reaped great benefits from the 1976 vote, but events and even the party's successes have saddled it with new problems. No less a figure than Berlinguer's brother, a leading party intellectual, has confessed that the PCI's analysis has lagged behind its gains in the real world.[38] Such an admission sounds ironic to long-term observers of the PCI, for the refrain in the sixties was that the party's analysis, the *via italiana*, suffered only from its failure to be translated into reality, not from any theoretical defects.

The *compromesso storico* originated when the fortunes of the left were at their lowest ebb, and many inside and outside the party have wondered whether the bleak outlook of the period did not lead Berlinguer to make too many concessions to moderation. The PCI's caution, even pessimism, not only appears to have deterred the party from proposing an aggressive series of initiatives at a time when they might have borne fruit, but also could mire it in a waiting game whose outcome would be very uncertain.

Not even the striking advances of the postreferendum period have budged the party from its stance. Indeed, after the 1976 election the PCI went out of its way to stress the positive side of its own archrival, the DC.[39] Communist statements to the effect that the DC had not become a "purely conservative" party and that it still had a sizable "popular" component obviously contain a good deal of truth, but they also forestall any discussion of whether and to what degree the DC may have changed as a result of the elections. As in the case of the PCI's arguments about bipolarization in Italy, it is frequently difficult to determine whether the Communists are discussing reality or a projection of the electoral pattern they would like to see—and that the historic compromise requires.

Theoretical clarity is an important issue. It is likely to become even more important as concrete policies must be enunciated. De-

---

[37] Vasco Calonaci and Ugo Pasqualetti, "Una logica da rifiutare" [A logic which must be rejected], *L'Unità*, July 15, 1976, p. 3; see also Romano Ledda, "Il volto laico dell'Italia" [The laical face of Italy], *Rinascita*, July 2, 1976, pp. 1-2.

[38] Giovanni Berlinguer, "La politica e le idee" [Politics and ideas], *Rinascita*, July 16, 1976, p. 2.

[39] Ledda, "Il volto laico"; see esp. Gerardo Chiaromonte's address to the July 1976 Central Committee meeting, *L'Unità*, July 3, 1976, p. 10.

tailed plans for economic recovery will have to specify which interests will be favored and which must suffer. If the waiting game or stand-off I have described can largely be attributed to the DC's unwillingness to alienate its own often tenuous support, it also is a result of the Communists' unwillingness to frighten off *their* supporters—or potential allies. In fact, both the PCI's lack of theoretical clarity and its insistence on entering a government that includes all the democratic parties in Italy grow out of this unwillingness to leave any flank exposed to possible right-wing manipulation. The point is not that the PCI is unable to make choices, but rather that it is unwilling to do so. It has consciously subordinated clarity to the exquisitely *political* goal of entering government with the broadest possible "cover." Convinced that the DC must be its ally in government if disaster is to be averted, the PCI has made all other considerations secondary.

Does this mean that the Communists, having focused their attention on how to enter the government without making Italy into another Chile, really do not have a very clear conception of what they would do in power? Some support for this interpretation can be found in the very broad goals the PCI has spelled out, in the stress it has placed on an emergency government, and in the self-conscious moderation of PCI positions in almost all major policy areas. This in turn raises the question of what, then, the PCI might hope to obtain from a coalition with the Christian Democratic party, which is by its very nature integral to some of Italy's most intractable problems. Surely the DC will not be inclined to cooperate in its own dismantling. Some observers suggest that the PCI might be setting itself up for a fate similar to that of the Socialists under the center-left, namely, that it might compromise itself into the structures of power without substantially changing them.

Party leaders have always been sanguine about the suggestion that they might suffer the same fate as the PSI. They point out the size and organizational health of the PCI and argue that these are the best guarantee against cooptation. While some leftist critics of the Communists see this as an overly optimistic interpretation of the party's abilities, there remains the compelling argument that the Communists' presence in civil society would give them a leverage, should they enter the national corridors of power, that even the DC could not resist for long.[40] A party which added the perquisites of state

---

[40] This point has been made consistently and cogently by Alessandro Pizzorno. See, for example, his "Il PCI e il ruolo dell'opposizione" [The PCI and the opposition's role] (mimeograph, 1972).

power to its own formidable capacity for social mobilization might well prove able to brush aside the stalling tactics and obstructionism that thwarted the Socialists' reformist aims.

When party leaders turn from their own organization to that of the DC, their responses are understandably less certain. Publicly the Communist position is to avoid any hint that the DC—or at least its "healthy" elements—cannot be convinced of the ultimate necessity of joining with the PCI. But is this faith in the DC, even the DC as it might be sometime in the future, widespread among Italian Communists? It certainly does not exist among the PCI rank and file, who have seen the Christian Democrats vilified as *the* enemy for thirty years. And many serious doubts exist even among party elites. This author's discussions with regional and provincial leaders in the immediate aftermath of the 1976 vote revealed much greater uncertainty than one might have expected in so single-minded a party. The evidence is admittedly impressionistic, but almost all of the leaders interviewed seemed to be persuaded that there simply is no alternative to Berlinguer's emergency formula and an eventual historic compromise. At the same time, many were quite obviously disoriented by the PCI's specific decisions. And while no one was starry-eyed about the prospect of an imminent conversion of the DC to even moderate reformism, many seemed to believe that a new course could be imposed little by little on the ruling party.

Some leaders, however, were unwilling to believe in the future conversion of the DC, even a forced conversion. They saw a different meaning in the *compromesso storico*. Following the PCI's traditional assessment of the DC, they argued that the *entire* Christian Democratic party would never consent to serious reforms in Italy. But the retrograde elements in the DC are large enough (and they exert influence beyond their numbers) to make a compromise strategy necessary to the PCI as the only way to neutralize the DC's right wing. To succeed in splitting the DC—long the goal of many Italian Communists—would, in this view, simply leave the vast bulk of the DC both in power and in the hands of its right wing. What the historic compromise makes much more likely is the eventuality that the schism in the DC (which real reforms will provoke) will be on the right so that only the right wing of the DC, rather than the full power of the state, will be arrayed against the PCI and its allies. This may be an overly optimistic interpretation of both the historic compromise and Christian Democratic corruption and unwillingness to change, but it certainly is not inconsistent with the broad outlines of Berlinguer's strategy.

Immediate Problems. Thus far, we have limited our considerations to the realm of theory and intentions. There are, of course, a number of important practical problems that face the PCI with great immediacy in the wake of the 1976 elections—especially in light of the DC's unwillingness to undertake even the moderate reform measures it promised in exchange for PCI abstentions in Parliament.

One such problem arises from the PCI's position in Parliament. The Communists are obviously strong there, as the many formal and informal concessions they have obtained since the election show. But the argument of some critics that the PCI enjoys all the perquisites of power without the attendant responsibilities can just as easily be reversed. Theoretically, the PCI can end its policy of abstention at any time, thereby bringing down the government. But could it do so in practice? As long as the Communists' primary goal remains eventual collaboration with the DC, the PCI will have to consider the consequences of new elections and a probable increase in political polarization for any future rapprochement with the DC. The DC, for its part, seems aware of this dilemma and willing to capitalize on it. Since the election the DC has been forced to make many galling concessions to the Communists, but it has frequently managed to obtain a moderated stance by the PCI in return (particularly concerning secularizing reforms such as abortion, or, more broadly, concerning calls for sacrifice and moderation on the part of the labor movement).

A second problem now facing the PCI is its vulnerability to pressures from the more militant sectors of its own rank and file and especially of the trade union movement. Beginning with its abstention on the government's severe austerity program, the PCI has had to defend its actions to restive militants. Although it has done so effectively so far, it cannot go on forever claiming that no other options exist. Indeed, the PCI's hesitance to propose specific programs has already occasionally allowed the initiative to slip from the PCI's grasp to that of the union movement. More than once the unions have stepped forward to make preemptive statements about what the working class will or will not accept, and the PCI has had no choice but to follow the unions' lead. This was glaringly evident when the unions spoke out, late in 1976, against any serious alteration of the workers' cost-of-living wage index. However this tension evolves, it will be a thorn in the side of the PCI. The Communists' ability to control the union movement is not as great as some observers believe, and it is bound to diminish even further as the PCI edges closer to power.

181

A third crucial constraint on the PCI's freedom to maneuver grows, ironically, out of the unprecedented successes of the PCI at the local level. The PCI's expanded role in local government makes the party increasingly dependent on the national government, source of the vast bulk of local funds under Italy's centralized administrative system. The Communists' reputation for honesty and responsibility is based on their laudable track record in local government. Thus, the PCI's entry into so many more local administrations since 1975, including the country's debt-ridden major urban centers, powerfully increases pressure on it to enter the national government. It is true that in almost all cases the PCI is only the heir to the crumbling cities' problems, but it now is under intense pressure to prove its mettle by delivering the goods. And the economic crisis, combined with the DC's reluctance to furnish enough aid to reinforce the PCI's position, either directly or through decentralizing fiscal powers to the regions, leaves the Communists highly vulnerable on this front. A good deal of give-and-take between the country's two largest parties is likely to occur around this issue.

These factors, as well as others, underline the seriousness of the impasse that faces the Italian political system and the PCI. Although the Communists are now in the most advantageous position of all the major political parties, they remain able, at best, to influence but not to dictate the terms of the evolution of the Italian crisis. With so inherently unstable a situation as the current stand-off and with the DC obviously unwilling to make major concessions to the left, the PCI's goal of a formal governing role is likely to remain thwarted for the time being.

The option most likely to be exercised under these difficult circumstances would not solve the crisis, but it would at least buy time for the major protagonists. This would be some sort of coalition built around PSI-DC collaboration, with the formal but external support of the Communists. The DC would probably try to woo the Socialists away from their insistence on full Communist participation and responsibility and the PCI would be equally ardent in its use of such a coalition as the prelude to its own formal entry into government. The Socialists, traditionally buffeted between the two giants of the Italian political system, would not consent easily to such an arrangement, in which they would feel highly uncomfortable. Moreover, even this least problematic option would only postpone the very uncertain stage that lies beyond the present impasse.

6

THE ITALIAN SOCIALIST PARTY: AN IRREVERSIBLE DECLINE?

Gianfranco Pasquino

The Italian Socialist party played a key role in causing the premature end of the sixth Parliament and in highlighting the issue—more immediate in 1976 than at any time since 1948—of Communist participation in the government. Nevertheless, the outcome of the 1976 elections was disappointing for the Socialists. Their poor showing can be traced to three major weaknesses of the party: (1) its inadequate organizational structure, (2) its ambiguous stand on the fundamental issue of governmental coalitions, and (3) the progressive decline of the PSI's ability to acquire and maintain a good working relationship with the more dynamic sectors of Italian society.

The "Socialist Area" and the Socialist Party

According to Socialist politicians and scholars, the number of Italians potentially inclined to express a political preference for Socialist proposals and solutions is higher than the number of votes polled by the Socialist party in recent elections; indeed, it is increasingly so. The voters who believe in Socialist ideas but cast their votes for leftist parties other than the PSI constitute the so-called Socialist area. This concept indicates a political space which the PSI might reasonably expect to occupy, were it better organized and more disciplined. The tragedy of Italian Socialists is that "their" space has been largely and gradually preempted by the Italian Communist party. By 1976, the idea that there was a pool of disillusioned Socialist voters waiting to be brought back into the PSI fold was probably wishful thinking.

Over the years many parties stressing their kinship with the "Socialist family" have emerged, fragmenting the Socialist area.

This has tended to confuse the voters and weaken their party identification; ultimately, it has brought a decline in the overall percentage of Socialist votes (see Table 6–1).

If one starts by looking at the evolution of the non-Communist leftist parties, one notices not only a multiplication of parties, but also the decline in both comparative and absolute terms of the PSI. While in 1946 the Socialist party was electorally strong, the only representative of non-Communist Socialist voters, in subsequent elections it has had to compete with one or more parties in the same political space.

Moreover, while in 1946 the Socialist party occupied one-half of the leftist area and was still stronger than the Communist party, today it represents only one-fifth of all leftist voters, while the Communist party has won the support of three-fifths in a seemingly irresistible ascent (see Figure 6–1). The result is that we find at the same time (and probably *pour cause*) the smallest Western European Socialist party and the largest Western European Communist party in the same country. Since this situation cannot be simply dismissed by pointing to the overwhelming organizational capacities and great

Table 6–1
FRAGMENTATION AND DECLINE OF THE "SOCIALIST AREA" IN ITALY, 1946–76
(in percentages of the total vote)

	Election							
Party	1946	1948	1953	1958	1963	1968	1972	1976
PSI	20.7	12.4[a]	12.7	14.2	13.8	14.5[b]	9.6	9.6
PSDI		7.1	4.5	4.5	6.1		5.1	3.4
PSIUP						4.4	1.9	
DP							0.7	1.5
MPL[c]							0.4	
PR								1.1
Total	20.7	19.5	17.2	18.7	19.9	18.9	17.7	15.6

[a] Estimate based upon the number of seats allotted to the Socialists within the popular front group in Parliament.

[b] PSI and PSDI together in the Unified Socialist party (PSU).

[c] Workers' Political movement, a Catholic splinter group which later largely joined the PSI.

Source: Author's compilation based on data from Alberto Spreafico, "Risultati elettorali ed evoluzione del sistema partitico" [Electoral results and evolution of the party system], in Mario Caciagli and Alberto Spreafico, eds., *Un sistema politico alla prova. Studi sulle elezioni politiche italiane del 1972* [A political system on trial. Studies on the Italian political elections of 1972] (Bologna: Il Mulino, 1975), p. 39; and *Il Corriere della Sera*, June 23, 1976, p. 1.

Figure 6-1
ELECTORAL EVOLUTION OF THE PSI AND THE PCI, 1946-76

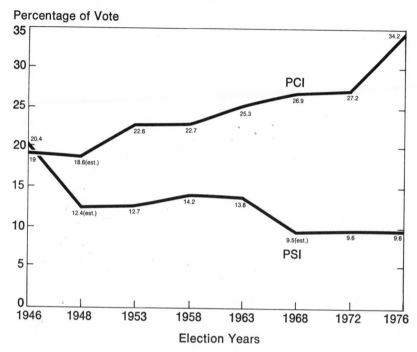

Percentage of Vote

Source: See source for Table 6-1.

political imagination of Italian Communist leaders, we must seek an explanation in the organizational structure of the Socialist party and in the political role the PSI has played, distinguishing as clearly as possible between objective constraints and subjective choices.

There have been many turning points in the postwar history of the PSI, each in turn reducing the party's political space. In January 1947, the issue of a too close relationship with and alleged subordination to the PCI led to the first split on the party's right and the birth of the Italian Social Democratic party. In 1948, the PSI's participation in an electoral popular front alliance with the PCI resulted in its being crushed by the superior discipline of the Communists in channeling preference votes to their candidates. The slow and painful process of emancipation from the PCI culminated in the inauguration of a costly governmental alliance with the DC: the center-left (launched in 1962–1963), which provoked the secession

185

of the Socialist left wing and the creation of a competing party, the Italian Socialist party of Proletarian Unity, in January 1964. Finally, a hastily organized and ill-fated merger with the Social Democrats in October 1966 was followed by another split in July 1969.[1]

Inevitably, this tortuous evolution had profound repercussions not only upon the leadership,[2] but especially upon the electorate. The center-left should have been a very favorable period for the expansion of the party. The PCI had to face both the attempts of the governmental coalition to isolate the Communists and the succession crisis following Togliatti's death in August 1964, as well as, later on, the bewilderment following the Soviet invasion of Czechoslovakia and the consequent defection of many young members. During this period, the economic resources available to the Italian population were still abundant and growing, and the governmental parties could claim credit for prosperity. Nevertheless, the PSI was unable to profit from these exceptionally favorable conditions.

It must be added that, in the center-left decade, the Socialist vote appeared to be positively correlated with many indicators of modernity—that is, it was high where industrialization, urbanization, literacy, and income figures were high. It might have been inferred that the continuation of socioeconomic progress would produce a greater increase of votes for the PSI than for any other party. However, the split-off of the PSIUP and the PSI merger with the PSDI, conservative and entrenched among backward sectors of Italian society, discouraged actual and potential Socialist voters from supporting the PSI. Both in absolute terms and in comparison with the PCI and DC votes, the PSI vote became much more volatile.[3]

Sources of Decline. At the leadership level, the most disruptive phenomena were the "parliamentarization" of party office holders and

---

[1] On these phases, see Liliano Faenza, *La crisi del socialismo in Italia (1946-1966)* [The crisis of socialism in Italy, 1946-1966] (Bologna: Alfa Edizioni, 1967), and Felice Rizzi, "From Socialist Unification to Socialist Scission, 1966-1969: Socialist Unification and the Italian Party System," *Government and Opposition*, vol. 9 (Spring 1974), pp. 146-164.

[2] "Overall, as many as twenty-nine out of ninety-six politicians who became members of the several Socialist executive committees [from 1945 to 1965] have left the party. Fourteen of them have joined groups to the right of the PSI and fourteen have joined a party which, declaring itself the heir to Morandi's political line, located itself to the left of the PSI." (The twenty-ninth member left active political life altogether.) From Franco Cazzola, *Carisma e democrazia nel socialismo italiano* [Charisma and democracy in Italian socialism] (Rome: Collana di studi e ricerche dell'Istituto Luigi Sturzo, 1967), p. 34. Author's translation.

[3] Here I fundamentally accept Giorgio Galli's interpretation as formulated in *Il difficile governo* [The difficult government] (Bologna: Il Mulino, 1972), pp. 204-205.

186

the transformation of the party apparatus into a middle-class organization run by local government department heads (assessori), as the party's president Pietro Nenni put it. Table 6–2 shows only the tip of the iceberg. A very far-reaching and prolonged process has produced, and at the same time reflects, two very disturbing tendencies for the party: the southernization and the embourgeoisement of PSI membership, both most pronounced at the leadership level but characteristic of the electorate as well. Tables 6–3 and 6–4, which present data on the geographical and occupational distribution of the mem-

Table 6–2
OCCUPATION OF PSI MEMBERS, SECTION SECRETARIES, AND ELECTED REPRESENTATIVES, 1973
(in percentages)

Occupation	Party Members	Section Secretaries	Elected Representatives	
Industrial workers	35.2	20.4	17.5	(2,869)
Professionals and white-collar workers	20.9	35.9	43.1	(7,048)
Self-employed workers a	7.4	13.9	13.3	(2,170)
Agricultural workers	13.0	6.1	13.5	(2,209)
Inactive b	13.5	10.2	8.7	(1,432)
Others	10.0	13.5	3.9	(641)
Total				(16,639)

a Includes artisans, shopkeepers, and small entrepreneurs.
b Includes retired people and housewives.
Source: Il Partito Socialista. Struttura e organizzazione (Padua: Marsilio, 1975), pp. 343 and 347.

Table 6–3
GEOGRAPHICAL DISTRIBUTION OF PSI MEMBERSHIP, SELECTED YEARS
(in percentages)

Year	North	Center	South	Italy
1961	44.0	22.1	33.9	100.0
1963	42.1	22.2	35.7	100.0
1965	37.7	20.8	41.5	100.0
1967	37.5	20.2	42.3	100.0
1972	38.4	18.1	43.5	100.0

Source: Il Partito Socialista, p. 316.

Table 6-4
OCCUPATIONAL DISTRIBUTION OF PSI MEMBERSHIP, SELECTED YEARS
(in percentages)

Occupation	1945	1961	1970
Industrial workers	62.0	30.0	35.2
Agricultural workers	13.5	31.4	13.0
Self-employed workers[a]	—	6.1	7.4
White-collar workers	6.0	14.5	20.9
Others[b]	18.5	18.0	23.5

[a] Includes artisans, shopkeepers, and small entrepreneurs.
[b] Includes retired people, housewives, and probably salaried party workers and professional politicians (no official figures are given because this is a sensitive political issue).
Source: *Il Partito Socialista*, p. 317.

bership, speak for themselves. They indicate a clear shift from the north to the south and from the industrial working class to the white-collar sectors, as well as a probable increase in the number of paid party workers and professional politicians to be found in the "others" category.

The other traditional problem of the PSI—inadequate leadership renewal—while it still affects the executive committee and parliamentary group, has been overcome at the level of local cadres. Nevertheless, the implications of this development at the local level are not all positive. As official party sources have remarked,

The extensive turnover of our local leadership [starting in the mid-sixties], which involves as many as 50 percent of the section secretaries with less than ten years of activity in the PSI, takes on ambiguous implications when one keeps in mind two facts. (1) The turnover has come about through a generational change: increased numerical weight of cadres in the 30 and 40 year old cohorts. But at the same time, (2) there has been a substantial reduction in the number of cadres of working-class and peasant origins—precisely the groups which, not only in the red regions but also in the South, have constituted for years the political reference point of any change-oriented action undertaken by Italian leftist parties.[4]

---

[4] *Il Partito Socialista. Struttura e organizzazione* [The Socialist party. Structure and organization] (Padua: Marsilio, 1975), pp. 320-321. Author's translation.

There is no doubt that the *embourgeoisement* of the PSI has accelerated conspicuously since the center-left period and has continued unchecked. Previously excluded from most city and provincial governments, playing only a subordinate role in joint Socialist-Communist administrations where the PCI was by far the leading element, the Socialists found their bargaining power suddenly increased during the center-left period. After 1962, their role became pivotal: at the level of local government they could in most places form either a center-left coalition or a leftist alliance; in both cases they were often able to reap more than their due share of patronage. Political opportunities and socioeconomic spoils expanded with the creation of fifteen elected regional councils in 1970, and this further increased the PSI's political influence and governing opportunities. It also provoked a series of bitter Christian Democratic accusations that the Socialists were supporting one political formula, the center-left, at the national level and different ones, including leftist alliances, in many local governments.

It is a fact that the Socialists have always found it difficult to give full and unambiguous support to governmental decisions, for two specific reasons. First, they have had to maintain working relationships with social groups that were often in opposition to the government, not least with the PCI itself as the representative of large sectors of the working class. Second, as time went by the Socialists realized that a coalition with the DC could not implement incisive reforms. They became increasingly restless; by the late sixties, their role in government was a shirt of Nessus. Not only did the so-called independent press and the DC constantly blackmail the Socialists by threatening to hold them responsible for any crisis or sign of political instability, but the PCI itself put continuous pressure on the PSI. The Communists had come to consider the center-left a lesser evil and wanted the PSI to play its governmental role in order to prevent the emergence of a power vacuum, the eruption of a long governmental crisis, or the return to a center-right coalition.[5]

During the center-left period, the PSI slowly wore itself out, organizationally and politically. A major element in this process of

---

[5] Center-left governments were rightly considered less dangerous than any other type of coalition by the PCI. As a matter of fact, a temporary return to a centrist coalition (PLI-DC-PRI-PSDI)—the so-called Andreotti-Malagodi government, June 1972-July 1973—not only increased the level of sociopolitical tensions, but caused irreparable damage to the public finance system: specifically, a disproportionate rise in public expenditures due to a law allowing early retirement for public employees and another granting exaggeratedly high salaries to the so-called superbureaucrats, a cherished DC political clientele.

deterioration was the fragmentation of the party: not so much the emergence of organized factions, which can be traced back to the fifties and even the forties, but their consolidation, increased aggressiveness, and growing influence upon the internal decision-making process.[6] The strains between the factions that were unwilling to accept ministerial responsibilities but were unable to provoke a sharp break with the DC, and those that had vested interests in the continuation of governmental collaboration because patronage was vital to their functioning became unbearable and paralyzed the party.

It is well known, and understandable, that the appearance of ideological factions within the party in the immediate postwar period was connected with the PSI's relationship with the PCI. Not even the Social Democratic split resolved this issue: the PSI continued to have a rightist anti-Communist wing, a centrist faction, and a leftist pro-Communist faction. What differentiates the Socialist factions in the forties and fifties from the ones of the sixties and seventies is not only the degree of organizational autonomy (most factions today have their own news agencies and publications, independent headquarters, and special financial sources), but their structural persistence, the extent of their members' identification with them, and, above all, the fact that political and material spoils are carefully allocated to them on the basis of their proportional strength.

No Socialist activist and, for that matter, no Socialist leader would deny the factional degeneration of his party in the last fifteen years. The old cleavage over the attitude to be taken towards the PCI has been supplemented by a new one, the distinction between factions inclined to perpetuate the center-left coalitions (the followers of Nenni and De Martino and, in a more equivocal position, the factions led by Mancini and by Bertoldi) and those opting for a return to the opposition (mostly, if not solely, Lombardi's leftist faction).

By and large, the factional degeneration of the PSI is the product of two factors: ideological cleavages concerning the attitude to be

---

[6] As Samuel H. Barnes has ascertained in his *Party Democracy: Politics in an Italian Socialist Federation* (New Haven and London: Yale University Press, 1967), p. 50: "The inflexibility of the factions in 1963 was recognized by both leaders and militants in the province of Arezzo. They complained that the factions had hardened into separate political parties cohabiting a single organization; as such, they inhibited rather than facilitated internal discussion and exchange of ideas. This was true on the national level as well. Factional leaders negotiated with one another more like chieftains of separate parties than colleagues in a common cause. The issues selected by top factional leaders became the focus of discussion at lower levels; local problems became subordinated to national considerations. Paradoxically, factions thus encouraged centralization despite the relative independence of strata within the party."

taken vis-à-vis the DC and the PCI, and the internal struggle for ministerial and patronage positions. Control of these positions—which depended on the governmental alliance with the DC—ended in the creation of faction machines staffed not by ideologically motivated members but by opportunistic and power-thirsty characters. Obviously, this development had pernicious consequences for the functioning of the party at all levels.

In fact, "the organized presence of the factions, whose proselytizing activity has as its predominant purpose the weakening of the organized strength of competing factions more than the enlargement of the consensus area to be acquired by the party," [7] has three major negative consequences. In the first place, the image that the PSI projects to the electorate is that of a party torn by rifts. The relevance of these internal conflicts is not often apparent to the public, which perceives only the equivocations and unreliability of the PSI. Second, the existence of organized factions not only slows down the internal decision-making process, but also impedes the implementation of those decisions that are finally taken. Finally, all the factions need increasing resources for their sheer survival, and their financial maneuverings associate the PSI as a whole with clientelistic practices, particularly in some regions and in some sectors (such as public works). [8]

While the process of factional fragmentation is very complex and cannot be attributed simply to the prolonged participation of the PSI in center-left governments, [9] it must be said that the Socialist leaders have never decided to confront the issue squarely and, therefore, bear the responsibility for the degeneration of their party. Always formally condemned by PSI spokesmen, factionalism has been widely accepted in practice as a convenient formula for guaranteeing a fair share of benefits to all leaders and subleaders. That it is short-sighted politically (as well as fundamentally undemocratic) is evident today when a policy-oriented and more principled electorate is rewarding the discipline and unity of the PCI and punishing the equivocations of the PSI.

---

[7] Il Partito Socialista, p. 316.

[8] The need for resources should have been eliminated or at least limited by a rather generous law on the public financing of political parties passed in April 1974. Instead, this law seems to have only allowed the PSI to pay for its cumbersome central apparatus and to support the Socialist daily, which is running a tremendous deficit.

[9] Barnes, Party Democracy, pp. 47-48, has rightly emphasized that "factionalism in the PSI has a number of bases: personal differences among national leaders, historical memories and attachments, ideological preferences, local issues and personalities, interests, and clientelistic relationships."

Since factionalism by now has deep roots in the PSI, its mere abolition by decree, attempted by the central committee in July 1976, will not suffice. There is no evidence that the headquarters of the various factions have been dismantled, their news agencies taken over by the party, or their special financial reserves absorbed in the party coffers. Above all, there is no evidence that spoils and benefits are no longer distributed on the basis of factional identification.[10] Much remains to be done if the PSI is serious about recreating a united, disciplined, and democratic party, avoiding both the Scylla of authoritarian decision making and the Charybdis of factional fragmentation.

The Candidate-Selection Process

By 1976 most Italian parties had realized that they needed a profound renewal of their parliamentary representation, and some of them proceeded to work towards it. While the Communists have consistently respected and implemented their informal principle of renewing at least one-third of their parliamentary representatives at each election, DC members of Parliament and to a large extent Socialist ones have tended to have long tenures in Parliament. Furthermore, the low DC and PSI turnover rates have been due not so much to the inability of the two parties to find or to back attractive new candidates (though this has been one element of weakness) as to the ability of the incumbents to retain their ranking order in the constituency lists and to win reelection through their control of vital patronage resources, better exposure, and good connections.[11]

In the search for appealing and competent new faces in 1976, the PSI had, of course, to confront competition from the Communists and, even more, to overcome some structural obstacles. Relying upon its well-functioning organizational machine, the discipline of its electorate, and the increasing availability of safe House and Senate constituencies, the PCI picked up candidates prominent in a variety of occupational fields with the aim of reproducing in the parliamentary party a microcosm of Italian society. Five well-known dissenting

---

[10] As a matter of fact, the seats in the new executive committee elected in July were allocated on the basis of membership in the very factions that had just been disbanded.

[11] For a discussion of the overall problem with particular reference to the motivations of the major parties, see Gianfranco Pasquino, "Ricambio parlamentare e rendimento politico" [Parliamentary turnover and political performance], *Politica del diritto*, vol. 9 (October 1976), pp. 543-565.

Catholics, a prominent judge, a famous retired general, a couple of brilliant economists, the EEC high commissioner for industry, and a diversified group of administrative and technical experts became PCI candidates in 1976. A similar strategy was followed by the Christian Democrats, who were able to attract trade unionists, economists, judges, and some industrial entrepreneurs, notably Umberto Agnelli.

Compared with the DC and the PCI, the PSI has very few House constituencies where it is confident of electing more than two or three deputies and even fewer safe single-member senatorial constituencies. Therefore, it needed not only nationally known candidates, but personalities with *independent vote-getting power.* The DC and the PCI did not face this constraint. In fact, it is rather unlikely that the so-called independent candidates running for the DC and the PCI brought many votes of their own to the two parties. Probably only a few entrepreneurs and the candidates supported by the aggressively militant Catholic youth group "Comunione e Liberazione" mobilized new votes for the DC. The Communists have openly recognized that their independent Catholic candidates did not bring votes of their own, since most rank-and-file dissident Catholic voters had already joined the Communist electorate in preceding years.

Having rejected an electoral alliance with the Radicals, the PSI found itself deprived of new candidates from precisely those sectors of Italian society which the party had courted in recent years—young voters, women, the civic-minded bourgeoisie, civil rights associations, and so on—and was unable to draw upon the mobilizing skills of such groups in its own campaign.

The unwillingness of some second-string PSI candidates to renounce their safe constituencies and make way for newcomers was responsible for the defection of a brilliant young economist and columnist for *Il Corriere della Sera* and a prominent advocate of European unity, both of whom became independent Communist candidates (and eventually deputies). These defections of candidates previously closely associated with the PSI tarnished the image of the party.[12] In addition, the PSI was unable to make inroads in the trade union movement (most trade unionists decided not to become candidates for any party) and the various feminist groups. The result was that the very few independents who finally ran under the PSI banner

---

12 The economist, Luigi Spaventa, had been invited to sit on the executive board of the Fortieth Socialist Congress, and the advocate of European political unity, Altiero Spinelli, was the author of the chapter on foreign policy in the *Progetto socialista* [Socialist project] (Bari: Laterza, 1976), a collection of essays by Socialist intellectuals.

and were elected were not prominent at all and utterly lacked autonomous vote-getting ability.[13]

As for women representatives, while the PCI has forty-seven of them in the new Parliament, of whom thirty-one are newly elected, and the DC ten, the PSI has only one woman deputy among its eighty-six members of Parliament, just as it did in 1972. The Republicans, with a total of twenty seats, and the Demoproletarians, with a total of six seats, also have one woman member each, while the Radicals have two women deputies out of four as a result of deliberate party policy. Of course, this outcome only reflects the subordinate and marginal role played by women within the PSI. Only 3.7 percent of the 3,409 party officials are women; only 29 percent of the women members have a high school diploma compared with 46 percent of the men; 59 percent of the women are housewives, 40 percent white-collar workers, and 1 percent professionals; and 71 percent of them have been members of the party for less than ten years as compared with 47 percent of the males.[14]

To sum up, the net outcome of this half-hearted attempt at renewal was that in 1976 the only prestigious independent among the Socialist representatives was former navy commander Falco Accame. A sizable majority of the PSI members of Parliament come from the executive and the central committees of the party. The tendency known as the parliamentarization of the executive committee antedated the 1976 campaign, but it was reinforced at a time when the party was attempting to credit itself with representing the most important Italian collective movements: those launched by the students in 1968, by the workers in 1969, and by the feminists in 1974.

The choices of the party's leaders made the representation of these movements at the parliamentary level impossible. A very large proportion of the members of the executive committee have exploited their party office as a stepping stone to Parliament. Specifically, eight members of the executive committee elected in March 1976 obtained good positions in the party's lists in safe electoral districts so that seven deputies and one senator were elected to Parliament for the first time. There now exists a remarkable overlapping of top party

---

[13] Some Radical candidates and movement activists could have brought votes to the PSI. Moreover, the PSI proved unable to enlist as a candidate the prominent philosopher Norberto Bobbio who has acquired nationwide renown through his essays, later collected in *Quale socialismo?* [Which socialism?] (Turin: Einaudi, 1976). Bobbio probably could have attracted support from non-Socialist voters.

[14] All the data are from *Il Partito Socialista* except those on women in Parliament, which come from *Noi donne* [We women], July 25, 1976, pp. 20-34.

Table 6–5
OVERLAPPING BETWEEN PARTY AND
PARLIAMENTARY OFFICES, 1976
(real figures in parentheses)

Overlap	March 1976	June 1976	July 1976
Percentage of PSI deputies on executive committee	28.0 (15)	42.1 (24)	36.8 (20)
Percentage of PSI senators on executive committee	6.0 (2)	2.7 (1)	none
Percentage of PSI executive committee members in Parliament	46.0 (17)	67.5 (25)	64.5 (20)

Note: In the 1972-1976 Parliament there were sixty-one Socialist deputies and thirty-three senators; in the current one there are respectively fifty-seven and twenty-nine. The executive committee had thirty-seven members up to July 1976; since then it has been made up of thirty-one members.

Source: The names of the Socialist deputies and senators of the 1972–1976 Parliament and of the current one can be found in the official publications by the Camera dei Deputati [House of Deputies] and the Senato [Senate], respectively June and August 1972, and for both, July 1976. The names of the members of the executive committees elected in March and July 1976, as well as their factional affiliations, can be found in the booklet by Giovanna Zincone, *I partiti tra due elezioni* [The parties between two elections] (Turin: Centro di ricerca e documentazione "Luigi Einaudi," 1977), pp. 89-91.

and parliamentary offices, although this is not unprecedented in the postwar period (see Table 6–5).[15]

The failure of the PSI's renewal effort looks most dismal when set against the success of the efforts of the PCI and the DC. The percentages of freshmen in the three parties' groups in the House and Senate are as follows:

	House	*Senate*
PSI	28	44.8
PCI	54	56
DC	33.5	53.3

---

[15] For a series of historical data, see Cazzola, *Carisma e democrazia nel socialismo italiano*, pp. 24-32, according to whom the mean percentage for double member-ship in Parliament and in the executive committee in the postwar period has been 70.5 (but in that period, 1945-1965, the executive committee was composed at most of only twenty-one members). See also Cazzola, *Il partito come organizzazione. Studio di un caso: il P.S.I.* [The party as an organization. A case-study: the PSI] (Rome: Edizioni del Tritone, 1970), chap. 3, pp. 103-143.

Moreover, the high percentage of Socialist freshmen senators is misleading: it was due more to the electoral defeat of incumbents than to a deliberate renewal of the senatorial candidates, since only five incumbent Socialist senators, 15.1 percent, were not renominated, compared with 40.7 percent for the DC and 34 percent for the PCI.

The Target Groups

The PSI addressed its electoral appeal above all to unionized workers, dissident progressive Catholics, women, and civil rights supporters organized in various more-or-less spontaneous movements.

By 1976 the PSI had long since ceased to be a predominantly working-class party. In particular, its ties with many unionized workers had been severed after the split of the party's left wing in December 1963–January 1964 [16] when the Italian Socialist party of Proletarian Unity emerged. Nevertheless, the PSI had never renounced the attempt to exert some influence in industrial working-class sectors. For instance, the enactment in 1970 of a major legislative reform, the Statuto dei Lavoratori (bill of workers' rights), must be attributed to the unrelenting efforts of a Socialist minister of labor as well as to the contributions of Socialist jurists. The bill represented a real breakthrough for the unions and the workers. The former were allowed to play an important political role within each factory through commissions and delegates. The latter obtained better protection of their social and political rights. Policies of indiscriminate dismissal were forbidden and the requirement that an employer find a "just cause" for dismissal was made compulsory. Freedoms of speech, of assembly, and of political activity within each factory were explicitly granted for the first time.

In the wake of the bill of workers' rights, the unions were so strengthened in their relationship with the rank-and-file and in their

---

[16] According to Mattei Dogan, "Political Cleavage and Social Stratification in Italy and France," in Seymour M. Lipset and Stein Rokkan, eds., *Party Systems and Voter Alignments* (New York: Free Press, 1967), p. 152, industrial workers and the urban proletariat accounted in 1958 for 51 percent of the combined electorate of the Socialist and Social Democratic parties. According to Celso Ghini, *Il voto degli italiani* [The Italians' vote] (Rome: Editori Riuniti, 1975), p. 516, the evolution of the vote in working-class towns has been as follows:

	1946	1948	1953	1958	1963	1968	1972
PCI	25.85		25.00	25.19	28.08	31.00	31.39
PSI	26.76	39.87	16.32	17.33	16.54		10.81
PSDI		7.97	5.47	5.67	6.59	15.55	5.45
PSIUP						5.04	2.27

proselytizing activities as to become a fundamental force to be reckoned with in the formulation of socioeconomic policies. They even went so far as to launch their own proposals for pension schemes, housing projects, health insurance, and transportation improvement, known collectively as the "strategy of reforms."

The PSI never hid its ambition to become the privileged representative of the trade union movement, the spokesman for their demands and their channel of access to the government. It attributed such great importance to this role that it was willing to subordinate its policy choices in the socioeconomic field to the desires of the unions.

However, the Socialists cannot yet compete for influence, either with the Communists in the General Confederation of Italian Labor (CGIL) or with the Christian Democrats in the Italian Confederation of Workers' Unions (CISL), the two major union organizations. Within the CGIL the Socialists have a significant number of members but far fewer militants than the Communists. In 1976 they enjoyed a relative majority of members only in the small Italian Union of Labor (UIL), and even this did not allow them to control the executive committee of the organization or the position of secretary general until very recently. At most, therefore, through their deliberate representational activity they could have acquired some additional support from the rank-and-file unaffiliated workers, but this would have been very limited given the rigid boundaries placed upon Socialist expansion by the Communist and Christian Democratic organizational dominance as well as by the emergence of far-leftist groups.[17]

As to dissident progressive Catholics and the feminist movement, the Socialists had already tried to attract their support during the referendum on the divorce law, which had been sponsored jointly by a Socialist deputy and a Liberal deputy. The PSI hoped that Catholics and women who had abandoned the DC in 1974 (and in 1975) would choose their party over the PCI. One issue in the 1976 campaign was the abortion bill introduced by Socialist deputy Loris Fortuna, and the likelihood of a new referendum on abortion was lurking in the background; indeed, the Radicals had already collected more than the necessary 500,000 signatures. In their bill the

---

[17] For an analysis of these developments, see Gianfranco Pasquino, "Capital and Labour in Italy," *Government and Opposition*, vol. 11 (Summer 1976), pp. 273-293. In October 1976, a Socialist trade unionist, Giorgio Benvenuto, former secretary of the metalworkers, was elected secretary general of the UIL, replacing a Republican, both as a consequence of the Socialists' attempt to increase their influence among unionized workers and in an effort to stiffen the policy of UIL.

Socialists supported the most progressive option—legalizing abortion for any woman who wanted one—while the PCI, over the opposition of its women's organization, was trying to reach an agreement with the DC.

Thus the Socialists were confident of acquiring the support of the burgeoning militant feminist groups as well as of many dissident Communist women. But they greatly overestimated the size of the first group—in which, moreover, the Radicals had very strong support—and underestimated the party loyalty of Communist women.

Among the dissident Catholics the Socialists encountered serious obstacles that they tried in vain to minimize. Even those Catholics who were favorably inclined towards the PSI could only object to some features of Socialist ideology and practice which are repellent to ordinary Catholics. In particular, Socialist libertarian positions seemed to some to border on "anarchical patterns of individualistic behavior" far from the Christian ideal of communal life. To others, the very model of a Socialist society, as articulated by prominent PSI leaders and characterized by a sharp separation between the private and the public spheres of action, was considered largely incompatible with "many of the fundamental goals of the politically involved Christian." [18]

Finally, one must not discount the hypothesis that the most important challenge in the race for Catholic votes came from the PCI, which supplied an alternative *Weltanschauung* based on dogmatic beliefs and embodied in a quasi-monolithic party which is appealing to less politicized Catholic voters.[19] Be that as it may, while the Communists attracted some prominent Catholic dissidents by offering them safe parliamentary seats, the Socialists were unable to do so. It is doubtful whether they won the votes of more than a few progressive Catholics.

The civil rights movement developed outside the parties and often in opposition to them. It was the Radical party that worked as a leavening agent, while the Socialists, who openly supported several groups, hoped to reap the electoral benefits. However, two unforeseen obstacles severely impaired the PSI's ambition to become recognized as the parliamentary representative of these heterogeneous coalitions of militant workers, dissident Catholics, radical students,

---

[18] Articles contributed by Domenico Rosati of the Italian Christian Workers' Association (ACLI) and Franco Bentivogli of the metalworkers' federation (FIM-CISL), *Mondoperaio*, February 1976, respectively pp. 48 and 55.

[19] Federico Coen, "Questione cattolica e questione socialista" [The Catholic question and the Socialist question], *Mondoperaio*, May 1976, p. 68.

progressive soldiers, emancipated women, and members of the under-
privileged classes.

The first obstacle has been identified by a sociologist of Socialist
leanings.

The Socialist party considers itself a party embodying a
movement, because it has some of the dynamic tendencies
of a movement. This does not mean, however, that it is
penetrated by the great collective social movements or that
it absorbs them or, even less, that it guides them. It repeatedly recognizes itself in them all: in the Catholic dissident
movement, in the student movement, in the workers' movement and, today, in the feminist one. It understands them,
it offers them its support, it is responsive to their issues and
backs their requests at the parliamentary or governmental
level. Extremely sensitive to the demands which emerge
from the collective movements, it becomes their defender,
their advocate.

But this function of representation or advocacy lasts only
as long as the movement does. When the movement withers
away or becomes institutionalized, the party no longer has
a firm sense of direction. Not having absorbed their leadership and not having created alternative leaderships, it has
not grown. . . . That is, the party does not function as a pole
of aggregation and a center for debate and for critical elaboration of what the movement is and expresses. The PSI
does not foster the political growth of the movement nor
does it work to bring about the institutionalization of the
movement within the party structure.[20]

The only systematic attempt to endow the PSI with a strong
organizational apparatus was implemented, for a very short time,
in the first half of the fifties by Rodolfo Morandi, with mixed results.
Since then, the party's organizational weakness, particularly the lack
of a stable network of voluntary party workers and differentiated
flanking organizations, has appeared endemic. This was most striking when the left wing split from the party in 1964 and, later, when
repeated attempts to recreate the conditions for a mass party or at
least for a flexible organization appealing to large sectors of public
opinion miserably failed, or perhaps were never fully put into practice.[21]

---

[20] Francesco Alberoni, "L'immagine del PSI" [The image of the PSI], *Mondoperaio*, March 1976, p. 8. Unfortunately, my translation can by no means convey
the literary excellence of Alberoni's style.
[21] So far this has been the destiny of the National Socialist Convention devoted
to organizational problems, whose proceedings have been published in *Il Partito
Socialista*.

In the seventies the PSI has had to confront two challenges in its ambition to represent the newly emerging interest groups. The first has come from the PCI, which has superior organizational ability and is articulate and flexible enough to accommodate, at least at the grass-roots level, elements not completely in tune with the party's leadership and policies. The second has come from the new left, whose membership, though fluctuating and limited in size, is composed essentially of full-time, devoted militants. Many Socialist party members and some leaders share a core of beliefs with these groups, particularly regarding the nature of the Christian Democratic regime and the struggle for the rights of conscientious objectors, soldiers, policemen, prisoners, and asylum inmates. But the decision of the new left to present its own electoral list under the label of Proletarian Democracy (DP) probably deprived the PSI of more than 200,000 votes.

The Campaign

In the electoral campaign, the PSI had to overcome one initial disadvantage: the fact that it was considered largely responsible for the premature death of the sixth Parliament. For the second time in a row, Parliament had been dissolved a year before the completion of its normal term. According to the Socialists, the responsibility had to be placed upon the Christian Democrats, who had obstinately insisted on keeping alive an inefficient DC-PRI government (with additional parliamentary support coming from the PSDI and the PSI itself), whereas the country's problems could be solved only by achieving a working relationship with the PCI.

On the other hand, the Socialists feared the creeping establishment of a historic compromise between the DC and the PCI behind their backs. The PSI considered itself, rightly or wrongly, the indispensable link, the go-between, in this alliance, or at least it hoped to play this role and to reap electoral and political benefits from it. Thus it decided to push for the creation of a new majority either openly including the PCI or enjoying external Communist support.

In a leading article in the party's daily, *Avanti!*, of December 31, 1975, Secretary General Francesco De Martino expressed disagreement with the government's economic policies and, above all, with the project of industrial restructuring (an issue which has not yet been resolved). This provoked the fall of Moro's fourth cabinet (Italy's thirty-seventh since the overthrow of fascism) which had been voted into office on November 21, 1974, one of the longest-lived cabinets in postwar Italian history. All subsequent attempts to create a stable government failed and a caretaker DC minority government, again led by Moro, was established in February 1976.

The Party's Appeal. Before and after their fortieth congress in March 1976, the Socialists clearly stated their position. The fundamental meaning of the PSI's abstention in the vote on Moro's fifth cabinet was "to mark the end of a political phase, that of the center-left, which is by now completely exhausted. The Socialist initiative is addressed to creating the conditions for a new kind of politics, conditions which do not exist yet, but which must be pursued with tenacity and consistency." [22] Not surprisingly, the Socialist congress of March 3–7, 1976, gave its unanimous approval to a motion declaring that the center-left era was over and that the PSI would not participate in any governmental coalition that excluded the PCI.

De Martino's report to the congress—*"L'impegno socialista per uscire dalla crisi e per realizzare l'alternativa"* (The Socialist commitment to overcome the crisis and to implement the alternative)— tackled, as is usual in Italian party conventions, all the problems of the country, the governmental coalitions, and the party. Albeit somewhat hesitantly, the party's secretary general declared his support for a leftist government ("the alternative")—a government, that is, that would exclude the Christian Democrats from power.

With varying degrees of enthusiasm, all of the major factions within the PSI approved the final document. The headline in *Avanti!* on March 9—*"Il PSI sceglie la strategia dell'alternativa"* (The PSI opts for the strategy of the alternative)—was formally correct. However, it grossly understated the differences of emphasis among the factions. Furthermore, De Martino himself had been less sanguine about this very strategy in his concluding speech than he had been at the beginning of the congress. In fact, with reference to the likelihood of the PCI's being called upon to become part of a *governmental majority* (which does not automatically imply the allocation to the PCI of ministerial portfolios), De Martino said: "In this hypothetical case, we will not be able to remain adamant in our preference for an 'alternative' and to reject the important progress which would

---

[22] Resolution of the executive committee, *Avanti!*, February 6, 1976, p. 1. Author's translation. Later on De Martino added that the real and most fundamental meaning of the decision taken on January 7 was to put an end to a period of Italian politics that had become inadequate to meet the serious difficulties facing the country and to open another phase: "Il PSI intende muoversi per una nuova situazione politica" [The PSI intends to bring about a new political situation], *Avanti!*, February 21, 1976, p. 1.

be made in Italian society through the creation of governments or parliamentary majorities in which Socialists, Communists, and even Christian Democrats were included."[23]

One month later the executive committee of the PSI went even further, putting forward a proposal for an emergency government, an agreement among all democratic and constitutional forces to deal with the country's crisis. The sine qua non of this proposal was that Communist support be openly requested and accepted by the Christian Democrats. Despite the efforts of the PRI to win acceptance for the Socialists' proposal, the Christian Democrats rejected it, and the way was open for the dissolution of Parliament and new legislative elections.

Not unexpectedly—and probably not very shrewdly—the Socialists singled out as their paramount campaign target the DC, both as a party and as the dominant element in all governmental coalitions, the founder of a "regime."[24] The Socialists' electoral campaign was dominated by the slogan launched by De Martino: Let us defeat the DC's hegemony in order to accomplish a profound change in the life of the country.[25]

Caught up in a whirlwind of rising electoral expectations, the Socialists called for "a government created on the basis of an alliance among all democratic and constitutional forces, without any exclusions, defeating the DC's absurd pretension to assign the parties in advance a role either in the majority or the opposition."[26] They even talked about forming a Socialist minority government, an exaggerated ambition and a ridiculous proposal for a party representing about one-tenth of the electorate. "In the event that a weak leftist majority were elected and that nobody else would take part in a governmental coalition," De Martino said, "the PSI—of course, after re-

---

[23] Ibid., March 9, 1976, p. 1 ff.

[24] *Avanti's* headlines are illustrative: "Sconfiggere la Democrazia Cristiana per un reale rinnovamento" [Defeat the DC for a real renewal], June 4, 1976; "Battere lo strapotere della DC per costruire una nuova società" [Beat the DC's excessive power in order to build a new society], June 5, 1976; "Fanfani rinnova propositi liberticidi" [Fanfani reiterates anti-liberty intentions] and the leading article "La svolta reazionaria della DC" [The DC's turn toward reaction], June 6, 1976; "Ricadono sulla DC le responsabilità della crisi economica" [The DC is responsible for the economic crisis], June 8, 1976; and, finally, the day before the election: "Un voto contro l'egemonia della DC per rinnovare nella libertà" [A vote against the DC's hegemony to bring about change and preserve liberty], June 19, 1976.

[25] De Martino's report to the central committee published by *Avanti!*, May 21, 1976, p. 1 ff.

[26] "Le nostre garanzie e le nostre proposte" [Our guarantees and our proposals], *Avanti!*, May 16, 1976, p. 1.

flecting deeply—would not evade the responsibility . . . of providing the country with a government." [27]

The DC and the system of power and clienteles it had built up in its uninterrupted thirty years in government were easy targets for the propaganda of the opposition (Communists and Radicals included), but neither before nor during the campaign was the PSI able to identify and underline the features that distinguished the Socialists from the other leftist parties, especially the PCI. To many voters the Socialists' insistence that the PCI should participate in any future government seemed to be an invitation to vote for the PCI if one wanted to make things really change. After all, had not the PSI had its chance as a participant in the government for the last fifteen years?

Some of the Socialists' campaign pitches were effective and appealing: "The Italian problem can't be solved in either Moscow or New York. The solution is a free, European and socialist Italy"; "All over Europe socialism is struggling for liberty and democracy, both in power and in the opposition"; "With a strong PSI there will be no leap in the dark"; "This time you are voting to bring about change. The PSI is the political force that strives most consistently for change while preserving liberty and democracy. The alternative is socialism." In sum, the PSI campaign put the emphasis on the independence of the party from foreign powers and on its qualities as a progressive, democratic, and libertarian party.

Weaknesses of the PSI Campaign. Nevertheless, though one of the major purposes of the electoral campaign of the PSI was necessarily to recapture votes from the PCI, the most important differences between the two parties were not convincingly brought out by the Socialists. The PSI did not either formulate a coherent political strategy in opposition to the Communists' historic compromise or challenge the PCI on its evaluation of the Eastern European experience of bureaucratic socialism. Partly, this was a deliberate precaution against weakening the left; its motivation was opportunistic since the weakening of the left usually produces a reduction of the PSI vote. But it also revealed that the political imagination of Socialist leaders, their single-mindedness, and their unity were far inferior to those of the Communists.

As the Christian Democrats had done after their crushing defeat of June 15, 1975, the Socialists often complained of their coverage in the media and put a large part of the blame for their poor showing

---

[27] See De Martino's above quoted report and Giancesare Flesca, "L'Amleto socialista" [The Socialist Hamlet], *L'Espresso*, May 30, 1976, pp. 6-7.

in June 1976 upon the hostility of the press. They pointed to the allegedly changed political preferences of some major dailies, specifically the influential *Corriere della Sera*, which they accused of giving covert as well as open support to many Communist positions.[28]

In fact, however, the PSI had never had so much support from the mass media in an electoral campaign. A new daily, *La Repubblica*, manifestly pro-Socialist and edited by Eugenio Scalfari, a former Socialist deputy and widely respected journalist, was launched in January 1976. With a circulation of between 100,000 and 150,000 copies, it quickly reached a rather wide readership by Italian standards and, moreover, a highly political one. Second, the executive board of the state radio and television company, selected by the government in March 1976, appointed the directors and editors of the two television channels and the three radio stations. The appointments, made more with reference to party loyalty than to technical competence, gave the Socialists an unheard-of opportunity of filling several top-level positions in the second television channel and the first radio station. In turn, the DC acquired control of the first television channel and the second radio station. Finally, a few days before the elections, in one of its extremely rare electoral pronouncements, *Il Corriere della Sera* published an explicit endorsement of the PSI and the PRI.[29]

But these unprecedented advantages proved to be of no avail, for a reason related to the structure of the PSI itself. As we have seen, the party simply does not possess the organizational resources, in terms of flanking organizations, and the energies, in terms of number and quality of activists, to get out the Socialist vote and to channel it toward the Socialist party.

In addition to these objective and subjective difficulties, the party's leadership also made a fundamental blunder in mid-May 1976 when, after negotiations were held at the initiative of the Radical leaders, it decided to reject an electoral agreement with the Radical party. True, the PSI could not afford to deprive itself of any of its very few safe seats by allocating some of them to Radical candidates. Nevertheless, the ex post facto justification offered by De Martino leaves much to be desired: "The executive committee has never rejected an electoral agreement and, on the contrary, it has advanced

---

28 A widely respected journalist for *Il Corriere della Sera*, Giampaolo Pansa, has unmasked these petty claims and justifications. See his "Partiti e giornali 'cattivi'" [Parties and "naughty" newspapers], *Problemi dell'informazione*, vol. 1 (April-June 1976), pp. 233-287.

29 Alberto Sensini, "Due voti per rinnovare" [Two votes for renewal], *Il Corriere della Sera*, June 13, 1976, p. 1.

it even though many harbored serious doubts regarding its suitability. The refusal came from the Radicals who wanted to link the presentation of joint lists with political commitments by the PSI."[30] The weakness of the justification lies in the fact that the Socialist party was already so closely identified with "radical" struggles that it could not in any case hope to win votes from those who would reject accusations against the Christian Democratic regime. Moreover, by rejecting an electoral agreement with the Radicals, the PSI deprived itself of one of the very few reservoirs of youthful and energetic militants available to it and showed once more its fundamental indecisiveness and ambivalence. It lent its support to most if not all radical causes and struggles, but not to their most innovative representatives.

The ambiguity of the PSI position on civil rights had already revealed itself in other instances. After all, the party that hoped to stand for civil rights had voted in favor of a very repressive law on public order approved in May 1975 and, in March 1976, had taken part in the very disreputable distribution of spoils when the allocation of top executive positions of the radio and television company was made on the basis of party affiliations.

Thus, if one considers both the ambiguity of Socialist positions on some important issues and the party's organizational weakness, one is less surprised than one would otherwise be by the results of a Demoskopea survey taken in October 1975 (see Table 6–6). Seventy-one percent of the respondents believed that civil rights issues were very important or extremely important: an unexpectedly high percentage. But even more unexpected is the fact that the respondents singled out the PCI as the party which had contributed most to civil rights struggles, the PSI coming in second, and the Radicals third (see Table 6–7). This was due not only to inadequate information, but to the PCI's ability to exploit successfully even causes it had never strongly supported, thanks to its superior network of political communications. Finally, it is possible that the respondents identified civil rights with the protection of the workers, that is, with the PCI.

In summary, one must emphasize that the PSI found it impossible to overcome a somewhat tarnished and negative image in the

---

[30] De Martino's report to the central committee, *Avanti!*, July 13, 1976, p. 1 ff. See also the interpretation advanced by Angelo Panebianco, "Analisi di una sconfitta. Il declino del PSI" [Analysis of a defeat. The decline of the PSI], in Arturo Parisi and Gianfranco Pasquino, eds., *Continuità e mutamento elettorale in Italia* [Electoral continuity and change in Italy] (Bologna: Il Mulino, 1977), pp. 175-178.

Table 6-6
VOTERS' PERCEPTION OF THE IMPORTANCE OF
CIVIL RIGHTS STRUGGLES, 1975

Importance Rating	Percentage of Respondents
Extremely important	34.5
Very important	36.5
Moderately important	18.0
Not very important	5.6
Not important at all	5.4
Total	100.0

Note: The survey question was: "How important are civil rights struggles in the life of the country: divorce, abortion, minority rights, objective reporting by the RAI-TV and freedom of the press, moralization of public life, drugs, individual rights, anticlericalism, struggles against Fascist and authoritarian laws and against militarism?"

Source: Demoskopea survey in *Panorama*, October 23, 1975, p. 33.

Table 6-7
VOTERS' PERCEPTION OF PARTIES AND
GROUPS THAT HAVE CONTRIBUTED MOST TO
CIVIL RIGHTS STRUGGLES, 1975

Parties and Groups	Percentage of Responses
Italian Communist Party (PCI)	63.1
Italian Socialist Party (PSI)	57.8
Radicali e Movimenti per i Diritti Civili	33.1
Christian Democratic Party (DC)	20.8
Republican Party (PRI)	16.7
Partito di Unitá Proletaria per il Comunismo	13.5
Lotta Continua[a]	13.1
Social Democratic Party (PSDI)	11.9
Liberal party (PLI)	10.2
Avanguardia Operaia[a]	10.1
Italian Social Movement— National Right (MSI-DN)[b]	3.4
Comunione e Liberazione[c]	1.2
D.K.	14.8
None	1.8
Total	100.0

[a] Leftist extraparliamentary groups.
[b] Neo-Fascist party.
[c] Militant Catholic organization.

Note: The survey question was: "Which of the following parties and political organizations has contributed most to civil rights struggles?" (multiple responses allowed).

Source: Demoskopea survey in *Panorama*, October 23, 1975, p. 33.

eyes of some voters—in particular dissident Catholics and militant civil rights fighters—through its use of the mass media, largely because of its weak organizational machinery and its contradictory policies. Thus, precisely when Italian society was feeling the winds of change, the party which had usually supported and often promoted modern solutions to many Italian problems found itself left behind. Paradoxically, while the sector of the electorate that shared Socialist ideals was becoming larger, the impact of the PSI and its electoral support were, if anything, shrinking.

It is now time, therefore, to devote our attention to the nature, quality, quantity, and evolution of the Socialist vote.

The Elections

Polls and Expectations. In May 1972, the PSI polled 3,208,497 votes (9.6 percent) and elected sixty-one deputies and thirty-three senators; in June 1976, it polled 3,541,383 votes (9.6 percent) and elected fifty-seven deputies and twenty-nine senators. In spite of the loss of only four deputies and four senators, the party's leaders and activists as well as the mass media and the other parties unanimously interpreted these results as a serious defeat for the PSI.[31]

The disappointment of the Socialists, which provoked an agonizing reappraisal within the party, was all the greater because they had entered the elections with high expectations. Their optimism had been based on three main factors: the results of the regional elections of 1975, the poll forecasts, and the hope of winning votes from the Social Democrats and the Communists. In the regional elections of June 15, 1975, the PSI had drastically reversed a declining electoral trend which had started in 1963 by polling 4,235,416 votes (12 percent). These favorable regional results seemed to confirm that the rising Socialist vote was connected with the expansion of the left in general and the political awakening of Italian society. This awakening had already manifested itself in the referendum on divorce and in a growing awareness of citizens' rights vis-à-vis the state.

In May 1974, 59.1 percent of the Italian voters had rejected the repeal of the divorce law, demonstrating the growing maturity of

---

[31] See especially the article by Renzo Di Rienzo, "Compagni, cosí non va . . ." [Comrades, we cannot go on this way], *L'Espresso*, July 4, 1976, pp. 18-20, and the essays in the Socialist monthly *Mondoperaio*, July-August 1976, by Federico Coen (the editor), "La questione socialista dopo il 20 giugno" [The Socialist question after June 20] and Sisinio Zito, "Per il rinnovamento del PSI" [For the renewal of the PSI], pp. 2-4 and pp. 20-23.

Italian society as well as the beginning of the emancipation of centrist and rightist voters from their traditional parties (the left had until then always polled less than 45 percent of the votes). More generally, Socialist leaders were encouraged by the willingness of Italian public opinion to support an enlargement of citizens' rights vis-à-vis the police and the judiciary, the rights of soldiers vis-à-vis the military hierarchy, the rights of workers vis-à-vis the entrepreneurs, and by the increasingly flexible interpretation of the laws by the judiciary itself.

Meanwhile, the public opinion polls were raising the Socialists' hopes. The forecasts of many different preelection surveys all pointed to very considerable gains for the PSI (see Table 6–8). Particularly significant were the results of a widely publicized survey by the Demoskopea polling organization published for four successive weeks in *La Repubblica* (see Table 6–9).

The third factor inflating the expectations of the Socialists was their overly optimistic assessment of the electoral gains they might make from the Social Democrats. Social Democratic dissidents who had left the PSDI and organized a political movement called MUIS after the June 1975 administrative elections would vote Socialist, the PSI reasoned; moreover, the PSI hoped and believed that the PSDI was a declining party, bound to lose many additional votes to the Socialist party. This proved to be a very mistaken assumption; the Social Democratic electorate moved toward the DC. Finally, there was the conviction that some voters who had chosen the PCI in the past because of its well-known administrative competence would shift to the more reassuring and soundly democratic PSI when the

Table 6–8
PSI ELECTION RESULTS AND SURVEY FORECASTS, 1976
(in percentages)

	Date	PSI Share of Vote
Election Result, House of Deputies	June 20	9.6
Pollster and Newspaper		
Demoskopea, *La Repubblica*	June 16	12.5
Pragma, *L'Espresso*	June 6	15.7
Doxa, *La Stampa*	May 23	12.5
Makno, *Il Mondo*	May 23	12.3
Metra, *Il Giornale*	May 19	15.0

Source: Adapted from *Il Mondo*, June 30, 1976, p. 18.

Table 6–9
DEMOSKOPEA FORECASTS FOR THE LEFTIST PARTIES
AND THE DC, 1976 ELECTIONS
(in percentages)

| Party | Date Survey Published | | | | | | Election Result, House of Deputies |
	May 26	June 2	June 9	June 16	June 20[a]	June 20[b]	
DC	34.2	35.3	34.4	34.0	32.5	34.6	38.7
PCI	32.4	32.4	32.9	32.9	33.5	31.2	34.4
PSI	11.6	11.3	12.0	12.5	12.5	12.8	9.6
DP	1.7	1.7	1.8	2.1	2.2	2.1	1.5
PR	1.0	1.0	0.9	0.9	1.1	0.9	1.1
Percentage of sample responding[c]	69.5	75.4	82.2	87.8			

[a] Undecided respondents distributed on the basis of the statement: "I have not yet decided, but I think I will vote for . . ."
[b] Undecided respondents distributed on the basis of the statement: "I have not yet decided, but at last year's regional elections I voted for . . ."
[c] Percentages do not add up to 100 nor to the percentages given because respondents indicating their preference for other parties have been excluded here.

Source: *La Repubblica*, dates indicated.

prospect of a profound change in the composition of the national government became an immediate issue. Though the presence of a militant Radical party presented a challenge to the Socialists, it was widely discounted as a minor problem compared with all the positive factors that seemed to promise success.

The forecasts made by PSI sympathizers and potential voters may have been both cause and effect of the expectations nourished by Socialist leaders. Tables 6–10 and 6–11 offer some interesting data on this point. Table 6–10 reveals that respondents chosen from the electorate at large had more confidence in a Communist electoral victory than in a Socialist one, while the expectation of a decline for the Christian Democrats was very widespread.

Table 6–11 supplies two indications based upon the forecasts of Socialist and Communist sympathizers. First, almost all of those who intended to vote for the Communist party were very confident that the PCI would increase its votes, while slightly more than two-thirds of the potential Socialist voters were equally optimistic about the

Table 6–10
VOTERS' FORECASTS OF ELECTORAL OUTCOME
FOR THE THREE MAJOR PARTIES, 1976 ELECTION
(in percentages)

Predicted Outcome	PSI May 16	PSI June 6	PCI May 16	PCI June 6	DC May 16	DC June 6
More votes	35.3	38.3	55.6	66.2	11.3	14.8
No change	27.3		18.8		22.4	
Fewer votes	17.8	10.5	10.4	4.8	53.2	59.1
Don't know	19.6		15.3		13.0	

Note: The survey question used in the May 16 survey was: "Do you think that in the next elections the PSI will have more or fewer votes than in the last elections? And the PCI? And the DC?" The survey question in the June 6 survey was: "Apart from your political preferences, for which party do you foresee success in the next elections? For which do you foresee a notable loss of votes?" Of the respondents, 15.4 percent could not say which party would increase its votes and 18.8 percent could not say which would lose votes.

Source: Doxa survey in *La Stampa*, May 16, 1976, p. 2; Demoskopea survey in *Il Tempo*, June 6, 1976, p. 30.

Table 6–11
PSI AND PCI SYMPATHIZERS' PREDICTIONS OF
THE SUCCESS OF THEIR PARTY AND THE LEFT
(in percentages)

Respondent's Party	Respondents' Predictions Success for party	Loss of votes for party	Majority for the left
PSI	69.9	13.7	80.1
PCI	92.7	0.6	66.4

Note: The survey questions for the three columns respectively were: "Do you foresee a success for your party?" "Do you foresee a loss of votes for your party?" and "Will the left get a majority of votes?"

Source: Adapted from a Demoskopea survey, in *Il Tempo*, June 6, 1976, pp. 29–30.

chances of their party. On the other hand, Socialist sympathizers were far more inclined than Communist sympathizers to believe that the left would get over 50 percent of the votes.

To sum up, Communist sympathizers were both more partisan and more realistic than Socialist sympathizers, who were at the same time less optimistic about the electoral chances of their own party and slightly unrealistic about the electoral chances of the left. From Table 6–11 one can infer a stronger sense of party identification of Communist voters as well as the fluctuation of the Socialist electorate.

The Electoral Results. The hope and fear of many Socialist leaders and spokesmen that the Socialist area was larger than the percentage of votes polled by the PSI, especially in 1976, has already been mentioned. Even if they were right, however, one cannot refrain from stressing two general and seemingly irreversible trends which act counter to the Socialists' hope of recovering their past strength, at least in the short run.

The fact is that not only has there been a progressive shrinking of the Socialist vote overall, including the various splinter groups (see Table 6–1), but the PSI vote itself has sharply decreased. The second and more ominous sign for the PSI is that its shrinking is taking place in a period of great expansion for the left as a whole. For the first time in Italian electoral history, ten representatives purportedly to the left of the PCI were elected to Parliament. But the expansion of the left is almost completely due to the increase of Communist votes consolidated since the imposing leap forward made in 1975. Even in a period of accelerated political change and expansion of the electoral body following the lowering of the voting age to eighteen, the PSI has actually seen its electoral strength reduced in absolute and especially in comparative terms.

Figure 6–1 may have suggested an inverse relationship between the PCI vote and the PSI vote, but, while direct transfers of votes from the PSI to the PCI occur,[32] the actual pattern of defections is much more complex. The challenge to the Socialist party came as much from the Radicals as from the PCI, and the poor electoral showing of the PSI was due to a combination of factors: foremost among them were the inability to attract progressive Catholic voters and the rather disappointing performance of the party among the working class, but also the defection of a section of what was believed to be the progressive bourgeoisie.

Let us start with some general comments. Figure 6–2 shows that Socialist losses between 1975 and 1976 were uniformly widespread in all regions and were larger than Radical gains (the only exception is the minor one of Trentino-Alto Adige). This may be taken as an indication that some Socialist votes were absorbed by the PCI—which

---

[32] Interesting indications regarding defections and acquisitions of voters by and from the different parties emerge from the survey made by Makno and published in *Il Sole-24 Ore*, May 12, 1976, p. 3.

Figure 6-2

SOCIALIST LOSSES AND GAINS BY REGION, COMPARED WITH COMMUNIST AND RADICAL RESULTS, 1976, 1975, 1972

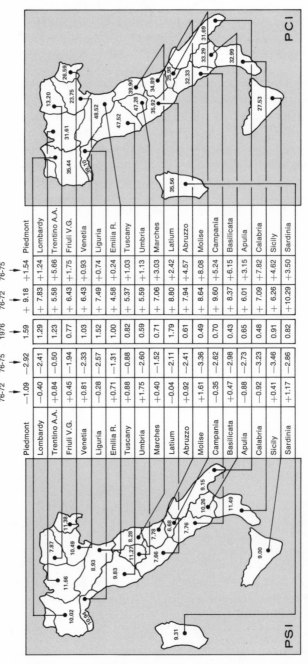

Region	PSI diff. 76-72	PSI diff. 76-75	PR Radicals 1976	PCI diff. 76-72	PCI diff. 76-75
Piedmont	-1.09	-2.92	1.59	+ 9.18	+1.54
Lombardy	-0.40	-2.41	1.29	+ 7.83	+1.24
Trentino A.A.	+0.84	-0.50	1.23	+ 5.58	+5.66
Friuli V.G.	+0.45	-1.94	0.77	+ 6.43	+1.75
Venetia	-0.81	-2.33	1.03	+ 6.43	+0.93
Liguria	-0.28	-2.57	1.52	+ 7.49	+0.74
Emilia R.	+0.71	-1.31	1.00	+ 4.58	+0.24
Tuscany	+0.88	-0.88	0.82	+ 5.37	+1.03
Umbria	+1.75	-2.60	0.59	+ 5.59	+1.13
Marches	+0.40	-1.52	0.71	+ 7.06	+3.03
Latium	-0.04	-2.11	1.79	+ 8.80	+2.42
Abruzzo	+0.92	-2.41	0.61	+ 7.94	+4.57
Molise	+1.61	-3.36	0.49	+ 8.64	+8.08
Campania	-0.35	-2.62	0.70	+ 9.60	+5.24
Basilicata	+0.47	-2.98	0.43	+ 8.37	+6.15
Apulia	-0.88	-2.73	0.65	+ 6.01	+3.15
Calabria	-0.92	-3.23	0.48	+ 7.09	+7.82
Sicily	+0.41	-3.46	0.91	+ 6.26	+4.62
Sardinia	+1.17	-2.86	0.82	+10.29	+3.50

Source: *Rinascita*, June 25, 1976, p. 6.

made steady progress between 1975 and 1976—and/or by the DP in a few areas.

On the other hand, the PSI made small gains over its 1972 results in twelve out of nineteen regions. Table 6–12 shows this progress to have been greatest in the islands and in the central regions, where the PSI vote has still not reached the national PSI average. The most discouraging outcome was in the northwestern regions. Here the Socialist party suffered a defeat as compared with both 1975 and 1972. Moreover, even in the southern regions the PSI vote declined from its 1975 level, notably in the Socialist stronghold of Calabria, where the clientelistic politics of the powerful faction leader Giacomo Mancini (former secretary general of the party and former minister of public works) apparently no longer pays off (see Table 6–13).

On the whole, compared with 1972 the party lost more votes in the northwestern than in the southern regions. It gained votes in the northeastern and central regions and in the islands, though in many cases without reaching its national average of 9.6 percent.

Yet, looking at the overall regional distribution of Socialist electoral strength, one cannot accept the blunt assertion often heard that the PSI is "southernized" in terms of electoral success. The party still attains higher average percentages in northern than in southern regions with the exception of Calabria. Nevertheless, the PSI is comparatively weak, and is becoming even more so, precisely where a modern Socialist party should be strong: that is, in the regions where most of the Italian industrial working class is located; in the red belt

Table 6–12
SOCIALIST LOSSES AND GAINS, 1976–75 AND 1976–72,
BY GEOGRAPHICAL AREA
(in percentage points)

Area	1976–1975	1976–1972
Northwest	−2.8	−0.8
Northeast	−1.6	+0.7
Center	−1.2	+0.9
South, islands	−1.7	+1.2

Note: Northwest: Piedmont, Lombardy, and Liguria; Northeast: Trentino A.A., Friuli V.G., and Venetia; Center: Emilia-Romagna, Tuscany, Marches, Umbria, and Latium; South and Islands: Abruzzo, Molise, Campania, Apulia, Basilicata, Calabria, Sicily, and Sardinia.

Source: Author's computations based on data from *Rinascita*, June 25, 1976, pp. 26-27.

Table 6–13
EVOLUTION OF THE SOCIALIST VOTE
IN THREE NORTHERN INDUSTRIAL REGIONS
AND IN THREE SOUTHERN REGIONS

	PSI Vote (in percentages)			Difference (in percentage points)	
	1976	1975	1972	1976–1972	1976–1975
Northern Regions[a]					
Piedmont	10.1	12.9	11.1	−1.0	−2.8
Lombardy	11.7	14.1	12.1	−0.4	−2.4
Liguria	10.9	13.5	11.2	−0.3	−2.6
Southern Regions[b]					
Campania	7.7	10.4	8.1	−0.4	−2.7
Apulia	9.1	10.0	11.9	−2.8	−0.9
Calabria	11.5	14.7	12.4	−0.9	−3.2

[a] Total voters, approximately 11,300,000.
[b] Total voters, approximately 7,400,000.
Source: *Il Corriere della Sera*, June 3, 1976, p. 4 for the 1972 and 1975 data; ibid., June 25, 1976, p. 6 for the 1976 data.

where a strong leftist subculture and leftist participation in local government should have created favorable conditions for the Socialist party, as they have for the PCI; and in all the major cities where the two favorite Socialist reference groups (the technicians and the "productive" middle strata) are concentrated.

On the contrary, in fewer than half of these cities does the PSI poll more than its national average. An explanation may be found by looking at the results of its two rivals, the PCI and the PR. On the basis of their electoral showing, one can assume that the PSI must have lost votes to the PCI in working-class constituencies and to the PR in the large cities, where the leftist children of the bourgeoisie live.

To be more specific, it is necessary to take into consideration first of all the electoral districts of the northern industrial triangle. Here the PSI lost an average of 0.7 percentage points compared with 1972 and 2.9 percentage points compared with 1975 (see Table 6–14). In only three out of seven electoral districts did Communist and Radical gains exceed Socialist losses, and, significantly, this occurred in the three most industrialized ones, including Milan and Turin where the Radical party is quite strong. However, since Radical gains in these

Table 6-14
EVOLUTION OF THE SOCIALIST VOTE IN THE
"INDUSTRIAL TRIANGLE," 1972-76
(in percentages and percentage points)

Electoral District	PSI				PR	PCI
	1976	1975	1972	1976-1975	1976	1976-1975
Turin-Novara-Vercelli	10.2	12.9	10.9	−2.7	1.7	+1.4
Cuneo-Asti-Alessandria	9.5	12.9	11.6	−3.4	1.3	+1.8
Genoa-Imperia-La Spezia-Savona	10.9	13.5	11.2	−2.6	1.5	+0.7
Milan-Pavia	11.9	13.9	12.3	−2.0	1.6	+0.8
Como-Sondrio-Varese	11.8	14.7	12.7	−2.9	1.1	+2.0
Brescia-Bergamo	10.2	12.7	9.6	−2.5	0.9	+1.5
Mantua-Cremona	13.5	16.9	14.6	−3.4	0.9	+1.7

Source: Author's computations based on data from *Il Corriere della Sera*, June 23, 1976, p. 8.

cities were less than Socialist losses, one can hypothesize that many Socialist defectors were working-class voters who shifted to the PCI.

This hypothesis is backed by data from some major cities (see Table 6-15). Socialist losses were higher than Radical gains precisely in the most industrialized cities: Turin, Genoa, Venice, Bari, and Catania as well as Milan, all of them very industrialized and very bourgeois at the same time. Of course, only an accurate ecological analysis could transform this very plausible hypothesis into a well-supported generalization.[33] On the basis of the available evidence, however, one can state with some confidence that the PSI probably lost some working-class votes to the PCI and some bourgeois votes to the PR, further weakening its penetration into some dynamic social groups and modern geographical areas.

One additional phenomenon needs some elaboration to complete the picture: the success of the PSI among young voters. The absolute number of *new voters* for the House of Deputies was 5,304,626 out of a total electorate of 36,715,577, which indicates the importance of this group. It is not easy to evaluate precisely the distribution of the youth vote among the various parties. The procedure normally utilized consists of subtracting the percentage of votes obtained by

---

[33] See Barbara Bartolini, "Insediamento subculturale e distribuzione dei suffragi" [Subcultural implantation and suffrage distribution], in Parisi and Pasquino, eds., *Continuità e mutamento elettorale in Italia*, pp. 103-144.

Table 6–15

**PSI LOSSES AND GAINS AND RADICAL VOTE
IN TEN MAJOR CITIES, 1976, 1975, AND 1972**

(in percentages and percentage points)

City	PSI		PR
	1976–1975	1976–1972	1976
Turin	−3.3	−0.2	2.3
Milan	−2.3	−0.4	2.4
Genoa	−2.6	−0.6	1.7
Venice	−3.3	+1.1	2.0
Bologna	−0.8	+0.4	1.8
Florence	−1.3	+0.1	1.6
Rome	−1.9	−0.1	2.5
Naples	−1.9	−1.4	1.1
Bari	−4.4	−3.0	1.5
Catania	−3.1	+0.5	1.6

Source: Author's computations based on data from *Il Resto del Carlino*, June 23, 1976, p. 12.

each party for the Senate from that obtained for the House, since the minimum voting age for the Senate remains twenty-five. The difference indicates, according to some, the size of the youth vote for each party.

This procedure starts from the assumption that vote splitting is negligible. As a matter of fact, vote splitting must be taken into account for two reasons. First, it has been repeatedly shown that when a voter has more than one vote—as in elections for city, provincial, and regional governments—he makes differentiated choices, and thus there is no reason why he should not do so when he has two ballots.[34] Second, parties often present candidates for the House of Deputies only—the PSIUP and other leftist parties did so in 1972 and the DP did so in 1976 (except in Lombardy)—and invite their supporters to cast their votes for other leftist parties in the Senate race.

On the other hand, even if vote splitting is widespread, it is likely to take place *almost exclusively* within political areas. It is extremely unlikely that a Christian Democratic voter will select the DC for the House and a leftist candidate for the Senate or that a Socialist voter will shift to the Liberal party for the Senate. It is more plausible that a voter who supports the PLI in the House contest will

---

[34] The Communist electoral expert Celso Ghini has drawn attention to this phenomenon, perhaps overemphasizing it. See especially his *Il terremoto del 15 giugno* [The earthquake of June 15] (Milan: Feltrinelli, 1976).

vote for the DC in the Senate race, especially since the percentage required for election to the Senate is much higher than that necessary for election to the House and, thus, a Senate vote for a minor party is likely to be wasted. The most probable of all combinations in 1976 was a Radical vote for the House and a Socialist vote for the Senate; this was true not only in constituencies where the PR was not present but in other constituencies as well since a Radical vote for the Senate would have probably been wasted.

On the basis of this general assumption and of additional evidence collected and analyzed by Giacomo Sani,[35] one can evaluate the distribution of the youth vote between the two major political areas: the center-right and the left. The available evidence suggests a marked increase at the national level of the youth vote for the leftist parties, particularly after the lowering of the voting age in 1975. This process, however, had probably already started in 1972 (as we will see in the case of Lombardy).

It is generally difficult to allocate exact percentages of youth votes to the parties making up the leftist area. Any analysis of House-Senate differences by region and by party involves risks and elements of arbitrariness. With this caveat in mind, we may examine the major findings: that the PCI polled higher percentages for the House than for the Senate in all regions in 1976, with the minor exceptions of Calabria and Tuscany, and that the PSI did the opposite, though the differences between the House and Senate votes were smaller in 1976 than in 1972. As expected, the Radical party polled higher percentages for the House than for the Senate in all regions with the exception of Friuli-Venezia Giulia. The exception is explained by the fact that the Radical party did not present candidates in the electoral district of Udine-Belluno-Gorizia, where its supporters were invited to cast their preferences for the incumbent Socialist deputy, Loris Fortuna, the sponsor of the law on divorce and of an abortion bill.[36]

---

[35] See Giacomo Sani, "Le elezioni degli anni settanta: terremoto o evoluzione?" [The elections of the seventies: earthquake or evolution?], in Parisi and Pasquino, eds., Continuità e mutamento elettorale in Italia, pp. 67-102, and Sani's contribution to the present volume.

[36] For all these comparisons see Arturo Parisi and Gianfranco Pasquino, "20 giugno: struttura politica e comportamento elettorale" [June 20: political structure and electoral behavior], in Parisi and Pasquino, eds., Continuità e mutamento elettorale in Italia, pp. 21-48. For a good and well-documented analysis of the Radical vote as well as for an explanation and a reaffirmation of "the correctness of the choice" not to present candidates in competition with "comrade" Fortuna, see Gianfranco Spadaccia, "Analisi del voto radicale" [Analysis of the Radical vote], Prova Radicale, vol. 1 (July-August 1976), pp. 16-22.

217

Additional evidence on the youth vote can be gathered by analyzing the case of Lombardy. This is the only region where all of the leftist parties presented their own candidates for both the House and the Senate. Table 6–16 confirms once again that the youth vote was predominantly distributed among the PCI, the PR, and the DP. The PSI was slightly disadvantaged in terms of percentages, less so in absolute terms. In this case, then, the Socialists held their own even though Radical and Demoproletarian voters and sympathizers had the possibility of remaining loyal to their party in the Senate election. (Most of them probably did remain loyal, though it was very unlikely that Radical and Demoproletarian senatorial candidates would win, and none of them did.)

The available evidence seems to indicate that the PSI polled a greater number of youth votes in 1976 than in 1972, at least in Lombardy—admittedly an exceptional case in terms of leftist political awareness and activism among the young. One can tentatively conclude that the PSI seems still to maintain better ties with youth than with other social sectors such as the working class, women, and the productive middle strata. This, at least, is a positive element, but in itself it is not sufficient to brighten the party's future.[37]

Evaluation of the Results by the Party. The official Socialist interpretation of the vote was formulated on the one hand in *Avanti!* and on the other in the debates which took place first within the executive committee and then within the central committee. Needless to say, the official pronouncements emphasized different nuances according to the audiences to which they were addressed.

Avanti! did its best to assuage the disappointment of militants, voters, and sympathizers and at the same time to present a dignified image to the other parties and the public. One of its first issues after the elections carried the headline:

The PSI Retains Its Positions in the House and the
Senate after an Electoral Campaign Dominated by the
DC-PCI Confrontation
The Final Results Confirm that the PSI Has Stood Up
to the Confrontation
Party's Political Strength Unchanged

The article made three major points: (1) the PSI had stood the test; the challenge coming from the Radicals sufficed to account for

---

[37] However, Giacomo Sani, *Generations and Politics in Italy*, paper presented to the seminar on the Italian crisis, Turin, March 24-27, 1977, has found a declining percentage of young voters who identify with the Socialist party.

Table 6-16
YOUTH VOTE (HOUSE-SENATE DIFFERENCES) FOR LEFTIST PARTIES, LOMBARDY, 1972 AND 1976

	1976				1972			
	House	Senate	Difference	Youth vote (in percentages)	House	Senate	Difference	Youth vote (in percentages)
In Percentages								
PCI	31.6	30.7	+0.9	37.6	23.8	24.5	+1.4	37.2
PSIUP	—	—			2.1			
DP	2.3	1.6	+0.7	7.7	0.7	—	+0.7	7.6
PSI	11.7	11.8	−0.1	10.8	12.1	13	−0.9	3.0
PR	1.3	0.9	+0.4	3.6	—	—		
Other leftist groups					0.8		+0.8	8.3
In Absolute Figures								
PCI	1,892,445	1,597,160	(+295,285)		1,304,339	1,219,259	(+201,430)	
PSIUP	—	—			116,350			
DP	138,884	78,055	(+60,829)		41,153	—	(+41,153)	
PSI	698,104	613,194	(+84,990)		661,254	644,494	(+16,560)	
PR	76,668	48,672	(+27,996)		—	—		
Others[a]					45,602		(+45,602)	
Total left			(+469,100)	59.7			(+304,745)	56.1
Total young voters			(785,494)				(541,785)	

[a] Workers' Political Movement, 29,901 (0.54 percent); and Marxist-Leninist Communist party, 15,701 (0.29 percent).

Source: Author's computations based on data from *Il Corriere della Sera*, June 22, 1976, p. 7, for the Senate; ibid., June 3, 1976, p. 4, for the House in 1972, and ibid., June 23, 1976, p. 8, for the House in 1976.

the small decline; (2) the issues upon which the party had based its campaign had proved valid: opinion had converged around them, reducing the originality of PSI proposals in the eyes of the mass electorate; and (3) the parliamentary strength of the left had become greater and the DC itself had been compelled to recognize explicitly the PSI's irreplaceable function in the Italian political spectrum.[38]

Nevertheless, there is no doubt that the results did not live up to Socialist leaders' and activists' expectations. They were unable to hide their disappointment and openly vented their frustration and bitterness, once again presenting the image of a deeply divided party.

Both in his brief assessment to the executive committee [39] and in his long report to the central committee, De Martino frankly underlined all the major features and problems of the party's policies. He recalled the expectations of success in the wake of the PSI's good showing in 1975, emphasized the difficult position of the PSI, oscillating between radicalization and yielding to the enticements of the DC. He rejected "the statement that the PSI has the most encrusted leadership group," but proceeded to criticize himself and the party for not having fully anticipated the consequences of early elections. Some of the blame he placed upon those who had deluded themselves by looking to the Mitterrand model of a Socialist party, some upon the party leaders in general for their confusion about the leftist alternative, emergency government, and other hypothetical formulas, which had conveyed the impression of a party uncertain about its prospects. Finally, the Socialist secretary reasserted his conviction that the PSI was a political force that still had a decisive role to play in Italian politics.

In his analysis of the vote, De Martino recognized that the beginnings of a decline were evident but defended the party's decision not to accept an electoral, even less a political, agreement with the Radicals. However, he criticized the state of the party organization and some party leaders' and activists' exaggerated attention to and interest in their own electoral success.

On the basis of an evaluation of the results obtained by the party in three geographical areas, De Martino stressed "the constant divergence between the results of the legislative elections and the results of the local elections." He went on to say:

---

[38] *Avanti!*, respectively June 22 and 23, 1976, p. 1.

[39] "La Direzione esamina i problemi che il voto ha posto al Partito e al Paese" [The executive committee analyzes the problems the vote has posed for the party and the country], *Avanti!*, June 25, 1976, p. 1.

This divergence does not manifest itself only in different periods, as between the 1975 administrative elections and those of 1976, but also within periods. This was true last year—when the party polled a higher percentage in the municipal elections than in the regional ones, which had assumed a more political content. The same occurred in 1976, at least in a number of towns where the party polled a greater number of votes in the municipal than in the legislative elections. This divergence cannot have any other explanation than the limited capacity of grass-roots organizations to operate as such through pervasive activity and commitment.

At the local level the party has left the task of winning support for the party lists to the individual candidate's initiative and activity. This phenomenon reveals the serious weakness of the PSI organization which must be tackled with the necessary energy by the [provincial and regional] federations and the center by transforming all party members into activists.[40]

In conclusion, De Martino remarked that the PSI had set three main goals for itself: to defeat the DC hegemony, to strengthen the party, and to make possible a change in the political leadership of the country through the establishment of an emergency government from which the left would not be excluded.[41] While the first two goals had not been reached, the third remained, according to De Martino, within the realm of present possibilities.

Although De Martino had interpreted and implemented rather faithfully, albeit not very energetically, the line chosen at the fortieth congress, the central committee ousted him during a stormy meeting. He not only resigned from the office of secretary general, but also renounced his seat on the executive committee.[42]

Through a formal and largely ineffective document, the party factions were dissolved and a new secretary and executive committee

---

[40] *Avanti!*, July 13, 1976, p. 3.

[41] This formula had been "appropriated" by the PCI, but its elaboration must be credited to De Martino himself. See the interview by Giuliano Zincone, "De Martino per un governo d'emergenza anche in caso di vittoria delle sinistre" [De Martino wants an emergency government even if the left wins], *Il Corriere della Sera*, June 17, 1976, pp. 1-2.

[42] Antonio Padellaro and Mario Pendinelli, "La delusione del 20 giugno nel PSI scatena accuse tra il vertice e la base" [The disappointment of June 20 in the PSI sets off accusations between the leaders and the rank-and-file], *Il Corriere della Sera*, July 10, 1976, p. 2.

were elected.[43] In the meantime, negotiations on the formation of a new government were going on. Within and outside the PSI, debate revolved around two main themes, closely interwoven but analytically distinguishable: the new role of the PSI in the Italian political system, if any, and the nature and structure of the party and its policies.

While the government was formed rather quickly by Italian standards,[44] the issue of the renewal of the PSI, its nature and its role, remained paramount for PSI leaders and received increased attention. After all, the PSI's unflinching opposition to any government that adopted a rigid attitude towards the PCI had been instrumental in modifying the political situation. It had compelled the DC openly to recognize the importance and the necessity of the PCI's abstention on the confidence vote indispensable for the formation of Andreotti's government. Yet the PSI's predicament remained, and its bargaining power did not increase. The crisis has as much to do with its political role and choices as with its organizational structure.

The Present and the Future

The PSI still fluctuates between a subordinate position in an alliance with the Christian Democrats (the *asse preferenziale,* not yet clearly abandoned, indeed, according to some commentators the formula for which the new party secretary Bettino Craxi is working) and a subordinate position in a coalition with the PCI. Perhaps this is inevitably the destiny of a party polling less than 10 percent of the votes in any alliance with parties polling between 34 and 39 percent of the votes.[45] On the other hand, while it is true that the majority

---

[43] Paolo Mieli, "Il terremoto socialista. E il terzo giorno Mancini creó Craxi" [The socialist earthquake. And on the third day Mancini created Craxi], and Renzo Di Rienzo, "Compagni, da ora in poi . . ." [Comrades, from now on . . .], both in *L'Espresso,* July 25, 1976, respectively pp. 10-12 and 13-15. On the new secretary, see Alfonso Madeo, "Craxi, un figlio del partito" [Craxi, an offspring of the party], *Il Corriere della Sera,* July 16, 1976, p. 2. See also the interesting comparison between the replacement of Fanfani by Zaccagnini as DC secretary in July 1975 and the substitution of Craxi for De Martino in July 1976 drawn by Panebianco in "Analisi di una sconfitta," pp. 177-178.

[44] See Gianfranco Pasquino, "Before and After the Italian National Elections of 1976," *Government and Opposition,* vol. 12 (Winter 1977), pp. 60-87, and "Per un'analisi delle coalizioni di governo in Italia" [For an analysis of governmental coalitions in Italy], in Parisi and Pasquino, eds., *Continuità e mutamento elettorale in Italia,* pp. 251-279.

[45] This is the conclusion reached in the articulate analysis by Norberto Bobbio, "Questione socialista e questione comunista" [The Socialist question and the Communist question], *Mondoperaio,* September 1976, pp. 41-51.

Table 6–17
SOCIALIST SYMPATHIZERS' ATTITUDES
TOWARD POTENTIAL GOVERNMENTAL PARTNERS
(in percentages of responses)

Attitude toward Alliance	Potential Partners of PSI									Don't Know
	DC	PCI	DP	PR	PSDI	PRI	PLI	MSI	None	
Favorable	17.4	51.4	4.7	1.9	6.0	13.4	1.9	0.6	8.7	18.1
Unfavorable	26.5	10.4	1.1	0.2	8.5	2.2	13.2	73.8	1.9	5.3

Note: The two survey questions were: (1) "Can you tell me which party (or parties) you would like your party to form a governmental coalition with?" and (2) "Which party (or parties) would you like your party never to accept as allies?"
Source: Adapted from a Demoskopea survey, in *Il Tempo*, June 6, 1976, p. 31.

of Socialist sympathizers would like to form a governmental coalition with the PCI and that the percentage of those who oppose entering a government with the DC is higher than the percentage of those willing to resort to it, it is also true that the Socialists, from the leadership down to mere sympathizers, are still divided on the question of governmental coalitions (see Table 6–17).

Interestingly enough, the best debate on the Socialist party was launched by the Communist weekly *Rinascita* which provided a forum for the representatives of the various factions. Not unexpectedly, these leaders diverged widely in their analyses of the nature of the party, their assessments of its present role, and their predictions for the future. Party leaders and intellectuals seemed to take for granted that it would be impossible for the party to enlarge its electoral support, at least in the short run, and attempted to define its role on this assumption.

Four positions, ranging from right to left, emerged. Giacomo Mancini put the emphasis on the elaboration of a Socialist policy. He opposed accepting the movement of the Italian party system toward two-party competition in the belief that the conservative pole would probably remain the stronger for a long time.[46] Silvano Labriola, a faithful collaborator of De Martino's and often his spokesman, emphasized the role of the PSI (presumably a policy role) in an emergency government. Such a government, he added, should be a

---

[46] Giacomo Mancini, "Rifiutare la rassegnazione" [Let's not give up], *Rinascita*, August 6, 1976, pp. 6-7.

transient coalition including all democratic parties, and therefore both the DC and the PCI. But he did not identify any alternative scenarios.[47] Fabrizio Cicchitto, representing the left wing, summed up his view by pleading for a leftist government including minor lay parties (the PSDI, the PRI, and the PLI) under the leadership of the PSI.[48] Finally, Antonio Giolitti, the defeated candidate for secretary general, also believed that the PSI could play an active and fundamental role in promoting a democratic alternative to the Christian Democratic regime. Giolitti maintained that there was no space and no need for mediation between the DC and the PCI, but that there was a need for a PSI alternative to the dangers of both the historic compromise and a frontal clash between the PCI and the DC.[49]

These statements suggest several important roles that the PSI might play: it might be a key element in coalitions either in the government or in the opposition; it might act as a guardian, a sort of check on PCI and DC behavior in case of a deep reaching historic compromise not limited to the enactment of a few exceptional measures; it might fulfill a policy role aimed at putting forward a coherent plan and/or a series of policies to improve the Italian situation and around which to rally all non-Communist and non-Christian Democratic public opinion; or it might perform a programmatic role in a dynamic period of transition to a new socioeconomic organization.

The prerequisite for any of these roles is the renewal or restructuring of the party. Those who emphasize the participation of the party in coalitions, who coolly appraise this role as the only possible one in the near future, are not preoccupied with the state of the party. But only a new type of party could effectively perform any of the other roles. So far Italian Socialists have only been able to identify two models of a Socialist party which might be implemented: the Morandi type and the Mitterrand one.

Rodolfo Morandi was a very capable organizational leader of the late forties and early fifties who tried to create a solid network of

---

[47] Silvano Labriola, "I socialisti e l'emergenza" [The Socialists and the emergency], *Rinascita*, August 6, 1976, p. 7.

[48] Fabrizio Cicchitto, "Il dibattito sull'autonomia tra e con i socialisti" [The debate on autonomy among and with the Socialists], *Rinascita*, September 3, 1976, pp. 14-15. It must be stressed that a coalition including the PSDI, the PRI, and the PLI plus the leftist parties is the only one that could enjoy a parliamentary majority and keep the DC in the opposition.

[49] Antonio Giolitti, "Autonomia e alternativa" [Autonomy and the alternative], *Rinascita*, September 17, 1976, pp. 5-6. Giolitti's is the most lucid contribution to the debate.

party sections and to educate a core of devoted and well-trained cadres all dependent upon the center.[50] The Mitterrand type of party is identified with a more flexible and diversified and far less cumbersome apparatus that permits open working relationships with a variety of social and economic groups. The idealization of the second model by some Socialists and the debunking of the first by others have not been accompanied by a deep and thorough analysis of the temporal and political limitations of either.

For instance, no Italian Socialist leader has been willing or able so far to point out the fact that the French Socialist party benefits highly from the existence of a very appealing leader. His qualities are magnified by the French constitutional and electoral systems which offer him extensive exposure during the presidential campaigns and make the creation of tight alliances necessary. This asset, of course, is not easily transferable to a different sociopolitical context. And no Socialist leader has yet come to the conclusion that Morandi's model is no longer applicable to the PSI in the present Italian situation. No thorough analysis of Morandi's work exists; moreover, this model was never fully implemented. Thus, there is no reason why the degeneration of the party should be attributed to the organizational innovations introduced by Morandi.

In attempting to formulate solutions to the party's crisis and to advance proposals for change, some party leaders apparently would like to have it both ways, to reconcile a strong apparatus with a flexible organization.[51] Others dismiss one of the models out of hand,[52]

---

[50] "In the Morandi era," Barnes wrote, "reports increased in length and attention to detail, membership drives were carefully organized and executed, and statistical services were given great attention. An effort was made to emulate not only the centralization and discipline of the PCI but also its success in involving the membership in party activities," *Party Democracy*, p. 66. To my knowledge, no fully satisfactory and comprehensive analysis of Morandi's activities has been written.

[51] Cicchitto, "Il dibattito sull'autonomia tra e con i socialisti," p. 6, recognizes that the enterprise is difficult but is willing to rely upon the central committee "to build a party that is really structured and at the same time truly open."

[52] "The PSI can no longer be a mass party according to the old Morandi model . . . the bureaucratic apparatus, the operational structure, are absolutely disproportionate to the political and electoral result the Socialists achieve. Furthermore, they often become a hindrance to more widespread penetration of the party in the society, to an osmosis with lively and spontaneous forces existing within the 'movement' and facilitate the closing of the leadership group at the various levels and the ossification of the party. . . . The PSI, instead, is more and more clearly a party of cadres and of movement (not simply an opinion party)." Claudio Signorile, "La crisi socialista: troppi burocrati lontani dalla base" ["The Socialist crisis: too many bureaucrats far from the grass-roots], *La Repubblica*, June 24, 1976, p. 3.

while still others have formulated a completely "ideological" plan. One has described this as "a party which should not be a sum of power groups, but a political 'collective' in which all the forces and the movements that identify themselves with the Socialist endeavor would be represented, and in which these forces and movements would find opportunities not for modifications but for stimuli to their own autonomous political creativity." [53]

Judging from these statements, the party and its leaders have a long way to go before they can formulate and implement a viable reform. The party's apparatus is overstaffed and its relationship with politically sympathetic outside groups is rigid and unconducive to mutual strengthening. In the meantime, a creeping historic compromise may well produce irreversible changes in the distribution of political power—not to mention a showdown between the DC and the PCI, which would provoke a further polarization of the electorate and reduce the PSI's electoral strength.

Conclusion. Today the Italian Socialist party finds itself in the most difficult period of its entire existence since its founding in 1892. It has many important assets: it is still in power, either with the DC or with the PCI, in most local governments and therefore has access to patronage and spoils; it is an indispensable coalition partner in local administrations; it enjoys full domestic and international legitimacy; and, finally, it may be the party around which many progressive sectors of Italian society will rally. Nevertheless, its pivotal role might be severely endangered by the implementation of any form of historic compromise, whatever the Communists might say about the unity of the Catholic, Socialist, and Communist masses.

It is safe to conclude that the Italian Socialists will have to struggle against time in order to find both a political program appropriate for a politicized and changing society and a party organization adequate to withstand the challenges coming from the two giants of Italian political life.[54] While the evolution of the international system

---

[53] Federico Coen, "La questione socialista dopo il 20 giugno" [The Socialist question after June 20], *Mondoperaio*, July-August 1976, p. 4.

[54] The analysis and suggestions contained in Bettino Craxi's first report to the central committee as secretary general, "I socialisti per lo sviluppo del Paese e per la costruzione dell'alternativa" [The Socialists in favor of the development of the country and the construction of an alternative government] and in his rebuttal "La soluzione d'emergenza unica via d'uscita dalla crisi del paese" [An emergency solution the only way out of the country's crisis], *Avanti!*, respectively November 16 and 18, 1976, p. 1ff. are indicative of the difficulties to be faced in the formulation of new policies for the party as well as for the Italian political system.

and the support of other European Socialist parties might help the PSI, the present challenge to a small and declining party and to its unimaginative leadership is great indeed.[55] Yet, without a strong Socialist party the solution of the Italian crisis will be all the more difficult and painful.

[55] For a counterweight to my perhaps overly pessimistic view, see the balanced and articulate assessment of Craxi's report by Giorgio Galli, "Questo PSI é meglio" [This PSI is better], Panorama, November 30, 1976, p. 47. For a theoretical argument generally supportive of my views, see the essay by Stefano Bartolini, "Per un'analisi dei rapporti tra partiti socialisti e comunisti in Italia e Francia" [Toward an analysis of the relationships between the Socialist and Communist parties in Italy and France], Rivista Italiana di Scienza Politica, vol. 6 (December 1976), pp. 439-480.

7

THE SMALLER PARTIES IN THE 1976 ITALIAN ELECTIONS

Robert Leonardi

Overview of the Elections

The smaller or minor Italian parties are those that normally attract less than 10 percent, and in many cases even 5 percent, of the popular vote. Despite their feeble electoral strength, however, these parties have enjoyed considerable power in governmental coalitions since the beginning of the post-Fascist period. For this discussion of the 1976 elections the smaller parties can be divided into two groups: (1) the traditional minor parties, which have been in existence since at least 1948, namely the Social Democrats, the Republicans, the Liberals, and the neo-Fascist Italian Social Movement, and (2) the new parties which succeeded for the first time in 1976 in electing candidates to Parliament, that is, the Radicals and the Demoproletarians.

The 1976 Italian parliamentary elections had paradoxical results for the smaller parties: never before have so many divergent political forces found themselves on the parliamentary map, yet never before have these parties found their political space so drastically reduced. In 1976 the mass parties—the Christian Democrats, the Communists, and the Socialists—were able to attract 82.9 percent of the vote and claim 86.8 percent of the seats in the Chamber of Deputies. There remained only 17.1 percent of the vote and 13.2 percent of the Chamber seats for the minor parties—the smallest shares the minor parties have ever won since the first parliamentary elections in 1948 (see Table 7–1). Even in 1968, when the Socialists and Social Democrats ran on a common slate under the banner of the Unified Socialist party (PSU), the other small parties still managed to attract 19.5 percent of the vote. The 1976 decline is even more striking com-

Table 7–1

DISTRIBUTION OF VOTES AND SEATS FOR THE MASS AND SMALL PARTIES, CHAMBER OF DEPUTIES ELECTIONS, 1948–76

Election	Mass Parties [a] Percentage of vote	Mass Parties [a] Seats in Chamber	Small Parties [b] Percentage of vote	Small Parties [b] Seats in Chamber
1948	79.5	85.0	20.5	15.0
1953	75.4	81.5	24.6	18.5
1958	79.3	83.4	20.7	16.6
1963	77.4	81.4	22.6	18.6
1968	80.5[c]	84.8	19.5	15.2
1972	75.6	80.5	24.4	19.5
1976	82.9	86.8	17.1	13.2

[a] Mass parties: DC, PCI, PSI.

[b] Small parties: PSDI, PRI, PLI, MSI-DN, PDIUM, PP Sud Tirol, and others.

[c] Includes the PSDI which formed a common slate with the PSI known as the PSU.

Source: "Storia delle elezioni in Italia" [A history of elections in Italy], *L'Europeo* June 24, 1976, special supplement, and Ufficio Elettorale e di Statistica del PCI [Electoral and Statistical Office of the PCI], *Elezioni Politiche 20 giugno 1976: Elezioni della Camera dei Deputati* [June 20, 1976 political elections: elections for the Chamber of Deputies] (Rome: 1976), p. 2.

pared to the result in 1972, when the small parties won their second all-time high, 24.4 percent of the popular vote.

On the other hand, in 1972 one of the major elements in the small-party spectrum, the Socialist party of Proletarian Unity, failed to meet the minimum quota for parliamentary representation although it attracted 648,800 votes (1.9 percent of the total vote). In 1976 the number of small parties represented in Parliament increased to six, yet three out of the six won fewer votes than the total for the PSIUP in 1972. Why were the minor parties so unsuccessful in attracting votes from an electorate that for nearly a decade had actively demonstrated its dissatisfaction and its willingness to look for new political leaders and ideas?

The answers to this question must be sought in the general crisis of the Italian political system which came to a head in the "hot autumn" of 1969 and in the "strategy of tension" in the years 1969–1975. These two developments proved to have long-range effects in shifting the basic political orientations of the electorate and opening the political arena to new forces. Table 7–2 presents the

Table 7–2

**DISTRIBUTION OF THE VOTE AMONG
THE SMALL PARTIES, 1972–76**

Party	Vote (in percentages)			Change in Vote (in percentage points)	
	1972 Chamber of Deputies elections	1975 regional elections	1976 Chamber of Deputies elections	1975–76	1972–76
DPa	0.7	1.2	1.5	+0.3	+0.8
PR	—	—	1.1	+1.1	+1.1
PSDI	5.1	5.6	3.4	−2.2	−1.7
PRI	2.9	3.3	3.1	−0.2	+0.2
PLI	3.9	2.5	1.3	−1.2	−2.6
MSI-DN	8.7	6.8	6.1	−0.7	−2.6
Others	0.6	1.1	0.6	−0.5	0.0

a What became the DP ran as *Il Manifesto* in 1972 and as the PDUP *Manifesto* in 1975.

Source: Ufficio Elettorale del PCI, *Elezioni Politiche 20 giugno 1976*, p. 2.

fluctuating fortunes of the small parties between 1972 and 1976. In 1972 when the ex-Communists of the *Manifesto* group (expelled from the party when they refused to stop publishing the magazine of the same name) first attempted to form a viable political organization to the left of the PCI, they attracted a mere 0.7 percent of the vote. The neo-Fascists, on the other hand, scored a resounding victory, adding more than 1 million new votes to their 1968 electoral base and bringing their total share of the vote to an all-time high of 8.7 percent. However, as time went on the political space for the right started to shrink, and new possibilities opened up for the left. Contrary to almost everyone's expectations, the referendum on divorce in 1974 was won by the pro-divorce forces. In the 1975 regional elections, the slow but persistent shifts in the Italian electorate finally began to produce massive results. The 1975 electoral map bore witness to the sudden increase in Communist votes and the erosion of the Christian Democratic voting base. For the small parties the 1975 elections saw for the first time the partial success of the extraparliamentary forces on the left grouped around the PDUP *Manifesto*, a political alliance of the former *Il Manifesto* group with the remnants of the ex-PSIUP leadership which had not joined either the PSI or the PCI. The PSDI and PRI seemed to be doing well, while the Liberals and neo-Fascists showed their first serious signs of decline.

In preparation for the 1976 electoral campaign there were a number of attempts on the left to create new political formations. The former PDUP *Manifesto* successfully negotiated a common electoral program and list of candidates with the other major far-left groups including the Worker's Vanguard (AO), Continuous Struggle (LC), and the Workers' Movement for Socialism (MLS). It was this amalgamation of diverse political organizations that presented itself under the label Proletarian Democracy in the 1976 elections. The Radicals ran a separate list as a result of their failure to formulate a common program with the Socialist party, which had long been the institutionalized party closest to the libertarian line advocated by the Radical leadership. In fact, it had become common practice for Radical party members to have two party cards: one for the Radical party and one for the PSI. In 1976 the Socialists, who felt that they could make greater electoral gains without the Radicals, proposed certain compromises that the Radicals could not accept.

In the center and on the right there were timid attempts to present new faces and political formations. The neo-Fascists launched their "constitution of the right" campaign which attempted to amalgamate all of the right-wing forces dissatisfied with the soft-line policies and compromise measures proposed by the centrist parties (the Christian Democrats, the Liberals, the Social Democrats, and the Republicans) in relation to the PCI. Three of the lay parties—the PLI, the PSDI, and the PRI—undertook to present common candidates for Senate seats in which their separate candidates had traditionally not done very well. However, at the insistence of the Republican leader Ugo La Malfa, this temporary alliance dissolved after the elections rather than serving as the basis for a new political formation or common program. The Republicans, aware of the organizational and political difficulties of the other two lay parties, hoped that a conspicuous shift of votes away from these two temporary allies would allow the PRI to build its way past the 5 percent mark. But the 1976 electoral results proved disappointing for almost all concerned.

The 1976 results showed a noticeable contraction of the traditional small parties of the center and right—the PSDI, the PLI, and the MSI—with the minor exception of the PRI. Meanwhile, the new small parties of the left—the DP and the PR—advanced, though less than expected. Proletarian Democracy increased its vote from 1.2 percent in 1975 to 1.5 percent in 1976, and the Radicals did better than most observers expected with 1.1 percent of the popular vote and four seats in the Chamber. Returning to Table 7–2, we can see that, except for the Radicals (who hardly count since this was their first election and they therefore could not have lost votes) and the Demoproletarians, all of the minor parties did badly in comparison to their showing in 1975. The losses ranged from 0.2 percentage points for the Republicans to 2.2 percentage points for the Social Democrats. Taking 1972 as the base year for comparison does not significantly improve the picture: in four years the PLI has lost 66 percent of its voting base, the MSI 30 percent, and the PSDI 33 percent.

What happened? Undoubtedly, the main reason for the poor performance of the small parties in 1976 was the successful comeback of the Christian Democrats from their disappointing showing in 1975. While the DC did not necessarily woo back all of the voters who had abandoned it in 1975, it seems to have been able to compensate for its loss by attracting votes from its former allies in the center and on the right. As a result, the nature of the longstanding alliance between the DC and the minor parties was called into question. It was felt by many party leaders that the inability of the small parties to successfully differentiate their policies from those of the DC permitted the larger party to erode their voting bases in a moment of acute political crisis produced by the prospect that the Communists would become the largest party in Parliament. Thus, the defense of the status quo became the defense of the DC.

Before the Elections

Prior to 1976, political power in Italy was exercised by the Christian Democrats with the direct or indirect support of the Republicans, Social Democrats, and Liberals depending on the nature of the government coalition. The DC was the political sun around which orbited the minor planets of the Italian political system. This system of government was first instituted in 1947 when the DC succeeded in expelling—with the financial and political support of the U.S. government—the Communist and Socialist parties from the ruling coalition and forged a solid relationship of mutual dependence with the PRI, the PSDI, and the PLI.[1] Even after the 1948 elections, which

[1] See Robert Leonardi and Alan A. Platt, "The U.S. Political-Military Penetration of Italy: A Case Study of the Role of American Foreign Policy Preferences in Regulating the Internal Political Choices in a Mediterranean Country, 1945-1975," paper presented at the American Political Science Assoc. meeting, Chicago, Ill., September 2-5, 1976.

had given the Christian Democrats an absolute majority of seats in both the Chamber and Senate, the DC leadership preferred to rule with the support and direct participation of the three small lay parties rather than go it alone. Through the centrist experience, the DC was able to dominate the Liberals, the Social Democrats, and the Republicans in a way that made it difficult for them to criticize the DC. Within this context, however, each of the small parties attempted to influence the course of the government according to its own political beliefs.[2]

The Italian Social Movement. The neo-Fascist Italian Social Movement has been historically confined to the ghetto of Italian politics. Despite its efforts to find political room for maneuver in the postwar system, the MSI has been excluded from power. The DC has always turned first to the minor parties of the center and has sought aid from the MSI only as a last resort, usually clandestine. It has been difficult for the DC to openly draw the MSI into the administration of national power because of the bitter memory of Fascist collaboration with the German occupation forces in northern Italy between 1943 and 1945.

Benito Mussolini was deposed on July 25, 1943, by the Fascist Grand Council and placed under arrest by King Victor Emmanuel III, but he was soon rescued by German SS troops and brought to Salò, a town on Lake Garda, to head a new version of the Fascist regime. The new regime went under the official title of the Italian Social Republic (RSI) but was popularly referred to as the Salò Republic. What made the RSI particularly offensive to many Italians was that it operated under the direct auspices of the Germans and supported the German war effort in Italy against the Allies and the official Italian government. Nevertheless, the political program and experience of the Salò Republic served as the ideological and spiritual base upon which the neo-Fascist party was reconstructed in the postwar period.

The MSI no longer openly claims allegiance to pre-1945 fascism, but many of the party leaders and activists were involved in various ways in the Mussolini regimes. Indeed, all of the MSI party secretaries—Giorgio Almirante, Arturo Michelini, and Augusto De Mar-

---

[2] See Robert Leonardi, "The Politics of Choice: An Inquiry into the Causes of Factionalism in the Italian Christian Democratic Party" (Ph.D. diss., University of Illinois at Urbana-Champaign, 1974), pp. 75-76 and 116, and Giuseppe Di Palma, *Surviving without Governing: The Italian Parties in Parliament* (Berkeley and Los Angeles: University of California Press, 1977), p. 244, for the dates and composition of all Italian governments between 1945 and 1973.

sanich—were at one time either members of one of the Mussolini governments or officials of the National Fascist party.[3]

The influence and electoral strength of the MSI have fluctuated according to the fortunes of the right wing of the Christian Democratic party. During the collapse of the centrist coalition in 1953, for example, and the period of conflict within the center-left coalition in 1972, the DC experienced sizable losses of votes to the far right. The MSI has also been able to influence the DC in moments of acute discord among the governmental parties by offering its votes in Parliament in support of Christian Democratic proposals. MSI support was particularly important in the governments headed by Giovanni Pella (1953–1954), Adone Zoli (1957–1958), Antonio Segni (1959–1960), and Giuseppe Tambroni (1960). Under this last, the MSI reached the zenith of its parliamentary power; the Tambroni government was actually constituted with the explicit support of the neo-Fascists. However, this center-right experiment generated social unrest throughout the country, and Tambroni was forced to resign after only four months.[4] In the late 1960s and early 1970s the MSI became increasingly identified with the strategy of tension, a program of sporadic attempts to create conditions of disorder and promote a military takeover. The bombings and attempted coups that took place between 1969 and 1975 were inspired by a superficial analysis of sociopolitical conditions in Italy, which in reality were not favorable to a rightist coup.[5]

In 1972 under the leadership of Giorgio Almirante the MSI tried to project a more respectable image by absorbing the Monarchist party (PDIUM) and rebaptizing itself the Italian Social Movement-National Right (MSI-DN). This new formation did much better in the 1972 elections than had the neo-Fascists and Monarchists running separately in 1968, but the 8.7 percent it won was still well

---

[3] For a history of the MSI and the backgrounds of the leaders, see Petra Rosenbaum, *Il Nuovo Fascismo: Da Salò ad Almirante, Storia del MSI* [The new fascism: from Salò to Almirante, history of the MSI] (Milan: Feltrinelli Editore, 1975), and Pier Giuseppe Murgia, *Il vento del nord* [The wind from the north] (Milan: Sugar Editore, 1975), pp. 295-331.

[4] For a detailed account of the Tambroni experiment, see Robert K. Nilsson, "Italy's Opening to the Right: The Tambroni Experiment of 1960" (Ph.D. diss., Columbia University, 1964), and Pier Giuseppe Murgia, *Il luglio 1960* [July 1960] (Milan: Sugar Editore, 1968).

[5] Rosenbaum, *Il Nuovo Fascismo*, pp. 230-242. Between 1969 and 1975 there were a number of bombings that were initially attributed to anarchists and leftists but which were later revealed to have been carried out by right-wing sympathizers in an attempt to create a climate of uncertainty and disorder that could justify the staging of a military coup along the lines of the Greek colonels' coup of 1967.

under the 12.7 percent of the vote the two separate parties had attracted in 1953.

In 1976 the MSI-DN was still trying to shake its hard-line right-wing image and present itself as a more moderate rightist party that could attract the support and participation of former Christian Democrats and Liberals for its program of keeping the Communists out of power. The MSI-DN argued that it was the only true bulwark against the advance of communism in Italy. According to the electoral propaganda of the MSI-DN the parties of the center (the DC, the PSDI, the PRI, and the PLI) took an anti-Communist stance for electoral purposes but were quite capable of making deals with the left after the elections in order to preserve their own power. The MSI-DN campaign against the "traitors" of Italian anticommunism was especially virulent in its attacks on the DC. In an editorial that appeared in the MSI-DN newspaper *Secolo d'Italia* on May 29, 1976, Cesare Montavani denounced the DC for wooing the anti-Communist vote and then, once elected, substituting exchange for confrontation, searching for a meeting of minds. This policy, the editorialist said, had done nothing but increase the electoral strength and political weight of communism in Italy.[6]

It was clear to the MSI-DN leadership that to increase its votes the party would have to convince traditional Catholic voters that the only alternative capable of blocking further advances of the Communist party in Italian affairs was the radical right. To this end, the MSI-DN in 1976 launched the idea of a renewal of the right through the formation of a new political organization, *Costituente di Destra*, the constitution of the right, which could serve as a front organization for the neo-Fascists. Leadership positions in the movement were assigned to former DC members of Parliament Agostino Greggi and Enzo Giacchero. In the first television broadcast for the MSI-DN electoral campaign, Greggi explained his reasons for joining Almirante's party and abandoning the DC:

(1) Because I saw that the DC of the center-left was no longer fighting but giving in . . ., and by giving in it betrayed, one by one, my ideals and those of Luigi Sturzo [founder in 1919 of the first Italian Catholic political party, the Italian Popular party, which was later outlawed by Mussolini] and Alcide De Gasperi [leader of the DC from 1943 to 1954].

---

[6] Cesare Montavani, "Onesti voti" [Honest votes], *Secolo d'Italia*, May 29, 1976, p. 1.

(2) Because I saw that the center-left was bringing Italy toward disaster, and I didn't want, and couldn't be in any way associated with, responsibility for this disaster.

(3) Because at this point the DC under Moro and Zaccagnini has become the antithesis, the opposite, of the DC of Sturzo and De Gasperi.

(4) Because by now we need other alternatives, formulas, new programs, new alliances. The Constitution of the Right of which I am the national secretary is the alternative, is the new program, is the new alliance. . . .[7]

The rightist offensive against the DC and the expectation that the MSI-DN would improve on its 1972 result by four percentage points were brutally disrupted on May 28, 1976, when a neo-Fascist member of Parliament, Sandro Saccucci, was implicated in the shooting death of a PCI member and the wounding of another leftist sympathizer. The shooting took place after an MSI-DN political rally in a small town, Sezze Romano, to the south of Rome. Saccucci had gone to the rally armed and accompanied by similarly armed neo-Nazi sympathizers. In one blow, the incident neutralized all that the MSI-DN had done to present a respectable image and to convince the public that the new right-wing party had excluded hotheads and outright Nazi-Fascists. For the rest of the campaign the MSI-DN had to defend itself from the attacks of all of the other parties and, even more damaging, of all of the independent press of the nation. The party leadership attempted to cut its losses by expelling Saccucci from the MSI-DN's party organization and parliamentary group in the Chamber, but the damage had already been done.

In subsequent debates and interviews the leadership, including Party Secretary Almirante, attempted to regain the initiative by accusing the DC of having framed the MSI-DN by planting an official of the Italian intelligence service (SID) in the group accompanying Saccucci when the shooting occurred; it was suggested that the whole incident had been orchestrated by the government to block the shift of DC votes to the right. After the shootings it became difficult for the MSI-DN to hold political rallies anywhere in Italy; nobody wanted to come to the aid of the neo-Fascists. Almirante hammered away at the point that only he could prevent the radical right from taking to the streets and that he was wise enough to see the trap

---

[7] Agostino Greggi, "La DC di Moro e Zaccagnini non è quella di De Gasperi" [The DC of Moro and Zaccagnini is not the DC of De Gasperi], *Secolo d'Italia*, May 27, 1976, p. 2. This article is a transcription of the MSI-DN broadcast that appeared on television on May 26, 1976. Author's translation.

that violence held for the right as a whole. "I am committed with all of my conscience and will," Almirante wrote, "to preventing the extremism of the right from facilitating the subversive maneuvers of the left. It would be the greatest folly for supporters of the right in Italy—any of them—to maintain that only a violent right can stop the left."[8] Despite these and other attempts to reassure the public that Saccucci was not representative of the MSI-DN or its parliamentary leaders, the neo-Fascists faced the electorate on June 20 with a blotted reputation and very little hope of success.

The Liberals. The need to nominate new, more socially minded leaders was felt by all of the parties in 1976, including the Liberals. Prior to the elections, the Liberals chose a new party secretary, Valerio Zanone, and decided to cultivate the mildly reformist image that it had lost in 1954. Gone were the strident attacks against the center-left experience and the calls for reform of the social, economic, and political structures of the Italian Republic that had been the PLI's principal appeals from the mid-1950s to the mid-1970s.

The Liberals had enjoyed an almost absolute control of power from the unification of the Italian state in 1860 to the advent of fascism in 1922. From the beginning the Liberal party was a loose association of notables principally characterized by a strong lay view of society but somewhat less certain of how far social and economic reforms had to go to create a modern nation-state.[9] As a result, they championed political and institutional reforms that created a strong centralized national government dedicated to eradicating the Church's long established control of social institutions.

The Liberals emerged from the Fascist period with far fewer voters than before and strong rivals on the left for the lay vote. After a brief period of collaboration with the other anti-Fascist parties, the Liberal party became increasingly oriented toward an all-out defense of the market economy and dropped its stress on lay social issues. As a result, the PLI found itself one of the chief opponents of the structural reforms advocated by the Communists and Socialists. Basic to the success of the PLI's anti-leftist policy was the continuation of the centrist formula. The PLI, unlike the DC, never wavered in its support of centrism, and it quickly assumed the political initiative to

---

[8] Giorgio Almirante, "L'estremismo giova ai nemici della Destra" [Extremism favors the enemies of the right], *Secolo d'Italia*, June 1, 1976, p. 3.
[9] The early history of the Italian state is covered thoroughly in Dennis Mack Smith, *Italy* (Ann Arbor, Mich.: University of Michigan Press, 1969).

stop the other parties of the center from casting their lot with the Socialists through the formation of a center-left coalition. In 1954 Giovanni Malagodi was elected secretary of the party on a platform that rejected reformism and the idea that an alternative on the left could be found to the current centrist formula. Malagodi's virulent opposition to social and economic reforms and the center-left coalition brought the PLI to 7 percent of the vote in the 1963 elections (double its 1958 vote), but the party was unable to capitalize on its success. In 1968 the DC won back the support it had lost to the Liberals, and the Liberals were left stranded on the right in the company of the MSI.

Under Malagodi the PLI escaped from its political isolation for two brief moments: (1) in 1972–1973 during the first Andreotti government, which was based on a new version of the centrist formula, and (2) in 1974 during the referendum campaign, when the Liberals joined forces with the other lay parties to combat the anti-divorce positions of the Christian Democrats and neo-Fascists. However, the impetus generated by the pro-divorce campaign was not followed up by an attempt to refurbish the party's image and organization. In retrospect, what happened to the PLI's voting base in the 1975 elections was inevitable: the only political solution offered by the Liberals was a centrist coalition that did not have the necessary popular support to rule. Their long absence from government had deprived the Liberals of the positions of influence that had long compensated for their lack of a viable party organization. In 1976 the alternatives before the PLI were to drastically change course or to face extinction.

Under Zanone the PLI attempted to escape from its ideological isolation and reestablish its political contacts with the other lay parties by presenting common candidates where possible and by pressing its claim to being the first and only authentic liberal, democratic force in the political system. This point was forcefully made by Zanone in the televised press conference reserved for the PLI on June 9, 1976.[10] Zanone discussed the new role of the PLI in occupying the political space between the twin hegemonies of the DC and PCI. The lay parties, he said, must find a third road:

---

[10] During the 1976 electoral campaign the Italian state television network, RAI-TV, set aside prime evening time to broadcast individual hour-long press conferences with spokesmen for each of the parties represented in Parliament. The Radicals and Demoproletarians conducted a vigorous fight to be included in the series of broadcasts, and succeeded.

The autonomous position of our party is, in the last analysis, the position from which operate the democratic liberal forces in all of the democratic representative systems in Europe. We believe that only from this position can we conduct a vigorous attack on the two hegemonic powers in our country that are responsible for the great political defects of Italy—that is, the Christian Democratic hegemony, which is declining, and the Communist hegemony, which could succeed it. This is our political location, and this is the fundamental theme upon which we are conducting our electoral campaign, the initiative of the democratic alliance between the Liberals, the Republicans, and the Social Democrats; this is the base of our program and the foundation of our expectations for June 20—the hope that our moderate democratic position can be reenforced by these elections.[11]

In describing the PLI's newly found vocation of democratic moderation between the DC and the PCI, Zanone readily admitted that the PLI's past advocacy of the centrist formula had traditionally relegated it to a position of subordination to the DC. Now was the time to formulate an autonomous position for the PLI and for the other two lay parties in order to put to rest their past subordination to the DC and the possibility that in the future they would become equally subjugated by the PCI.

However, if Zanone had succeeded in bringing the PLI from a position right of the DC to a position left of it, between the DC and the PCI, it was also true that this area had already been occupied by other parties. In constituencies where there was no common centrist candidate, the PLI had to compete with the PRI and the PSDI for support from a single voting base. In contrast to the Republican and Social Democratic leadership, the PLI leaders rejected the possibility of collaborating with the PCI in any national coalition, but they made it clear that the PLI would equally reject the possibility of working together with the MSI-DN in a rightist coalition. The new liberalism, Zanone noted, had been born in the postwar period from a victorious struggle against fascism; the PLI would take no part in resurrecting what he called a "moral disease that has been eradicated" from the body politic.[12] Nevertheless, the problem remained of making sure that the conservative elements that had sustained the PLI's struggles against the center-left would be convinced by the new

---

[11] Valerio Zanone, "Conferenza Stampa del PLI" [PLI press conference], *Tribuna Elettorale, 1976* [1976 electoral forum], June 9, 1976, mimeographed (Rome: RAI-TV, June 9, 1976), p. A/9.

[12] Ibid., p. C/16.

leadership's arguments and would follow the party to the left; otherwise, the PLI would have to face another cut in its votes and hope that enough could be salvaged to provide the basis for a regrouping of the party in the coming years.

The Republicans. In contrast to the Liberals, the Republican party expected to make major gains in the 1976 elections. Much of the Republican strategy was based on the PRI's ability to build upon its positive showing in the 1975 administrative elections where it had made major inroads into the electoral bases of the other centrist parties, including the DC. The 3.2 percent of the vote that the PRI had won in 1975 held forth the promise that the party might finally emerge from its traditional role as the mini party of the Italian political system. To many political observers the possibility that the PRI would attract over 5 percent of the vote seemed one of the sure bets of the 1976 elections.

The Republicans have always been the smallest of the small parties in the Italian postwar political system. Much of their support in the past has come from well-defined but restricted geographical areas (for example, the provinces of Ravenna and Forlì in the North) and from socioeconomic groups that are now shrinking (like the small independent farmers). The PRI had historically based much of its political program on the radical lay philosophy of Giuseppe Mazzini, the prophet of Italian unification, and had made its first inroads into the social fabric of Italy through the organization of production cooperatives and mutual aid societies.[13] During the Fascist period, republicanism was severely repressed, but it nevertheless served as a major ideological component in the formation of one of the foremost anti-Fascist groups, Giustizia e Libertà (Justice and Liberty) which became the Action party in 1943.[14] After the dissolution of the Action party on the heels of the 1946 elections, many of its most prominent leaders—for example, Ferruccio Parri (national leader of the Armed Resistance partisan forces that fought against the German occupation) and Ugo La Malfa—became leading figures in the Republican party. La Malfa in particular has had a major role

---

[13] See Giuseppe Mazzini, *The Duties of Man and Other Essays* (New York: E. P. Dutton, 1966), and Maurice F. Neufeld, *Italy: School for Awakening Countries* (Ithaca, N.Y.: Cornell University Press, 1961), for discussions of the theoretical background and experiences of the Republican cooperative movement.

[14] See Charles F. Delzell, *Mussolini's Enemies: The Italian Anti-Fascist Resistance* (Princeton, N.J.: Princeton University Press, 1961) for a full discussion of the various branches of the anti-Fascist movement in Italy.

in transforming the party program in accordance with his own technocratic approach to economic problems.

In 1976 the Republican campaign stressed the deflationary economic measures that La Malfa had attempted to implement under the last DC-PRI government headed by Aldo Moro. The PRI placed the blame for the country's economic ills on the PCI and the PSI, which had tried to placate their mass bases with the adoption of irresponsible economic programs: "the mass parties have been responsible for the parasitism, nonproductivity, and high costs that characterize our system of public enterprise," La Malfa said.[15] To combat Italy's financial and economic difficulties, the PRI proposed: (1) to limit public expenditures, (2) to enforce a rigid incomes policy at all levels, (3) to restructure the executive branch of government by the creation of a vice-prime minister for economic affairs with the power to coordinate government economic policies, and (4) to institutionalize the role of all social forces by a social compact between government and labor unions along the English model that would limit the conflicts between trade union demands and government economic policies.[16]

The question remained, however, of where the PRI would find the necessary political consensus to implement such a stringent economic program. In this regard the PRI's position vis-à-vis the Communists was less rigid than that of the Liberals. La Malfa refused to exclude categorically the possibility of collaboration with the PCI. The Republicans would not take part in any government of the left that took the form of a popular front—a government with the PCI to the exclusion of the DC—but they would consider the possibility of participating in a government that was based on the collaboration of the two major parties if certain conditions could be guaranteed. The first condition was the maintenance of the Western alliance, the second a social compact between the government and the trade unions.[17]

Not all of the PRI was in accord with this attempt by La Malfa to walk the tightrope between the DC and the PCI. Certain party

---

[15] Ugo La Malfa, "Un richiamo alla ragione e al senso critica della realtà" [A call for reason and a critical attitude toward reality], *La Voce Repubblicana*, June 5, 1975, p. 1.

[16] The social compact that the Republicans were pushing as an essential element in any governmental economic program would have required the government to sit down with the unions to agree on price and wage scales. The wage scales thus determined would govern all negotiations between workers and employees, and prices would not be allowed to rise beyond the agreed level.

[17] Oddo Biasini, "Essenziale per il governo del paese il ruolo del partito repubblicano" [The role of the Republican party is essential to the governing of the country], *La Voce Repubblicana*, June 16, 1976, p. 1.

leaders in Milan and Turin believed that the PRI should not exclude a priori the possibility of participating in a popular front government. Others—foremost among them Pietro Bucalossi, former minister for public works in the Moro-La Malfa government—maintained that it was a mistake not to exclude from the beginning any cooperation with the PCI. A strong stand against collaborating with the Communists, these Republicans believed, would attract ever growing numbers of middle-class voters who had become suspicious of the economic policies of the DC and who, in the last analysis, had been responsible for the advances made by the PRI in the 1975 elections. Any other policy would inevitably force these moderate voters back into the DC, which was strenuously attempting to present itself as the only credible and convinced opponent of the PCI. As the campaign progressed, it became increasingly difficult for the PRI to maintain its independent stance and propose itself as a serious alternative to the frontal collision of the two major parties.

The Social Democrats. The impending clash between the PCI and the DC and the possibility that the PCI would become the majority party served to reduce the political room for maneuver of the minor parties between the two major blocs. One of the parties most directly affected by this turn of events was the Social Democratic party, which in the last five years had adopted right-wing policy stands despite its leftist tradition. The PSDI had traditionally found support for its reformist policies among skilled workers, but after the split with the Socialists in 1968, the PSDI began openly to court moderate middle-class voters with a bitter campaign against the reformist policies adopted by the PSI and the PCI. With this shift in position the PSDI made major electoral gains. In 1970 the PSDI received 7 percent of the vote, which seemed to provide ample legitimacy for its new vocation as a moderate party to the right of the DC. Things began to return to normal in 1972 when the party fell to its pre-1970 levels with 5.1 percent. The 1975 regional elections confirmed the party's relative stability in percentage terms, but since the PSDI has always done better in local than in national elections, the 1975 result was the first warning that hard times lay ahead. Analyses of the 1975 elections suggested that the PSDI had lost some votes to the PSI, its arch rival for the past six years.[18]

The love-hate relationship between the PSDI and the PSI has

---

[18] Robert Leonardi and Gianfranco Pasquino, "Le elezioni in Emilia-Romagna" [The elections in Emilia-Romagna], Il Mulino, vol. 24 (July-August 1975), pp. 559-582.

historical roots in the struggles between the reformist and radical wings of the Italian Socialist movement.[19] For most of the postwar period the Social Democrats and Socialists have existed as two separate parties, but there have been important groups in both parties that have long nurtured the dream of Socialist unity. The feat was finally achieved in 1967 as one of the basic requirements of the center-left experience.[20] Unity was short-lived. In 1969 the two parties split again over the emphasis that should be placed on basic socio-economic reforms and the nature of the party organization. The leader of the post-1969 Social Democratic party was Mario Tanassi, the chief disciple of Giuseppe Saragat who had founded the PSDI in 1947 and had served as president of the Republic between 1964 and 1971.[21] Tanassi's moderate approach to Italian politics and lackluster performance as defense minister proved very costly to the party in the 1976 elections.

Between the 1975 and 1976 elections the PSDI seemed to be coming apart at the seams. The sudden explosion of the Lockheed scandal in early 1976 cast a heavy shadow of suspicion over former Defense Minister Tanassi, who was accused of having personally taken money from the American corporation before agreeing to sign the final purchase order for nineteen C130 Hercules transport planes for the Italian air force. The PSDI's 1976 party congress in Florence was more noteworthy for name calling and shoving matches between rival factions than for the level and content of the political debate. After the congress Giuseppe Saragat had to be asked to reassume the secretaryship of the party in an attempt to save it from total disintegration. The PSDI's record of policy shifts, opportunism, and scandal left the party militants in open revolt. Thus, the 1976 campaign underlined the need for a redefinition and reorganization of the party in a moment of acute crisis.

It was difficult for the PSDI to present a reassuring image to the electorate. One of the first responses of the party organization was to completely drop any mention of Mario Tanassi in the electoral campaign: he effectively became a nonperson for the party press. No mention of Tanassi's electoral activities, speeches, or candidacy was carried in the party newspaper, *L'Umanità*, in the entire three

---

[19] The best treatment of the early history of Italian socialism is Richard Hostetter, *The Italian Socialist Movement* (Princeton, N.J.: Van Nostrand, 1958).

[20] For a complete history of the center-left experience, see Giuseppe Tamburrano, *Storia e cronaca del centro sinistra* [History and events of the center-left] (Milan: Feltrinelli Editore, 1971).

[21] See Ugo Indrio, *La presidenza Saragat* [The Saragat presidency] (Milan: Arnoldo Mondadori Editore, 1971).

weeks prior to the election despite the fact that Tanassi led the PSDI's list of candidates in the Rome electoral district. The PSDI attempted to minimize the negative effects of the Lockheed scandal by ignoring it and by counterbalancing the notoriety of Mario Tanassi with the heroic reputation of Giuseppe Saragat, one of the fathers of Italian socialism and a dedicated anti-Fascist.[22]

If the Saragat cult of personality was the most conspicuous feature of the PSDI campaign, its guiding purpose was to reestablish the party's credentials as a viable force of the Italian left and bring to an end its subjugation to the DC. The PSDI joined the Liberals and Republicans in the campaign against the hegemonic pretentions of the DC toward its minor allies. One of the more interesting changes brought to bear on Social Democratic policy making by the electoral campaign was the soft line taken by Saragat and other PSDI leaders toward the Communist party. In 1976 the PSDI dropped its ideological opposition to the PCI and accepted the possibility of cooperating with the Communists in government coalitions at the local level but not at the national level. Saragat made it clear in his television presentation on June 10, 1976, that he did not consider a popular front government a viable alternative in the present crisis. He feared that the PCI, once in power, would not be able to resist the attraction of the Soviet Union. However, he had faith in the good intentions of many of the Communist leaders, and in time, he believed, the problem of the international orientation of the PCI could be resolved.[23]

The only alternative that seemed available to Saragat was a new center-left coalition, not in its traditional form but in a form that would see the power of the DC balanced by that of the lay parties—the PSDI, the PSI, and the PRI. The era of the need to accept a Christian Democratic hegemony over governmental coalitions had come to an end. Now it was time to share power in a rational way so as to face the pressing needs of the country. Uppermost in the minds of the Social Democrats was the need to increase the efficiency of the state and push forward a policy of economic planning. "But to launch an economic upturn," wrote one PSDI leader, "it is not enough to have the means necessary to finance it: we need to make the government efficient again and resume with greater conviction and seriousness a policy of planning. The efficiency of the state can

---

[22] See *L'Umanità*, especially issues of June 8 and 19, 1976.

[23] Giuseppe Saragat, "Conferenza Stampa del PSDI" [PSDI press conference], *Tribuna Elettorale, 1976*, mimeographed (Rome: RAI-TV, June 10, 1976), p. B/4.

245

be reestablished by eliminating useless agencies from the bureaucracy and moving public employees to sectors that are short of personnel."[24]

Before such a policy could be implemented, the DC would have to lose the elections and the PSDI and PSI would have to emerge strengthened in a political context that pointed neither to a strong leftist nor to a rightist direction. Such a prospect was difficult to imagine given the political forces at work. In particular, both the PSI and the PCI were being hounded by two new parties on the left: the Radicals and the Demoproletarians.

The Radicals. In the two years between the referendum on divorce and the 1976 elections a new party, the Radicals, had built up a reputation as the indefatigable champions of radical solutions to difficult legal and social problems that perplexed the nation—abortion, women's rights, opposition to compulsory military service, and so on. The 1976 parliamentary elections would measure their political and organizational strength. In 1975 the Radicals had supported the Socialist party, of which they felt themselves to be the libertarian wing, and they probably contributed significantly to the increase in Socialist votes in the regional elections. The attempt to reach an accord with the PSI for the new parliamentary elections, however, was foiled by the PSI's unwillingness to give the Radicals free rein in the campaign. Thus, the Radicals presented an independent list of candidates in direct competition with the Socialists and all of the other parties of the Italian left. Marco Pannella, the charismatic leader of the Radicals, described the 1976 election as a popular referendum on the reforms for which the PR had crusaded in the 1970s.[25]

The political program of the Radical party was based on a militant attack on the repressive nature of the Italian state apparatus and the influence enjoyed by the Catholic Church in domestic affairs. Many of the old anticlerical positions of the left that had been laid to rest by the PSI and PCI in their attempts to court the Catholic voter were revived by the PR. Nevertheless, the Radicals saw their cause as constituting an integral part of the general movement to the left in the country and proposed in their political program a resolution of the current crisis by a government of the left that would

---

[24] Stefano Sandri, "Le nostre proposte per la crisi economica" [Our proposals for the economic crisis], *L'Umanità*, June 4, 1976, p. 4.

[25] Marco Pannella, "Conferenza Stampa del Partito Radicale" [Radical party press conference], *Tribuna Elettorale, 1976*, mimeographed (Rome: RAI-TV, June 7, 1976), p. A/2.

include all of the Marxist-oriented forces: the DP, the PCI, the PSI, and the PR. As a consequence, the question surfaced many times during the campaign whether the Radicals could maintain their independence and liberty of action within the confines of a leftist coalition in which the PCI would have the lion's share of the popular support. Pannella replied that if the Radicals were capable of saying no to the present Christian Democratic authoritarian regime they could say no to a government dominated by the Communists.

In contrast to the other political forces, the Radicals did not spare either their opponents or their future allies from bitter attacks. On television Pannella accused the Republicans, the Social Democrats, and the Liberals of outright opportunism before and after the 1975 elections:

> But everyone in Italy would agree that no guarantee of autonomy and liberty under a government of the left will come from the La Malfas, the Republicans, the Social Democrats, the Liberals, or from the people who after June 15 [1975] began to flock around the PCI and the Radicals in all of the regions—people who, having served the DC for thirty years, were suddenly ready to serve the left.[26]

In a heated reply to a journalist from L'Umanità, Pannella accused the PSDI and the other lay parties of blindness and insensitivity toward the opposition in their willingness to exercise political power in harmony with the DC. He attacked the PSDI for having accepted the clientelistic and antidemocratic rules for the conduct of politics laid down by the DC over the past thirty years. As a result of these policies, new parties had been denied time or exposure in the government-controlled television and radio networks, and it had only been through the personal sacrifices and bitter struggle of the Radical leaders, Pannella said, that a semblance of democratic behavior and tolerance for the opposition had been introduced into the public mass media. However, the most serious mistake of the PSDI had been to sell out its Social Democratic ideals for "petty governmental clientelism." [27] In turn, Pannella accused the parties of the left, especially the Communists and the Demoproletarians, of intolerance and physical violence against PR activists who were attempting to awaken the nation's conscience over social and legal injustice.

It is undeniable that the Radicals were responsible for many innovations in the 1976 campaign. The Radical political rallies had

---

26 Ibid., p. B/2.
27 Ibid., p. B/5.

more the atmosphere of cultural events than of campaign meetings, and the Radicals introduced into their political speeches the jargon of the Italian youth culture. They were giving voice to social frustrations that had long been overshadowed by the dialectic of class conflict that has historically dominated political debate in Italy. What the Radicals offered to the Italian voter in 1976 was the chance to introduce a new type of political dialogue and style within the confines of the traditional parliamentary system.

Proletarian Democracy. Proletarian Democracy represented a composite group of extraparliamentary leftist movements and parties that traced their origins to the events of the hot autumn of 1969, their ideological inspiration to Mao's Cultural Revolution. The first edition of the DP was formed on a limited basis in the 1975 regional elections through the coordination of electoral lists and strategies by the group known as Proletarian Vanguard (AO) and the Democratic party of Proletarian Unity (PDUP), itself an amalgamation of the former *Manifesto* group and remnants of the old PSIUP led by Vittorio Foa. The new party judiciously selected ten regions in which to run its candidates and succeeded in electing six representatives to regional councils. The expectation for the 1976 election was an increase from the 1.2 percent the extraparliamentary alliance had polled in 1975 to 3 percent through the addition of two other far-leftist groups, the Workers' Movement for Socialism (MLS) and Continuous Struggle (LC). With 3 percent of the vote, the DP expected to tip the balance of the 1976 electoral scale in favor of a leftist government that would finally relegate the DC to the opposition.

It was the conviction of the Demoproletarians that only a government involving all of the leftist parties could deal with Italy's concrete problems:

> Only a government of the left, united behind a long-range program, can effectively take even the immediate steps that can launch . . . a new mechanism for the development of the society and the state; and only a government of the left that is committed to change can create in the country the hope and, thereby, the moral and social mobilization without which one cannot escape from a crisis such as this.[28]

Despite constant disagreements with the PSI and PCI leadership on goals and tactics, the DP felt that only the two large parties of the

---

[28] Lucio Magri, "Conferenza Stampa di Democrazia Proletaria" [The press conference of the Proletarian Democracy], *Tribuna Elettorale, 1976*, mimeographed (Rome: RAI-TV), p. A/3. Carried by *Il Manifesto*, June 6, 1976, p. 5.

left could bring about the creation of a leftist government. If a leftist government became statistically possible—that is, the left as a whole gained over 50 percent of the vote and seats in Parliament—the Socialist and Communist leaders would have no other choice than to go along with the groundswell of sentiment in favor of a leftist coalition that would inevitably sweep the country. A government of the left was the only way to defeat the DC and punish it for its long career of corruption and mismanagement of power.[29] Once in power the left would have to implement an economic program based on the strict enforcement of the tax system, the reduction of superfluous consumption, the rationing of certain goods, such as gasoline and meat, and the freezing of incomes above a certain minimum.

This stringent economic program, according to the DP, had to be coupled with a series of political measures that would organically link Parliament with numerous initiatives at the local level to promote popular participation in the management of community affairs. As Lucio Magri, party secretary of the PDUP, put it:

> The new goal of democracy is to ask people not only to vote every five years but also to participate in an organized way, as workers, residents, women, students, in concrete political decisions, from urban planning to the direction of investments, from the administration of justice to the running of schools.[30]

In launching this program to the left of the PCI, the DP hoped to emerge from its isolation in the political system. If the shift to the left registered by the Italian electorate in 1975 continued but still favored disproportionately the moderation of the PCI, the far left would remain in its ghetto and eventually would be smothered by the hegemony of the Communists. The goal of the DP in the 1976 election was, therefore, to radicalize the campaign to such an extent that the dissatisfied voters of the left could be convinced to give their support to the authentic revolutionary commitment of the Demoproletarians.

Election Results and Future Prospects

The 1976 elections had mixed results for the minor parties of the left and center: all succeeded in having candidates elected to Parliament

---

[29] Luigi Pintor, "Ma dove é il nemico?" [But where is the enemy?], *Il Manifesto*, May 25, 1976, p. 1.
[30] Magri, "Conferenza Stampa," p. C/4.

but none won as many seats as it had expected. Moreover, the DC recuperated its 1975 loss at the expense of its centrist allies, and the PCI made further gains at the expense of all the other groups on the left. Excluding the Radicals, who were running for the first time, two of the small parties—the DP and the PRI—made better showings than in 1972, but only the Demoproletarians did better than in the administrative elections of 1975. All of the rest suffered substantial setbacks: the Social Democrats and neo-Fascists lost approximately one-third and the Liberals close to two-thirds of their 1972 electoral bases. Nevertheless, all succeeded in inserting themselves into the institutionalized political process for the next five years—partly because of the vagaries of the electoral system.

Geographical Analysis of the Vote. The Liberals entered the Chamber on the basis of their turnout in the First Electoral District, comprising the provinces of Turin, Novara, and Vercelli in the northwestern part of the country; the Demoproletarians in the Fourth Electoral District (Milan and Pavia); and the Radicals in the Nineteenth Electoral District (Rome, Viterbo, Latina, and Frosinone). What is immediately striking is that the three smallest parties made their way into the Chamber through the support they received in the three largest cities (Turin, Milan, and Rome) in the northern and central parts of the nation. These three large metropolitan areas proved to be the salvation of the three mini parties. But urban centers were also the scene of major losses for three of the six minor parties (the MSI-DN, the PSDI, and the PLI).

This point is illustrated in Table 7–3, where a distinction is drawn between provincial capitals, the poles around which most urban growth has occurred, and the "periphery," the territory outside the provincial capitals, which is usually characterized by smaller cities. The table shows the relative importance of the small-party vote in these two areas for all of Italy in the 1972 and 1976 elections. In 1972, with the exception of the Social Democrats and *Il Manifesto*, all of the small parties won approximately twice as many votes in the provincial capitals as they won in the periphery: for the MSI-DN, 12.7 versus 6.5 percent; for the PLI, 5.8 versus 2.8 percent; and for the Republicans, 4.0 versus 2.2 percent. In 1976 the same three parties suffered losses across the board, but their losses were slightly smaller in the periphery than in the capitals. For example, the neo-Fascists lost 35 percent of their 1972 voting base in the provincial capitals but only 23 percent in the periphery; the Liberals suffered a 72 percent cut in the capitals and 60 percent in the periph-

Table 7–3

DISTRIBUTION OF THE SMALL-PARTY VOTE BETWEEN THE PROVINCIAL CAPITALS AND THE PERIPHERY, 1972–76

(in percentages)

Election	MSI-DN	PLI	PRI	PSDI	PR	DP[a]
Provincial capitals						
1976	8.3	1.7	4.3	3.2	1.8	1.7
1972	12.7	5.8	4.0	5.5	—	0.7
Periphery						
1976	5.0	1.1	2.5	3.4	0.7	1.4
1972	6.5	2.8	2.2	5.0	—	0.6

[a] In 1972, *Il Manifesto.*

Note: The provincial capitals are the most urbanized areas in the country; the periphery includes the territory outside the capitals, including both smaller cities and rural areas.

Source: Calculated from Ufficio Elettorale del PCI, *Elezioni Politiche 20 giugno 1976,* pp. 2 and 158.

ery; and the Social Democrats 42 percent in the capitals and 32 percent in the periphery. Thus, in all cases the largest cuts into the small-party vote occurred in the capital cities.

An attempt to distinguish in more detail between various types of peripheries was made for Emilia-Romagna, a region which presents political characteristics different from those of the nation as a whole but which in many cases has manifested trends that later became the national norm.[31] In Table 7–4 we can see that in Emilia-Romagna the PSDI and the MSI-DN had their heaviest losses in the capital cities and did much better in all types of peripheral areas—plains, hills, and mountains. However, it was in the mountain areas, characterized by the most remote and smallest urban concentrations, that they lost the fewest votes, while in the plains their losses were similar to those suffered in the provincial capitals. Thus, voters who had access to numerous and varied sources of information and lived in relatively complex political environments abandoned the PSDI, the PLI, and the MSI-DN more readily than voters living in comparatively homogeneous, isolated communities. The loss of votes, on

---

[31] See Robert Leonardi and Gianfranco Pasquino, "Il 20 giugno in Emilia-Romagna e a Bologna" [June 20 in Emilia-Romagna and Bologna], *Il Mulino,* vol. 25 (July-August 1976), especially pp. 501-502.

Table 7–4
ANALYSIS OF PSDI, PLI, AND MSI-DN VOTE IN
EMILIA-ROMAGNA, 1976

Geographic Area	Percentage of 1972 Voting Base Retained in 1976 (1972 vote = 100 percent)		
	PSDI	PLI	MSI-DN
Provincial capitals	61	25	74
Cities in plains	69	24	77
Cities in hill areas	69	27	87
Cities in mountain areas	70	34	86
Total, Emilia-Romagna	67	26	74
Italy	67	34	70

Source: Calculated from Robert Leonardi and Gianfranco Pasquino, "Il 20 giugno in Emilia-Romagna e a Bologna" [June 20 (1976) in Emilia-Romagna and Bologna], *Il Mulino*, vol. 25 (July-August 1976), p. 510.

the other hand, did not vary from one location to another according to the strength of the DC.[32]

It is not possible to analyze trends in the Radical vote since 1976 was the PR's first election, but it is significant that in 1976 the Radicals received twice as many votes in the provincial capitals as in the periphery. In the capitals, the PR vote was considerably higher in middle and upper-class neighborhoods than elsewhere.[33]

Surprisingly, the results for the DP were similar: the DP vote was higher in the provincial capitals than in outlying areas, and the urban votes did not come predominantly from the working class. In a number of cities in the North, the DP did better in middle-class neighborhoods than in working-class ones, and it is a good bet that these middle-class votes were predominantly from students and intellectuals. Working-class votes apparently continued to flow to the PCI rather than its leftist rivals.

Another geographical dimension of the vote—the highly important north-center-south distinction, which corresponds roughly to a socioeconomic breakdown—sheds more light on the 1976 result. Table 7–5 reveals that the MSI-DN has been much stronger in the south than in the center or north and shows the PLI to be a dis-

[32] See the discussion of the DC increase in votes in Arturo Parisi and Gianfranco Pasquino, "20 giugno: struttura politica e comportamenti elettorali" [June 20: political structure and electoral behavior], *Il Mulino*, vol. 25 (May-June 1976), pp. 368-370.

[33] Leonardi and Pasquino, "Il 20 giugno," pp. 525-526.

Table 7–5

SMALL-PARTY VOTE IN THE NORTH, CENTER, AND SOUTH, 1972 AND 1976

Geographic Division	MSI-DN	PLI	PRI	PSDI	PR	DP[a]
1972						
North	5.2	5.0	3.1	6.0	—	0.6
Center	9.4	3.0	3.1	4.9	—	0.9
South	13.7	2.6	2.4	4.0	—	0.6
1976						
North	3.7	1.6	3.6	3.8	1.2	1.7
Center	6.4	0.8	3.1	2.8	1.2	1.3
South	9.6	1.2	2.4	3.1	0.7	1.3

[a] In 1972, *Il Manifesto*.

Source: Calculated from Ufficio Elettorale del PCI, *Elezioni Politiche 20 giugno 1976*, pp. 4-6.

tinctly northern party. Comparing the losses since 1972 suffered by each party in 1976, one discovers that the MSI-DN lost approximately 30 percent of its vote in all regions of the country. Similarly, the PLI lost two-thirds of its electorate in all three areas. The situation was slightly different for the other small parties. First, the PSDI lost less heavily in the south than it did in the center and north. Second, a good part of the PRI increase can be attributed to the party's greater attraction for northern voters. Third, the Radicals demonstrated a strong ability to draw votes in the center and north while the Demoproletarians enjoyed a much larger share of the vote in the north than in the center or south.

Tables 7–3, 7–4, and 7–5 suggest a number of points. It is clear that in 1976 the MSI-DN was afflicted by a general loss of voter support throughout the country. When asked to explain the nature of this dismal result, the head of the electoral office for the MSI-DN, Ferruccio de Michieli-Vitturi, answered that a large portion of the potential MSI-DN voting base had been dissuaded from voting according to their true beliefs by the incessant scare tactics used by Christian Democrats against all the minor parties. MSI-DN leaders and militants had been provoked again and again, de Michieli-Vitturi said, by the inflammatory charges of DC spokesmen, designed to soil the reputation of the MSI-DN and prevent it from attracting DC voters with its "constitution of the right" campaign. Unfortunately for the MSI-DN, he added, one of the party representatives, Sandro Saccucci, had fallen into the trap:

Q. Do you think that the case of Saccucci had a negative influence on the electoral result for the MSI-DN?
A. Of course it had a negative effect. We knew that we were recuperating votes because of the people's conviction that the DC wanted to prevent elections and continue its dialogue with the PCI. Just when we were gaining votes, the Saccucci incident occurred and was very damaging psychologically. For a number of days we were unable to hold rallies in certain places. One doesn't vote for a party that is being persecuted at a time when the electoral climate is so tense, difficulties are on the increase, and the threat of communism is so present.[34]

Equally damaging, according to the MSI-DN spokesman, was the American intervention in the Italian electoral campaign in favor of the Christian Democrats. For certain sectors of the middle class that are sensitive to the views of Italy's Western allies, the pronouncement of Secretary of State Kissinger on the need to reenforce the DC was another element that favored the shift of votes from the MSI-DN to the DC.[35]

The MSI-DN lost votes in a wide variety of social classes that had previously provided solid foundations for rightist candidates. Unable to capitalize on their advance in the 1972 elections, the neo-Fascists quickly lost their momentum among the lower classes of the south, who continued to see no visible changes in their socioeconomic conditions. The MSI-DN had been unable to convince any of the other parties in the political spectrum to give it any real power at the national or local level. As a consequence, in 1975 the votes of the working classes in the south began to flow toward the Communist party, and in 1976 the flow became a torrent. One of the most important examples of this decline for the MSI-DN was the loss of support among the lumpenproletariat of Naples.

In 1976 Naples elected a Communist mayor. This de Michieli-Vitturi interpreted as a result of the protest vote of the large poor classes, which tend to support whatever party seems to offer an alternative to the status quo, and of the PCI's clientelistic practices. The city is the largest employer in Naples, and the Communists, he

---

[34] Author's interview with Ferruccio de Michieli-Vitturi, June 30, 1976.
[35] See statements by Henry Kissinger in New York Times, November 9, 1975, p. 1.

claimed, won the election partly by promising spoils to their supporters.[36]

The Lessons of 1976. Even though the MSI-DN leaders resorted to conspiracy theories and charges of clientelism to explain away the party's significant losses, the 1976 elections brought home to them the realization that the right was increasingly being ignored. Its maneuvers for political power, which had occasionally been successful before 1975, had failed. The DC no longer had enough power or room for maneuver to permit the existence of a strong right-wing party like the MSI-DN, and in this moment of crisis it needed the rightist vote for itself to compensate for its losses on the left. A majority of the parliamentary wing of the MSI-DN soon realized that if the party wanted to survive it had to radically change its image so that it would be thought of not as a neo-Fascist movement but as a constitutionally oriented moderate party. Otherwise, the party base and leadership would eventually be reduced to the hard-core Fascists who were seeking a violent confrontation with the left. In accordance with this line of thought, the more moderate leadership split off from the parent MSI-DN organization on December 23, 1976, in an attempt to bridge the gap that separates the MSI-DN from the other parties in the political system.

In contrast to the MSI-DN, the PLI—despite its even heavier losses—seemed fairly sanguine about its chances for rebuilding its decimated voting base. It was clear to PLI leaders like Giovanni Malagodi that the DC had capitalized on the voters' fears of a PCI majority and role in government.[37] To get back the votes that the Liberals had lost to the DC, in the opinion of Malagodi, the PLI had to continue its attempt to redefine the role of the party in Italian politics, but it had to remain steadfast on certain principles: above all, its rejection of Communist participation in a national government coalition.

The PLI party secretary, Valerio Zanone, and the more progressive elements of the party felt that the PLI had to adopt more autonomous and dynamic political strategies. The party had to come out energetically in favor of civil rights and social equality, and in accord with this new attitude the PLI decided to abstain in the August 1976 vote of confidence for the Andreotti government, along with the PCI. There is some evidence to support the thesis that the PLI bottomed out in the 1976 elections (for example, the Liberals' improved

---

[36] Interview with de Michieli-Vitturi.
[37] Author's interview with Giovanni Malagodi, July 7, 1976.

showing in the elections for neighborhood councils held in November 1976 in cities like Novara, Florence, and Perugia), but the fate of the party will depend on its ability to fully realize the internal renovation that it began in the 1976 campaign, resisting the temptation to fall back on traditional policies at the first sign of success.

The Social Democrats, too, took the 1976 election results to heart. Having lost ground in their central and northern strongholds to the DC on the right and the PSI (and maybe the PCI) on the left, they were determined to radically change course. The PSDI leadership regarded the party's losses as due to its inability in twenty-five years to break the DC hegemony over the exercise of power and to implement policies favorable to a Social Democratic view of society. As a result, one party leader said, the "Communists have become the most credible implementors of Social Democratic policies." [38] The 1976 election showed that the PSDI had no future in remaining subject to the influence of the DC; it had to rediscover its popular roots and its reformist programs. One way of doing this was to reestablish its close working relationship with the Socialist party and assume a direct role in leftist coalitions at the local level. In late 1976, the PSDI joined the leftist governments of the Lazio region and the communal administration of Naples. Thus, one of the major casualties of the DC "victory" in 1976 was the hard-line anti-Communist policy that had long characterized the Social Democratic party.

The Republicans arrived at a similar conclusion, but they did not feel the immediate political imperative to translate it into action. In 1976 the PRI had, on the whole, confirmed its 1972 showing. It had made some headway among the northern urban electorate. What seemed to escape the notice of the party leadership was that it had also lost votes in peripheral areas in which it had previously enjoyed a certain ascendency. For example, in the provinces of Forlì and Ravenna the PRI lost ground in thirteen out of fifteen noncapital cities in which it had won over 10 percent of the vote in 1972, and these losses in the classical Republican stronghold of Romagna probably went to the PCI.[39] The implications of this exchange of votes between urban centers and periphery are that the PRI has increasingly assumed the characteristics of an "opinion" party—that is, a party lacking a capillary organization and dependent on middle-class votes—and has lost the popular base that had served as its basic

---

[38] Author's interview with Michele Di Giesi, July 2, 1976. Di Giesi is the head of the PSDI's party organization office.

[39] Leonardi and Pasquino, "Il 20 giugno," pp. 514-518.

building block since the end of the postwar period. In the coming years, the PRI will have to resolve this dilemma if it hopes to retain its political bargaining power and flexibility to influence the course of politics.

The outlook for the Radicals and the Demoproletarians seems equally ambiguous. After the elections, it became clear that the Demoproletarians had been unable to coalesce popular sentiment to the left of the PCI, and the electoral alliance between the far-left groups quickly broke down. The Italian working class had shown little interest in the programs advanced by Proletarian Democracy, and a revolutionary party cannot proceed with the votes of students and intellectuals alone. In an editorial of May 26, 1976, Lucio Magri wrote that if the groups around Proletarian Democracy did not register substantial success in the 1976 elections they would be cast back into the extremism and malaise that had given them birth.[40] That prophecy seems to have come true in the demonstrations and student rioting of 1976 and 1977.

The 1976 elections gave the Radicals an institutional platform from which to play their gadfly role in Italian politics. The difficult problems to be resolved by the new Parliament—that is, abortion, the renewal of the Concordat with the Church, and the adoption of policies to resolve the economic crisis—will provide ample scope for the PR's libertarian struggle. However, the problem remains of defining the political and social base upon which to orient the party over the next five years. Can the PR survive as an urban opinion party representing the disinherited groups in society? The answer to this question will depend on the efficacy of the strategy and arguments adopted by the Radicals in Parliament. If these fail, the party may find itself no longer the gadfly but the court jester of the system. The problems facing Italy are too serious to permit the Radicals, or any other party, this luxury.

If the minor parties are really serious about escaping from their subordination to the two giants of the system, they must work out a common strategy for assuming the initiative rather than being constantly the objects of the political maneuverings set in motion by the DC and the PCI. Perhaps the most important legacy of the 1976 elections for the small parties is their new sense of autonomy and the conviction that they must begin to define an independent course between the two large power blocs.

---

[40] Lucio Magri, "Democrazia Proletaria" [Proletarian Democracy], *Il Manifesto*, May 26, 1976, p. 1.

257

8
THE MASS MEDIA IN THE
ITALIAN ELECTIONS OF 1976

William E. Porter

Few kinds of social research are as unrewarding as the attempt to systematically describe and evaluate the role of the mass media in a political campaign. The variables are too many, solid evidence too slight; there are more leaps of faith than determinations of causality.

For that reason the chapters on the media in the previous volumes in this series of election studies have tended to be descriptive and suggestive, and the same is true of this chapter. It begins with a description of some of the more important characteristics of the Italian press and broadcasting systems, including some discussion of that most uncommon of professionals, the Italian journalist. Since there have developed during the last ten years some substantial changes in the media and the profession, these are laid out in some detail. Campaign coverage then will be discussed, and finally some speculations will be offered about the connections between what was printed and said and some outcomes of the election. Few hard answers will be provided, but perhaps eventually some of the hard questions will be better understood.

The Italian Journalist

Let us begin with people before moving to institutions. Journalism is among the professions defined by statute in Italy, along with law, medicine, engineering, and eight others. With that status goes a requirement that each working journalist in either printed or broadcast media be licensed; those who practice the profession without licenses can be prosecuted and heavily fined.

The journalist not only is a member of a legally defined profession, or *Ordine*, he also automatically is a member of a powerful trade union called the *Federazione Nazionale della Stampa Italiana*. This body negotiates a national contract, including minimum salary levels in each major city, every two years. In practice, journalists' salaries are well above those minimums. The profession in Italy probably is the second-best paid in the world, not much behind its U. S. counterpart—and Italian journalists may well be the best paid if one takes into account their numerous perquisites, including extraordinary fringe benefits, substantial discounts on a wide range of purchases, and easy access to bribes if they wish to seek them. Many have. Evidence surfaced some time ago that all the major political journalists in the Giolitti era (1906) received regular payoffs,[1] and, though hard evidence is lacking, there is no reason to believe the practice has declined. Most Italians simply assume journalists take bribes. This is not to imply an endemic promiscuity, with favors routinely going to the highest bidder; Italian journalism is a gentleman's game, with its own rules.

Long before the social legislation which makes it difficult to dismiss any employee in Italy today, journalists were protected by severance compensation so high that newspapers seldom undertook to pay it; it was cheaper to retain out-of-favor journalists and give them trivial assignments. Severance pay for the well-paid journalist who simply quits, however amicably, to take another job may be over $20,000. If the journalist is impelled to resign by a change in his employer's political line, the figure may be as high as three years' pay.

The profession can be entered only through a tightly controlled apprenticeship system; admittance to *L'Ordine* follows the completion of apprenticeship and the passing of comprehensive examinations. There are no legal educational requirements, but in fact almost every journalist in the country is university trained, generally in political science, economics, history, or law. Italian journalists write with erudition and style, although not necessarily with clarity.

For years these well-paid, secure professionals concentrated on personal flair and the civilized life; they were highly political, but in a kind of intellectual salon sense. During the last decade, however, a spirit of reform has begun to move through the profession, and journalists have begun to seek more control of the content of the publications and broadcasts they turn out. They have succeeded

---

[1] Giovanni Spadolini, "La stampa libera ieri oggi e domani" [The free press yesterday, today, and tomorrow], *Nuova Antologia*, n. 2006 (February 1968).

to a considerable extent in the most important dailies in the country, to a lesser degree in other papers and in Radiotelevisione Italiana (RAI), the country's state-operated broadcasting system. This change was underway at the time of the elections of 1972. It had progressed a good deal further, as we shall see, by the time of the campaign of 1976.

The Italian Broadcasting System

Television. The elections of 1976 found Radiotelevisione Italiana in the early stages of a revolution. Six months earlier, RAI (Italians like acronyms, and the system is invariably referred to as "rye") had lost its monopoly role through court rulings, and private broadcasting had begun a wild and disordered growth. During roughly the same period, the corporation's programming policies governing news and the reporting of politics were drastically changed. There was general agreement that almost any new direction would be for the better.

Broadcasting always has been under the control of the government in Italy, as in most European countries. Although RAI appears to be a free-standing state enterprise along the lines of the British Broadcasting Corporation (BBC), it technically is a private corporation with a contractual relationship with the government. Most of its stock is held by IRI (Istituto per la ricoztruzione industriale), one of Italy's mixed government-and-private holding companies. There are few traces of direct interference with the corporation's affairs by its legal owners. The hand of party politics is visible, however, in almost everything it does.

After the Opening to the Left which brought the Christian Democrats into a tenuous alliance with the Socialists in 1962, official control of RAI became a matter of a careful balance between the two parties; although a Christian Democrat served as director general, the remainder of the administrative posts, from the nine-member directors' committee down to on-the-air personnel, were divided equally between Socialists and Christian Democrats. The result was a rigorous censorship of all political journalism which frequently reached the point of the ludicrous.

There was, for example, a set procedure for reporting government crises. No politician's voice was ever heard, nor were his words quoted directly. Instead, party leaders appearing for consultation with the president of the republic were each shown from the same camera angle and for the same amount of time; upon his exit, each was shown in turn speaking at a microphone, but without sound. While this went on, a disembodied voice—what RAI calls a "speaker" —read a carefully written and approved summary of what the man had said. In every newscast, the last action of the news director before air time was consultation behind closed doors with a group of political censors over the finished script. Arrigo Levi, once a major RAI personality himself and since 1973 editor of La Stampa, once described Italian politicians on television as resembling fish in an aquarium—"their mouths move, but no sound emerges."[2]

Since almost all civil unrest has political overtones, traditionally none was reported on the air. The Milanese who was delayed getting home at the end of the day by an uproar in the Piazza San Babila would never learn about it on that evening's news broadcast; the Roman who saw pitched battles between radical students of the right and left wielding chains and monkey wrenches could be certain that his favorite medium would carry not a word of it. RAI is a member of Eurovision (EVN), a network of European telecasting systems. As such it is responsible for providing film of Italian news for other members, but in the past no film of civil crisis was ever available.

For more than a decade the major evening news broadcast typically began with the fish in the aquarium, moved from that to a series of what television journalists call talking heads—RAI correspondents reporting from London, Paris, Bonn, sometimes Vienna or North Africa—and concluded with a feature or two about the monuments of the past and the beautiful countryside. As craftsmen, Italian film and television crews have always been superb, but their reputation has been made by what they do when they're away from home. Their coverage of papal trips all over the world, for example, has included technical feats such as the assembly of a satellite relay station in Uganda.

Add to this extreme caution in covering politics a general practice of not covering crime or highway accidents and the country was left with what were for years the world's dullest news broadcasts. These did not reflect the competence of RAI journalists. It has been a common observation, even among professionals from the print media, that the brightest young journalists go to RAI. Members of the news staff belong to L'Ordine, and there have been occasional attempts at remaking the system from within, none of which bore much fruit until 1975.

---

[2] Arrigo Levi, Televisione all'Italiana [Television Italian style] (Milan: Etas Kompass, 1969), p. 79.

In May of that year a law providing for the reform of RAI was passed by Parliament. Its first provision was the establishment of a commission of fifteen members, politically balanced with representatives from the major parties, with wide powers to collect information and change both structure and executive personnel. Within a few weeks a new structure for broadcast news was in the planning stages. It established two news broadcasts, one controlled by the DC, very much in the traditional style and identified as *Telegiornale 1* (TG1); the other, TG2, *laico* [3] and basically reflecting the views of the parties of the left—*Panorama*, one of Italy's weekly news magazines, referred to the Socialist party as its "spiritual father" [4]—and of the Republicans and Liberals. The development of a competitive spirit between the two gave powerful assistance to the breaking of old taboos. The staff of TG2 turned their attention to things Italians had never seen covered on television before. Its reporters covered national congresses of the major political parties, catching leaders for impromptu interviews and asking embarrassing questions. TG1 followed suit. Panel discussions on hot issues such as abortion were set up. Disorder in the streets began to be covered; so did domestic scandals.

To some extent RAI journalists were permitted to choose between the two services when the split came; the TG2 staff, although considerably smaller, is considered by many to be the better, and this has produced considerable belligerence on both sides. The RAI establishment did not do everything possible to ease the path of the new agency. TG2 began operations from an informal, if not cluttered, studio—because, its staff charged, RAI wouldn't provide anything better. TG2's work force was inadequate, not because few journalists and technical staff chose that direction, but because the RAI heirarchy managed the budget.

Whatever the facts in the internal warfare, Italy's television viewers in the final days before the election suddenly found themselves with access to more and better information about their government and social institutions than they had ever had before. Suddenly politics seemed much more real, populated by human beings.

---

[3] Although this word literally means "secular" in English, it has a much sharper meaning in Italian. The *Dizionario Garzanti* identifies it with the concept of "autonomy or indifference with respect to ecclesiastical authority." Affiliation with—or independence from—the Vatican is, of course, part of the bedrock of the structure of Italian politics.

[4] *Panorama*, vol. 13, no. 489, p. 77.

Radio. Major changes also came to radio. There are three radio networks under RAI's supervision; the prototypes are the classic three services of the BBC. Although the difference between *rete* (network) 1 and *rete* 2 has not, in recent years, been as sharp as the old BBC distinction between "home" and "light" services, *rete* 3 always has been modelled closely on the Third Programme. This has meant programming so intellectually refined that it could only be described as esoteric; the first winter this writer spent in Italy, a solid hour every Friday evening on network 3 was given over to lectures on volcanology, which must have drawn an audience about the size of that generated by the BBC's Third Programme reading of the entire text of the *Canterbury Tales* in Middle English. At the time of the TG1-TG2 split in television, the news operations of the two major radio networks were similarly divided. There was little concern about the third radio network; as one magazine said, "It covers only about 15 percent of the country's territory, has a reputation for boring programs, and nobody wants it." [5]

Nevertheless within a year the *terzo* began originating programs which would have been unimaginable earlier as RAI projects. Not only were they completely free of censorship, but also they involved appearances by spokesmen for unconventional causes: militant feminists, organizers of inmate protests in Italy's appalling prisons and mental hospitals, homosexuals, and leaders of a movement to democratize the military.

These breaks with the past were not merely the initiative of a few broadcasters. The changes taking place in the media were part of a broad front of change which began moving through Italian culture toward the end of the 1960s. What happened might be summed up as a breakdown of the conventions which governed some forms of societal behavior in Italy and some of the established ways of thinking. Consider the treatment of sexuality in the mass media. Twenty-five years ago there were no publications in Italy resembling "girlie" magazines; there was no nudity in films, and too lingering a shot of Lollobrigida's completely decorous blouse might prompt the government to rate a film unsuitable for minors. There were no descriptions of sexual relations in popular literature, and even in the most serious works such things were handled with almost Victorian indirectness; no scatological words were encountered in a public context. Today in every major Italian city newsstands display books and magazines (sometimes labeled "Swedish type" on the bands that seal them against browsers) which could be purchased

---

[5] *Panorama*, vol. 13, no. 477, pp. 53-54.

in the United States only in porno shops. Some enterprising independent broadcasters have even invented pornographic radio. Traditionally Italian political campaigns have been even more highly ritualized than those in other parliamentary systems. All campaigning was national, however local the actual focus of the voting; only a few carefully arranged candidates at the top of the party pyramid were visible, and these had highly specialized functions. Each party had its orators who spoke at important meetings, and each a figure or two symbolic of leadership. These were never seen in spontaneous give-and-take situations, and most reporting of their activities in party-line papers was closer to hagiography than to serious comment.

It will be some time before the changes of the late 1960s and 1970s greatly affect the mass of the Italian electorate. What they have brought about is a considerable expansion of the group of attentive, knowledgeable, and active participants in political life. Some of the best evidence to that effect came from the sudden appearance of a new mass medium in early 1976. It was called *radio libere*— literally "free radio," of course, but "liberated radio" might better convey its spirit.

RAI's monopoly over broadcasting was challenged several times in the courts over the years, but invariably it was upheld, notably in a decision by the Constitutional Court as late as 1974. Then in January 1976, RAI brought suit to shut down a station in Milan which had begun broadcasting on the unused portion of the FM band; the court of first jurisdiction denied the request, and the case moved to the Constitutional Court. On June 25, 1976, that body upheld the lower court's decision, opening the way to private broadcasting in Italy for the first time and giving legal standing to the hundreds of new stations that had appeared in recent months. The court held that RAI did hold a monopoly on national broadcasting, but only on national broadcasting, permitting the private use of both FM and television frequencies, which are short range. The court also made clear that RAI's retention of any control had to be related to its providing impartial and comprehensive coverage, along with the opportunity for expression of a variety of points of view.

Thus, in the spring of 1976 the FM band began to fill up with wildly undisciplined broadcasting initiatives. There has not yet been an accurate census of the numbers involved, and estimates have varied greatly. By election time RAI executives were estimating that there were 400 new radio stations, and in September the announcement of a new magazine called *Altrimedia*—devoted largely to instructions for starting up and operating a broadcasting station—cited the figure 800.

Most of the new stations grew up around Milan and Rome. A correspondent for the *Washington Post* put them in three categories: political, commercial, and esoteric.[6] One of the most spectacular fell into the last group. It was called Radio L, and among other programs it featured a late-night recorded music show called "Vai a letto con me" (Come to bed with me). Magazines carried photographs of the show's new-style disc jockey, a young woman wearing only a set of headphones and holding a microphone.

The "political" stations, of course, were those most directly involved in the electoral campaign of 1976, and the public response to some of their activities was perhaps the most telling evidence of a new spirit among Italian voters. We shall turn to that, along with analysis of the coverage by the other media, later in this chapter.

The Press

Newspapers. Some historians of the press have said that every nation's newspapers have developed out of one of two traditions.[7] Newspapers in such countries as the United States and the United Kingdom came out of a "mercantile" tradition; that is, their primary function in the beginning was the accurate and efficient transmission of business information (for example, shipping news and prices abroad). This led to a tendency to emphasize succinctness, speed, and at least enough objectivity to make the numbers trustworthy. The other tradition is described as "literary"; newspapers came out of the life of the cafés, salons, and universities of the eighteenth century. The development of newspapers in France and Italy, in particular, was associated with this tradition.

Until recently the *terza pagina* (third page) of all serious Italian newspapers was given over to short essays, critical commentary, and short works of fiction. As the papers have sought to renew themselves, the *terza* tradition has faded, but a substantial influence remains; it is suggestive that on June 20, the first day of the voting in 1976, *Corriere della Sera* carried a new short story by Alberto Moravia.

---

[6] Sari Gilbert, "Pirate Radios Mushroom in Italy," *Washington Post*, July 25, 1976.

[7] See, for example, chapter 6 of the first edition of Frank Luther Mott, *American Journalism* (New York: Macmillan, 1947), and chapter 1 of Francesco Fattorello, *Il Giornalism Italiano* [Italian journalism] (Udine: Casa Editrice Idea, 1941).

The tradition extends to news writing. The journalist is held responsible for the literary quality of his work, and he is expected to display his skills. Perhaps nothing about the Italian newspaper business so startles the American journalist as the discovery that there is no such thing as a copy editor on an Italian paper—no one who condenses, rearranges, rewrites leads, makes one story out of two or three. The only restraint is a specified length (and even that does not always apply); sometimes a department editor may wish to cut a story, but under the present labor contracts in most papers he may do so only after consulting the author.

This kind of respect for personal expression leads, naturally, to the development of ornate styles. It is partly for this reason that many educated Italians find reading newspapers tedious, if not difficult—and the undereducated, of whom there are still millions, cannot read them at all.

The "inside" quality of Italian publications is not just a matter of literary style. There always has been an enormous amount of political talk in the papers, typically consisting of a news "peg" followed by columns of commentary and insiders' gossip. Such stories occupied a prominent place on the front page of every major Italian newspaper almost every day for years. Journalists refer to them as *pastone Romano* (*pastone* is pig feed, largely garbage); essentially they are show pieces and an instrument for arcane communication among an elite within an elite. Enzo Forcella, an eminent writer and editor, once wrote a famous article entitled "The 1500 Readers" which asserted that only about that number of people in Italy could read Italian political journalism.[8] During the past five years some papers—for example, *Il Messaggero*—have thrown out the *pastone Romano* or moved it to an inside page in abbreviated form.

The hope is to create a front page that will attract more readers. Italian newspaper circulation is shamefully low: about 100 copies per 1,000 of population; the U. S. figure is more than three times that, and the British and Swedish figures are five times as high. Several elements contribute to this low circulation. Newspaper style which makes for difficult reading is part of it; so is the elaborate coverage of news which interests few people, and the pervasive feeling that all journalists are prone to take bribes. Price may also be a factor. Although the government tries to keep the price of newspapers down because it is one of the items on the list of prices upon which cost-

---

[8] Enzo Forcella, "Millecinquecento lettori—confessioni di un giornalista politico" [1500 readers—confessions of a political journalist], *Tempo Presente* (November 1959), pp. 451-458.

of-living escalator clauses are based, at the time of the election of 1976 the price of the average newspaper was 150 lire (around eighteen cents) a copy. Whatever the explanations, the years between the elections of 1972 and 1976 saw circulation continue a decline that began in 1950. This suggests that newspapers have minimal influence on the electorate as a whole.

This said, two points should be added immediately. First, one of the most important functions of newspapers in any society is to serve as a channel of communication among the operating elite. Because that elite does pay attention to newspapers—more than to any other medium—the smaller and more closely articulated the elite, the more significant that function. The influence of the *New York Times* and the *Washington Post* in the United States grows not so much from their impact upon the voters as from their impact upon the people who control the government, run for office, and contribute to political parties. They also influence the other media. In a country where the operating elite is as small and well-defined as Italy's and the enthusiasm for politicking reaches Byzantine extremes, the role of newspapers is critical.

Second, the fact of a slow, continuing slide in public acceptance suggests stagnation, a failure to change in response to the mood of the times. In fact, however, Italian newspapers have not stagnated and have tried not to ride along passively. Like the broadcast media, they have undergone remarkable upheavals.

In the decade before the election of 1976 there were large-scale changes in the ownership of newspapers which eventually resulted in a highly concentrated ownership pattern. During that period there were four major national dailies, and it is upon them that most of this analysis will be concentrated: *Corriere della Sera* and *Il Giorno* in Milan, *La Stampa* in Turin, and *Il Messaggero* in Rome. All are generally available throughout the country; *Corriere*, with the highest circulation figure is the most pervasive. Like most of Italy's dailies, all four are *giornali d'informazione*—that is, not party papers.

A decade ago *Corriere della Sera* belonged to the Crespi family, rich from textiles, manufacturing, and *Corriere* itself (historically one of the few Italian papers that consistently made money). *La Stampa* belonged to the Agnellis, whose chief interest was Fiat. *Il Giorno* belonged to ENI, a vast holding company built by Enrico Mattei around petroleum and natural gas with heavy governmental participation. *Il Messaggero* was the property of the Perrone family, primarily identified with steel manufacturing. Through a complicated series of mergers which began in the early 1970s, *Corriere della Sera* and *Il Messaggero*—along with a number of papers of local and regional circulation—passed to the control of Angelo Rizzoli, one of the sons of the founder of the Rizzoli book publishing firm. *Il Giorno*'s controlling owner, Eugenio Cefis, was deeply involved in the burgeoning of Rizzoli; so, some contend, was the house of Rothschild. The pattern has been complex even by Italian corporate standards. It is essentially accurate to say in summary that all the Italian national dailies with the exception of Agnelli's *La Stampa* are now in the hands, in effect, of a single conglomerate.

A question comes immediately to the mind of any observer who watched this process of concentration going on: why would anybody want to own a big Italian newspaper? By 1971, when the wave of consolidation began, all of the major papers in the country were losing money heavily. The total losses in the newspaper field in Italy in 1976 were estimated at $45 million; they were expected to rise 80 percent in 1977.

A possible explanation might be the desire to acquire a mouthpiece; through the ownership of major papers it should be possible to exercise powerful influence upon public opinion. When the remarkable changes within the newsrooms of those same major papers during the last few years are taken into account, however, this explanation loses much of its persuasiveness and raises a second question: why buy papers which not only lose money, but over which the owners' control is highly imperfect?

From the beginning of the 1970s, some journalists, increasingly restless despite their well-paid sinecures, began seeking a larger role in the critical decisions of the newsroom. To do so they took advantage of a provision of their national contract which had been adopted in 1954 but utilized only in an offhand way. It called for the establishment in each newsroom of a *comitato di redazione*—an editorial staff committee—with a vague mandate for some staff involvement in policy making.

For a good many years this amounted, in most newsrooms, to no more than a small group of staff members who occasionally sat in while the bosses talked; in some papers, no committee was even organized. Signs of a changing mood came in the national meeting of the Federation of the Press in Salerno in 1968, out of which came a minority alignment which called itself the *movimento democratico*. That first initiative died, but a direction had been established and a force set in motion. Several factors gave it impetus. The continental "reporter power" movement, which began at *Le Monde* in 1951,[9] had been watched with much interest. There was growing unhappiness on the part of most journalists (who considered themselves not only political men but intellectuals) with a Christian Democratic regime which, despite superficial signs of instability, had been substantially unchanged for decades. ("Remember," one of them told this writer once, "Italy has had only two governments since the end of the First World War.") A group of well-documented and devastating books attacking the contemporary Italian media had appeared, some written by fellow professionals, and there was developing an aching conscience about the lack of credibility of the press and its irrelevance for most Italians. The transfer of leading newspapers from family ownership to conglomerates, always without consultation with the staffs and in some cases accompanied by deliberate efforts to mislead the staffs, rankled. The national federation acquired young and energetic leadership when Luciano Ceschia became national secretary in 1968.. All this fueled the push for more say in the employers' affairs.

The most convenient point at which pressure could be brought to bear on the managers was the *comitato di redazione*. The national contract already gave the journalists more power than they actually exercised; both union contracts and new social legislation made it almost impossible to fire in-house organizers, and the powerful printers' union provided further support. The objective at most papers was a contract specifying the division of powers in the newsroom between ownership and staff.

The contract in force at the time of this writing at *Il Messaggero* of Rome provides a striking example of such an agreement. The owner's direct representative *(direttore responsabile)* has no control over content; actual administration is provided by two vice-directors, one of whom is elected by the staff. The paper's political staff is formally defined in the contract as being *laico*, progressive, and anti-Fascist. News judgments are measured against that definition; if someone objects to a story or a headline, a meeting of the *comitato* may be called to change it—or if the matter seems of major importance, a meeting of the entire news staff may be called. There is much monitoring at *Il Messaggero* of tendentiousness in headlines and lead paragraphs; meetings of the full staff to argue about such

---

[9] A 1951 confrontation between the owners of *Le Monde* and its editor, Hubert Beuve-Méry, triggered a rebellion by the staff in support of Beuve-Méry which developed into a successful push for part ownership and a considerable voice in policy making for employees.

matters between editions are not uncommon. Neither are direct attacks upon the proprietors.

Although the *direttore responsabile* has a bit more power at *Corriere della Sera* and the weekly newsmagazine which it publishes, *Il Mondo*, the arrangements in force there are similar; both specifically prohibit management's overruling any decision by section editors about content, for example. *La Stampa* and *Il Giorno* also have strong editorial staff committees.

All this makes it somewhat improbable that a Cefis or Rizzoli would aspire to own as many papers as possible for the sake of the influence which it might give him. The hope of eventual profit is a more likely explanation, despite the present state of the newspaper industry. Government subsidies to the press began in 1974; by 1976 they were still relatively modest and aimed primarily at reducing the cost of paper. Much more elaborate plans were afoot in 1977 which would involve the virtual abolition of taxes in the newspaper business, major government assistance in the acquisition of new equipment, and the remodeling of the industry's obsolete plants, financial support for a variety of employee perquisites including severance pay during staff reduction, and millions of dollars in subsidy.[10] Less ambitious proposals call for short-term help of equal generosity, but only until the industry might get back on its feet. Either way, if the government assumes enough of the burden, private profit is eventually assured. A special parliamentary commission went to work in the fall of 1976 to consider drafting such legislation.

As of January 1, 1976, there were eighty daily newspapers in Italy. Sixty-seven of these described themselves as *giornali d'informazione*. The group includes three primarily concerned with financial and economic matters. Six more were official publications of political parties and another three of Catholic organizations. There were, in addition, four dailies devoted entirely to sports.

The country's four nonparty, nationally circulated dailies were: *Corriere della Sera* (Milan), circulation 660,000; *La Stampa* (Turin), circulation 511,000; *Il Giorno* (Milan), circulation 330,000; and *Il Messaggero* (Rome), circulation 315,000.

The major regional papers included: *La Nazione* (Florence), circulation 254,000; *Il Tempo* (Rome), circulation 260,000; *Il Giornale Nuovo* (Milan), circulation 250,000; and *Il Mattino* (Naples), circulation 148,000. Among the official political party newspapers, only *L'Unità*, published by the PCI, has major national circulation. It is

[10] Claudio Rinaldi, "Su un trono di carta" [On a paper throne], *Panorama*, vol. 14, no. 548, pp. 149-152.

the third largest daily in Italy, with a circulation of 450,000. It should be remembered that Italian newspaper circulations are not audited; these figures are claims, and are based on the number of copies printed (*la tiratura*) rather than on actual sales.

Magazines. A UNESCO survey made in the late 1960s indicated that Italy was the only country in Europe in which the per capita circulation of magazines (326 per 1,000 inhabitants) was higher than that of daily newspapers. There has been some decline in circulation during the last five years, but the numbers remain high, and the weekly magazine—increasingly scarce in the rest of the world—remains a major medium. During the campaign of 1976 there were six nonparty, general-circulation weeklies which were primarily concerned with politics. *L'Espresso, Panorama, Il Mondo, L'Europeo, Tempo,* and *Il Settimanale* are news magazines resembling *Newsweek* and *Time* in the United States. The circulations of Italian newsmagazines are relatively modest, somewhere around 200,000 in most cases, and four are owned by corporate giants: *Il Mondo* and *L'Europeo* belong to Rizzoli, *Panorama* to Mondadori, and *Il Settimanale* to Rusconi. *L'Espresso,* reminiscent of France's *L'Express,* and *Tempo* were independent in 1976. All were to some extent antigovernment during the campaign; *Il Settimanale* was generally friendly but sometimes attacked from the right. The others were to the left; *L'Espresso* was the most strident of the lot. *Panorama* is fat with advertising, but the others tend to be slender. All are put together with style, erudition, and wit, in the best tradition of Italian journalism. It is common to find among Italian intellectuals people who never read a newspaper; it is almost impossible to find any who do not read magazines.

That fact might lead to the assumption that magazines are more influential than newspapers in opinion formation. Such matters are difficult to investigate in a systematic way, and there are no good studies on the subject. Research does indicate that the magazine audience in any society is elite in social status, education, and income, and it is possible to demonstrate in several countries that some national issues of consequence have surfaced first in the magazines. The case for broad political influence, however, is hard to make.

Magazine audiences are completely self-selected, for one thing; in a sense, the list of successful magazines at any given moment anywhere represents the ingenuity of publishers and editors in ferreting out special groups heavily predisposed to them. Newspapers reach at least a certain number of people who disagree with much of their content but still feel the need to read a newspaper, and television set owners in every country watch the tube almost regardless of what is on. Both of these media, then, and particularly television, have at least some potential for changing attitudes through involuntary exposure. Magazines spend most of their energy exhorting the converted.

The Media in the Campaign

In setting out to analyze the performance of each of the media during the electoral campaign of 1976, one might do well to begin with some observations about one medium that was surprisingly uninspired.

Posters. Wall posters always have been a striking and provocative part of the Italian urban scene. Superb commercial graphics are a national tradition, and they have always been put to use during political campaigns. During the spring of 1976, however, most of the political posters on display consisted of little more than the word "Vota" and the party's name and device. One of the most commonly seen, produced by the Christian Democrats, consisted of just that in blue ink on white paper; even the usual red accent on the emblem was missing. By comparison, the simple red, white, and green emblem of the Liberals seemed almost flashy, and the most striking artistic innovation was the rose in a clenched fist used by the Radicals.

There is no simple explanation for the lack of flair in wall-poster design for this campaign. Lack of time might well be the most important factor; the period from the call for elections to the voting was less than six weeks. Costs of production also were involved; the powerful printers' union has made prices high. For the first time in 1976 broadcast commercials could be bought, and these may have held more promise of influence upon the wavering voter. It is even possible that the wit and imagination of the poster makers, which had given previous elections a touch of the carnival spirit, seemed inappropriate in this grim year.

There have been no major studies of the effectiveness of posters. In modern times they have been most clearly functional in China, where they serve as a basic communication system between government and the people and where even the act of their manufacture has been an important form of political behavior.[11] In pre-World

---

[11] See Frederick T. C. Yu, *Mass Persuasion in Communist China* (New York: Frederick A. Praeger, 1967), pp. 137-142.

War II Italy, when illiteracy and poverty were widespread, they had an important information function (and most Italian dailies still post the separated pages of their latest edition outside their offices).

Clearly no one thought posters would play such a role in this election. Lietta Tornabuoni of *Corriere della Sera*, in a final summary story before the election, noted, a little sadly, perhaps, "the absolute lack of satire; from the most noted creators of political satire no party commissioned even a single drawing." [12]

The Television Campaign. RAI played a major role in the electoral campaign of 1976. It did so under the detailed supervision of the parliamentary *commissione di vigilanza*, which exercised control down to the level of choosing each of the journalists who would ask questions in the staged press conferences of "Tribuna Elettorale." Within this carefully articulated scheme, each party had two chances, in effect, to make its case on national television. (Two final summary programs, involving all the parties, also were presented; RAI television provided, all told, somewhere around twenty-five hours of official, special campaign programming.) Each party had total responsibility for the content of one of its two major appearances; in the other segment, "Tribuna Elettorale," a spokesman provided by the party answered questions from journalists.

RAI had provided something resembling question-and-answer sessions between candidates and journalists during earlier campaigns, as well as its regular program called "Tribuna Politica." These tended to be stiff and carefully managed affairs, however, with little chance for follow-up questions or real debate. In 1976, "Tribuna Elettorale" was different. It also had a unique tone of self-consciousness since, as Furio Colombo of *La Stampa* pointed out in a thoughtful piece, this was the first time Italian political leaders had had to improvise answers to hard questions while face-to-face with the voters.[13]

Each "Tribuna Elettorale" lasted about forty-five minutes; RAI, like most European broadcast systems, tends to be casual about time slots. The program appeared simultaneously on both of RAI's television channels, and an audio tape of most sessions was later broadcast on radio. A panel of ten reporters was chosen for each session by the parliamentary commission. The guideline for selection was, as the *commissione* put it, the pitting of "activists against activists" —in other words, there were to be no shills asking questions de-

[12] *Corriere della Sera*, June 20, 1976.
[13] *La Stampa*, June 19, 1976.

signed to make a particular candidate look especially good. Most of the journalists chosen were political reporters who might be described as well-known journeymen; the big names from newspapers and magazines did not appear. Members of the RAI news department staff appeared only as moderators.

Early on there was a prospect of the minor parties being disregarded in the allocation of time for "Tribuna"; both the Radical party and the party of Proletarian Democracy were extraparliamentary, that is, neither held seats in the Chamber of Deputies. Apparently in part through leverage generated by their appearances on TG2, however, each eventually received a regular turn.

Each broadcast in the series was devoted to a particular party, and each began with a statement by the party spokesman which generally ran less than five minutes. Then questioning began, with each reporter having time during his turn for two or three questions; there was no provision for general catch-as-catch-can questioning.

Benigno Zaccagnini appeared for the DC (this session was not broadcast on radio; Aldo Moro appeared instead on the radio), Enrico Berlinguer for the PCI, Francesco De Martino for the PSI, Giuseppe Saragat for the PSDI, Ugo La Malfa for the Republicans, Valerio Zanone for the Liberals, Giorgio Almirante for the MSI, Marco Pannella for the PR, and Lucio Magri for the DP. By the standards of the Ford-Carter-journalists sessions which took place a few weeks later, the Italian journalists were much more rhetorical than probing, and much more inclined to make speeches. The open political activism of almost all Italian journalists, those of the *giornali d'informazione* as well as the representatives of the party papers, makes the questioner feel that he represents something more than a newspaper and helps produce harangues instead of inquiry.

Old antagonisms sparked some of the most bitter exchanges. A spokesman for *Avanti!* (the PSI's party daily) asked Giuseppe Saragat, leader of the PSDI, a "question" which amounted to an accusation of lying about the issue of a popular front government in 1948. Saragat replied in kind, and a violent personal exchange followed. For some viewers it was a jarring reminder of the continuing importance of unhealed wounds of thirty years before, but to the mass of Italian voters the exchange must have been close to meaningless. A journalist from the Vatican's *Osservatore Romano* was equally belligerent when his turn came with De Martino of the PSI, but De Martino, the most low-key of the party leaders in the series, turned him aside with soft answers. Almost everybody who questioned

Almirante of the MSI was more interested in establishing his own antifascism than in inquiring about the positions of the MSI.

The most common subject for questions (about one-fourth of all those asked) was the mechanics of coalition after the election. Zaccagnini and Berlinguer were pressed on their plans in case of a stand-off, both in terms of DC-PCI collaboration and possible allies in other coalitions; De Martino was asked if the PSI would really stick by its commitment not to return to the center-left arrangement; Saragat tried to develop the case for a centrist government; La Malfa was asked about the PRI's possibly acting as a broker for and eventually a participant in a rightist coalition; even Almirante was asked how he would put together his proposed antileft, law-and-order government.

None of the replies said very much. In effect, party leaders said, "Trust us; it might be easier than you think, there are possibilities you don't understand, and anyhow our side is going to do better than the polls indicate." (Several newspapers and magazines commissioned surveys by commercial pollsters during the campaign, and on the "Tribuna" programs both journalists and politicians demonstrated their close following of the findings.) The nearest thing to hard news in the entire series, perhaps, was De Martino's reaffirmation of the Socialists' refusal to try again with the DC. Equivocal replies are to be expected of politicians on television, but these were a long way from the enthusiastically detailed analysis of the political dynamics which always has characterized Italian political comment in newspapers and magazines.

Some profound questions were raised in the television series, but waffling answers and the journalists' failure to follow up blunted their impact. A journalist from *Il Manifesto*, published by one wing of the radical left, pursued Zanone of the Liberals with a question that could have been directed with equal relevance to most of the other party leaders: in effect, what real differences are there among you corrupt and tired old men, whatever your party, who make up the national political establishment? Several speakers were also asked about the reasons for political violence in Italy. And there were questions from special interest groups: a female journalist asked about school reform, a representative of *24 Ore*, a financial paper, asked Zanone why there were no businessmen on the Liberal candidate list, and a reporter from *Tutto Sport* asked why none of the candidates ever commented on sports. There were no questions on divorce or abortion, perhaps because there already had been so much debate on those matters that the journalists felt the subjects to be exhausted. The only reference to the growing feminist movement in Italy was practically an aside, made by Berlinguer.[14] Only slight reference was made to corruption in government, although the Lockheed scandal was at its height during the campaign.

The most important effect of these programs upon the conduct of Italian politics was not demonstrated by the range or acuity of the journalists' questions, but by the behavior of the political leaders in responding. None seemed as much concerned with issues as with presenting the most effective image of his party to the voters. Most were models of cool gentility and sweet reasonableness. Berlinguer was probably the best at this, but most carried it off well. De Martino almost overdid it, sometimes seeming barely interested. Only Almirante, whether by calculation or by lack of self-control, showed sharp edges; he began the confrontation with arrogance and ended with jeering contempt for his questioners.

There was, of course, none of the bite of controversy in the programs staged by the parties in the time provided by RAI. Two designs were most common. Several parties chose simply to put their best-known orator in front of the cameras to make the kind of speech that, in the piazzas of Italy, had long been a ritual of political life; Furio Colombo saw these speakers as living for a moment in a dream, "speaking on both channels, with no one in between, without obstacles and without objections." [15] It was the most old-fashioned campaigning of the election.

Another favorite format was some variation on the round table idea—a group of people in a circle, praising the party (and sometimes each other) seriatim. The Communists used major party officials and the popular mayor of Naples in a domestic living room setting. The Christian Democrats adopted a more elaborate approach, using Zaccagnini, film clips from the recently concluded DC national congress, and staged questions.

---

[14] Nino Nutrizio, from La Notte, brought props to illustrate his question. Holding a packet of rice in one hand and one of spaghetti in the other, he pointed out that they could not be cooked in the same pot; if cooked long enough for spaghetti al dente, the rice would be half-raw; if cooked long enough to prepare the rice properly, the spaghetti would be suitable only for putting up wall posters. What makes you think, he asked Berlinguer, that you and the DC can function in the same government? Berlinguer answered: "I don't want to follow your gastronomical reasoning very far, except to observe that it does not appear to me that your notion that women belong in the kitchen is very progressive. . . . There are many women who are forced to do only housework. . . . This is one of the fundamental problems of Italian social life." Stenographic text of "Tribuna Elettorale" for June 15, 1976; author's translation.

[15] La Stampa, June 19, 1976.

The Radio Campaign. *Radio libere* was reaching important dimensions by the time of the campaign and played a major role, though it was too ephemeral to have chroniclers or analysts. Several aspects of its contribution need underlining. There was widespread use of the new commercial stations for political advertising. Prices for broadcast time ran from around $25.00 per hour in the early days of the campaign to more than $1500.00 per hour during the final push. And because low-power radio is an especially efficient form of communication with small, localized audiences, it calls for a special campaign style. Speakers tended to adopt a conversational tone, and they were concerned with appealing to women. Communal and regional elections also were being held, and for the first time candidates for local administrative posts found in commercial radio a means of access to the voters' homes.

Finally, the phone-in talk show came into its own. The arrangement is standard on radio stations in the United States, but the management of phone-ins keeps the talk away from politics because of possible difficulties with federal regulations. In Italy in the spring of 1976 the phone-in radio shows were almost entirely political, at least in the larger sense of the word. Perhaps the most successful call-in program was that conducted by the leader of the Radical party. Marco Pannella conducted a series of open-line programs on *Radio Radicale* after each broadcast of "Tribuna Elettorale," generally beginning with his own comments. The number of incoming calls ran as high as 600 a night, and the talk went on until the early hours of the morning.

The difficulty in trying to connect any of these activities with what Italian voters did at the polls has already been pointed out. There is even a lack of simple audience data; although RAI has an excellent research department, it made no surveys of audience size for political programs, the results of which might have had political effects inappropriate to a neutral agency. It can be pointed out, however, that the effect upon politicians is identifiable. Their awareness of a vast national audience was palpable, not only in what they said on "Tribuna Elettorale" and other programs, but in their constant efforts to project an attractive image. The new availability of small and unregulated local radio gave new emphasis to local administrative issues which are less partisan than the great national issues. The ordinary Italian, for his part, began to get accustomed for the first time to the politicians' presence in his living room—and even to the possibility that he could call up his candidate and talk back.

Newspapers in the Campaign. The root of the most important break with the past in the newspapers' treatment of the 1976 campaign was the increased power over policy acquired by newsroom committees. The effect was a pronounced antigovernment tone in three of the country's four biggest *giornali d'informazione*.

This had not been the case for more than twenty-five years after the end of World War II. During that period the PCI's daily *L'Unità* had the country's third highest circulation, behind *Corriere della Sera* and *La Stampa*, while the DC's *Il Popolo* was a skimpy throwaway sheet. The contrast between the two sometimes led to speculation as to why the DC did not put more talent and money into producing a competitive paper. The explanation was conveyed in a wry remark, common among Italian journalists, to the effect that the Christian Democrats did not need a newspaper to speak for them; the national dailies were their mouthpieces.

By the time of the 1976 campaign, that explanation no longer served. The most important newspapers which unequivocally spoke for the DC were *La Nazione* of Florence, Montanelli's *Il Giornale Nuovo* (produced by a group of ex-staff members of *Corriere*), and *Il Tempo* of Rome, all regional papers. *Il Messaggero*, *Corriere della Sera*, and *Il Giorno* were non-Communist, but somewhat more radical than De Martino socialism; most of all, they were bitterly antigovernment and anti-DC. *La Stampa*, while not as persistently hostile to the nation's political establishment, was hardly recognizable as the voice of Fiat. Its move to the left, together with a general upgrading under the editorship of Arrigo Levi, had gone just far enough to leave it somewhere in the middle. *Il Messaggero's* streamer headline the morning the voting began read, "A Vote for Change"; the page-one editorial was headed "We Must Save the Country." *La Stampa's* streamer the same morning read "Forty Million Citizens Vote; the Whole World Watches Italy," and the main commentary was headed "The Ways of Democracy"; its substance was that some changes were to be hoped for but that in any case the country would muddle through.

That was as close to a progovernment stance as could be found in any of the big four during the campaign. Generally, coverage of government was characterized by continuing emphasis upon various aspects of the Lockheed scandal, although it could be argued that this simply was part of the regular flow of the news. The story centered on the activities of a parliamentary commission which could, in effect, bring in indictments; it adjourned on June 16, four days before the election, and on an eleven-to-nine vote decided to make no arrests; most papers made much of the narrowness of the margin and the curious minority coalition of PCI-PSI-MSI.

Stories speculating about the involvement of such DC leaders as Rumor continued, however; so did accounts of a strike of bank employees and one scheduled by farm workers for the period immediately after the election. Stories about the gloomy fears of DC leaders about the results of the election were common; *Corriere della Sera* carried a typical one on June 17, headlined "DC is Pessimistic about Postelection Period."

The amount of attention given to the Socialists seemed disproportionately large, considering both the party's recent history and its acceptance by the public as measured by the election results. Several factors may contribute to the explanation. The center-left idea had been around for a quarter of a century, and such a coalition had recently governed the country. Its revival seemed to many the only hope for a stable postelection government, even though the PSI during the campaign renounced that notion in favor of a broadly based "emergency" government.

Nevertheless, the tendency to cover the last few days of the campaign in terms of the "big three" parties seems to have reflected more than a little the political commitments of the staffs of the leading *giornali d'informazione*. *Il Messaggero* and *Il Giorno* were openly pro-PSI, and the direction of *Corriere della Sera* also was strongly leftward; only *La Stampa*, although well to the left of its position of a decade earlier, conveyed a general impression of neutrality.

On the eve of the voting, for example, *Il Messaggero* devoted all of page three to three interviews: Andreotti (DC), Mancini (PSI), and Pajetta (PCI). No other parties received serious attention. *Corriere della Sera* ran comprehensive interviews with Berlinguer on June 17, De Martino on June 18, and Zaccagnini on June 19; its final front-page editorial made no endorsements, but castigated the DC and spoke highly of both the PSI and PCI. *Il Giorno* ran a profile on De Martino the same day as its formal interview with Zaccagnini, with the De Martino story receiving the bigger play.

Almost all of the Italian dailies made use of set-piece interviews with party leaders. The space given to each was carefully balanced against that accorded to the others. Their format was the presumably literal transcription of questions and answers. The questions tended to be more probing and answers more precise than those that arose in the television broadcasts; for example, Berlinguer in several newspaper interviews made detailed analyses of the differences between Italian communism and other forms.

280

The emphasis on the PSI became even more pronounced after the election. De Martino's resignation from the post of party secretary made major headlines, and the possibility of a DC-PSI government continued on front pages, despite the lack of any evidence of interest in a new center-left coalition on the part of party leaders; *Corriere* was asking what the Socialists would do more than a week after the voting.

The feeling that Italy was involved in one of the most critical periods of its history was widespread, of course, even before the campaign began on May 10. For two years there had been outbreaks of violence between the fringes at either end of the political spectrum, including street killings, political assassinations, and bombings. The general assumption was that the campaign would be violent, and there was an inarticulate but very real sense that the country was nearing the precipice.

The major newspapers handled this issue cautiously, seldom referring to the possibility of severe disturbances, but steadily emphasizing the seriousness of what was going on. When June 20 arrived there was a good deal of relief and congratulation in the press. *Il Giorno* proudly quoted Minister of the Interior Cossiga in his praise of the police: "You have performed a service not to this or that political sector, but to the whole country." *La Stampa* spoke in headlines of the conclusion "without incident" of a "tense" campaign. Each of the major papers made repeated reference to the number of foreign newsmen in Italy for the balloting, by far the largest group ever; *La Stampa* said "the whole world watches Italy," and *Corriere's* Washington correspondent wrote in detail about the way the *New York Times*, the *Wall Street Journal*, and the *Washington Post* were covering "changing Italy." *La Nazione* of Florence referred in a headline to the most important election in years and spoke with pride of the absence of an atmosphere of fear. This reinforcement by the press of a sense of crisis and historical importance probably had its effect upon the voting.

It should be noted that there was little coverage of the Movimento Sociale Italiano/Destra Nazionale or its leader, Almirante, and none that could be considered favorable. The Italian constitution forbids the revival of a Fascist party, and, though the MSI is careful never to use the word "Fascist" and has always contended that it has no connection with the Mussolini regime, Italian journalists have generally taken the position that the MSI is not a legitimate party under the constitution. Certainly, they took steps to minimize attention to it during the campaign. The vigilance of the *comitati di reda-*

zione about what they considered tendentiousness favoring the right became particularly acute.

Generally, these newsroom committees assumed a role which was more tactical than strategic during the campaign. There was no need for elaborate consideration of broad objectives in the offices of the national dailies; these had been hammered out, almost on a case-by-case basis, in the negotiations for the in-house contracts and in the daily preparation of the paper. There was no question that *Il Messaggero, Il Giorno,* and *Corriere della Sera* would be firmly committed to the left or that *La Stampa* would lean in that direction while remaining in the center. The second level of *giornali d'informazione,* the major regional papers—*Il Giornale Nuovo, Il Tempo,* and *La Nazione*—had an equally clear conservative commitment. It is not too much of an oversimplification to say that these newspapers had no more need of philosophical discussions in approaching an election than, say, the *Chicago Tribune* or *Pravda.* The only decisions to be made were short-range.

Thus, it is not surprising that the most important actions by the *comitati* on the big papers had to do not with news coverage, but with advertising. None of the four national dailies accepted advertising from MSI candidates. In this election the MSI added the explanatory subtitle *Destra Nazionale* (nationalist right) to its name, but the *comitati di redazione* always have insisted that, whatever its name, the MSI is neo-Fascist. Much of the bitterness many Italians feel toward the DC has grown out of the occasional collaboration of the government with the MSI, especially on the issue of abortion, and Almirante's protestations that Moro has pronounced the MSI legal have had little effect. The major papers' boycott of the MSI extended to news columns almost as completely as to advertising, except for stories which suggested ties between the party and rightist violence.

One particularly striking illustration of the influence of the *comitato* occurred at *Il Messaggero.* The PSI bought a full-page ad which included a list of what the Socialists considered the most sinister figures in Italy. One of the men named was Eugenio Cefis, who at that time indirectly owned *Il Messaggero.* Needless to say, the top management wanted the name of Cefis omitted; the *comitato di redazione* refused and made its decision stick.

Magazines in the Campaign. The campaign coverage in the news magazines in Italy was, in a way, old-fashioned. With the exception of Rusconi's *Il Settimanale,* it was bitterly antigovernment, leaning heavily upon such stories as the Lockheed scandal, neofascism in the armed forces, and the sometime DC-MSI alliances. The classic tools were used to the fullest: caricature, satire, and epithets bordering on the surrealistic. *Panorama's* last preelection cover showed Fanfani in a Mussolini-style uniform decorated with death's-heads; *Tempo* (in no way connected with the Roman daily of the same name, it must be remembered) showed Moro behind bars. As in the *giornali d'informazione*, the Socialists received much favorable attention. There were also, at various times during the campaign, analyses in several publications of the extent to which the PCI was really Italian and could be trusted. Competition among this set of magazines in Italy is fierce, and their tone frequently approaches the hysterical.

Tempo's election-day cover summed up both the tone and the central themes. It carried small facsimiles of six earlier covers, including one of Leone caricatured as a masked antelope ("antelope cobbler" was the code name of the recipient of the Lockheed payments), another a montage of clenched red fists with the caption "To the Left is Great!" and the Moro cover mentioned above. "June 20/ the New Left Enters Parliament," the cutline said. "The New Prime Minister is a Socialist/ Italy Turns the Page."

After the Voting

In 1976 there was, for the first time, considerable use of polling and pollster projections by the media. Both newspapers and magazines commissioned their own polls, generally from Doxa, an affiliate of the Gallup organization, or Demoskopea. These tended to indicate major losses by the DC, major gains by the PCI, and relatively small changes for the minor parties. Because of the long voting period (all day Sunday, until noon on Monday) and the complexity of the ballot (Romans were voting in this election, for example, for four different sets of officials, each on a separate ballot), results traditionally have come in very slowly. Each of RAI's news services also hired its own survey service—TG1 had Doxa, TG2 Demoskopea—and each was making projections of the final results by early Monday evening. The national dailies also carried stories based on projections in their first editions late Monday night.

All of these erred, but modestly. Since both the regional elections of 1975 and the prevote polls had indicated heavy losses for the DC, during the first hours there was a tendency to overestimate the extent of the DC recovery and to underestimate the PCI gains suggested by the early returns. *Corriere della Sera's* early edition was

283

headlined "The DC and PCI Both Reinforced"; *Il Giorno's* three-line comprehensive streamer began by referring to the DC recovery and then mentioned gains by the PCI; *Il Messaggero*, in large type, said "DC Recovers; PCI Stronger"; *La Stampa* was a bit more cautious, with a streamer which began "DC Still Leading in the Chamber." In each case, the better-than-expected performance of the Christian Democrats was cited first. Both RAI news services conveyed essentially the same message, and the party papers amplified it; *Il Popolo* screamed "Victory to the DC!" (and appended some highly misleading figures); even *L'Unità,* while hailing in a torrent of red ink the "impetuous advance" of the PCI, conceded in the second line the recovery of the DC.

In fact, the DC lost three seats and the PCI gained more than forty. By Wednesday the papers not only had it straight, but were gripped again by the crisis mentality. "The Most Difficult Parliament of the Republic," *Corriere della Sera* said.

Effects of the Media on the Election. There was a warning early on in this chapter that the effects of the media on behavior are always difficult to identify, even when the behavior is as specific as the act of voting. Any assertions that media influence makes or breaks can be disposed of, in this case, by citing the fortunes of the Socialists and the Radicals. The great amount of attention given the PSI has been discussed earlier; that party's share of the vote was almost exactly the same as in the national election of 1972, 9.7 percent; it lost four seats in the Chamber of Deputies, and was off 3 percentage points from its showing in the regional elections of 1975. The Radical party was never seen as a major force, but it was the darling of the intellectuals and artists; it had its own radio station, apparently much listened to, had the most striking graphic symbol, and got much attention from journalists. It polled 1.1 percent of the vote.

Obviously media effects are much more complicated than the first common-sense insight would suggest. What follows here is, if not mere speculation, at best a matter of judgment.

Since the end of World War II, Italian politics has been essentially a matter of an antiestablishment, secular left led by intellectuals and philosophical revolutionaries in the classic European pattern set against a right which represents the heirarchical structure of the society and is led by an elite with money, status, and the power that grows out of that combination. In this alignment during the past thirty years there has been no real center; the center, as represented by the Christian Democrats, has been essentially rightist. For many reasons, including tradition and a love of politics for its own sake, a variety of political parties, the differences among which often are subtle, have stayed alive at the superficial level. As institutions, the media of mass communication have reinforced this fractionation; political parties have spent heavily to keep their official newspapers going, and the Italian journalist, proud of his identity as a political man, has reinforced the variety through his elaborate attention to the arcane dynamics of both intraparty and interparty relations. This has resulted in a political journalism beyond the understanding of most of the voters. The most pervasive of all the media, radio and television, in the past were so shorn of obvious political involvement that they seemed not involved in party politics at all.

The confluence of several trends made the election of 1976 different. Continued economic crisis and civil unrest helped create an atmosphere of deep concern for the country's future; the media, and especially newspapers and magazines, reinforced it, and the electorate responded by setting aside the joy of voting for style, wit, and delicate differences; instead, it soberly voted on the basis of a two-party world, and in the process demolished the minor parties.

Developments within the media, in addition to reinforcing the sense of national crisis, gave an additional thrust to the trend toward the simplification of politics. With the single exception of L'Unità, party papers either died or, by the time of voting, had shrunk almost to the point of extinction. The country's major nonparty papers, presumably without party identification but in the past for the most part on the side of the government, began to move sharply to the left; losing not only tremendous amounts of money but also circulation, they began seeking reforms that might renew the interest of the public. This coincided with major changes in ownership and with the rise of some control by working journalists over content and editorial policy.

Similarly, a confluence of pressures brought change to RAI. Court decisions produced a parliamentary commission charged with making political access to broadcasting much easier; a later set of court rulings limited the RAI monopoly to national broadcasts and permitted the rapid and thus far completely unregulated growth of local broadcasting.

All this did much to dilute the elitism of Italian party politics. Politicians, suddenly aware of addressing huge numbers of people—hundreds of thousands of whom might be possible converts—began to turn their attention to projecting a favorable personal image on behalf of their parties and to seeking to offend no one; (only sure losers are ever willing to be offensive on television). In the case of the two leading parties this was especially true; neither the PCI, on the verge of power, nor the DC, trying to retain it, could afford any appearance of irresponsibility.

The total effect of all these factors was to produce a sober election resembling, much more than any past Italian election, the pattern of politics in countries like the United States, Germany, the United Kingdom, and Japan. A year after the election of 1976, the enfeebled minor parties of Italy were complaining about the tyranny of the majority—a majority consisting, operationally, of the DC and the PCI. The graffiti on university walls were often as bitter toward Berlinguer as toward Andreotti, and the Communist daily *L'Unità* was fiercely attacking the radicals of the left.

That is not to say that the Communists and the Christian Democrats will be indistinguishable in the near future, or that the consensus which came out of the election is permanent. It is to suggest that Italian politics is moving toward the blurring of elegant intellectual differences, the simplification of dialectic, and a concentrated push to get a broad base in the electorate. The media of mass communication are, and will continue to be, primary tools in bringing about that kind of change.

9

ITALIAN FOREIGN POLICY: THE EMERGENT CONSENSUS

Robert D. Putnam

Throughout the thirty-year history of the Italian Republic foreign policy debates have focused on the two fundamental choices made by the postwar governments of Alcide De Gasperi: the *scelta di civiltà* (choice of civilization) embodied in the Atlantic Alliance, which bound Italy to an anti-Communist defense pact led by the United States; and the commitment to Western European integration, embodied most enduringly in the Treaty of Rome, which created the European Economic Community. Fidelity to this European and Atlantic *collocazione internazionale* (international alignment) has been the quintessential article of faith of the moderate parties that have ruled Italy throughout the postwar period, above all the Christian Democrats, whereas hostility to both NATO and the EEC has been the continuing theme of the left opposition, led by the Italian Communist party. Beginning with the bitter elections of 1948, acrimonious conflict about these foundations of Italian foreign policy has characterized every electoral campaign, as well as the interelection periods.[1]

Perhaps the most remarkable fact about the 1976 election, however, is that foreign policy ceased to be the kind of issue that it had been. In 1976 Italy's *collocazione internazionale* was transformed from a "position issue," like abortion, on which the parties took con-

Among the numerous friends who have helped me to think through the argument of this chapter, I want especially to thank Ronald Inglehart, Robert Keohane, Norman Kogan, Celinda Lake, A. F. K. Organski, and Franco Pavoncello.

[1] For useful introductions to postwar Italian foreign policy, see Norman Kogan, *The Politics of Italian Foreign Policy* (New York: Praeger, 1963); F. Roy Willis, *Italy Chooses Europe* (New York: Oxford University Press, 1971); and Primo Vannicelli, *Italy, NATO, and the European Community: The Interplay of Foreign Policy and Domestic Politics*, Harvard Studies in International Affairs, no. 31 (Cambridge, Mass.: Harvard University Center for International Affairs, 1974).

trasting stands, into a "valence issue," like economic growth, about which the only visible disagreement was which party would more successfully and enthusiastically pursue the policy goals shared by all.[2]

Party platforms testified to this surprising convergence. Except for the Proletarian Democrats on the extreme left, each party sought the resolution of Italy's economic difficulties in the free flow of international trade and capital, firmly rejecting autarky and protectionism. Each party (again with the exception of the DP) made the European Community a centerpiece of its foreign policy, and each called for progress toward supranational integration, including direct elections to the European Parliament. East-West détente was universally praised, but pledges of allegiance to the Atlantic Alliance were almost as universal. Even on the left, only the isolated DP remained faithful to "the watchword of such glorious tradition—Italy out of NATO." By all odds, the most striking feature of the new convergence was the PCI's endorsement of Italy's political, economic, and military ties to the West.

Given this apparent agreement on the main lines of foreign policy, the debate in 1976, unlike that in past campaigns, focused on the parties' respective abilities to carry out a European and Atlantic strategy. The parties of the center and right argued that, however sincere might be the new-found commitment of the PCI to the West, an Italian government that included the PCI would inevitably find itself excluded from full participation in NATO and the EEC. The PCI replied that Italy's much-feared *emarginazione* (isolation) derived instead from the economic and administrative failures of previous governments, failures that could be overcome only by the inclusion of the PCI within the governing coalition. Such "anything you can do, I can do better" argumentation is the classic mark of a valence issue.

I shall discuss later some of the remaining differences among the parties' foreign policy positions. Our point of departure, however, must be this striking convergence on the fundamentals of Italian foreign policy, a convergence acknowledged by leaders across the political spectrum. Before the election Sergio Segre, foreign affairs spokesman of the PCI, observed, "For more than 20 years foreign policy was probably the major point of contention among Italian political forces, [but] today, there are no substantial disagreements

---

[2] On the distinction between position and valence issues, see David Butler and Donald Stokes, *Political Change in Britain* (New York: St. Martin's Press, 1969), p. 189.

288

on the major options of Italian foreign policy."[3] This view was echoed later by the Christian Democratic foreign minister, Arnaldo Forlani, who reported to the United Nations General Assembly that "on the basic choices [of Italian foreign policy] there exists a full measure of agreement in our national parliament, between our political forces, and throughout the country."[4]

To assess the depth, the significance, and the implications of this emergent consensus, we must understand its origins. It shall be my thesis that both the consensus and its limits must be traced to several hard international and domestic realities that have emerged in the course of the last decade to constrain the foreign policy choices of any political force that aspires to help govern Italy. The underlying theme will be the growing recognition on the part of those who would make Italian foreign policy that, at least for the foreseeable future, Italy will remain a dependent country in an interdependent world.[5]

Thus, to understand the unexpected role of foreign policy in the elections of 1976, we must examine (1) Italy's international economic position, (2) its role in the international strategic balance, (3) the changing views of the electorate on international issues, and (4) the evolving domestic and transnational alliance strategies of the political parties, especially the PCI.

Economic Interdependence

Italy's Economic Ties to the West. The economic miracle of the 1950s and 1960s radically transformed Italy's economic relations with the rest of the world.[6] Lacking natural resources, Italy became an ever more successful exporter of low-technology manufactured goods, tourist satisfactions, and manpower and an ever increasing importer of energy, foodstuffs, and raw materials. Foreign trade grew

---

[3] Sergio Segre, "The 'Communist Question' in Italy," *Foreign Affairs*, vol. 54 (July 1976), p. 699.

[4] Arnaldo Forlani, "Statement to the XXXI Session of the General Assembly" (New York: Permanent Mission of Italy to the United Nations, October 1, 1976), p. 13.

[5] For a more detailed version of the argument presented here, together with additional supporting evidence, see my "Interdependence and the Italian Communists," *International Organization* (forthcoming).

[6] For useful introductions to the postwar Italian economy, including its international dimensions, see George H. Hildebrand, *Growth and Structure in the Economy of Modern Italy* (Cambridge, Mass.: Harvard University Press, 1965), and Gisele Podbielski, *Italy: Development and Crisis in the Post-War Economy* (New York: Oxford University Press, 1974).

rapidly and consistently, not merely in absolute terms, but even as a share of the swiftly expanding Italian economy, rising from roughly one-tenth of GNP in 1948 to more than one-fifth in 1976.

By the mid-1960s observers noted one important consequence of this profitable involvement in international commerce: "The Italian economy is 'open and vulnerable' to shocks from the outside world, indeed . . . more so than most countries."[7] As the international economic storms of the 1970s broke, Italy's vulnerability had grown greater still, now compounded by serious domestic structural weaknesses, a wage explosion, and very low levels of investment. The explosion of world prices for energy and raw materials in 1971–1974, followed by the unprecedented collapse in demand for manufactured goods during the worldwide recession of 1974–1976, devastated Italy's balance of payments. In particular, because of Italy's extraordinary dependence on Middle Eastern oil, no country in the industrialized world was harder hit by the oil price increases.[8] These adverse trends were accentuated by speculative capital flows that forced a series of drastic devaluations of the lira. Nor did Italy's public institutions enjoy the legitimacy and efficiency that would have enabled them to respond effectively to these crises.

In the face of these multiple ills, economic nationalism might seem a tempting option. But the economic realities created by nearly three decades of export-led expansion have largely foreclosed that alternative. To understand these new realities, we must glance at how Italy's trading partnerships have changed during the postwar era. In terms of both imports and exports, Italy's trade with the industrialized West, particularly within the EEC, and most particularly with Germany and France, has grown even faster than its foreign commerce generally. By contrast, commercial ties with the Third World (apart from the oil-producing countries) and with Eastern Europe have stagnated or even declined in relative (though not in absolute) terms. For example, West Germany alone has accounted for roughly one-fifth of Italy's exports in recent years, a share that has grown at the rate of about 5.4 percent per decade over the postwar period, whereas all of Eastern Europe (including the

---

[7] Hildebrand, *Growth and Structure*, p. 79.

[8] On Italy and the aftermath of the oil crisis, see Robert J. Lieber, *Oil and the Middle East War: Europe in the Energy Crisis*, Harvard Studies in International Affairs, no. 35 (Cambridge, Mass.: Harvard University Center for International Affairs, 1976), and the very useful annual volumes of *L'Italia nella Politica Internazionale* [Italy in international politics], edited by the Istituto Affari Internazionali of Rome (Milan: Comunità, 1973 and following years).

USSR) has accounted for roughly one-twentieth of Italian exports in recent years, a share that has "grown" at the rate of 0.1 percent per decade over this period. By 1976 the EEC alone accounted for nearly half of Italy's foreign trade and the countries of the Organization for Economic Cooperation and Development (OECD)—the industrialized West—for nearly three-quarters.

None of these commercial trends is peculiar to Italy, of course. Indeed, Italy's dependence on trade with Western Europe is just about on a par with that of its major EEC partners. Nor do these patterns imply that trade with the Second and Third Worlds is of negligible importance, particularly in helping to right a weak balance of trade. Nevertheless, trade data illustrate that Italy has shared fully in the growing economic interdependence among the nations of the North Atlantic.

These economic ties extend well beyond commercial flows to include less easily measurable, but no less significant, transfers of capital and technology. With the onset of the oil crisis in 1974, Italy began to draw heavily on loans from the International Monetary Fund and from the EEC countries, especially West Germany. The rapidity and intensity of the 1976 collapse of the lira illustrated the degree of interdependence in contemporary financial markets. Equally important, Italy's needs for imported capital will continue to be immense in the coming years, not merely to cover the rising cost of oil, but, more fundamentally, to finance the investment needed to regain international competitiveness and to meet the credit needs of prospective customers, especially in Eastern Europe and the Third World outside of the Organization of Petroleum Exporting Countries (OPEC). Though some of these capital requirements can be met by the direct recycling of OPEC wealth, the bulk of Italy's financial needs will have to be satisfied through bilateral and multilateral loans and investments from the West, especially the United States and West Germany.

These capital and commercial flows are supplemented by other sorts of transnational economic links. Only slightly less intensively than other European nations, Italy hosts a substantial number of multinational corporations, including several important ones based in Italy, such as Fiat and Olivetti. Italian expenditures on research and development are quite low even by European standards, so that the expansion of new high-technology industries, less subject to growing competition from the Third World, is in turn dependent on international collaboration and technology transfers. Receipts from tourism and remittances from emigrant workers are still important entries in Italy's national accounts.[9]

For all these reasons, Italy's well-being is clearly dependent on continued integration with the world economy, and most especially with the industrial nations of Western Europe and North America. As one of the PCI's leading economists has written:

> Some attribute the instability of the Italian economy to its high degree of foreign dependence, but every illusion, all wishful thinking about self-sufficiency should be rejected, [for] the increasingly marked interdependence of Italy with respect to the world market is determined by the peculiar, objective nature of the country, by the relative scarcity of material resources.[10]

Arrigo Levi, a leading non-Communist journalist, points out, "By now, no country could leave the European Community without seriously risking falling into a kind of medieval era economically."[11] Of none of the Nine is this more true than of Italy. In sum, the fears of *emarginazione* widely expressed in Italy today have a firm foundation in economic reality.

Italy's relations of interdependence are reciprocal, of course, in the sense that its primary economic partners are also vulnerable to disturbances in their relations with Italy. The German economy, for instance, would be seriously harmed if its markets in Italy were to be restricted. German loans to help restore stability to the Italian economy are not selfless. But interdependence can be reciprocal

---

[9] On Italy's transnational linkages, see Karl Kaiser, "Le relazioni transnazionali" [Transnational relations], in *Il Caso Italiano* [The Italian case], Fabio Luca Cavazza and Stephen R. Graubard, eds. (Milan: Garzanti, 1974), vol. 2, pp. 401-419. On Italy's expenditures on research and development, see Henry R. Nau, "Collective Responses to R & D Problems in Western Europe: 1955-1958 and 1968-1973," *International Organization*, vol. 29 (Summer 1975), p. 640. A detailed, quantitative analysis of Italy's interdependence with the West would need to go well beyond the evidence presented here, but more subtle measurements would lead very likely to the same conclusions. For useful discussions of economic interdependence and international politics, see Richard N. Cooper, "Economic Interdependence and Foreign Policy in the Seventies," *World Politics*, vol. 24 (January 1972), pp. 159-181, and Robert O. Keohane and Joseph S. Nye, *Power and Interdependence: World Politics in Transition* (Boston: Little, Brown, 1977).

[10] Umberto Cardia, in *Politica ed Economia* (August 1976), as quoted in Giacomo Luciani, *Il PCI e il Capitalismo Occidentale* [The PCI and western capitalism] (Milan: Longanesi, 1977), p. 112.

[11] Arrigo Levi, "Gli ultimi dei primi e i primi degli ultimi" [The last of the first and the first of the last], in *Il Caso Italiano*, vol. 2, p. 426.

without being symmetrical. As Robert O. Keohane and Joseph S. Nye explain,

> We must be careful not to define interdependence entirely in terms of situations of *evenly balanced* mutual dependence. It is *asymmetries* in dependence that are most likely to provide sources of influence for actors in their dealings with one another. . . . A less dependent actor in a relationship often has a significant political resource, because changes in the relationship (which the actor may be able to initiate or threaten) will be less costly to that actor than to its partners.[12]

To be sure, debtors have some power over creditors, but in the end it is creditors, not debtors, who set terms, who exact "letters of intent," and so on. Speaking crudely, the other countries of the West, and especially those of the EEC, need Italy, but Italy needs them even more.

Interdependence and Foreign Policy. Asymmetric interdependence imposes *two* sorts of constraints on governments, each with far-reaching political implications. First, because of the high costs of withdrawal from the interdependent relationship, external actors acquire considerable potential control over the dependent nation's behavior. German loans to Italy, for example, have been accompanied by severe strictures both on domestic and foreign policy and on domestic political alliances. Chancellor Schmidt's public proclamation of such political strings in July 1976 was a brutally clear illustration of the politics of asymmetric interdependence.

More subtly, interdependence constrains a nation's ability to undertake autonomous domestic policy initiatives, quite apart from intentional foreign interventions. This constraint is clearest in the case of national monetary policy, which can be easily subverted by international financial flows. In addition, as Richard N. Cooper has shown, "The international mobility of firms and funds erodes the tax policies of nations, [as well as] the national capacity to impose and enforce limitations on business behavior."[13] No Italian government could impose radical socioeconomic reforms and still hope to remain a competitive member of the EEC, unless those reforms were to some degree imposed throughout the Community.

---

[12] Keohane and Nye, *Power and Interdependence*, pp. 10-11 (emphasis in original).

[13] Cooper, "Economic Interdependence," pp. 164-165. See also Richard N. Cooper, *The Economics of Interdependence: Economic Policy in the Atlantic Community* (New York: McGraw-Hill, 1968).

In short, economic interdependence among the industrialized nations of the West has effectively foreclosed any possibility of "socialism in one country," unless that country is willing to forgo the substantial benefits of economic integration. This fact is well understood by the strategists of the PCI. Defending the party's acceptance of supranational European institutions that might limit the autonomy of a leftist government in Rome, Giorgio Amendola explains:

> Today the national sovereignty of every country is already limited in fact. It is a consequence of economic interdependence, of the need for loans, of the development of multinational firms, of every sort of bond, apart from the political conditions tied to the existence of military blocs. One has to give up the idea that there is a national, sovereign state that can decide its own fate in full autonomy; it is an anachronistic idea.[14]

Widespread recognition of the implications of asymmetric economic interdependence helps explain the transmutation of foreign policy from a position issue into a valence issue in the election campaign of 1976. Virtually all parties dismissed the siren calls of economic autarky. Debate about Italy's economic ties to the West was limited to accusations by each party that victory for its opponents would aggravate the risks of economic isolation. The Christian Democrats argued that Western aid would be jeopardized by Communist electoral gains. This argument was conveniently supported by expressions of official concern about the Italian elections emanating from Washington, Paris, London, and Bonn.[15]

The PCI replied that Western aid and investment were discouraged instead by the ineptitude of the government's economic policies and by political instability, both maladies curable only with a stronger Communist presence in the policy-making process. Indeed, while rejecting the imposition of political conditions on Western assistance to Italy, the Communists' economic spokesman, Luciano Barca, welcomed the imposition of stringent conditions on Italian economic policy.[16] Behind the partisan campaign polemics lay an important premise shared by all sides: that Italy's well-being depends on continued integration into the Western economy.

---

14 "Intervista con Giorgio Amendola" [Interview with Giorgio Amendola], appendix to Luciani, *Il PCI*, p. 176.

15 In fact, the strong U.S. public warnings about the consequences of Communist gains were apparently prompted privately by the Christian Democrats themselves. See "Italian Leaders Prompted U.S. Stand on Communists," *New York Times*, June 13, 1976, p. 1.

16 *Corriere della Sera* (Milan), July 2, 1976, p. 2.

International Security and Italian Foreign Policy

Italy and NATO. To understand the role of international security considerations in Italian foreign policy debates, we must first understand what NATO means to Italy and vice versa. Although Italy has been a loyal—even docile—member of this military alliance for nearly three decades, its motives for membership have never been primarily military. Italy's initial decision to join NATO was in fact reluctant. American diplomatic pressure, Italian dependence on Marshall Plan aid, fear of diplomatic and economic isolation, and a desire for international guarantees against radical shifts in domestic politics were more important factors in the decision than was fear of Soviet aggression.[17]

Throughout the cold war, despite the occasional hyperbole of Italian leaders, latent neutralism was very widespread. Italians who favored membership in NATO were outnumbered by those who had never heard of it, and those who thought that Italy should side with the West in the case of a "hot" war were even more outnumbered by those who thought Italy should remain neutral. Though most common among leftists, this denial of the principle of collective security was also characteristic of supporters of the pro-American parties of the center and the right.[18]

Détente and diminished fear of the Soviet Union further attenuated Italian strategic concerns. By 1974, both ordinary citizens and the attentive public were distinctly less enthusiastic about the military aspects of NATO and distinctly less eager to maintain a strong defense force than their counterparts in other NATO countries.[19] To be sure, Italians are no less concerned to defend their national independence and territorial integrity than other peoples, but their sense of shared danger from Soviet aggression is less acute than that of Germans, Britons, or Americans, so that their assessment of the military significance of the alliance is more modest. In this sense, we

---

[17] See Kogan, *Politics*, p. 136, and Willis, *Italy Chooses Europe*, pp. 18-27.

[18] On the attitudes of Italy's governing parties to the Atlantic Alliance, see Stefano Silvestri, "Il dibattito sulla NATO in Italia" [The NATO debate in Italy], *Lo Spettatore Internazionale*, vol. 3 (January-February 1968), pp. 121-141; Willis, *Italy Chooses Europe*, pp. 252-285; and Kogan, *Politics, passim.* For survey evidence on Italian attitudes to national defense and the Atlantic Alliance, see Lloyd A. Free and Renzo Sereno, *Italy: Dependent Ally or Independent Partner?* (Princeton, N.J.: Institute for International Social Research, 1957), p. 79; Kogan, *Politics*, pp. 24-28; and Richard L. Merritt and Donald J. Puchala, eds., *Western Europe Perspectives on International Affairs* (New York: Praeger, 1968), esp. pp. 201; 220-222; 328-331; 338-351.

[19] Lloyd A. Free, *How Others See Us* (Lexington, Mass.: Lexington Books, D.C. Heath, 1976), pp. 75-88.

may appropriate Pierre Hassner's label for Italy's attitude to the Western alliance: "pacifist Atlanticism."[20]

Nor is the evidence on this point merely verbal. Despite rhetoric about the importance of NATO's southern flank, Italy's material contribution to the alliance is remarkably low.[21] By virtually any comparative measure, Italy's defense spending has always ranked well below average for NATO's European members. In proportion to population or national wealth, Italy spends roughly half as much on defense as its NATO and non-NATO neighbors on the northern shores of the Mediterranean. Moreover, until very recently, an unusually high share of Italian military spending was devoted to personnel and a correspondingly low proportion to equipment and supplies. Large numbers of poorly armed soldiers suggest a force structure designed more for internal security than for external defense. Recently inaugurated ten-year defense modernization programs and a sharp reduction in military manpower in 1976 have tended to redress this imbalance between manpower and matériel, but have placed Italy with Luxembourg at the very bottom of the NATO roster in terms of military manpower as a percentage of males aged eighteen to forty-five. In sum, Italy's relatively modest defense effort tends to confirm that Italian involvement in NATO reflects, and is constrained by, domestic economic and political factors, rather than deeply felt imperatives of collective defense.

On the other hand, one must also consider what Italy means to NATO. Italy's primary role in Western defense consists in the provision of bases and logistic support for American naval and nuclear forces. In short, Italy is much more important for where it is than for what it does. Pacifist Atlanticism is formally inconsistent with Italy's NATO obligations, but it fits Italy's effective role within the alliance.

One important consequence is that Italian defense needs are largely met as a byproduct of the American presence at very low cost to the Italians. In the language of game theory, Italy is the classic "free rider" in the Western defense system. Any more independent system of national defense would be considerably more expensive, as indicated by the defense budgets of such European neutrals as Sweden, Switzerland, and Yugoslavia. NATO is for the Italians a "best buy."

---

20 Pierre Hassner, "The Political Evolution of Italy and the International Context: A Personal View," prepared for a joint meeting of the Istituto Affari Internazionale and Chatham House, Manziani, November 20-22, 1975.

21 Data on defense expenditures and manpower from *The Military Balance: 1976-1977* (London: International Institute for Strategic Studies, 1976) and earlier volumes in that series.

NATO, the Elections, and the PCI. Given Italy's characteristic orientation to NATO, it is hardly surprising that military issues were virtually undiscussed during the campaign.[22] Only the minor parties (the Liberals, the Social Democrats, and the Republicans) expressed concern about NATO's defense capabilities, for which they were ill-rewarded by the electorate. But if the military aspects of NATO were ignored, the political implications of Italy's membership in the Alliance featured prominently in the campaign. Here emerged the most important novelty in Italian foreign policy discussions in nearly three decades: the Communists' acceptance of Italy's membership in NATO. What lay behind this dramatic development?

The PCI's opposition to NATO had its roots in the earliest years of the cold war.[23] Immediately after the Liberation, the party entertained some hopes of coexistence with the United States. But during 1947–1948 the full force of the East-West conflict broke over Europe, and the PCI adopted an increasingly anti-American line. Subordination to Soviet strategy was an important element in this line. But fundamentally the Communists opposed NATO for the same reason that the Christian Democrats and their moderate allies endorsed it: Italian membership in NATO implied international guarantees of the domestic status quo.

With the gradual development of détente and with greater autonomy from Moscow, the party's hostility to the West slowly softened, most noticeably with regard to Western European integration. Yet the party's position on NATO and the United States remained essentially unchanged throughout the 1960s: the bipolar system of military blocs must be dismantled. Italy must leave NATO, and NATO must leave Italy.

At the party's Fourteenth National Congress in March 1975, however, Enrico Berlinguer reported a remarkable revision of the party's attitude to NATO:

---

[22] In addition to the party platforms, see the statements by party representatives in *La Stampa* (Turin), June 13, 1976. The platforms of the Socialists, Communists, and Christian Democrats did discuss proposals for reforms within the armed forces, aiming at more protection for the civil rights of soldiers, greater efficiency, and closer links between the armed forces and civil society. Such reforms may be highly desirable, but they are only marginally relevant to the exigencies of NATO or Italian national defense.

[23] On the evolution of the PCI's international policy, see Donald L. Blackmer, *Unity in Diversity: Italian Communism and the Communist World* (Cambridge, Mass.: M.I.T. Press, 1968); Donald L. Blackmer, "Continuity and Change in Postwar Italian Communism," in Donald L. Blackmer and Sidney Tarrow, eds., *Communism in Italy and France* (Princeton, N.J.: Princeton University Press, 1975), pp. 21-68; and Willis, *Italy Chooses Europe*, pp. 287-299.

We do not pose the question of Italy's departure from the Atlantic Pact, because this eventuality, and every other unilateral exit from one bloc or the other, in a situation like the European one, not only is not feasible, but would end up hampering or even reversing the process of international détente.[24]

This statement capped a revision of the PCI's views on defense and national security that had been quietly underway for several years. The party had already begun to retreat from its traditional opposition to military spending. Indeed, in the 1974 parliamentary debates on the military budget, the Communist spokesman had criticized the Socialist rapporteur for "veiled antimilitarism, which takes [us] back to outmoded times that did not take account of popular patriotic sentiments."[25] The PCI accepted Italian membership in NATO's integrated defense system and dropped its demand that the American bases in Italy be closed.

The Communists' new attitude toward the Western alliance was the most discussed aspect of foreign policy during the 1976 campaign. The party's opponents on the far right argued that the PCI was simply aiming to become a Trojan horse within NATO. Most moderate politicians, however, did not contest the sincerity of the party's leadership. Rather, they argued that, willy-nilly, Communist gains would weaken Italy's involvement in NATO and strengthen Soviet influence in the Mediterranean.

For example, Giuseppe Saragat, long-time leader of the pro-Western Social Democrats, argued:

It isn't that I have suspicions about Berlinguer, Longo, or Amendola, who are good people and who are probably in good faith. But the fact is that the existence of a popular front in Italy would immediately give Russia a pretext for practically imposing its hegemony on our country. We would be excluded from the Atlantic Alliance. . . . Countries like Yugoslavia, which have defended themselves courageously and continue even today to defend themselves against Soviet hegemony, would probably be forced to surrender. . . . The PCI declares itself to be independent. But *could* it be, if Russia could interfere in our internal affairs with arms and with tanks, as it did in Czechoslovakia and Hungary, and as it would do in Italy, if there were no American umbrella?[26]

---

[24] Enrico Berlinguer, *La politica internazionale dei comunisti italiani: 1975-1976* [The international policy of Italian Communists: 1975-1976], Antonio Tato, ed. (Rome: Editori Riuniti, 1976). This is a useful collection of Berlinguer's speeches on international affairs during this pivotal year.

[25] *L'Italia nella politica internazionale: 1973-1974*, p. 464.

This evocation of Italian fears of isolation from the West was an effective electoral argument in the hands of the non-Communists, reinforced as it was by suggestions from NATO official circles that Communist participation in the government would automatically exclude Italy from full participation in the alliance. In response, the PCI argued that, just as Italy had an interest in staying in NATO, NATO had an interest in keeping Italy in.[27] Moreover, the Communists stressed repeatedly their desire for friendship with the United States and went to great lengths to avoid polemics with the Americans, dismissing attacks by U.S. officials as not representing the full spectrum of opinion among American leaders. Not for thirty years had anti-Americanism played so small a role in an Italian election campaign.[28]

But what if the Soviet Union should try to impose its will on Italy? Party spokesmen at first limited themselves to the position that, given détente, this contingency would not arise. But many non-Communists whose votes the PCI sought were not so convinced of the benign character of Soviet foreign policy. Thus, in the closing days of the campaign the party was forced to a significant elaboration of its attitude toward NATO. During an interview granted by Berlinguer to *Corriere della Sera* (and revised by him line by line before publication) the following remarkable exchange occurred:

> [Interviewer] You don't fear that Moscow will make happen to Berlinguer and his Eurocommunism the same thing that happened to Dubcek and his "socialism with a human face"?
>
> [Berlinguer] No. We are in another area of the world. And admitting that there is the will, there is not the least possibility that our path to socialism could be hindered or conditioned by the USSR. You can discuss whether there is a desire of hegemony on the part of the USSR over the countries that are allied to it. But not a single act reveals any intention of the USSR to move beyond the frontiers fixed at Yalta.
>
> [Interviewer] In sum, the Atlantic Pact can even be a shield useful for the building of socialism in liberty?

---

[26] *Il Tempo* (Rome), May 26, 1976.

[27] *L'Unità* (Rome), June 1, 1976.

[28] On the other hand, the United States has been a convenient target of PCI distrust and hostility for many years, and one should not exaggerate the degree to which this visceral suspicion and antipathy have diminished. For abundant illustrations of the persistently anti-American tenor of PCI publications, see Giuseppe Are, "Italy's Communists: Foreign and Defense Policies," *Survival*, vol. 18 (September-October 1976), pp. 210-216.

[Berlinguer] I want Italy not to leave the Atlantic Pact also for this [reason], and not just because our exit would upset the international balance. I feel more secure on this side. But I see that here too there are serious attempts to limit our autonomy.[29]

That the leader of the Italian Communist party would "feel more secure" under the protection of NATO was indeed a remarkable declaratic... It was welcomed by non-Communist Italian commentators as another indication of growing international realism on the part of the PCI. Although its impact was blurred by Berlinguer's subsequent insistence that he feared interference from the West as well as from the East, the statement remained politically significant, as the PCI's first public recognition that Italy's national security interests were best served by membership in NATO. What could explain this reversal of hallowed party policy?

The official justification was relatively simple:

The unilateral withdrawal of Italy from NATO would disturb the entire process of détente, which is based on the strategic equilibrium of forces between NATO and those of the Warsaw Pact. To introduce an element of disequilibrium in that process would be contrary to the interests of peace, contrary to our own interests, and to those of other countries.[30]

Clearly, the continued success of the PCI does depend heavily on détente. But less than a decade earlier the party had argued that "Italy can and must contribute to détente . . . rejecting the American thesis according to which peace should be founded on the division of the world into zones of influence and on the balance of terror."[31] What had happened in the intervening ten years to make this "American thesis" more plausible to the PCI?

A rounded interpretation of this reversal of the PCI's international strategy must await the fuller evidence and longer perspective that will be available to the historian. But several elements in the explanation seem clear now. First, some important obstacles to the PCI's reconciliation with NATO faded between 1973 and 1976, espe-

---

[29] *Corriere della Sera* (Milan), June 15, 1976. Reprinted in Berlinguer, *La politica internazionale*, pp. 159-160.

[30] Berlinguer, *La politica internazionale*, p. 70.

[31] "La lotta per la pace, per una nuova politica estera dell'Italia, e per l'unita del movimento operaio internazionale" [The struggle for peace, for a new Italian foreign policy, and for the unity of the international workers' movement], *L'Unità*, November 7, 1965, as cited in Massimo Bonanni, "I partiti italiani e la politica estera: PCI" [Italian political parties and foreign policy: PCI], *Lo Spettatore Internazionale*, vol. 1 (January-February 1966), p. 74.

cially American involvement in Vietnam and, within the Mediterranean, the right-wing dictatorships in Greece, Portugal, and Spain. Given its passionate antifascism, the PCI would have found it virtually impossible to join an alliance that included several Fascist regimes.[32]

Two other international events were probably even more decisive in encouraging the PCI to accept the logic of a bipolar system of blocs: the overthrow of Dubcek and the overthrow of Allende. As is well known, the events of Czechoslovakia accelerated the PCI's progress toward autonomy from the Soviet Union, while the events of Chile occasioned a fundamental reexamination of the PCI's domestic strategy. More relevant here, both events provided final confirmation that East-West détente in no way undermined the logic of Yalta, according to which geography, not domestic politics, determines international alignments. It is, as Kremlinologists are wont to say, hardly an accident that Berlinguer referred to "the frontiers fixed at Yalta" in his interview with the *Corriere della Sera.*

Italian Communists themselves emphasized yet another international factor in explaining the new line—the need to ensure the nonaligned status of Yugoslavia in the post-Tito period. The "vital" and "profound" interest of the PCI in Yugoslav autonomy and the necessity of Italian membership in NATO to "avoid instability in the Central Mediterranean" were underlined by party spokesmen throughout the 1976 campaign.[33] However, it was left to Altiero Spinelli to make the point explicit.

> If a country like ours, which lies at such a critical spot, were to exit from NATO, this would impair stability. Strategic instability could be dangerous. The Communists have a clear, even if not manifest, motivation in this connection: the nearest critical point would almost certainly be Yugoslavia. They understand: if Italy assumes a neutralist position, then it is possible that Yugoslavia would end up the same way as Czechoslovakia. This they do not want.[34]

---

[32] See Berlinguer's comments on the passing of Mediterranean fascism at the Fourteenth Party Congress, as reprinted in Berlinguer, *La politica internazionale,* p. 22.

[33] See, for example, Berlinguer's statement on NATO at the Fourteenth Party Congress, reprinted in Berlinguer, *La politica internazionale,* p. 20, as well as the statements of Sergio Segre in *La Stampa* (Turin), May 31, 1976, and Alberto Jacoviello in *La Repubblica* (Rome), June 2, 1976.

[34] *L'Unità* (Rome), June 6, 1976. It is symptomatic of the PCI's "new look" in foreign policy that much of the responsibility for campaigning on this topic was assigned to two prestigious non-Communists, running as independents on the Communist slate for Parliament: Spinelli, former EEC commissioner and Italy's most renowned Europeanist, and General Nino Pasti, former supreme NATO vice-commander for nuclear affairs.

Historically, the independence of Yugloslavia has been considered an essential national interest by Italian statesmen. The "after Tito?" problem was quite salient for the Italian political class in 1975 and 1976, and indeed was an important motive for the normalization of relations between the two countries in November 1975, including the final settlement of the Trieste dispute. Any Italian party preparing to share government responsibilities would have had to weigh carefully its stance on this sensitive issue.

For the PCI, however, the question has added significance. The reaction of Italians to Soviet interference along Italy's eastern border would seriously compromise the PCI's long march along the democratic path to power, unless the party were to break irrevocably with the Soviets and support NATO defensive actions. As one distinguished leader of the Italian left, long sympathetic to the PCI, said privately in July 1976, "The last thing we want is Soviet troops on our border." Publicly, PCI leaders expressed confidence that no attempt would be made to upset Yugoslav nonalignment, but this public optimism did not preclude private concern about Soviet intentions, especially following the Soviet demands for increased Yugoslav military "cooperation" made during Brezhnev's visit to Belgrade in November 1976. In sum, Yugoslav neutrality is a vital strategic interest shared by NATO, Italy, and the Italian Communists.

Public Opinion and Italian Foreign Policy

Like citizens elsewhere, most Italians devote little attention to foreign affairs, and most have no firm views on the practical issues facing decision makers. Thus, public opinion rarely determines foreign policy. In representative democracies, however, no party competing in the electoral marketplace is likely to be successful if it consistently violates firmly held preferences of potential voters. Thus, over the long run, public consensus on international issues exerts a steady pressure on the foreign policies of party leaders. Therefore, it is instructive to examine the changing state of Italian public opinion toward the two main anchors of Italy's international alignment: Western Europe and the United States.

Italians and European Integration. At the creation of the Common Market in 1958 Italian support for European unity was quite lukewarm, compared to public attitudes elsewhere in Europe.[35] But the

---

[35] Ronald Inglehart, *The Silent Revolution: Changing Values and Political Styles among Western Publics* (Princeton, N.J.: Princeton University Press, 1977), pp. 344-349.

succeeding decades witnessed a steady increase in Italian enthusiasm for Europe. Italians readily recognized the benefits they derived from the Common Market, and they hoped for progress toward a federal Europe. By 1976 mass support for supranational European integration was actually higher in Italy than anywhere else in the Community. About nine Italians in ten endorsed such specific steps toward European unity as direct elections to the European Parliament and common European policies on such matters as economics, labor relations, civil rights, and foreign relations.[36] Doubtless much of this enthusiasm for European government was uninformed and represented disillusionment with Italian government. Nevertheless, it had become impolitic for any party to oppose this consensus for Europe.

Behind this transformation of Italian opinion on Europe lay a remarkable shift in party alignments. Figure 9–1 shows that in the mid-1950s Socialist and (especially) Communist voters were quite skeptical about Europe, following their parties' line that European integration was a capitalist trap. But the obvious benefits of the EEC converted first Socialist, and then Communist, voters into increasingly enthusiastic supporters of European integration. By 1976 Socialist voters were among the staunchest Europeanists in Italy, and the support for European unification expressed by Communist-voting survey respondents was only ten to fifteen percentage points behind that expressed by other Italians.[37]

Meanwhile, at the official level the PCI's attitude to European integration was also evolving.[38] In 1958 Communist deputies alone had voted against the Treaty of Rome, but the exhilarating spurt of

---

[36] Data from unpublished Eurobarometer surveys in 1975 and 1976, conducted for the Commission of the European Communities, under the direction of Jacques-René Rabier. I am grateful to Dr. Rabier and to Professor Ronald Inglehart for making these data available for my analysis, for which I am naturally responsible.

[37] In the 1976 Eurobarometer survey, for example, 81 percent of Communist voters favored a common European economic and monetary policy, as compared to 94 percent of non-Communists; 85 percent of the Communists, as compared to 92 percent of the non-Communists, favored direct elections to the European Parliament; and 76 percent of the Communists, as contrasted with 90 percent of the non-Communists, would accept European legislation concerning foreign relations. See also Figure 9–1.

[38] On the evolution of the PCI's attitude to Western European integration, see Donald L. Blackmer, "The International Strategy of the Italian Communist Party," in Donald L. Blackmer and Annie Kriegel, *The International Role of the Communist Parties of Italy and France*, Harvard Studies in International Affairs, no. 33 (Cambridge, Mass.: Harvard University Center for International Affairs, 1974), pp. 19-25; Blackmer, *Unity in Diversity*, pp. 263-329; Willis, *Italy Chooses Europe*, pp. 287-299; and Neil McInnes, "The Communist Parties of Western Europe and the EEC," *The World Today*, vol. 20 (February 1974), pp. 80-88.

Figure 9-1

SUPPORT FOR WESTERN EUROPEAN UNITY
IN THE ITALIAN PUBLIC, 1954-75

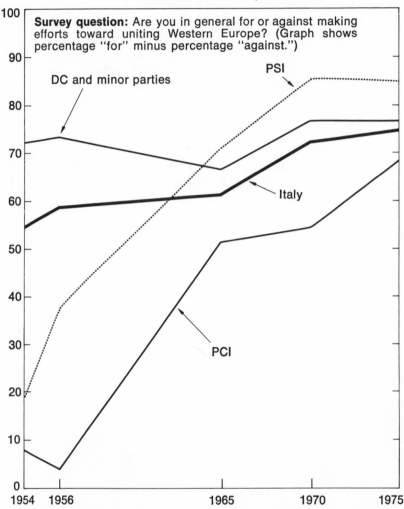

Survey question: Are you in general for or against making efforts toward uniting Western Europe? (Graph shows percentage "for" minus percentage "against.")

Source: For 1954-1965, surveys sponsored by United States Information Agency, data stored and analyzed by the Roper Public Opinion Research Center (Williamstown, Mass.); for 1970-1975: Eurobarometer Surveys, data originally collected by Jacques-René Rabier, special adviser to the Commission of the European Communities and made available through the Inter-University Consortium for Political and Social Research. Neither the collector of the data nor the consortium bears any responsibility for the analyses or interpretations presented here.

economic expansion that had characterized the first years of the Common Market had soon made outright opposition untenable. By 1962 the party reluctantly acknowledged the EEC's contribution to Italian prosperity, but on most practical issues involving national sovereignty and Europe's future the PCI found itself somewhat embarrassingly aligned with the Gaullists.

This position, too, was soon overtaken by reality. In 1969 the first PCI delegates were named to the European Parliament and there assumed a posture of constructive criticism. The Communists' public and private commitment to supranational European integration accelerated, and by 1976 party campaign propaganda even chided other Italian parties for not having pushed European unification beyond a mere customs union.[39] The party still called for greater European autonomy from America and for more "democratic" Community policies and institutions. Nevertheless, the PCI's basic stance toward Western European integration had been profoundly transformed in the space of barely a decade.

Doubtless, the shifting positions of the party and of its electorate were mutually supportive. Interestingly, however, evidence suggests that the voters were not taking cues from party leaders, but instead that the party itself may have been responding to the electoral marketplace. Four sorts of evidence support this interpretation:

(1) Figure 9–1 shows that the major shift in opinion among Communist voters occurred several years *before* any marked change in the party's official stance.

(2) Parallel surveys of voters and politicians in 1970 showed clearly that while nearly three-quarters of the Communist electorate favored major progress toward European integration, roughly three-quarters of Communist leaders still opposed such steps.[40] The PCI leadership was visibly lagging behind its own supporters, and, as Figure 9–1 shows, pro-European sentiment among Communist voters would accelerate again between 1970 and 1975. The party leaders were shooting at a moving target.

---

[39] *L'Unità* (Rome), June 20, 1976.

[40] The mass survey data in question were collected by Ronald Inglehart and Jacques-René Rabier on behalf of the European Communities, and were graciously made available for my analysis. At the suggestion of Professor Inglehart, I inserted identical questions in surveys conducted contemporaneously with national and regional Italian legislators. Analogous results were obtained with two separate questions, one concerning "the political formation of the United States of Europe" and the other, "a European government responsible for foreign affairs, defense, and the economy." These items were virtually unanimously endorsed by non-Communist voters and elites.

(3) Voters in 1970 were also asked where their parties stood on European integration. While virtually all non-Communists expressing an opinion described their parties (correctly) as favorable to European unity, Communist voters were thoroughly confused: 31 percent thought the PCI favorable, 26 percent thought it opposed, and 43 percent were completely unsure. Nevertheless, almost three-quarters of these same voters had already made up their own minds for Europe.

(4) These voters were also asked whether or not they would vote for another party, if their present party "took a position in regard to European unification contrary to your own ideas." Given the minimal impact that foreign affairs normally have on electoral decisions, the responses must be interpreted with caution. Nevertheless, it is interesting that while only one in twelve of the total Communist electorate said they "definitely" would defect if the party adopted a pro-European stand, nearly one Communist voter in *three* said he or she would switch allegiances if the party were to oppose European unification. In the short run, mixed signals might minimize losses, but in the long run, ambiguity on this central issue was not a tenable strategy. Moreover, the party's hopes for further gains rested among the solidly pro-European non-Communist electorate. Thus, by the 1970s the PCI's electoral calculus showed much to gain and little to lose from a clearer commitment to Western European unity.[41]

Public opinion is, to be sure, only part of the explanation for the PCI's changed position on European unity. Most fundamentally, Italy's increasingly irreversible integration into the Western economy encouraged reconciliation with Europe on the part of any party hoping to share governmental responsibilities. Indeed, from the very signing of the Treaty of Rome, trade unionists within the PCI had pushed the party toward an accommodation with Europe. Moreover, as we shall see later, the PCI's alliance strategy also required a more pro-European stance.

Yet the evolution of a popular consensus favoring European unity must have exerted steady pressure on Italian Communist leaders, whose hopes for increased power depended ultimately on increased popular support. Moreover, as Altiero Spinelli pointed out during the 1976 campaign, "The Communists know that Europeanism

---

[41] Evidence from a variety of surveys in the early 1970s suggests the existence of a small minority of PCI voters—perhaps 10 percent of the PCI's 1970 electorate and perhaps 7 percent of the party's 1976 electorate—who continued to adhere strongly to the party's earlier opposition to Western European integration. Note that this group was much outnumbered (and diluted) by the voters newly attracted to the PCI in 1975-1976.

unites Italians, while its disappearance would fatally divide them into an American party and a Russian party, which they do not want."[42] One reason why the PCI wished to avoid this fatal division can be clarified by turning now to evidence on Italian attitudes toward America.

The Italians and the Americans. Throughout the postwar era the Italian public has displayed a strong sense of solidarity with the United States and its purposes. Useful statistical evidence of this substantial reservoir of good will comes, for example, from a survey question posed repeatedly over the last two decades: "In your opinion are the basic interests of our country and those of the United States very much in agreement, fairly well in agreement, rather different, or very different?" Over these twenty years, respondents emphasizing shared interests have outnumbered those emphasizing divergent interests on average by more than two to one. Moreover, at least through 1974 the long-term trend line for these successive soundings of opinion was essentially flat, suggesting no secular tendency for this reservoir of solidarity to be drained by the frictions of alliance politics or the charms of East-West détente.[43]

Figure 9–2 provides a more detailed picture of the evolution of Italian attitudes to the United States, adding for comparison's sake a summary trend line for similar data from Britain, Germany, and France. These data show that in the short run Italian sentiment has tended to vary in harmony with the attitudes of other Europeans, rising from a relatively favorable level in the Eisenhower years through the Kennedy years to a peak in 1965, falling sharply in

---

[42] *La Stampa* (Turin), June 13, 1976.

[43] Most of these data come from a uniquely valuable archive of foreign survey data systematically compiled by the United States Information Agency since 1956. Since the percentage of "don't know" responses varies significantly from survey to survey, the most revealing summary measure consists of the net number of responses favorable (or unfavorable) to the United States, as a percentage of the total sample. Time series data from another indicator of "general opinion of America" follow roughly the same pattern over these two decades, and in fact show an even greater net margin favorable to the United States. See Merritt and Puchala, *Western European Perspectives;* Free and Sereno, *Italy;* Free, *How Others See Us;* and Alvin Richman, "Trends and Structure of Foreign Attitudes toward the United States and the USSR," paper prepared for the 1973 annual meeting of the American Political Science Association, New Orleans, Louisiana, September 1973. I am very grateful to Russell Dalton and Leo Crespi of the United States Information Agency for their assistance and counsel in connection with these data and, in particular, for making available data from the 1976 surveys. I am also grateful to Lloyd Free for graciously making available data independently gathered in 1974.

Figure 9-2

ITALIANS' CHANGING SOLIDARITY WITH THE UNITED STATES, 1957-76

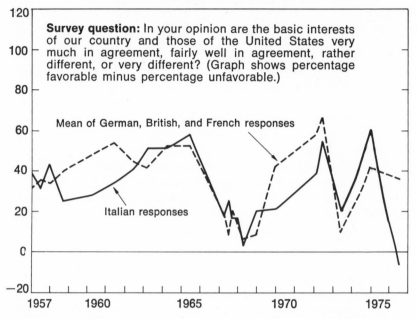

Survey question: In your opinion are the basic interests of our country and those of the United States very much in agreement, fairly well in agreement, rather different, or very different? (Graph shows percentage favorable minus percentage unfavorable.)

Mean of German, British, and French responses

Italian responses

Note: The non-Italian datapoint for April 1973 is estimated on the basis of French data only, in the absence of directly comparable German and British data. Related German data for that period are consistent with this estimate.
Source: See footnote 43.

reaction to American involvement in Vietnam, and then fluctuating rather sharply in response to the triumphs and tragedies of the Nixon administration.

Yet throughout these years, Italians, like their European neighbors, remained fundamentally sympathetic toward the United States. (I shall discuss later the remarkable results from postelection surveys in July 1976.) Even after the Tet offensive of January 1968, the nadir of American prestige in Europe as recorded in these surveys, Italians on balance perceived more convergence than divergence between their national interests and those of the United States. Despite the traumas of the late 1960s and early 1970s, surveys found Italians more favorably disposed to the Americans than to the English, the French, the Russians, the Germans, or the Chinese; indeed, only the innocuous

Swiss were more trusted than the Americans.[44]

Throughout this quarter-century, the Italians' sense of solidarity with the United States has been based less on admiration for American foreign policy than on a recognition of Italian dependence on American beneficence. Summarizing elite and mass opinion in the early 1950s, Lloyd Free and Renzo Sereno wrote that "explicitly or implicitly, it is Italy's relationship with this unbelievably rich and powerful giant which begins—and ends—almost all discussions of international problems in Italy, . . . no matter how much Italians may aspire for a more independent posture vis-à-vis America. . . . A pro-U.S. policy is still looked upon as the only *safe* policy."[45]

Two decades later, Free reported that, although Italians were more likely than any other European public to want somewhat more autonomy from the United States, they were also more likely than other Europeans to express a favorable opinion of the United States and a sense of shared interests with this country. Italians in the mid-1970s saw their country as very weak. They longed to be a bit less dependent on the United States, but they were realistic about the costs and the risks of autonomy.[46] On balance, the American connection seemed, as it had two decades earlier, "the only safe policy."

To assess the domestic impact of Italians' international sympathies, we must first recognize that attitudes to the United States and to the Soviet Union divide supporters of the left and the right systematically, but *not* symmetrically. In the early 1970s sympathy for America was still most common among conservative voters with close ties to the Church and to rightist parties, especially the Christian Democrats, while favorable attitudes to the USSR were found most often among voters with leftist affiliations.[47] However, sympathy for the United States was both deeper and less concentrated in party terms than sympathy for the Soviet Union. Whereas trust in the

---

[44] Unpublished data from a national survey directed by Samuel H. Barnes in 1968 (hereafter cited as "Barnes 1968 survey"), from a comparable 1972 survey directed by Barnes and Professor Giacomo Sani (hereafter cited as "Barnes-Sani 1972 survey"), and from the 1970 Inglehart-Rabier survey cited in footnote 40. I am grateful to Professors Barnes, Sani, Inglehart, and Rabier for making these data available for my analysis, for which I am solely responsible.

[45] Free and Sereno, *Italy*, p. 45.

[46] Free, *How Others See Us*, pp. 25, 30, 34, 72-73, 84-88.

[47] These generalizations are based on detailed analysis of the social and political correlates of sympathy for the United States and the Soviet Union, based on the Barnes 1968 survey and the Barnes-Sani 1972 survey. For this analysis, as well as much of the other statistical work for this chapter, I am deeply indebted to Ms. Celinda Lake.

Table 9–1
TRUST OF THE AMERICANS AND THE RUSSIANS
BY RESPONDENT'S PARTY, 1970
(in percentages of party supporters surveyed)

Response	PCI	PSI, PSDI, PSIUP, PRI	DC	MSI, PLI	Italy	Correlation (gamma) with Party Loyalty
"Some" or "much" confidence in the Americans	27	70	87	83	73	.36
"Some" or "much" confidence in the Russians	76	35	13	9	28	.51

Source: These data were originally collected in 1970 by Ronald Inglehart and Jacques-René Rabier and were made available by the Inter-University Consortium for Political and Social Research. Neither the original collectors of the data nor the Consortium bears any responsibility for the analyses or interpretations presented here.

Russians was largely confined to supporters of the PCI—and was incomplete even there—trust in the Americans was common among supporters of the left, as well as among centrist and rightist voters (see Table 9–1).

Moreover, although the United States and the Soviet Union symbolize for Italians two different social systems—broadly captured by the ideological distinction between capitalism and communism—the United States is *more* esteemed than the social system for which it stands, whereas the Soviet Union is *less* esteemed than its social system.[48] Being anti-American or pro-Soviet is apt to be more costly electorally than being anticapitalist or procommunist.

Thus, survey evidence significantly amplifies Spinelli's observation that Italians are divided into an "American party" and a "Russian party": despite détente and Vietnam, at the beginning of the 1970s the "American party" remained several times larger than the "Russian party." In electoral battles, foreign policy was unfavorable terrain for the PCI. This conclusion can be sharpened by examining the relative payoff to the PCI from domestic and foreign policy

[48] Data illustrating this point can be drawn from the 1970 survey cited in Table 9–1. At least "some" confidence in the Americans is expressed by 73 percent of the respondents, whereas only 28 percent express a similar level of trust in the Russians. On the other hand, only 58 percent of the same respondents rate "fighting communism" as a top priority, whereas 44 percent give top priority to "ending capitalism."

Table 9-2

VOTERS' PERCEPTIONS OF ISSUE SALIENCE, 1968 AND 1972

(in percentages of respondents)

Issue	Year of Survey	
	1968	1972
Economic development	80	—
Stopping inflation	—	90
Fighting crime	—	88
Improving health assistance	—	82
Development of education	66	—
Governmental stability	56	69
Just distribution of national income	54	48
Increasing wages	—	47
Independence of Italy from the United States	22	23
Passing/maintaining the divorce law	14	21

Note: The survey question was: "For each of the following problems, would you tell me if you consider it very important, more or less important, of little importance, or not at all important?" The entries are percentages of all respondents saying "very important." Dashes indicate alternatives not posed in one survey or the other.

Source: See footnote 44.

issues in the elections of 1968 and 1972, the background against which party strategists prepared for the national elections that were to come in 1976.

As I have already noted, most voters in most countries are much more concerned with domestic affairs than with international issues. Thus, it is hardly surprising that, as Table 9-2 shows, Italian voters in both 1968 and 1972 rated foreign policy at virtually the bottom of their list of priorities. Economic progress, social reform, and political stability were emphasized by three to four times as many voters as was autonomy from the United States.

Equally important for electoral strategy, between these two elections public opinion on the substance of each of these highly salient domestic issues shifted toward the PCI and away from the DC. For example, in 1968 equal numbers of voters thought the DC and the PCI likely to ensure a fair income distribution, but by 1972 the PCI had gained an edge of better than three to two on this issue. On the issue of governmental stability, the DC's 1968 lead of almost six to one had slipped by 1972 to a bit above three to one. The Communists' latent advantages on such domestic issues were ripe for exploitation.

On the other hand, another important trend lay concealed in the

311

patterns of opinion and party choice in 1972. Floating voters attracted by the PCI in 1972—those who reported having previously voted for some other party—were significantly less distrustful of Italy's ties to America than were the party's traditional supporters. The party was beginning to attract Italians who, though ready to vote for the PCI on domestic issues, were not nearly so anti-American and pro-Soviet as traditional Communist voters.

Events of the years following the 1972 elections reinforced this constellation of public attitudes. The continued decay of Italy's social, economic, and political institutions sharpened public discontent with the Christian Democrats and made the domestic reformism of the PCI increasingly attractive to non-Communist voters. On the other hand, the Italians' sense of identification with the West did not slacken. Indeed, as Figure 9–2 shows, solidarity with the United States reached unprecedented levels in this period. Asked in April 1976 to suggest changes that might make the two major parties more attractive, a national sample offered a myriad of criticisms of Christian Democratic domestic policies, but virtually no references to foreign policy or the American connection. On the other hand, undue dependence on the Soviet Union was the single most common criticism of the PCI.[49]

Electoral Strategies in 1976. Against this backdrop of public attitudes, the Communists' traditional emphasis on an anti-American line in foreign policy seemed singularly unproductive. Domestic issues were more important to most voters, and opinion on them was already moving toward the PCI. Party efforts in this domain worked with the grain of public opinion, not against it. Continued emphasis on foreign policy would merely alienate many voters otherwise attracted by the party's domestic reformism. Conversely, the rational strategy for the Communists' opponents was to stress Italy's ties to the West and the threat posed to those ties by Communist gains. Foreign affairs remained among the most powerful weapons in the electoral arsenal of the non-Communists.

In any event, the campaign strategies actually used by the Communists and their opponents in 1976 mirrored this logic almost exactly. Each side sought, above all, to control the campaign agenda. By endorsing Italy's Western alignment, the PCI sought to defuse foreign policy disputes, in order to concentrate the voters' attention on domestic issues. Conversely, the DC emphasized Italy's need for

---

[49] Giampaolo Fabris, *Il comportamento politico degli italiani* [The political behavior of Italians] (Milan: Franco Angeli Editori, 1977), p. 97.

help from its Western allies. "Italy's Salvation in Western Credits," screamed one headline. The Christian Democrats hoped thus to reawaken concern about the PCI's foreign policy and hence to shift the battle away from the uncongenial terrain of domestic issues. Not coincidentally, this Christian Democratic strategy was aided by warnings from Secretary Kissinger and other Western leaders about the "serious consequences" that would follow Communist gains. The PCI avoided making angry replies to these foreign pronouncements, for polemics would simply raise the salience of foreign policy, to the detriment of the party's electoral support. The joint effect of these strategies was to transform Italian foreign policy from a position issue into a valence issue.

Without electoral surveys from 1976 we cannot be sure just what effects these twin strategies had on the outcome. The massive gains of the PCI in 1975–1976, following the party's official acceptance of the Atlantic Alliance, are consistent with the notion that de-emphasizing foreign policy controversy helped the party. On the other hand, the recovery of the DC from its very low standing in straw polls in the winter of 1975–1976 suggests that the insistent evocation of international affairs by DC strategists and their supporters abroad did forestall losses that might have occurred had the PCI been allowed to continue to fight the campaign solely in domestic terms.

In confidential interviews just after the election, both PCI and DC leaders opined that the PCI had benefited from domestic discontent, whereas the DC had gained from international concerns. A senior Christian Democrat said, "An important element working against the PCI in these elections was fear that Communist gains would mean that Italy would be excluded from the Western Community. The average Italian agreed with the PCI on economic policy and with the DC on foreign policy." A leading member of the PCI offered a similar analysis:

> The Christian Democrats played the "American card" very effectively, even beyond Kissinger's own efforts. Without that, the DC would have lost much more ground. You must understand that we are now drawing many votes from people who are not wedded to the PCI. Many Italians wanted to vote for us for clean government and for social reform, but feared the Soviet Union and were concerned about Italy's ties to the West.

In the mid-1970s more and more Italians were cross-pressured between desires for domestic reform and contentment with Italy's international alignment. By modifying its foreign policy stance, the PCI had encouraged these electors to vote their domestic sympathies. The Communists' opponents, on the other hand, had accentuated the dissonance, hoping that international concerns would outweigh domestic temptations.

This tactic was not without risks, as its American defenders recognized privately. Forced to choose between their domestic and foreign sympathies, many Italian voters might renounce the latter, particularly in the face of what might seem improper international interference in Italian affairs. On the other hand, a quarter century's experience testified to the durability of the Italians' pro-Western loyalties. On balance, the risks seemed slight. On June 21 the electoral results were greeted as evidence that the tactical calculation had been correct.

However, surveys of Italian opinion in the aftermath of the election revealed the stark cost of this tactical victory. As the data in Figure 9–2 illustrate, the Italians' sense of solidarity with the United States plummeted from an all-time high at the end of 1974 to an all-time low in July 1976. For the first time in at least two decades (and probably much longer), Italians who saw a convergence between Italian and American interests were outnumbered by those who thought the interests of the two countries divergent. Anti-American feeling among Italians surged well above its previous peak, recorded just after the Tet offensive of 1968. Without much exploitation by Communist propagandists, the American intervention of 1976 (and the contemporaneous revelation of earlier interventions in Italian politics by Lockheed and the CIA) had accomplished what hundreds of Vietnam demonstrations had failed to do. Playing the "American card" had a price.

International relations is not a popularity contest. Nevertheless, in its relations with postwar Europe, the United States has been well served by a widespread sense of shared interests. Given the practical realities of democratic politics on both sides of the Atlantic, a naked imperium would hardly have been so durable. In the Italian case, popular solidarity with the United States has been a powerful factor ensuring governments sympathetic to American foreign policy. Moreover, this solidarity was an important element in the political context within which the PCI moved toward reconciliation with the West. The U.S. intervention of 1976 drew very heavily on this political capital to prevent an electoral victory for the Communists. Whether the loss of this asset, as reflected in the July surveys, will prove more transitory than the electoral gains purchased thereby is an important question for the future.[50] If the Italians' fundamental sympathy with the United States and its purposes is supplanted over the long run by indifference or active antipathy, the electoral constraints on Italian foreign policy makers will be altered fundamentally.

Foreign Policy and Party Alliances

Domestic Alliances. For more than twenty years the Italian Communist party has assiduously sought collaboration with non-Communists. Indeed, as Donald Blackmer has observed, the search for political and social alliances constitutes "the core of the *via italiana al socialismo*."[51] By the early 1970s broad agreement on domestic policy had developed among the parties of the center and the left, including the Communists. As one writer put it, "The opposing factions and interests appear to be approaching a consensus both on the diagnosis of the ills from which Italy is suffering and on the cures to be adopted. This would have been unthinkable only a short time ago."[52] Extensive under-the-table collaboration between the government and the Communists both before and after the elections of 1976—the so-called historic-compromise-by-telephone—testifies to this potential reformist coalition, as does a close comparison of the 1976 domestic platforms of the major parties.

Yet for many non-Communist reformers, foreign policy remained an insurmountable barrier to collaboration with the Communists. Ciriaco De Mita, a left-wing Christian Democrat, declared in 1974 that it was no longer "ideological irreconcilability," but foreign policy, that divided Christian Democrats and Communists.[53] By 1976 even Giuseppe Saragat, that venerable anti-Communist, ex-

---

[50] A Eurobarometer survey conducted for the European Communities in November 1976 yielded data comparable to that from 1970 in Table 9–1. The proportion of Italians expressing at least "some" confidence in the American people fell over this six-year period from 73 percent to 65 percent. This marginal decline suggests that the July 1976 USIA survey may have exaggerated somewhat the long-term impact of the events of the spring and summer of 1976, although the obvious differences in question wording between the two 1976 surveys make this inference a weak one. I am grateful to Professor Ronald Inglehart for making this latest data available to me.

[51] Blackmer, "Continuity and Change," p. 23.

[52] Podbielski, *Italy*, p. 64. Evidence of a trend toward ideological and political consensus within the Italian political elite is also available in a forthcoming study of mine, based on interviews with a national panel of regional politicians in 1970 and 1976.

[53] Quoted in P. A. Allum, "Italy: Republic without Government?" *The World Today*, vol. 30 (November 1974), p. 456.

pressed a similar position during a televised campaign press conference televised on June 10. "The problem is one of alignment on the international scene. This is the fundamental point that concerns us. We can contemplate a government in which there are Communists, who represent an important segment of the Italian people, but that is without taking account of the international alignment of our country."

Thus, if the Communists' main priorities were in fact domestic, as many observers have long maintained, the strategic implication was clear: they must drop their opposition to Italy's international alliances, including NATO. Berlinguer made this strategic calculation explicit in a remarkable preelection lecture to party members skeptical about the new line.

[Our] position, which envisions Italy remaining within the Atlantic Pact and NATO even if we were a part of a government coalition, has created problems and discussions. However, we maintain that a different position not only would be sterile, misleading, wishful thinking, but would open other equally difficult problems, both because unilateral departures from the two blocs would disturb and overturn the tendency toward détente . . . and because it would create a fracture among the Italian democratic parties. Both consequences would be fatal for the future of our country, as well as for our effort to begin the construction of a socialist society.[54]

The Communists lost no time in trying to capitalize on their foreign policy concessions. In a campaign round-table debate on foreign policy, for example, Sergio Segre addressed non-Communist reformists:

[You say to us], "Even if you had agreement among different political forces on political, economic, and social problems, agreement is lacking on the question of foreign policy." I think this claim does not take account of the present situation. The great new fact in Italy, I would say the great potentiality of Italy in the years to come, is that . . . perhaps for the first time since the unification of Italy, there exists general agreement on foreign policy among all the Italian political and democratic forces.[55]

The essence of foreign policy making in Italy, and perhaps in most dependent nations, was captured in an apothegm of Count Carlo Sforza, foreign minister under De Gasperi: "A foreign policy

[54] Berlinguer, *La politica internazionale*, p. 118.
[55] *Paese Sera* (Rome), June 8, 1976.

316

is only the mirror of an internal policy."[56] Italian politicians assume that the international environment affects domestic affairs more than Italy can affect that environment, and most of them care more about domestic policy than about foreign affairs. Hence, foreign policy positions are adopted more for their symbolic significance in the domestic arena than for their instrumental significance in the international arena.[57] As Norman Kogan has pointed out, "The principal issue in Italian foreign policy is whether to preserve or change the domestic social structure."[58]

For three decades, acceptance of the two fundamental elements of Italian foreign policy—Western Europe and the Atlantic Alliance —has been the most important credential demanded of those who would enter the "governing area."[59] The most striking previous illustration of this fact was the Socialists' about-face on foreign policy as the price for admission into the center-left coalition of the 1960s, but it is equally applicable to the PCI in the early 1970s. If Paris was worth a mass, surely, Rome was worth a naval base.

Transnational Alliances. As Western European interdependence grows, as socioeconomic forces and organizations vault national boundaries, as one government's decisions increasingly affect the vital interests of citizens of other countries, one would expect the gradual emergence of transnational political alliances. In fact, recent years have seen within Western Europe a resurgence of international links among kindred political parties—the Socialist International, the Liberal International, and so on. In the election campaign of 1976, such ties played a prominent symbolic role. Virtually every party's platform and campaign propaganda included glowing references to its collaboration with prestigious fraternal parties elsewhere in Europe.[60] François Mitterrand and Georges Marchais of France, Mario Soares of Portugal, and Santiago Carrillo of Spain held joint rallies with their Italian counterparts to demonstrate international party solidarity. Symbolically, such activities helped to shore up the shaky legitimacy of Italian parties in the eyes of Italian voters.

As European integration progresses, however, transnational party alliances come to have a more practical significance. Parties weak in

---

[56] Kogan, *Politics*, p. 135.
[57] Hassner, "Political Evolution of Italy."
[58] Kogan, *Politics*, p. 50.
[59] Gianfranco Pasquino, "Pesi internazionali e contrappesi nazionali" [International pressures and national counter pressures], *Il caso italiano*, vol. 1, p. 171.
[60] In addition to the official platforms, see the round-table debate in *La Stampa* (Turin), June 13, 1976.

one country seek aid from more powerful foreign allies.[61] Moreover, the politics of "arena-definition" becomes more important, as parties try to adjust the authority and the membership of decision-making units at various levels, so as to maximize the influence of the international political family to which they belong. Thus, one important reason for the enthusiastic Europeanism of Italy's Socialists, Social Democrats, Republicans, and Liberals is the strength of their natural allies in central and northern Europe.

The politics of arena-definition are especially problematic for the PCI. One of the prime motives for the party's initial opposition to Western European unity was its relative weakness in that wider arena. Nor has this disadvantage disappeared in recent years. In 1974, while the PCI held 27.2 percent of the seats in the Chamber of Deputies, Communists held 9.2 percent of the total seats in the national parliaments of the nine Community members. From such numbers, Neil McInnes concludes that "if the Community came into existence as a political entity, . . . it would be the desperate last act of West European Communism."[62]

Yet by the early 1970s, continued resistance to European integration had come to seem even more suicidal to the PCI, for the political and economic reasons that we have examined at length. Caught in a seemingly impossible political dilemma, the party reverted to its more enduring strategic traditions. In the words of Donald Blackmer, "The accent has always been on acceptance of unpleasant realities rather than stubborn resistance to them, on participating in alien institutions rather than boycotting them or pretending they do not exist."[63] Yet the Communists' conundrum remained: how to counteract their strategic inferiority in the wider arena?

The PCI's response, articulated between 1972 and 1976, was to extend the collaborative, alliance-seeking approach of the *via italiana* to the European level, that is, to attempt a less elaborate, but more portentous, European version of the *compromesso storico*. Only such a strategy could reconcile the hard constraints imposed by interdependence with the party's hopes for radical social change in Italy. Thus, after years of disparagement of "little Europe," the Fourteenth Party Congress heard its general secretary explain that "at the center

---

[61] The most prominent example of this phenomenon to date is the assistance of northern European Socialists to the Portuguese Socialists during the dark days of 1974-1975.
[62] McInnes, "Communist Parties," p. 88.
[63] Blackmer, "International Strategy," p. 25.

of our engagement in the international field will increasingly have to be the Western Europe initiative."[64]

The first practical step in this European strategy involved reaching agreement on the new line with the other major Communist parties of Western Europe. Months of negotiation culminated in joint declarations with the Spanish party in July 1975 and with the French party in November 1975, emphasizing among other things the parties' commitment to civil liberties, to competitive party systems, and to more intensive collaboration with other forces of the West European left.[65] It was the gestation of Eurocommunism.

Yet political arithmetic required that the search for allies extend well beyond the Communist ranks. The key to peace and social progress, Berlinguer explained, was "encounter and mutual understanding among the Socialist and Communist forces, the popular and progressive forces, the Christian and Catholic forces, the 'lay democratic' forces of Western Europe."[66] Progress on this front would not be easy, for it would require, above all, bridging the gulf that separated the Communists from the major Social Democratic parties of northern Europe. Yet as Altiero Spinelli pointed out during the 1976 campaign, "The PCI does not want to let itself be encapsulated in a purely Communist political formula (not even 'Eurocommunist'). It refuses to enter into a Mediterranean grouping to be counterposed to a Nordic one. It is instead methodically seeking to find contacts and convergences with other large working-class parties."[67]

By the summer of 1976 leaders of some of the major European Socialist parties, including Soares, Mitterrand, and even Willy Brandt, were beginning to take note of the PCI's overtures. Collaboration on some European issues no longer seemed an unrealistic goal for the medium term, though the obstacles, both symbolic and practical, remained substantial. But the new European strategy poses important constraints on the policies that can be followed by the PCI, if it is to acquire the trust and cooperation of its potential allies. Collaboration with the Social Democratic parties of northern Europe, for example, tends to limit the pace and nature of socioeconomic transformation that the party can pursue, both at the Community level and within Italy. Even clearer foreign policy limitations are implied by the new strategy. In particular, the British Labour party and the German Social Democrats would surely demand continued

---

[64] Berlinguer, La politica internazionale, p. 24.

[65] Ibid., pp. 194-199.

[66] Ibid., p. xvi.

[67] La Stampa (Turin), June 13, 1976.

Italian fidelity to the Atlantic Alliance as a precondition for any collaboration with the PCI. Indeed, at the Fourteenth Party Congress, Berlinguer defended the party's acceptance of NATO as necessary in part to facilitate "convergence among the diverse working class, leftist, and progressive forces of Europe."[68] Reneging on the PCI's acceptance of Italy's western alliances would undermine the party's entire European strategy.

Conclusions

By all odds, the most prominent element in the emergent Italian foreign policy consensus is the acceptance of Italy's western alliances by the Communist party. Among Italy's allies, the most common reaction to this metamorphosis has been to ask, can the Communists be trusted? This is almost surely the wrong question. Rather, we should ask, where do their interests lie? The penalty for transgressing the constraints traced in this chapter is not a guilty conscience, but political failure. Despite the PCI's recent celebrity, it remains a minority party in a second-rank, dependent nation. If such a party is to have any hope of success, it must adapt realistically to domestic and international constraints, both economic and political, guided by Thucydides' maxim that while the strong do what they can, the weak do what they must.

Thus, it is not surprising that many non-Communist Italian politicians find queries about the sincerity of the PCI leadership misplaced. "The impetus [for the new line] lies in reality, in the facts of economics, geography, and Italian society," said one influential leader privately after the election. "It is in the logic of things," explained another. "Any other line would simply be stupid."

To be sure, such realism has not always governed the foreign policy of Italian Communists. During the campaign Berlinguer replied revealingly to an interviewer's query about uneasiness within the party over the new strategy: "Certainly sentiments are important . . . but all our efforts for some years have been directed at the passage from myths to rationality. For some time there was the myth of the Socialist states, for example, but we have worked for years with growing success to outline a perspective of our own."[69] From the standpoint of western policy makers, this "passage from myths to rationality" may well be seen as a remarkable corroboration of their

---

[68] Berlinguer, La politica internazionale, p. 20.
[69] La Repubblica (Rome), June 8, 1976.

basic international strategy of the past three decades. The last significant opponents of that strategy within the West have yielded to reality.

This optimistic interpretation, though accurate and important in historical perspective, certainly does not mean that the PCI now wholeheartedly supports the West. Anticapitalism and anti-imperialism remain strong and uncontested within the party. Criticism of the foreign and domestic policies of the western powers is still common, though it is expressed in much more realistic and nuanced terms than in years past and is increasingly accompanied by sympathetic commentary.

Ideologically and publicly, Soviet foreign policy is still interpreted as essentially anti-imperialist, and the prizes at party festivals are still trips to Cuba, East Germany, and Russia. Privately, however, increasing numbers of PCI leaders and activists are ready to criticize Soviet imperialist tendencies. Only among a small and steadily diminishing fraction of the party membership is reflexive solidarity with the USSR still strong. Moreover, despite this continuing (though declining) importance of the Soviet link in terms of organizational solidarity and material support, we have seen that this link entails growing opportunity costs for the PCI in terms of election winning and alliance building.

From the Soviet point of view, the new Eurocommunist strategy is significantly more threatening than the traditional *via italiana*. The specter of a second major schism within the Communist movement, with ideological and geopolitical consequences at least as grave as the Sino-Soviet split, can no longer be dismissed, particularly because of the Eurocommunists' potential following among discontented East Europeans. Consequently, the threat of excommunication must now be contemplated by Italian Communist strategists, particularly in the wake of the Soviets' attack on the Spanish party leader, Santiago Carrillo, in June 1977.

To forestall this possibility, the PCI has followed a subtle strategy: while rejecting the Soviet model as nonexportable to Italy and criticizing specific domestic and foreign actions of the Soviets, the Italians (unlike Carrillo) have not questioned the basic legitimacy of the regimes of the East. Thus, while claiming autonomy to follow its own Eurocommunist line, the PCI has tried to avoid threatening the vital interests of the Soviet leadership, following once again the logic of Yalta.

Whether this attempt to avoid direct confrontation with the Kremlin can succeed in the long run may be doubted, though the strategy has the merit of postponing painful ruptures of traditional ties. More fundamentally, the PCI's autonomy is facilitated by—and in turn, facilitates—its domestic political gains and its domestic and transnational alliances. In the end, the potential sting of excommunication has been greatly reduced by the ever greater salience within the PCI of domestic symbols and domestic concerns—by "the passage from myths to rationality." Soviet strategists seeking supportive leverage within the ranks of the PCI should not be overly optimistic.

But bipolar politics are not necessarily zero-sum politics. Increasing distance from the Soviet Union need by no means imply increasing closeness to the United States. Within the party, commitment to Western Europe, both emotional and ideological, is by now quite pervasive, but the logic of the party's acceptance of NATO is much less widely appreciated. For most Italian Communists, the commitment to Western Europe is a matter of principle, while the commitment to the Atlantic Alliance is a matter of fact, a price to be paid, but a price to be minimized. The party's Europeanism is vastly stronger than its Atlanticism—of longer standing, more fully rationalized theoretically, more broadly and enthusiastically supported among party militants, more consequential in terms of policy initiatives.

Quite apart from the PCI's longstanding ideological and reflexive antipathy to American foreign policy, the party's unhappiness over the American presence in Europe can be interpreted in terms of the politics of arena-definition. Lacking natural allies on the American political scene, the party recognizes that to include the Americans in the European game is to shift the political center of gravity to the party's disadvantage. Moreover, the party's emphasis on European autonomy is consonant with that strand of Italian opinion that longs for more independence from America.

Formally, the party calls for an autonomous Europe equidistant between the United States and the Soviet Union. At one level, the equidistance thesis is quite unrealistic, for it ignores the manifold ties of ideology and interest—economic, political, military—that bind Western Europe to the United States. (This fact doubtless helps explain the Soviets' bitter attack on this thesis as "veiled anti-Sovietism.") Moreover, the equidistance thesis is fundamentally inconsistent with most other aspects of the PCI's new international strategy, including its acceptance of the Atlantic Alliance and its attempts to build bridges to non-Communist Europeans. Phrased and implemented more realistically, however, the party's stress on European autonomy might well create significant difficulties at the margins of the Atlantic relationship, in such areas as monetary policy, energy policy, defense planning, and relations with the Third World.[70] For American policy makers, this is the most serious challenge posed by the growing power of the Italian Communists: not a Western Europe more manageable for the Soviet Union, but a Western Europe less manageable for the United States. Only a blindly zero-sum, bipolar view of the world could confuse these quite different dangers.

It has been my thesis that the broadening consensus on Italian foreign policy is to be explained primarily in terms of narrowing constraints. Changes in the international environment and in domestic politics have induced a shared perception of Italian interests that transcends traditional ideological boundaries. This trend does not mean that all problems between Italy and its allies have vanished. On the contrary, on several counts the future is likely to be more difficult than the past. A growing role for the PCI in the governance of Italy is likely to exacerbate several of these difficulties, in part because the emergent consensus is as yet mainly about what *not* to do—leave the alliances—rather than about what to do in the context of those alliances. However, it is important to recognize that nearly every one of these problems will arise regardless of which parties are in power in Rome. Like the new strategy of the PCI itself, the new problems arise from "the logic of things." Let me illustrate.

The Middle East. Italy needs Arab oil. Since the oil embargo of 1973, the foreign policy implications of this simple fact have become increasingly obvious. As early as 1974, Italy joined France as the only European country to vote for Yasir Arafat's appearance before the UN General Assembly. Each year has seen further Italian concessions to the Arab position.[71] By 1976, differences on this issue between the Italians and the French—and differences between the Italian government and the PCI—had virtually disappeared. Whoever rules in Rome, Italian policy in the Middle East will probably diverge from American policy, particularly should Arab-Israeli hostilities intensify.

The Third World. Both sentiment and commerce have inclined many Italians to claim a special relationship with less-developed countries,

---

[70] On the other hand, the unwillingness of the PCI to support European unity in defense matters in effect perpetuates European dependence on the United States.

[71] See the annual autumn addresses of the Italian foreign minister to the United Nations General Assembly between 1972 and 1976.

particularly in Africa and the Middle East. In the postwar period the theme of solidarity with the poor and oppressed peoples of the world has been particularly characteristic of a substantial fraction of the DC, as well as of the left opposition. The practical consequences of this solidarity have been minimal, however, except when (as in the case of Enrico Mattei's oil agreements in the Middle East) it has been undergirded by economic interests. Italian foreign aid has been extremely modest and tied closely to Italian exports.[72] Rhetorical sympathy for black Africa has not prevented Italy from becoming a major arms supplier to South Africa.[73] Italy's aspirations as Mediterranean mediator have seldom been consequential.

For the foreseeable future, Italy's acute commercial needs are likely to encourage a neomercantilist policy, not unlike that of France and several other industrial nations. This policy will involve vigorous trade promotion and the search for advantageous bilateral links with raw materials producers. As Fiat's chairman, Gianni Agnelli, has explained, "Our particular geographic position and a certain tradition of political-economic relations with the emergent countries give Italy a position as hinge between Europe and the African and Middle Eastern world, which, if fully utilized, could increase Italy's international weight on the economic and industrial plane."[74] In some circumstances neomercantilism may cause Italian policy to diverge from American policy in world economic forums, regardless of who is in power, although Communist influence might encourage this tendency.

Intra-European Relations. The economic crises of the 1970s have made full and effective Italian participation in European integration more difficult. The Italian government's nominal commitment to Europe has been marred in practice by serious violations of EEC regulations, such as the imposition of import restrictions in 1974 without consultation with other members of the Community. The possibility of further de facto detachment from Europe cannot be excluded, particularly if economic disparities and political tensions along Europe's north-south cleavage line should increase.

---

[72] See, for example, Roberto Aliboni, "Italian Aid Policy in the 60's," *Lo Spettatore Internazionale*, vol. 7 (1972), pp. 49-68.

[73] *L'Italia nella politica internazionale: 1973-1974*, p. 439.

[74] Quoted in *Panorama* (Milan), December 21, 1976, p. 77. Agnelli's emphasis was on economics, rather than politics, and he added that "one must reject certain 'third-force' longings about an 'autonomous role' for Italy in the Mediterranean or a role of 'bridge' between the EEC and the Third World without belonging to either one."

Nevertheless, as we have seen, leaving the European Community would be terribly costly for Italy. The political consequences of a retreat into economic nationalism are difficult to foresee, but they are hardly likely to favor the left. Socialism in one country is much less probable than fascism in one country. On balance, therefore, increased Communist influence on Italian foreign policy is not likely to weaken Italian resolve to resume effective membership in the European Community.

On the other hand, no matter how well-designed and ably executed the PCI's new European strategy, the party and Italy face a grave danger of isolation, as the Communists move toward participation in government. Italy and the PCI may aspire to a special relationship with France, particularly if the left should gain power there too, but the mainstream of Europe today is not the Seine; it is the Rhine. The PCI's special efforts to develop collaborative links with the Brandt wing of the Social Democrats have not dissipated the deep anti-Communist skepticism of moderate and conservative Germans. More fundamentally, recent surveys of European publics have revealed widespread disaffection from Italy and the Italians.[75] Doubtless this estrangement is due in large part to the actions and inactions of Italy's past and present governments, but there is little evidence that the Italians' image abroad would be swiftly boosted by Communist participation in government.

International Security. Defense policy is the area in which the PCI has least adequately considered the implications of its new strategy. Throughout the 1976 campaign, party leaders avoided questions about the consequences of a possible reversal of East-West détente. Said one spokesman disingenuously of a possible collision of the United States and the Soviet Union in Europe: "The truth is that no European government today would know what it should do in that case."[76]

As we have seen, non-Communist Italians, too, often seem reluctant to accept the logic of collective security. Italy's minimal material support for the alliance is not likely to be increased by any

---

[75] This statement is based on surveys conducted on behalf of the USIA among the German, British, and French publics in July/August 1976. In Germany, respondents expressing solidarity with the Italians were outnumbered more than three to one by those who claimed German and Italian interests were fundamentally incompatible. In Britain, the skeptics outnumbered those favorable to Italy by more than two to one, and even the more sympathetic French are no more than evenly divided on the question. I am grateful to the USIA Office of Research for providing me these data.
[76] *La Repubblica* (Rome), June 2, 1976.

Italian government, in part because of persisting economic difficulties. Nevertheless, Western policy makers will continue to harbor doubts about the seriousness of the PCI's new strategy, so long as ambiguities on the practical implications of alliance membership remain.

Western policy makers must be attentive to unresolved inconsistencies in the PCI's commitment to its new strategy. But prudence should not preclude a sensitive assessment of the implications of this strategy. Important opportunities may be lost and unnecessary risks incurred by a failure to distinguish between the Kremlin and the Botteghe Oscure. Pierre Hassner has sorted out four possible Western strategies toward the Soviet Union and the Communist or leftist opposition in Western nations: "The first, the classic Cold War one, consists of being equally hostile to both [the Soviet Union and the left-wing movements of the different countries]. . . . The second, that of unconditional détente, consists of being equally conciliatory towards both." Two other, more subtle strategies distinguish between the Soviet Union and Western leftists. The strategy of former Secretary of State Kissinger, according to Hassner, consisted in being

> conciliatory towards the Soviet Union in the spirit of the age of negotiation, and intransigent towards all forms of leftward internal evolution in Western countries. . . . It would seem more reasonable to adopt the opposite attitude: that is, to be more vigilant about Soviet military power and more tolerant towards national change which cannot be prevented and which leads to consequences which the Soviet Union herself cannot control.[77]

At least in the Italian case, Hassner's argument is strengthened by a recognition of the interests and the constraints that have prompted the Communists' new international strategy.

---

[77] Pierre Hassner, "Détente and Political Change in Europe," *Survival* (London), vol. 18 (March-April 1976), p. 71.

10
THE CONSEQUENCES OF THE ELECTIONS: AN INTERPRETATION

Samuel H. Barnes

Winners and Losers

No one really knows the true consequences of the 1976 Italian elections—not the PCI, which is widely thought to have won; not the PSI, which is convinced that it lost; not the DC, which survived by cannibalizing its neighbors; not the small parties of the system, which became more marginal than ever. The only certain winner was the democratic process itself, for the election was a tranquil affair held amid spiralling violence and economic chaos; it demonstrated that the overwhelming majority of Italians were determined to abide by the existing rules of the game, that there is considerable consensus on the nature and functioning of these rules, and that there was no payoff for parties and individuals that sought to alter them. Of all the serious parties, only the MSI can reasonably be charged with lack of respect for the democratic electoral process, and even that party tried to have it both ways by proclaiming its constitutional intentions and simultaneously engaging in occasional electoral violence.

However real the problems of the Italian political system—and no party denied the existence of crisis—no analysis of this election should neglect the fact that the electoral process functioned smoothly. Nor should we overlook the fact that the present electoral system is virtually universally accepted, despite the complaint that it makes the achievement of a governmental majority impossible and permits the inclusion in Parliament of parties that claim only a small fraction of the electorate. The electoral system is one thing on which Italians are generally agreed.[1] Whatever the outcome of the current Italian

---

[1] There has been little serious discussion of reform of the Italian electoral law since 1953. In that year the DC sponsored the enactment of a revision that

crisis, the 1976 election increased the probability that the crisis would be dealt with through electoral and constitutional means. The threat of armed intervention from left or right, which appeared real enough during the period of tension preceding and following the 1972 elections, was hardly a factor in the recent campaign; though sporadic violence continued, it was increasingly unlikely to lead to a change in regime.

Winners and losers can be identified easily enough in quantitative terms. The PCI picked up 3.5 million additional votes over 1972 and increased its percentage of the national vote from 27.2 percent to 34.4 percent. The DC managed to secure 1.2 million votes over 1972 and to maintain a stable 38.7 percent of the total vote between 1972 and 1976. The losers were clearly the secular parties of the center and the MSI; both collectively and individually the center parties failed to live up to expectations. The PSI, in particular, which was blamed for precipitating the election, failed to surpass its vote percentage of four years before and, given its high expectations, this stalemate was viewed as a defeat. The Liberals were reduced to one-third of their size from one election to another. The Social Democrats were riddled by scandal, and the growing acceptance of the legitimacy of the PCI robbed the PSDI of much of its raison d'être. Moreover, the strategy of moving to the right that the PSDI had followed for the previous decade had carried it in a direction counter to the leftward movement of the electorate. The Republicans did not do badly in the polling, though their high expectations caused their modest success to be viewed as a defeat. The new Radical party secured representation, but its numbers gave it only the gadfly's role. The modest success secured by the extreme left, coupled with its disunity, showed the ability of the PCI to monopolize the credible left alternative.

There was much lamenting over the decline of the minor center parties, both from their own individual perspectives and from that of

would give 65 percent of the seats in the Chamber to the party or coalition of parties that received 50 percent of the popular vote. The 1953 election was bitterly contested, with the opposition parties—led by the PCI—accusing the DC of restoring the "swindle" law under which the Fascists had consolidated their power in 1924. When the DC-PSDI-PLI coalition received 49.85 percent of the vote in 1953, the previous electoral law was restored. The widespread acceptance of the current law as legitimate, combined with the previous history of manipulation of the electoral law, makes it unlikely that this form of political engineering will be used to deal with the problem of a majority. The Italian electoral system produces a Parliament—and a Chamber of Deputies in particular—that closely reflects the distribution of votes. For details, see the chapter in this volume by Douglas Wertman.

Italian democracy as a whole. These parties had in the past been a mediating force between the DC and the PCI. The growing monopolization of the vote by these two large parties is sometimes viewed as an increasing polarization of the Italian electorate. But, as Joseph LaPalombara notes in this volume, the DC and the PCI are in fact closer together than they have ever been; despite the move to the right that the recovery of the DC supposedly represents, the PCI has undoubtedly moved even further toward the DC.

The election inaugurated a period of uncertainty even greater than that of the preceding years.[2] From the perspective of a year's experience with the ensuing Parliament and the continuing public debate within and between the parties, it is evident that the election encouraged existing trends within the two largest parties and made even less viable the governing formula of the previous decade. The new situation was thus filled with possibilities for dramatic change, but the nature of the change was unclear. On the surface, the incorporation of the PCI into the governing coalition seemed inevitable. The form of the incorporation, however, remained to be worked out. The small parties feared a "historic compromise" between the DC and the PCI, a development that threatened to leave them out, with, from their viewpoint, grave dangers for Italian democracy. Another formula would have the PCI enter a government of national unity that would include the PSI and perhaps other parties as well. Still another method of accommodation would involve PCI support for governments that promised to enact specific programs worked out in collaboration with the PCI, but without the PCI's holding ministerial positions. This path could eventually lead to PCI participation when residual fear of that party had been dispelled.

Following extensive negotiations, this last form of accommodation was reflected in the formation in the fall of 1976 of a Christian Democratic *monocolore* (one-party) government headed by Giulio Andreotti. Its investiture was made possible by the abstention of the PCI, which was in turn obtained by negotiations between that party and the DC that resulted in agreement on a program of austerity and fiscal stabilization.[3] As remarkable as the achievement seemed

---

[2] The preelection period is analyzed in Samuel H. Barnes, "The Dark Side of Pluralism: Italian Democracy and the Limits of Political Engineering," in John H. Halowell, ed., *Prospects for Constitutional Democracy: Essays in Honor of R. Taylor Cole* (Durham, N.C.: Duke University Press, 1976), pp. 75-100.

[3] On the actual votes in both the Chamber and the Senate, the DC and the South Tyrol minority party voted for the DC *monocolore* government; the MSI, DP, and PR voted against; and the PCI, PSI, PSDI, PRI, and PLI abstained. See *La Stampa*, August 7 and 12, 1976.

to be, it was limited in scope. Furthermore, it was to test the ability of the PCI to maintain its influence over the unions and the left in general. Thus, the achievement of a government supported by but not including the PCI did not exhaust the possibilities for change. Increasing PCI involvement was widely expected.[4] What did not appear to be likely a year after the election was either the PCI's governing alone or a PCI-led coalition of left parties.

A brief analysis will suggest some of the complexities of the coalition game, and especially the constraints on extensive and rapid change in Italy. The election will then be viewed from the perspectives of the individual parties involved.

Electoral Change and Regime Change

A discussion of change must begin with an understanding of the point of departure—in this case, the nature of the present Italian regime. A fundamental issue in the 1976 election was the role of the PCI in the postelectoral political scene. Basic to this issue is the question of how a powerful PCI could go about altering the present regime—a much more difficult task than increasing its share of the vote. The PCI certainly recognizes the magnitude of the challenge before it, hence its extreme caution. The PCI must operate with great finesse; it can afford few tactical mistakes if its strategic goals are to be achieved. And success is by no means guaranteed. The Christian Democrats whom the PCI is trying to dislodge are not just a political party: they are the regime. A second fundamental issue affecting PCI policy is the integration of Italy into the Western economic and diplomatic bloc. These two issues will be considered in turn.

The DC is a catchall party with a number of components. It is a religious party, originally dependent on the Church for its links with the segment of the population that attends church regularly; it still needs the many large and small paths of access that its favored status within the Catholic subculture provides it. But processes of influence work both ways; the Church is dependent on the DC for its political clout. It needs the DC to fight its battles against the secularization of society, against divorce and abortion today, against the removal of religious influences from the schools tomorrow, against the watering down some time in the future of the favored status of the Church that is written into the republican constitution. More-

---

[4] The publicly expressed preferences of both the PCI and PSI were for a government of all democratic forces (DC, PCI, PSI, PRI, PSDI, PLI) to deal with the national emergency. See *La Stampa*, March 17 and 19, 1977.

over, it needs the DC in numerous small ways as well—to give it access to the bureaucracy, to support its clients, to preserve its standing in day-to-day life. The Church has moved away from the open partisanship of the years of Pope Pius XII and plays a more subtle role today; Catholic Action organizations no longer provide the front-line troops for the DC's political battles. But the Church is not neutral in Italian politics. Its involvement in the past election in favor of the DC was open and extensive, even if less organizationally focused than in the immediate postwar years.

The fact is that loyal Catholics know how they should vote— and vote accordingly. What is not known is just how many loyal Catholics there still are and what the cost in DC votes would be of policies that were strongly opposed by the Church. The DC must remain a religious party; but it must be a lot more than that, especially considering the decline in religious practice in Italy and the shrinking pool of confessional voters.

The Christian Democratic party dominates a Christian Democratic regime. It is often said—and only partly in jest—that Italy has had only two governments since 1922. The DC inherited a political system in which the state was viewed as party property, and it has continued to operate as if government were the private preserve of the party. State office is used to produce Christian Democratic votes. The state is politicized thoroughly at all levels and in all areas. In addition—and just as significantly—the very large portion of Italian economic life that involves state-owned property or that owes its prosperity to the state is likewise used as party property. Its swollen bureaucracies support an army of Christian Democratic followers chosen in large part because of their political connections and who view their positions as rewards for political ties rather than as public trusts. Office is property, and at the national level it is owned by the Christian Democratic party. The chief significance of the Opening to the Left was that it cut the PSI into the system, into the national establishment. But control remained in the hands of the DC; the Socialists were permitted a modest slice of the pie in lieu of reform.

The left—especially the PCI—has done much the same thing at the local and regional levels, and anticipation of that result was the principal reason for the DC's reluctance to establish the regions called for in the Republican constitution of 1948. This document recognized four special regions already in existence (Sicily, Sardinia, Valle d'Aosta, and Trentino-Alto Adige), and another, Friuli-Venezia Giulia, was created in 1963. Fourteen regular regions were also mentioned, but enabling legislation was delayed until 1970. One of the regular regions was subsequently divided into two, so there are currently fifteen regular and five special regions. The fears of the DC have been realized: the PCI participates in regional governments in several of the most heavily populated regions of the country. PCI local and regional bureaucracies have been closely watched by the DC, which is one of several reasons for their high levels of performance, especially when compared with DC achievements in local and regional government.[5]

It is impossible to say what would happen to the DC if it were to lose the patronage capabilities provided by the state and the parastate agencies. It is certain that the party would give up on almost any other front before it would make serious concessions in that direction, and this is an important factor in the current strategic thinking of Italian parties. Thus the PCI is unwilling to push for extensive nationalization of industry in the near future, not only because it might be unwarranted on economic grounds but also because it would simply add to the patronage potential of the DC. And the DC is not likely to take the lead in reducing the swollen and inefficient national bureaucracy, not only because it would increase unemployment but also because it would punish DC supporters.

It is widely believed, by the left and others, that the DC will begin to lose the support of these patron-client-oriented followers as soon as the party shows signs that it is loosening its iron grip on power. According to this point of view, these opportunistic elements will seek to make connections with the new rulers as soon as the "tipping point" is reached. In this event, the electoral decline of the DC would be swift and irreversible.

There are signs that this may be beginning. The changes in the operation of RAI, the state radio-television corporation, described in William Porter's chapter in this volume, reflect important developments in "liberating" the state from the DC; but broadcasting involves relatively few bureaucrats, despite its political sensitivity. More important is the development of the regional bureaucracies. Communal and provincial governments have long been the stronghold of the left in many areas, and now several important regions are dominated by the left. It is, of course, not certain that loss of patronage would be fatal for the DC, but that party will not want to run the risks involved in a genuine restructuring of the bureaucracy. Hence the precise nature of PCI-DC cooperation becomes of primary

---

[5] For an introduction to the regions, see Norman Kogan, "Impact of the New Italian Regional Governments on the Structure of Power within the Parties," *Comparative Politics*, vol. 7 (April 1975), pp. 383-406.

importance, and it seems unlikely that the needs of both the parties can be easily accommodated.

The second aspect of the Christian Democratic regime that sets severe constraints on the PCI is its integration into the Western economic and diplomatic alliance. Italy is part of the European Economic Community; its economy is modified capitalist with a substantial state-owned section that is managed largely independently of the cabinet. As several contributors to this volume have noted, it is a precariously balanced economy; Italy has few natural resources and is heavily dependent on trade. It is difficult to prevent the flight of domestic capital; and the high cost of labor, political unrest, and bureaucratic complications make it less attractive than many other countries to foreign capital investments. On the other hand, Italian economic well-being is greater now than in the past. A call for austerity and sacrifice would not be greeted warmly. There would not be much support—even on the left—for Italy's integration with the eastern bloc economies, and no one seriously advocates the Albanian or Chinese models as relevant for Italy. It is thus not surprising that the economic program of the PCI is vague—a point to which we will return—and that the continuation of the existing pattern of economic relationships is generally assumed. Along with economic ties there are also alliance strategies that would be difficult to alter.

Against this background of seemingly unalterable constraints— in the international field, in the economy, in the state machinery— the task of the PCI appears to be very difficult. Let us now look at how that party has reacted to the 1976 election and its aftermath.

The PCI and the Elections

Strategy and Tactics. The PCI is caught in a dilemma. In the long run it would like to change Italy dramatically, but it is far from having a strong electoral mandate to do so. It is the second largest party and has the potential of a plurality; it holds thousands of positions in communal, provincial, and regional governments; it is supported by overwhelmingly nonrevolutionary solid citizens who want change *and* order. Consequently, to achieve its strategic goal of change it must find ways to work with the dominant Christian Democratic party. But it must accomplish this miracle of accommodation without falling victim to the attractions of office for individual gain and without losing its appeal for those segments of the Italian electorate that want change. Tactically, it must try simultaneously to increase its power at the national level, consolidate its local and regional positions, maintain the loyalty of its activists and functionaries, and continue to extend its appeal in sections of the population that are distant from its core support in the industrial working class.

The PCI must balance these contradictory objectives while carefully altering its international positions so as to increase the credibility of its claim that a Communist government would respect Italy's international obligations. The PCI leadership appears to have accepted the constraints imposed by the logic of the electoral returns and the realities of international politics. The result is an apparent de facto abandonment of previous models of Communist systems. The nature of the new PCI model, however, is unclear. Although the party continues to reaffirm its commitment to structural change and extensive reform, the emphasis on strategy does not mask the vagueness of its programs. As Stephen Hellman says in this volume, "One gets the impression of a fundamentally incomplete strategy."

There is surprisingly little disagreement among the Italian parties concerning the foreign policy of Italy, now that the PCI's acceptance of the country's existing international obligations has brought its position closer to those of its rivals. While criticizing the Christian Democratic party's inability or unwillingness to seek an independent foreign policy for Italy—and while promising to implement such an independent policy itself—the PCI has explicitly endorsed the continued membership of Italy in the European Community and in NATO. As the party comes closer to power, the disadvantages—indeed, perhaps the economic disaster—that would ensue if Italy withdrew from the European Community are apparent to the PCI. But the integration of Italy into the European and world economies leaves little room for altering overall economic policies. How the Communists, once in power, would reconcile their strategy of change with their acceptance of the European economic system and their rejection of integration with the eastern economic bloc is an open question.

The possibility of Communist political power in Italy is extremely unsettling for Italian investment, both foreign and domestic. The task of the PCI is to reassure capitalists about their future in Italy—not an easy task, yet one necessary for Italian economic viability. The PCI must do more than reassure private investors; it must also be convincing at the governmental and intergovernmental levels. Italy's balance-of-payment problems are severe, and the country is, and will be, heavily dependent upon the International Monetary Fund and friendly governments for loans. It is possible that the

German and American governments cannot afford to permit Italian bankruptcy. But the task of dealing with these governments would be difficult for the PCI. Furthermore, the demands of domestic politics in other Western European countries and the United States may make cooperation difficult. For example, during the 1976 German electoral campaign, Chancellor Schmidt found it politically opportune to make undiplomatic and strongly anti-Communist statements concerning the Italian elections; the issue of support or opposition to a Communist government in Italy was also raised during the American presidential campaign. The Carter administration seemed to be outlining a more flexible policy toward the Italian Communists than its predecessors. But the very fact that Western leaders were expressing concern about an Italian campaign was a sign of the international constraints that might ultimately confront a PCI government.

As Stephen Hellman says in his chapter, the PCI is also worried about the example of the Allende regime in Chile. It is not necessary to debate what really happened in Chile; the message that the PCI derives from that experience is the impossibility of successfully imposing substantial change in a Western nation with only a bare statistical majority in favor of change and with institutional forces such as the state bureaucracy and the military opposed. It is impossible to know the extent to which Communist thinking is influenced by the postwar division of the world into spheres of influence and Italy's position outside of the Soviet orbit. Italian Communist leaders openly state their reluctance to attempt dramatic changes in Italy without a strong coalition of "popular forces" behind them. This motivates their electoral strategy of appealing to diverse groups of the population and their political tactics of attempting to expand the current coalition to include the PCI in a historic compromise or grand coalition of popular forces to bring about reforms. The current severe economic crisis afflicting Italy provides the PCI the opportunity to pursue a strategy of national cooperation and renewal, a policy that furthers the party's strategic goals at the same time that it promotes an image of cooperation and moderation.

The logic of the electoral returns suggests that the problem of 50 percent plus 1 is not likely to arise for the PCI in the near future. The growth of the PCI over the past thirty years has been constant from election to election. It is impossible to predict what the ultimate limits of the PCI's electoral potential may be, but it is unlikely that the party will be able to expand its share of the vote indefinitely. As Giacomo Sani's analysis in this volume has indicated, a substantial portion of the PCI's increase has come from new voters; these were especially numerous in 1976 because of the lowering of the voting age to eighteen. While PCI participation in the government might help the party win new votes, it might also embroil it in a fate similar to that of the PSI. What seems certain is that the PCI by itself is a long way from achieving an absolute majority in Parliament.

On the other hand, the possibility of a left majority is very real. Indeed, a potential left majority already exists, if the widest definition is given to the term left. However, a PCI-dominated government relying not only on the Socialists but also on the Social Democrats, the Republicans, and possibly even left-wing Christian Democrats would be quite different from a PCI *monocolore* government. Such a government would be one solution to the PCI's problems, though the party prefers an arrangement with the DC. But a left coalition would be unlikely to make substantial alterations in Italy's current economic system and its pattern of international alliances. And a left coalition seems extremely unlikely during the life of the present Parliament, though it cannot be discounted as an eventual outcome.

The probability of a successful right-wing coup to prevent the peaceful assumption of power by the PCI has receded considerably since 1972. The neo-Fascists split in late 1976 and are in decline. The possibility of independent action by the military or police is becoming less likely; their leaders, probably overwhelmingly conservative, are less able to control the rank and file with each passing year.

The Commitment to Democracy. The Italian Communist party is deeply rooted in the governmental structure of Italy; it has been presented with the opportunity of playing an increasingly important role within the political system; and it is the spokesman for a new generation that has grown up within the postwar democratic and constitutional order. It has a lot to lose and would not enter lightly into revolutionary adventures that were not guaranteed success.

This last point is very important. The generation that fought in the Resistance and survived the Stalinist years still dominates the top of the PCI. However, the most Stalinist elements have been retired or shunted aside. The present party membership is young, and a majority probably have joined the party within the past decade. The question of the fundamental devotion to democracy of the Italian Communists is often raised. What the party will eventually do is almost certainly not known to anyone, including the leading actors themselves, but study after study by social scientists, repeated statements by party spokesmen, and the viewpoints of scores of important non-Communist Italian leaders all suggest that the party is very much devoted to the procedures of the Italian constitutional system.[6] If this is merely a plot to mislead researchers and voters, it is one of the most successful mass conspiracies ever mounted—one involving hundreds of thousands of people, countless opportunities for unmasking the "real Communists," and the careful cultivation of deceptive images over the period of a generation. It seems highly likely that the present Communist leadership and rank and file are—in principle —overwhelmingly devoted to the constitutional order and the rights and liberties it defines. That situations might arise in which there were conflicts between these and other equally valued goals—such as reform or the maintenance of power—should be acknowledged. Similar conflicts, of course, could arise for substantial portions of the Christian Democratic party. Thus, though Italian democracy may not seem as securely entrenched as, for example, British or American democracy, one should not assume that the only threat comes from the Communists.

---

[6] The democratic commitment of the PCI is at the core of the present debate. The findings of numerous scholars who have studied Italian elite and mass opinions using the techniques of systematic interviewing have all reported attitudes consistent with the present constitutional system on the part of PCI elites and supporters. On the elite level, see, among others, Robert Putnam, *The Beliefs of Politicians* (New Haven: Yale University Press, 1973), and "The Political Attitudes of Senior Civil Servants in Western Europe: A Preliminary Report," *British Journal of Political Science*, vol. 3 (1973), pp. 257-281; Samuel H. Barnes, *Representation in Italy: Institutionalized Tradition and Electoral Choice* (Chicago: Chicago University Press, 1977); and Gordon J. DiRenzo, *Personality, Power and Politics* (Notre Dame, Ind.: Notre Dame University Press, 1967), who reaches conclusions inconsistent with his data. On the mass level, see Barnes, *Representation in Italy;* Giacomo Sani, "Mass Level Response to Party Strategy: The Italian Electorate and the Communist Party," in Donald Blackmer and Sidney Tarrow, eds., *Communism in Italy and France* (Princeton: Princeton University Press, 1975); and Sani, "Italian Communism on the Threshold," *Problems of Communism*, vol. 25 (November-December 1976), pp. 27-51.

A sampling of opinions on the future role of the PCI is contained in a round-table on "La democrazia italiana fra alternativa e confronto" [Italian democracy between alternatives and confrontation], *Il Mulino*, vol. 25 (September-October 1976), pp. 749-807.

Representative negative views of the PCI's democratic commitment are Giovanni Sartori, "I communisti al potere, e dopo?" [Communists in power, and after?], *Biblioteca della liberta*, vol. 11 (July-August 1974), pp. 92-98; and Domenico Fisichella, "L'alternativa rischiosa: considerazioni sul'difficile governo" [The risky alternative: considerations on the unlikely government], *Rivista italiana di scienza politica*, vol. 2 (December 1972), pp. 589-613.

Giuseppe Di Palma summarizes the problem succinctly. Writing of the PCI, he says, "It is not the sincerity but the clarity and endurance of their intents that are in question." "Eurocommunism?—Review Article," *Comparative Politics*, vol. 9 (April 1977), p. 361.

This discussion of the constraints under which the PCI operates does little to clarify the party's contemporary policy choices. Certainly, the PCI is "a party not like the others." There are several models of ruling Communist parties in existence, but the Eurocommunist is not one of them. It is an orientation, not a functioning system of government. What Eurocommunism will be like in practice has yet to be learned. The PCI is probably the party that will first be called upon to create "communism with a human face," and it has not disclosed the components of its model. No Communist economic system has been proposed, only short-term policies for pressing problems that the PCI hopes to deal with in cooperation with the DC. These policies are conventional and unalarming. Presumably the Italian road to socialism would consist of something more. But what? Mussolini is said to have made the trains run on time: Would the PCI settle for achieving less?

The PCI is much more centralized and disciplined than any other Italian party and maintains the principle and practice of democratic centralism. As first elaborated by Lenin and still followed in the PCI, democratic centralism permits intraparty debate until a policy is announced, at which point the entire party is required to accept and implement the directives of the party leadership. Adherence to this principle renders the open cultivation of factions impossible. Although identifiable currents of opinion exist alongside internal party groups based on geographical area and functional interests (unions, peasants, students, and so on), they have thus far not prevented the party from acting as a unified and disciplined organization. Dissidents, including the group around the journal *Il Manifesto*, have been expelled. Unlike other Italian parties, the PCI does not practice internal pluralism. The continued existence of democratic centralism is cited by critics as incompatible with the PCI's professed adherence to political pluralism in society as a whole. This is a difficult issue for the PCI. Much of its organizational and electoral strength stems from its structure, and the party cannot alter this greatly without changing its very nature. Yet democratic centralism in a governing party has frightening implications and is one of the chief causes of lingering suspicions about the democratic, western orientation of the PCI.[7]

---

[7] In 1977 the PCI began to substitute "democrazia unitaria e organica" [unitary and organic democracy] for democratic centralism. What this change will mean in practice is not evident at the time of writing. See the article of Fausto de Luca in *La repubblica*, January 20, 1977.

Ties with Soviet and European Communism. The second source of suspicion is the PCI's continued support of Soviet interests in foreign affairs. As both Hellman and LaPalombara have pointed out, the PCI's international stance continues to favor the positions of the eastern bloc far more than those of Italy's European and American allies. An Italy in which the PCI exercised considerable power would be an extremely unreliable member of NATO, regardless of the professions of loyalty made recently by PCI spokesmen. While the military value of Italy may be limited in any engagement involving central Europe, the emerging importance of the Mediterranean increases Italy's strategic value considerably. The Russian Mediterranean fleet, the resurgence of a democratic Latin Europe, the projected expansion of the European Common Market to include Greece and Spain, the association of the states of the Maghreb with the European Community, and the growing economic power of the oil-rich Middle Eastern countries all are shifting world concerns southward. Although the Mediterranean seems unlikely to attain its pre-Columbian centrality in the world, it is again becoming more than a mere geographical term, and Italy lies at its center.

It may not be a historical accident that the resurgence of Mediterranean Europe goes hand in hand with the growth of Eurocommunism. This unfortunate neologism—rightly rejected by the European Communist parties as being too restrictive a term for a type of party that includes the Japanese and other non-European parties as well—refers to the new combination of national communism and political democracy epitomized by the current PCI.[8] The French Communist party seems to share some of these characteristics; the recently legalized Communist party of Spain, which received just under 10 percent of the votes in the June 1977 election, is the third member of this Latin triumvirate. It is likely that these three Latin states will have important Communist parties and will be dealing with northern European countries in which Communist parties are politically insignificant. Thus, the nature and extent of the collaboration among these three parties will be very important for their further evolution.

Furthermore, the potential victory of the combined left in the next French parliamentary elections and the growing importance of the PCI make the question of relations between Communist parties

---

[8] Eurocommunism is a promising growth industry in political science. For introductions, see Neil McInnes, *The Communist Parties of Western Europe* (London: Oxford University Press, 1975), and Giuseppe Di Palma, *Comparative Politics*, pp. 357-375.

and the dominant Socialist parties of northern Europe of fundamental importance. The PCI, in particular, is seeking avenues for collaboration with these parties, and with the German Social Democratic party in particular. It is not an easy or promising path, though the way could be smoothed by the Communist parties' Socialist partners in France and Italy. Fear of isolation both internally and in Europe lies at the core of the PCI's strategy of trying to maintain contact with the PSI. At the same time, the Communists' wooing of the Christian Democrats fills the PSI with apprehension, since a successful DC-PCI coalition might deprive the PSI of any further historical role in Italy. This outcome, however, seems unlikely, for reasons that we will develop later.

The Left Electorate. The final point concerning the PCI is its relation with the left electorate. The electoral strategy of the PCI in 1976, as in previous elections, was to broaden its appeal as much as possible; to accomplish this, it developed specific aspects of its program to appeal to particular target groups as well as to general categories. Thus, it sought the support of all "progressive forces" and did not exclude the "productive" components of the capitalist class. From some perspectives, it appears that the party either now seeks to be all things to all people or is in fact engaging in deceptive campaigning. Whatever the truth, the party has not reconciled its appeal to traditional elements of the working class and others who are attracted by the promise of radical change with its conciliatory attitude toward more moderate segments of Italian society.

However compelling the need to appeal to more moderate segments in order to gain power through electoral means, the PCI cannot afford to jeopardize its stronghold on the left and especially within the working class. Its long-range maneuvers designed to give it a share of power on the national level harbor dangers precisely from this direction. Following the June 1976 election, PCI leaders worked hard to convince the lower leadership and the rank and file that the party was not abandoning its commitment to change. This operation has been largely successful, at least up until the time of writing. Furthermore, no other political grouping in Italy seems to be in a position to exploit the dissatisfaction with the PCI felt by leftist groups. The Socialists might want to do so, but they lack the grass-roots organizational capacity to compete seriously with the PCI at the mass level.

Potentially more serious for the PCI is the danger of the party's being outflanked on the left by newer radical movements outside its orbit of influence. Several chapters in this volume have referred to the dissident *Manifesto* group that was finally expelled and merged with others to form an electoral coalition, Democrazia Proletaria, for 1976. The DP was able to gain over half a million votes in the election, or 1.5 percent, and six seats in the Chamber of Deputies. These are votes and seats that might otherwise have gone to the PCI. On the other hand, the existence of these groups is not all bad for the PCI: they help the party to appear relatively moderate, make it possible for the party to warn against leftist adventurism, and serve as a perpetual reminder of the party's willingness to expel those who reject its discipline.

The PCI should have no fear of rivals on the left—as long as it is able to maintain its own internal discipline; if the PCI can remain united it will face little threat from the radical fringe. However, a deep party split, one that involved far more than the small group around *Manifesto*, would gravely threaten its effectiveness. As the party moves into a period of negotiation and compromise with the Christian Democratic party, it runs the risk of suffering the fate of the PSI in the Opening to the Left—that is, gaining the fruits of office but little in the way of substantive reform. A major difference, of course, is that the PSI had the PCI breathing over its left shoulder while the PCI has only scattered groups of intellectuals and dissidents to worry about at the present time.

The Significance of the Elections for the Christian Democratic Party

The ability of the Christian Democratic party to maintain its percentage of the total national vote between 1972 and 1976 was in many ways the most remarkable result of the electoral campaign. That a party in office for more than thirty years, with virtually no renewal at the top level,[9] suffering from charges of both corruption and incompetence, opposed by most of the country's intellectual spokesmen, and facing electoral opposition from every segment of

---

[9] The top leadership of the DC has been virtually unchanged since the immediate postwar years. All prime ministers had already served in the cabinets of Alcide De Gasperi; cabinet instability took the form of what P. A. Allum calls " 'musical chairs' of continuous coalition between the same partners: frequent changes of cabinet, less frequent changes of office and rarer changes of personnel. Indeed as a result of the frequency of cabinet reshuffles in Britain, more men have held cabinet office in postwar Britain than in Italy." *Italy— Republic Without Government?* (London: Weidenfeld and Nicolson, 1973), p. 119.

the left-right continuum could hold its own was quite an achievement. It is not clear whether this was a sort of Italian "last hurrah," for which the party marshalled every shred of influence and patronage, or whether the continued strength of the party reflected the beginnings of its reconstruction along coherent conservative lines. These questions will be answered only with hindsight, though few observers think that genuine renewal is likely. What is clear is that the party did indeed maintain its percentage of the vote but that, in the process, its geographical and socioeconomic bases were altered.

Preliminary analyses of the results reported in this volume and elsewhere suggest several fundamental changes in these bases of support. The Christian Democratic party gained in the south, and in Sicily in particular. It also gained in the red belt of central Italy and in Lazio, the area around Rome. As Figure 3–1 in Sani's chapter demonstrates, it is likely that the DC gained votes from the right of the political spectrum as well, though the evidence for this is far from conclusive. It is probable that many people who voted for the Liberal party and the neo-Fascist MSI-DN in 1972 went over to the Christian Democratic party in 1976. And it is likely that some of the DC's supporters in 1972 went over to the lay parties of the center and center-left, though it is also possible that the party gained votes from these same parties as well. The DC barely held its national percentage among the young, and perhaps did not even achieve that level of support among first-time voters. Considering the great successes of the Communists among the unusually large cohorts of new voters, the poor showing of the DC within this group is cited by many as evidence that the decline of the DC is inevitable.

Scattered analyses of the vote in northern cities suggest that the DC has lost most of its working-class following and that it is gaining in upper-middle-class areas of the larger cities. Insofar as this is indeed true, it represents a shift of the party to the right along the left-right continuum. Combined with its growing strength in the south, its decline in the north and its longstanding weakness in the central areas of the country make it more and more difficult for the party to reform itself in a dynamic direction.

Critics are virtually unanimous in the opinion that the party needs to make significant internal reforms, renew its leadership, and develop a more effective organization, but there are few signs that it will do so. It is true, as Douglas Wertman notes in his chapter in this volume, that the DC put forward more new faces in this campaign than previously. But the top levels of the party are still dominated by the same people who were already in charge in the 1940s.

Furthermore, the nature of internal party factionalism makes it extremely difficult for the party to act effectively to remedy its organizational weakness.

What is more foreboding for the Christian Democratic party is that the major problems of the Italian state—the swollen bureaucracy, the inability of the state machinery to formulate and execute programs in an effective manner, the unchecked operations of state-owned industry, and so on—are not the result of idiosyncratic circumstances, but rather reflect the very bases of Christian Democratic power. With the party and the machinery of state so closely intertwined, to ask serious reform of the Christian Democratic party is to ask it to destroy the bases of its strength in the society.

The current emphasis of the left on the development of the regions and on reform of the industrial bureaucracies of the state undoubtedly reflects a recognition of the difficulty of attacking the DC at its center. Whether the regions can be converted into effective instruments for the implementation of public policy or whether they will become simply another bureaucratic base for a somewhat different set of leaders—within the DC as well as the parties of the left—remains to be seen. What cannot be expected is a voluntary reform of the state machinery that would be detrimental to the DC in electoral politics.

The electoral results seem to push the Christian Democratic party in directions that may, in the long run, greatly affect its chances for successful competition with the resurgent left. One significant development is the decline in the role of the Church. Over the years since Vatican Council II, the nature of the ties between the party and organized religion have been modified considerably. But the emergence of divorce and abortion as central issues in Italian politics threatens to undo the movement toward the separation of religious and political questions. In particular, these issues serve to reinforce many of the less flexible elements in the DC. One of the few novelties in the campaign was the appearance of a militant Catholic movement, Comunione e Liberazione; its potential weight and particular policy orientation were uncertain at the time of writing.

Another significant result of the campaign was the increase in conservative votes going to the Christian Democratic party. The long-term consequences of this increase are difficult to interpret. While the immediate impact may be to push the party in a direction that will make it less able to compete with the left, a long-term consequence may be to alter considerably the structure of Italian partisan politics. The experience of other Christian Democratic parties in Europe suggests that it is quite possible for a religiously oriented party to become a conservative catchall party. The best example is, of course, the German Christian Democratic Union/Christian Social Union (CDU/CSU). This party has been successful as a Christian party in a country where church attendance is extremely low. Its southern wing, the Bavarian Christian Social Union, is more conservative than the Christian Democratic Union—a situation that has its parallel in Italy. The fact that it was, from its origins, interconfessional may render the CDU/CSU of doubtful utility as a model, but that party has been able to combine the defense of religious interests with the promotion of the conservative forces in German society. The Dutch Catholics, too, have been able to move away from an era of confessionalism into an alliance with Protestant parties. Thus, there is no reason why the Christian Democratic party of Italy could not continue to evolve in the direction of monopolizing the votes of those on the right and right-center of the political spectrum.

However, the presence of the Vatican in the country combined with the continued political saliency of emotionally charged issues such as divorce and abortion probably make this evolution more difficult in Italy than elsewhere. Moreover, the DC faces competition for the Catholic vote. The PCI views the Catholic rank and file as a genuinely popular force that must take its place in the national union of popular forces the Communists seek to promote. Consequently, the Communists are concerned not to antagonize the Catholic masses and thus attempt to minimize the significance of the highly emotional issues. This is the fundamental reason why it is the Socialists and Radicals who have taken the lead in pursuing policy questions that both the DC and the PCI would prefer to ignore.

Numerous observers, and Sani in particular in this volume, have emphasized that patterns of population replacement in Italy seem to favor the parties of the left, and the evidence strongly supports this view. One of the basic assumptions of PCI strategy is that continued leftist intrusion in the policy-making process will lead to a decline in the social bases of support for the right and center parties, and thus to their eventual demise. If this is true, the question of the Communists' having to give up power or alternate in power would not arise; once in power, the PCI could expect a long and tranquil period in which to remake Italian society.

However, forecasting is an imperfect art; it is unlikely that current trends will continue indefinitely. More probable would be a readjustment of the structure of the party system in the direction of the concentration of conservative—note well, conservative, not Fascist

344

—forces that could offer an electoral alternative to a triumphant left. It has been mentioned that, once deprived of its patronage in the state bureaucracy, the DC might shrink to a fraction of its present size. Of course, this could happen, but even that eventuality would not make impossible the restructuring of the party along classic conservative lines. Indeed, it might facilitate the reform of the party. But whatever happens, the DC is unlikely to give up its position in the state machinery easily.

Neither the DC nor the PCI has, or is likely in the near future to have, an absolute majority in Parliament, hence the importance of those political forces lying between the Communists and the Christian Democrats. It is to this subject that we now turn.

The Significance of the Elections for the Smaller Parties

The Socialist Party. In the aftermath of the elections, the Socialist parties in general and the PSI in particular underwent a period of intense self-examination, recrimination, and purging.[10] The expectations of the PSDI were perhaps modest; the change in the climate of anticommunism, which had been its original raison d'être, combined with serious scandals involving some of its leaders, weakened its potential. The PSI, on the other hand, entered the election with great hopes. The Socialists were primarily responsible for the dissolution of Parliament and looked forward to the substantial gains predicted by all the preelection polls (see Table 3–1 in the Sani chapter). When the party received a percentage of the vote no larger than it had obtained in 1972, its supporters viewed the result as a disaster.

With several months' hindsight, it appears that the PSI's feelings of loss were exaggerated, just as its hopes of gain had been greatly inflated. The reasons for its aberrations need to be recapitulated. As Gianfranco Pasquino has pointed out, the PSI pretends to possess much the same organizational structure as the PCI; it also seeks to appeal to most of the same groups and to share the left counterculture with the PCI. The weakness of the PSI is that it comes in second in every competition with the PCI. Although it has sub-

---

[10] Two analyses of the PSI's problems following the election are Angelo Panebianco, "Analisi di una sconfitta: il declino del PSI nel systema politico italiano" [Analysis of a defeat: the decline of the PSI in the Italian political system], *Il Mulino*, vol. 25 (September-October 1976), pp. 673-704; and Giuliano Cazzola, "Il PSI dopo il 20 giugno: le ragioni politiche di una crisi" [The PSI after June 20: the political reasons for the crisis], ibid., pp. 704-718.

stantial support in the popular sectors and can realistically claim to be a party of the working class, it is far behind the PCI among the most numerous groups such as the urban working class and agricultural categories. Its leadership is overwhelmingly middle class, which is true of all Italian parties with the partial exception of the PCI.

Moreover, the fact that the PSI is not a strong presence in mass organizations—unions, religious groups, reform movements—deprives its leaders of direct access to much of the electorate. Both the PCI and the DC can communicate directly with the semiliterate mass public, while the PSI must, to a large extent, rely on the mass media and other indirect forms of access. If Italian politics were largely a matter of image manipulation by the media, as is the case in so many countries, the PSI would not be so handicapped, but the institutionalization of the Italian electorate is an obstacle for parties that are not heavily represented in the mass organizations.[11] As a result, the PSI sometimes appears to be a party of generals with a sparse officer corps and poor linkage with the rank and file.

The PSI lost the battle in the trenches with the PCI. It lost the struggle for dominance of the mass organizations of the left; it maintained its presence, but with difficulty and with the sufferance of the PCI. The PSI had considerable potential as a democratic alternative to communism when the PCI was still viewed as Stalinist and dictatorial. Even today the PSI has a much stronger record than the PCI on such matters as internal democracy and commitment to civil liberties. But in the larger framework, the PSI has seen most of its positions adopted by the PCI. In a sense, it has won all the battles and still risks losing the war.

The PSI was weakened by its long collaboration with the DC. During the center-left period, in the 1960s and 1970s, the PSI acquired a share in the system of patronage, clientelism, and personal reward. For the PSI as well as the DC, these practices provided resources that could be converted into votes for the party and also into preference votes for individuals; these preference votes in turn brought power within the party and a claim on public office. While the PSI never gave up its pretention to being a working-class party, it attempted to play the ministerial game as well. The reforms

---

[11] At least this has been the case throughout the postwar period. A better educated electorate, the loss of DC monopoly over the state-owned electronic media, the proliferation of independent radio stations following a court ruling that ended the state monopoly of broadcasting, and the decline in the mass organizations of both the Church and the left may dramatically alter the patterns of mass mobilization in the future. For a discussion of the patterns that dominated through the 1960s, see Samuel H. Barnes, *Representation in Italy*.

achieved by the center-left government were perhaps substantial, but they were slow in coming and completely inadequate in the light of the massive needs of the country. It may be that the PSI needs nothing more than a *cure d'opposition*. However, it faces a severe historical test in achieving a strategic stance that differentiates it from the PCI. Its consistent advocacy of Communist involvement in the "government area" and its insistence on the inclusion of the PCI in some manner as a condition of its own support for a coalition raise serious questions about the continued need for a party such as the PSI.

The Socialist party has strongly supported the evolution of the parliamentary and democratic nature of the PCI. It has done this in large part out of the conviction that the PCI is a genuine mass party that holds the key to the achievement of socialism in Italy. The PSI always refused to join attempts to isolate the PCI; even during the Opening to the Left and the brief merger with the PSDI, the PSI kept open its lines of communication with the PCI. But the PSI's insistence on PCI involvement in national decision making stems also from two pragmatic considerations. The first is the realization that the PSI and the other moderate secular parties lack the strength to force substantial changes in the DC regime. With the weight of the PCI added, by means of some formula that would bring it more directly into the policy game, the DC could be coerced. A second reason for the PSI's insistence was more narrowly political: for years the PSI had suffered electorally from accepting responsibility for governmental policies. If the PCI were equally involved in government, negative reactions to governmental policies would not be automatically translated into votes against the PSI and for the PCI. On the other hand, this interpretation could be seen as an admission that the PSI could accomplish little without the PCI, in which case it would not be unreasonable for voters to support the PCI directly rather than the ineffectual PSI.

The PCI has come a long way toward eliminating the practices and loyalties that separate it from the PSI. In many respects, there are now few ideological reasons for preferring one over the other, while all of the organizational advantages and considerations of effectiveness favor the PCI. Yet there are still real differences between the two parties. The PCI has not matched the PSI on questions of internal party democracy, and this is a major distinction between them. However, the importance of this point is limited by two rather obvious factors. The first is that, despite the absence of organized factions, the PCI has a vigorous internal party life and probably better elite–mass linkages than exist in the PSI. The second is that the experience of factionalism in the other Italian parties, and especially in the PSI, hardly makes internal democracy appear to be a virtue. So an apparent PSI strength is, perhaps, on balance a handicap. Once again the ability of the PCI elite to adapt selectively is demonstrated.

The Opening to the Left was probably a historical blunder on the part of the Socialists. Whatever the real alternatives were for Italian democracy, the decision of the PSI to enter the majority caused it to leave a political space open on its left. The Opening to the Left was in fact a shift to the right by the PSI, and undoubtedly this greatly aided the expansion of the PCI, which had no other direction in which to expand. The wisdom of the PSI's action will be evaluated differently by people with different concerns. For those who emphasize cabinet stability and the need for a majority, the PSI's action was essential to the survival of Italian democracy, as there was no other democratic source of majority support. For them, the PSI simply acted responsibly. For critics who emphasize the need for change, the PSI made a mistake, sold out too cheaply. The past ten years have been very disappointing for Italian socialism.

Despite what has been said, Italian socialism has a future, albeit not the one to which it has historically aspired. The 1976 elections witnessed a sharp decline in the total vote for the secular moderate parties. The PCI and DC increasingly dominate the electorate. But neither is likely to approach an absolute majority of the votes soon. The small parties will continue to be necessary for all cabinets, assuming that there is no grand coalition limited to the PCI and the DC—a highly unlikely but possible outcome. The PSI will continue to play the crucial role of coalition partner. It is the role of the Free Democrats in Germany and of small liberal-oriented parties in other countries. The existence of a large Communist party extends the political space, so that in Italy the middle role is likely to be played by Socialists rather than by Liberals. The decline of the PLI undoubtedly reflects this interpretation of the political space. The decline in the PSDI also seems to reflect the expansion of the left. The union of the two Socialist parties would make little difference for Socialist strength and importance; the PSDI would simply become a faction within a larger Socialist party.

At the time of writing, the PSI appeared to be fighting against the vision of the future outlined above. The future is still open. But the PCI has quietly occupied the space on the left of the PSI, and it is hard to see where the latter can turn. Although the PCI has made very few mistakes in the past, a miscalculation in the next few years could greatly expand the range of choices available to the PSI. Just as it has throughout most of the past thirty years, the fate of the PSI rests on the strategic choices of the Communists. If there is still an Italian road to socialism—and that is uncertain—the Communists seem to have taken it over. The Socialist alternative lacks credibility. But the logic of the electoral returns appears to assure the PSI a crucial role in determining the nature of Italian politics over the next few years.

The Smaller Parties. It is more difficult to evaluate the significance of the election for the smaller parties in the system. The Social Democratic party, not unexpectedly, slipped badly in the electoral returns. It has embarked on a new course of reversing its long-term hostility to the PCI. As Leonardi points out in this volume, Giuseppe Saragat expressed the PSDI's willingness to cooperate with the PCI at the local but not the national level. But it is difficult to see a bright future for the party in the altered political situation. Its weak parliamentary strength renders it an unimposing ally; its leadership is in disarray; it occupies a shrinking political space.

The Republican party suffered a considerable disappointment in the election, though it retained its role as the secular conscience of the Italian system. It had an impressively articulated campaign document, but the complexity of the Republican program and the nature of the party's organization made it impossible for it to acquire any substantial mass following. Furthermore, the domination of the party by Ugo La Malfa, an aging lion of Italian politics, raised doubts about the continued vitality of the party.

The future of the Liberal party was perhaps darker than that of any center party. The Liberals' share of the vote slipped from 3.9 percent in 1972 to 1.3 percent in 1976. The desertion of much of its following, presumably to reinforce the conservative forces within the Christian Democratic party, may have been irreversible. On the other hand, the PLI has long had a highly educated and discriminating electorate that has switched votes from party to party more often than any other in the system. It is thus possible that the defections were not permanent, especially considering the efforts toward renovation being taken by the Liberal leadership. At present it is not clear that there is much of a future for the PLI in the unfolding Italian situation.

The MSI underwent changes following the election that appeared destined to permit at least some of its representatives a role in future governments, though at tremendous cost. Having fought the election as the MSI-Destra Nazionale, the party suffered a split in late

1976 when seventeen of its thirty-five deputies and nine of its fifteen senators defected to a new group calling itself Democrazia Nazionale (national democracy).[12] Spokesmen suggested that the group wanted to alter the anticonstitutional image of the MSI and eventually to join the governing majority. While such a move might add a few votes to a center-right coalition, it would certainly move the coalition and the Christian Democratic party further away from the center and, undoubtedly, in the long run would weaken the ability of the constitutional right to mount a credible alternative to the growing strength of the left. The DC was unlikely to attempt to stake its government on the support of the Democrazia Nazionale. The split weakened still further the already troubled neo-Fascists, to the point where it is difficult to envisage even a strong spoiler's role for the MSI.

The parliamentary role of the new Radical party is uncertain. The party ran an unusual campaign and insisted on tackling many of the untouchable subjects of Italian politics. Perhaps for this reason, it attracted considerable interest among Italian intellectuals. As the review of the preelection maneuvering has demonstrated, many of the party's leaders could have been part of the Socialist party had the negotiations between the two gone differently. Given the differences in style and interest, the Radicals did not seem merely another Socialist faction. But it appeared unlikely that there was much room for their party's growth.

The Proletarian Democrats were a coalition of groups on the extreme left, and their agreement barely lasted through the campaign. The now fragmented alliance is in a poor position to exploit leftist discontent with the PCI's policies.[13] Without an internal split in the PCI, which is unlikely, there is at present no strong leftist alternative to the current policy of accommodation.

Epilogue

What did the 1976 election settle? Nothing yet has been resolved. The Christian Democrats are still in office. While the PCI greatly increased its influence in the system, it seems little closer than before to implementing the thoroughgoing restructuring of society that is traditionally conjured up by the thought of a Communist victory. The problem of a government majority was not solved by the elec-

---

[12] See *Corriere della Sera*, December 22, 1976.
[13] *Corriere della Sera*, December 1, 1976.

tion. But then few problems are "solved" in Italy; people learn to live with situations, which is different from dominating them. Perhaps it is a peculiarly American belief that politics involves problems and solutions; perhaps it is unrealistic to expect more than repeated accommodation, which is, after all, a highly respected strategy when it is successful.

The slate is never wiped clean in Italy; there are no new beginnings. In Italy every deep probe of the terrain—in politics as in the construction industry—uncovers layers of the past that must be carefully examined, evaluated, and often preserved. The advance of the PCI represents a potential for change that is remarkable in a country that is the home of the Vatican and a member of the Western European economic and political system. The PCI accepts these realities and promises innovative reforms that will be compatible both with them and with its own sense of historical mission. It faces a difficult task that requires creative leadership and effective organization, both of which it has exhibited in the past. The success of the PCI's strategy also requires subtlety on the part of the other parties and especially the Christian Democrats; all must cooperate by accepting the logic of the electoral returns.

At least this was the dominant scenario to emerge in the aftermath of the elections. Historical trends seemed to favor the PCI. But projecting trends is a risky enterprise. It assumes no changes in the parameters; it discounts the political acumen of the DC; it requires that the PCI make few errors. A period of delicate maneuvering lies ahead.

APPENDIX

Election Results, Italian Chamber of Deputies, 1968, 1972, 1976, and Senate, 1976

Compiled by Richard M. Scammon

The data below are for party voting in Italy's thirty-one multimember proportional representation constituencies (*collegi elettorali*) in 1968, 1972, and 1976. Voting in the single-member Aosta Valley (constituency 31) is given below the voting statistics in a special note.

In several instances in the text, national vote and seat totals for the Chamber will vary slightly from those below. As indicated, these data are for 629 seats, excluding the single-member Valle d'Aosta; in the text, the figures may reflect a vote for 630 seats by assigning joint list votes in the Valle d'Aosta to national parties.

At the end of each table, below the national vote and seat totals for the seats won in the thirty-one proportional representation constituencies, are listed the seats allocated at the national level through the *Collegio Unico Nazionale* to secure a more proportionate distribution of deputies than that secured by relying only on the constituencies themselves.

Constituency 21 was reported as Campobasso in 1968, and as Campobasso-Isernia in 1972 and 1976. Constituency 30 was reported as Cagliari-Sassari-Nuoro in 1968 and 1972, with Oristano created and added for 1976.

The constituencies have been numbered as follows:

1. Torino-Novara-Vercelli
2. Cuneo-Alessandria-Asti
3. Genova-Imperia-LaSpezia-Savona
4. Milano-Pavia
5. Como-Sondrio-Varese
6. Brescia-Bergamo
7. Mantova-Cremona

8. Trento-Bolzano
9. Verona-Padova-Vicenza-Rovigo
10. Venezia-Treviso
11. Udine-Belluno-Gorizia-Pordenone
12. Bologna-Ferrara-Ravenna-Forli
13. Parma-Modena-Piacenza-Reggio nell'Emilia
14. Firenze-Pistoia
15. Pisa-Livorno-Lucca-Massa e Carrara
16. Siena-Arezzo-Grosseto
17. Ancona-Pesaro-Macerata-Ascoli Piceno
18. Perugia-Terni-Rieti
19. Roma-Viterbo-Latina-Frosinone
20. L'Aquila-Pescara-Chieti-Teramo
21. Campobasso-Isernia
22. Napoli-Caserta
23. Benevento-Avellino-Salerno
24. Bari-Foggia
25. Lecce-Brindisi-Taranto
26. Potenza-Matera
27. Catanzaro-Cosenza-Reggio di Calabria
28. Catania-Messina-Siracusa-Ragusa-Enna
29. Palermo-Trapani-Agrigento-Catanissetta
30. Cagliari-Sassari-Nuoro-Oristano
31. Valle d'Aosta
32. Trieste

The party names have been abbreviated as follows:

DC	Democrazia Christiana, Christian Democratic party
PCI	Partito Comunista Italiano, Italian Communist party
PSI	Partito Socialista Italiano, Italian Socialist party (1972 and 1976)
PSDI	Partito Socialista Democratico Italiano, Social Democratic party (1972 and 1976)
PSU	Partiti Socialisti Unificati, United Socialist party (PSI plus PSDI; 1968 only)
MSI	Movimento Sociale Italiano, Italian Social Movement

PDIUM	Partito Democratico Italiano di Unita Monarchica, Monarchist party (1968 only)
MSI-DN	Movimento Sociale Italiano - Destra Nazionale, Italian Social Movement - National Right (MSI plus PDIUM; 1972 and 1976)
PRI	Partito Repubblicano Italiano, Republican party
PLI	Partito Liberale Italiano, Liberal party
PSIUP	Partito Socialista Italiano di Unita Proletaria, Socialist party of Proletarian Unity (1968 and 1972)
DP	Democrazia Proletaria, Proletarian Democracy
PR	Partito Radicale, Radical party

1968 ELECTION RESULTS, ITALIAN CHAMBER OF DEPUTIES

Constituencies	Total	DC	PCI
1. Votes cast	1,974,991	654,827	562,452
% of vote	100	33.2	28.5
Seats	29	11	9
2. Votes cast	833,776	375,345	169,637
% of vote	100	45.0	20.3
Seats	13	7	3
3. Votes cast	1,232,693	410,302	381,325
% of vote	100	33.3	30.9
Seats	19	7	7
4. Votes cast	2,704,949	946,310	735,169
% of vote	100	35.0	27.2
Seats	44	16	13
5. Votes cast	961,529	459,394	160,172
% of vote	100	47.8	16.7
Seats	17	9	3
6. Votes cast	1,038,755	575,082	149,611
% of vote	100	55.4	14.4
Seats	19	12	3
7. Votes cast	482,043	185,314	144,118
% of vote	100	38.4	29.9
Seats	8	4	3
8. Votes cast	496,703	188,834	33,480
% of vote	100	38.0	6.7
Seats	8	4	—
9. Votes cast	1,462,252	829,503	222,937
% of vote	100	56.7	15.2
Seats	27	17	4
10. Votes cast	877,342	413,574	172,011
% of vote	100	47.1	19.6
Seats	15	8	3
11. Votes cast	721,280	334,250	123,751
% of vote	100	46.3	17.2
Seats	12	7	2
12. Votes cast	1,482,452	359,200	651,157
% of vote	100	24.2	43.9
Seats	25	6	12
13. Votes cast	1,094,662	328,453	463,790
% of vote	100	30.0	42.4
Seats	20	6	9
14. Votes cast	919,422	276,934	404,082
% of vote	100	30.1	43.9
Seats	14	5	7
15. Votes cast	848,413	282,333	296,343
% of vote	100	33.3	34.9
Seats	12	5	5
16. Votes cast	534,138	149,416	244,187
% of vote	100	28.0	45.7
Seats	9	3	5
17. Votes cast	866,410	341,142	279,205
% of vote	100	39.4	32.2
Seats	15	7	6

PSU (PSI + PSDI)	PLI	MSI	PSIUP	PRI	PDIUM	Other[a]
319,401	203,414	49,933	98,661	24,424	22,294	39,585
16.2	10.3	2.5	5.0	1.2	1.1	2.0
5	3	—	1	—	—	—
144,751	65,737	12,543	38,547	18,697	8,519	—
17.4	7.9	1.5	4.6	2.2	1.0	—
2	1	—	—	—	—	—
194,169	111,052	37,098	51,254	19,529	8,336	19,628
15.8	9.0	3.0	4.2	1.6	.7	1.6
3	2	—	—	—	—	—
480,379	256,541	99,671	115,733	35,646	20,072	15,428
17.8	9.5	3.7	4.3	1.3	.7	.6
8	4	1	2	—	—	—
175,435	66,940	24,555	58,620	7,278	7,056	2,079
18.2	7.0	2.6	6.1	.8	.7	.2
3	1	—	1	—	—	—
139,219	61,968	33,342	64,280	5,798	8,426	1,029
13.4	6.0	3.2	6.2	.6	.8	.1
2	1	—	1	—	—	—
82,766	22,171	15,546	25,473	3,598	3,057	—
17.2	4.6	3.2	5.3	.7	.6	—
1	—	—	—	—	—	—
64,341	22,141	14,394	12,750	3,961	1,984	154,818
13.0	4.5	2.9	2.6	.8	.4	31.2
1	—	—	—	—	—	3
201,313	78,012	38,718	74,613	10,213	6,943	—
13.8	5.3	2.6	5.1	.7	.5	—
4	1	—	1	—	—	—
142,194	42,186	21,840	49,095	9,020	3,997	23,425
16.2	4.8	2.5	5.6	1.0	.5	2.7
3	—	—	1	—	—	—
156,375	32,809	27,181	33,977	7,192	5,745	—
21.7	4.5	3.8	4.7	1.0	.8	—
3	—	—	—	—	—	—
213,888	68,209	37,972	70,247	72,564	4,529	4,686
14.4	4.6	2.6	4.7	4.9	.3	.3
4	1	—	1	1	—	—
157,072	51,671	24,572	57,230	6,863	5,011	—
14.3	4.7	2.2	5.2	.6	.5	—
3	1	—	1	—	—	—
120,430	43,329	26,046	37,358	7,765	3,478	—
13.1	4.7	2.8	4.1	.8	.4	—
2	—	—	—	—	—	—
127,295	29,978	36,646	46,101	22,447	4,086	3,184
15.0	3.5	4.3	5.4	2.6	.5	.4
2	—	—	—	—	—	—
67,741	15,443	17,728	26,235	11,196	—	2,192
12.7	2.9	3.3	4.9	2.1	—	.4
1	—	—	—	—	—	—
111,634	30,961	29,847	40,163	27,475	3,147	2,836
12.9	3.6	3.4	4.6	3.2	.4	.3
2	—	—	—	—	—	—

1968 CHAMBER RESULTS *(continued)*

Constituencies	Total	DC	PCI
18. Votes cast	607,512	192,049	238,533
% of vote	100	31.6	39.3
Seats	10	4	5
19. Votes cast	2,580,641	888,604	713,807
% of vote	100	34.4	27.7
Seats	44	16	13
20. Votes cast	685,502	333,878	174,322
% of vote	100	48.7	25.4
Seats	13	8	4
21. Votes cast	182,584	91,076	33,012
% of vote	100	49.9	18.1
Seats	3	2	1
22. Votes cast	1,698,861	633,910	444,394
% of vote	100	37.3	26.2
Seats	34	14	10
23. Votes cast	892,675	386,465	159,212
% of vote	100	43.3	17.8
Seats	18	9	4
24. Votes cast	1,047,957	458,847	307,924
% of vote	100	43.8	29.4
Seats	22	11	7
25. Votes cast	843,714	377,469	206,519
% of vote	100	44.7	24.5
Seats	17	9	5
26. Votes cast	323,608	158,051	84,481
% of vote	100	48.8	26.1
Seats	7	4	2
27. Votes cast	978,696	410,367	233,399
% of vote	100	41.9	23.8
Seats	23	11	6
28. Votes cast	1,263,141	509,977	279,735
% of vote	100	40.4	22.1
Seats	28	12	7
29. Votes cast	1,131,766	458,467	258,544
% of vote	100	40.5	22.8
Seats	26	12	7
30. Votes cast	755,310	324,113	178,663
% of vote	100	42.9	23.7
Seats	15	8	4
32. Votes cast	213,538	73,686	51,432
% of vote	100	34.5	24.1
Seats	3	2	1
ITALY			
Votes cast	31,737,315	12,407,172	8,557,404
% of vote	100	39.1	27.0
Seats won at constituency level	569	256	170
Seats assigned at national level	60	9	7
Total seats	629	265	177

a The "other" vote was as follows: 152,954, South Tyrol People's party (3 deputies elected); 100,044, Socialdemocrazia; 63,361, Unione Democratica Nuova Repubblica; 129,160, miscellaneous remaining parties.

PSU (PSI + PSDI)	PLI	MSI	PSIUP	PRI	PDIUM	Other[a]
77,179	16,216	34,233	32,530	13,899	2,873	—
12.7	2.7	5.6	5.4	2.3	.5	—
1	—	—	—	—	—	—
333,427	198,409	213,288	81,028	62,820	50,486	38,772
12.9	7.7	8.3	3.1	2.4	2.0	1.5
6	3	4	1	1	—	—
79,159	21,049	34,256	23,416	12,619	4,527	2,276
11.5	3.1	5.0	3.4	1.8	.7	.3
1	—	—	—	—	—	—
28,635	9,945	7,287	4,521	2,368	—	5,740
15.7	5.4	4.0	2.5	1.3	—	3.1
—	—	—	—	—	—	—
205,878	70,863	120,333	55,938	40,275	90,348	36,922
12.1	4.2	7.1	3.3	2.4	5.3	2.2
4	1	2	1	—	2	—
136,400	44,966	61,501	38,278	20,732	35,113	10,008
15.3	5.0	6.9	4.3	2.3	3.9	1.1
3	1	1	—	—	—	—
135,915	30,448	55,824	29,642	10,255	16,389	2,713
13.0	2.9	5.3	2.8	1.0	1.6	.3
3	—	1	—	—	—	—
107,606	28,576	69,764	25,044	16,375	8,942	3,419
12.8	3.4	8.3	3.0	1.9	1.1	.4
2	—	1	—	—	—	—
45,979	9,907	10,879	9,180	2,456	2,675	—
14.2	3.1	3.4	2.8	.8	.8	—
1	—	—	—	—	—	—
174,554	25,743	53,152	43,157	23,915	6,422	7,987
17.8	2.6	5.4	4.4	2.4	.7	.8
4	—	1	1	—	—	—
138,791	84,680	89,591	64,861	49,779	26,118	19,609
11.0	6.7	7.1	5.1	3.9	2.1	1.6
3	2	2	1	1	—	—
137,649	52,162	67,061	60,533	57,660	27,432	12,258
12.2	4.6	5.9	5.3	5.1	2.4	1.1
3	1	1	1	1	—	—
81,136	33,475	29,932	40,635	14,970	25,158	27,228
10.7	4.4	4.0	5.4	2.0	3.3	3.6
2	—	—	1	—	—	—
25,121	22,059	20,061	5,444	4,778	1,260	9,697
11.8	10.3	9.4	2.5	2.2	.6	4.5
—	—	—	—	—	—	—
4,605,832	1,851,060	1,414,794	1,414,544	626,567	414,423	445,519
14.5	5.8	4.5	4.5	2.0	1.3	1.4
82	23	14	15	4	2	3
9	8	10	8	5	4	—
91	31	24	23	9	6	3

Note: The total vote in the Aosta Valley (constituency 31) was 65,938, comprising 34,381 Christian Democratic and 31,557 UV (Union Valdotaine).

Source: *Elezione della Camera dei Deputati, 19 Maggio, 1968,* volume 2 (Rome: Istituto Centrale di Statistica, Ministero dell'Interno).

1972 ELECTION RESULTS, ITALIAN CHAMBER OF DEPUTIES

Constituencies	Total	DC	PCI
1. Votes cast	2,106,654	705,358	602,089
% of vote	100	33.5	28.6
Seats	30	11	10
2. Votes cast	849,805	379,114	174,328
% of vote	100	44.6	20.5
Seats	13	7	3
3. Votes cast	1,279,723	428,809	404,483
% of vote	100	33.5	31.6
Seats	20	8	7
4. Votes cast	2,867,343	982,468	808,005
% of vote	100	34.3	28.2
Seats	42	16	13
5. Votes cast	1,025,769	471,015	182,221
% of vote	100	45.9	17.8
Seats	15	8	3
6. Votes cast	1,105,541	612,971	169,185
% of vote	100	55.4	15.3
Seats	19	12	3
7. Votes cast	486,878	186,338	145,255
% of vote	100	38.3	29.8
Seats	8	4	3
8. Votes cast	510,733	200,313	38,853
% of vote	100	39.2	7.6
Seats	7	4	—
9. Votes cast	1,532,574	874,409	241,397
% of vote	100	57.1	15.8
Seats	26	17	4
10. Votes cast	926,142	438,488	188,742
% of vote	100	47.3	20.4
Seats	14	8	3
11. Votes cast	755,046	346,532	133,682
% of vote	100	45.9	17.7
Seats	12	7	2
12. Votes cast	1,545,930	379,951	693,342
% of vote	100	24.6	44.8
Seats	23	6	12
13. Votes cast	1,138,432	340,722	486,124
% of vote	100	29.9	42.7
Seats	17	6	9
14. Votes cast	972,428	288,698	438,510
% of vote	100	29.7	45.1
Seats	14	5	8
15. Votes cast	883,496	296,380	323,618
% of vote	100	33.5	36.6
Seats	13	5	6
16. Votes cast	549,626	159,740	251,890
% of vote	100	29.1	45.8
Seats	9	3	5
17. Votes cast	898,506	354,817	295,056
% of vote	100	39.5	32.8
Seats	14	7	6

PSI	MSI-DN (MSI + PDIUM)	PSDI	PLI	PRI	Other[a]
229,220	111,488	146,381	166,460	71,465	74,193
10.9	5.3	6.9	7.9	3.4	3.5
3	1	2	2	1	—
99,299	29,054	58,866	56,623	27,266	25,255
11.7	3.4	6.9	6.7	3.2	3.0
1	—	1	1	—	—
143,668	78,701	68,024	75,053	45,360	35,625
11.2	6.1	5.3	5.9	3.5	2.8
2	1	1	1	—	—
353,051	195,166	140,208	174,993	112,987	100,465
12.3	6.8	4.9	6.1	3.9	3.5
5	3	2	2	1	—
130,761	51,816	69,123	55,280	26,567	38,986
12.7	5.1	6.7	5.4	2.6	3.8
2	—	1	1	—	—
106,547	51,214	58,822	41,442	18,517	46,843
9.6	4.6	5.3	3.7	1.7	4.2
2	1	1	—	—	—
71,004	26,089	18,582	14,982	7,926	16,702
14.6	5.4	3.8	3.1	1.6	3.4
1	—	—	—	—	—
36,062	19,105	25,249	14,841	9,581	166,729
7.1	3.7	4.9	2.9	1.9	32.6
—	—	—	—	—	3
129,654	70,719	81,415	54,994	29,937	50,049
8.5	4.6	5.3	3.6	2.0	3.3
2	1	1	1	—	—
102,686	38,779	62,332	33,677	22,530	38,908
11.1	4.2	6.7	3.6	2.4	4.2
2	—	1	—	—	—
96,081	41,972	72,534	23,599	16,535	24,111
12.7	5.6	9.6	3.1	2.2	3.2
2	—	1	—	—	—
119,630	65,072	90,450	54,664	87,360	55,461
7.7	4.2	5.9	3.5	5.7	3.6
2	1	1	—	1	—
100,965	43,916	70,098	38,773	15,988	41,868
8.9	3.9	6.2	3.4	1.4	3.7
1	—	1	—	—	—
81,767	47,368	43,410	26,110	18,519	28,046
8.4	4.9	4.5	2.7	1.9	2.9
1	—	—	—	—	—
83,483	54,013	46,775	18,831	29,545	30,851
9.4	6.1	5.3	2.1	3.3	3.5
1	1	—	—	—	—
50,265	26,825	21,142	10,226	12,345	17,193
9.1	4.9	3.8	1.9	2.2	3.1
1	—	—	—	—	—
70,832	47,109	39,321	21,812	33,529	36,030
7.9	5.2	4.4	2.4	3.7	4.0
1	—	—	—	—	—

1972 CHAMBER RESULTS *(continued)*

Constituencies	Total	DC	PCI
18. Votes cast	625,567	201,649	244,643
% of vote	100	32.2	39.1
Seats	10	4	5
19. Votes cast	2,800,726	964,161	762,045
% of vote	100	34.4	27.2
Seats	44	16	13
20. Votes cast	714,885	344,585	192,611
% of vote	100	48.2	26.9
Seats	14	8	4
21. Votes cast	186,992	102,960	32,429
% of vote	100	55.1	17.3
Seats	4	3	1
22. Votes cast	1,806,061	642,369	460,661
% of vote	100	35.6	25.5
Seats	36	14	10
23. Votes cast	915,962	425,474	157,688
% of vote	100	46.5	17.2
Seats	19	10	3
24. Votes cast	1,089,439	435,797	301,596
% of vote	100	40.0	27.7
Seats	23	10	7
25. Votes cast	886,905	386,658	206,074
% of vote	100	43.6	23.2
Seats	17	9	4
26. Votes cast	328,475	161,476	81,868
% of vote	100	49.2	24.9
Seats	6	4	2
27. Votes cast	1,003,685	392,687	260,071
% of vote	100	39.1	25.9
Seats	22	10	6
28. Votes cast	1,333,526	519,706	275,473
% of vote	100	39.0	20.7
Seats	27	12	6
29. Votes cast	1,201,941	489,532	263,516
% of vote	100	40.7	21.9
Seats	26	12	6
30. Votes cast	801,334	327,823	202,654
% of vote	100	40.9	25.3
Seats	16	8	5
32. Votes cast	217,885	78,270	54,345
% of vote	100	35.9	24.9
Seats	3	2	1
ITALY			
Votes cast	33,348,009	12,919,270	9,072,454
% of vote	100	38.7	27.2
Seats won at constituency level	563	256	170
Seats assigned at national level	66	10	9
Total seats	629	266	179

a The "other" vote was as follows: 648,763, PSIUP; 224,288, Manifesto; 153,764, South Tyrol People's party (3 deputies elected); 120,061, Movimento Politico dei Lavoratori; 85,838, Communist (Marxist-Leninist); 49,756, miscellaneous remaining parties.

Note: The total vote in the Aosta Valley (constituency 31) was 66,770, comprising 32,192

PSI	MSI-DN (MSI + PDIUM)	PSDI	PLI	PRI	Other[a]
60,908	44,383	24,117	10,405	16,014	23,448
9.7	7.1	3.9	1.7	2.6	3.7
1	—	—	—	—	—
212,691	414,106	154,633	115,501	96,072	81,517
7.6	14.8	5.5	4.1	3.4	2.9
3	7	2	2	1	—
49,090	54,646	28,107	14,656	11,490	19,700
6.9	7.6	3.9	2.1	1.6	2.8
1	1	—	—	—	—
9,484	13,404	13,455	5,383	4,555	5,322
5.1	7.2	7.2	2.9	2.4	2.8
—	—	—	—	—	—
138,297	335,508	82,987	42,633	47,549	56,057
7.7	18.6	4.6	2.4	2.6	3.1
3	7	1	—	1	—
82,553	120,575	43,012	29,544	24,968	32,148
9.0	13.2	4.7	3.2	2.7	3.5
2	3	1	—	—	—
111,572	133,305	44,756	23,589	15,709	23,115
10.2	12.2	4.1	2.2	1.4	2.1
2	3	1	—	—	—
86,921	114,262	27,188	19,025	22,460	24,317
9.8	12.9	3.1	2.1	2.5	2.7
2	2	—	—	—	—
32,169	22,531	15,948	4,630	2,850	7,003
9.8	6.9	4.9	1.4	.9	2.1
—	—	—	—	—	—
124,503	122,371	33,237	16,405	20,271	34,140
12.4	12.2	3.3	1.6	2.0	3.4
3	3	—	—	—	—
101,754	243,697	44,440	50,659	36,690	61,107
7.6	18.3	3.3	3.8	2.8	4.6
2	5	1	1	—	—
116,046	158,913	48,437	38,720	40,557	46,220
9.7	13.2	4.0	3.2	3.4	3.8
2	4	1	—	1	—
65,213	90,690	30,848	26,636	20,012	37,458
8.1	11.3	3.8	3.3	2.5	4.7
1	2	—	—	—	—
14,251	27,350	13,642	16,959	9,443	3,625
6.5	12.6	6.3	7.8	4.3	1.7
—	—	—	—	—	—
3,210,427	2,894,147	1,717,539	1,297,105	954,597	1,282,470
9.6	8.7	5.2	3.9	2.9	3.8
51	46	20	11	6	3
10	10	9	9	9	—
61	56	29	20	15	3

Progressive Group; 31,963 Christian Democratic and associated parties; and 2,615 MSI-DN.

Source: *Elezione della Camera dei Deputati, 19 Maggio, 1968,* volume 2 (Rome: Istituto Centrale di Statistica, Ministero dell'Interno).

1976 ELECTION RESULTS, ITALIAN CHAMBER OF DEPUTIES

Constituencies	Total	DC	PCI	PSI
1. Votes cast	2,264,438	741,841	865,252	231,557
% of vote	100	32.8	38.2	10.2
Seats	33	12	14	3
2. Votes cast	889,700	384,340	252,169	84,641
% of vote	100	43.2	28.3	9.5
Seats	12	7	4	1
3. Votes cast	1,349,057	464,575	527,236	147,571
% of vote	100	34.4	39.1	10.9
Seats	20	8	9	2
4. Votes cast	3,107,647	1,092,254	1,113,369	368,246
% of vote	100	35.1	35.8	11.8
Seats	49	18	19	6
5. Votes cast	1,135,534	515,915	308,481	134,459
% of vote	100	45.4	27.2	11.8
Seats	16	9	5	2
6. Votes cast	1,229,663	654,729	283,537	125,910
% of vote	100	53.2	23.1	10.2
Seats	19	12	5	2
7. Votes cast	514,084	197,938	187,274	69,329
% of vote	100	38.5	36.4	13.5
Seats	7	3	3	1
8. Votes cast	567,382	186,190	74,822	44,681
% of vote	100	32.8	13.2	7.9
Seats	7	3	1	—
9. Votes cast	1,696,934	942,301	362,442	162,179
% of vote	100	55.5	21.4	9.6
Seats	26	16	6	2
10. Votes cast	1,023,925	466,092	284,076	118,756
% of vote	100	45.5	27.7	11.6
Seats	15	8	5	2
11. Votes cast	824,548	365,838	209,269	106,703
% of vote	100	44.4	25.4	12.9
Seats	10	6	3	1
12. Votes cast	1,664,120	430,104	819,224	147,273
% of vote	100	25.8	49.2	8.8
Seats	24	7	13	2
13. Votes cast	1,219,954	390,179	579,845	110,022
% of vote	100	32.0	47.5	9.0
Seats	16	6	9	1
14. Votes cast	1,051,172	319,031	529,458	91,952
% of vote	100	30.4	50.4	8.7
Seats	15	5	9	1
15. Votes cast	949,602	321,240	406,341	101,642
% of vote	100	33.8	42.8	10.7
Seats	13	5	7	1
16. Votes cast	587,072	172,999	293,040	60,510
% of vote	100	29.5	49.9	10.3
Seats	9	3	5	1
17. Votes cast	976,701	381,223	389,556	80,877
% of vote	100	39.0	39.9	8.3
Seats	15	7	7	1

MSI-DN (MSI + PDIUM)	PSDI	PRI	DP	PLI	PR	Other[a]
91,881	99,971	89,592	42,037	61,488	38,840	1,979
4.1	4.4	4.0	1.9	2.7	1.7	.1
1	1	1	—	1	—	—
25,886	48,455	34,398	15,638	32,996	11,177	—
2.9	5.4	3.9	1.8	3.7	1.3	—
—	—	—	—	—	—	—
58,672	39,972	51,670	14,089	24,064	20,484	724
4.3	3.0	3.8	1.0	1.8	1.5	.1
1	—	—	—	—	—	—
132,163	98,173	127,019	79,933	44,883	49,423	2,184
4.3	3.2	4.1	2.6	1.4	1.6	.1
2	1	2	1	—	—	—
41,224	42,539	37,849	23,152	20,029	11,886	—
3.6	3.7	3.3	2.0	1.8	1.0	—
—	—	—	—	—	—	—
40,992	40,977	25,901	29,383	16,900	11,334	—
3.3	3.3	2.1	2.4	1.4	.9	—
—	—	—	—	—	—	—
19,485	15,328	9,577	6,482	4,169	4,502	—
3.8	3.0	1.9	1.3	.8	.9	—
—	—	—	—	—	—	—
14,661	14,062	15,319	13,030	5,618	6,960	192,039
2.6	2.5	2.7	2.3	1.0	1.2	33.8
—	—	—	—	—	—	—
59,347	62,073	47,162	23,344	19,343	17,789	954
3.5	3.7	2.8	1.4	1.1	1.0	.1
1	1	—	—	—	—	—
30,778	47,434	35,107	18,552	10,709	11,925	496
3.0	4.6	3.4	1.8	1.0	1.2	—
—	—	—	—	—	—	—
32,779	54,864	27,222	14,609	9,831	—	3,433
4.0	6.7	3.3	1.8	1.2	—	.4
—	—	—	—	—	—	—
52,331	63,054	99,783	15,542	15,749	18,263	2,797
3.1	3.8	6.0	.9	.9	1.1	.2
—	1	1	—	—	—	—
34,863	47,460	23,605	13,139	10,157	10,684	—
2.9	3.9	1.9	1.1	.8	.9	—
—	—	—	—	—	—	—
32,312	23,929	25,142	13,220	6,011	10,117	—
3.1	2.3	2.4	1.3	.6	1.0	—
—	—	—	—	—	—	—
39,043	24,803	31,167	12,275	5,652	7,439	—
4.1	2.6	3.3	1.3	.6	.8	—
—	—	—	—	—	—	—
20,179	11,675	14,896	7,294	2,874	3,605	—
3.4	2.0	2.5	1.2	.5	.6	—
—	—	—	—	—	—	—
39,079	27,957	33,588	10,826	6,560	7,035	—
4.0	2.9	3.4	1.1	.7	.7	—
—	—	—	—	—	—	—

365

1976 CHAMBER RESULTS *(continued)*

Constituencies	Total	DC	PCI	PSI
18. Votes cast	672,837	215,618	303,770	74,571
% of vote	100	32.0	45.1	11.1
Seats	10	4	5	1
19. Votes cast	3,159,181	1,127,263	1,138,531	240,205
% of vote	100	35.7	36.0	7.6
Seats	50	19	19	4
20. Votes cast	789,938	349,123	275,536	61,325
% of vote	100	44.2	34.9	7.8
Seats	14	7	5	1
21. Votes cast	203,878	103,396	52,956	13,618
% of vote	100	50.7	26.0	6.7
Seats	4	3	1	—
22. Votes cast	2,037,550	739,177	730,693	146,968
% of vote	100	36.3	35.9	7.2
Seats	36	14	14	2
23. Votes cast	1,017,960	467,888	257,129	90,058
% of vote	100	46.0	25.3	8.8
Seats	17	9	5	1
24. Votes cast	1,224,394	497,345	398,490	110,597
% of vote	100	40.6	32.5	9.0
Seats	22	10	8	2
25. Votes cast	1,013,578	435,890	310,484	94,200
% of vote	100	43.0	30.6	9.3
Seats	16	8	6	1
26. Votes cast	360,955	160,491	120,341	37,065
% of vote	100	44.5	33.3	10.3
Seats	7	4	3	—
27. Votes cast	1,119,021	440,458	368,406	128,732
% of vote	100	39.4	32.9	11.5
Seats	21	9	8	2
28. Votes cast	1,486,713	612,595	410,588	124,241
% of vote	100	41.2	27.6	8.4
Seats	25	12	8	2
29. Votes cast	1,337,813	580,189	366,743	130,116
% of vote	100	43.4	27.4	9.7
Seats	23	12	7	2
30. Votes cast	930,128	370,682	330,585	86,529
% of vote	100	39.9	35.5	9.3
Seats	15	7	6	1
32. Votes cast	226,808	82,615	65,007	15,776
% of vote	100	36.4	28.7	7.0
Seats	3	2	1	—
ITALY				
Votes cast	36,632,287	14,209,519	12,614,650	3,540,309
% of vote	100	38.8	34.4	9.7
Seats won at constituency level	569	255	220	48
Seats won at national level	60	7	8	9
Total seats	629	262	228	57

a The "other" vote was as follows: 184,375, South Tyrol People's party (3 deputies elected); 42,689, miscellaneous remaining parties.

Note: The total vote in the Aosta Valley (constituency 31) was 75,291, comprising

MSI-DN (MSI + PDIUM)	PSDI	PRI	DP	PLI	PR	Other[a]
37,182	11,008	17,046	6,446	3,054	3,865	277
5.5	1.6	2.5	1.0	.5	.6	—
—	—	—	—	—	—	—
298,643	105,134	104,961	44,528	38,581	57,709	3,626
9.5	3.3	3.3	1.4	1.2	1.8	.1
5	1	1	—	—	1	—
50,011	19,943	13,744	10,308	5,083	4,865	—
6.3	2.5	1.7	1.3	.6	.6	—
1	—	—	—	—	—	—
12,188	7,349	6,220	3,266	3,885	1,000	—
6.0	3.6	3.1	1.6	1.9	.5	—
—	—	—	—	—	—	—
233,566	59,694	53,408	32,127	22,311	16,429	3,177
11.5	2.9	2.6	1.6	1.1	.8	.2
4	1	1	—	—	—	—
99,741	43,459	24,585	13,096	17,054	4,950	—
9.8	4.3	2.4	1.3	1.7	.5	—
2	—	—	—	—	—	—
119,863	41,317	22,352	12,729	12,920	8,781	—
9.8	3.4	1.8	1.0	1.1	.7	—
2	—	—	—	—	—	—
97,558	28,049	21,339	12,881	6,410	5,786	981
9.6	2.8	2.1	1.3	.6	.6	.1
1	—	—	—	—	—	—
21,778	8,842	3,367	4,317	2,454	1,572	728
6.0	2.4	.9	1.2	.7	.4	.2
—	—	—	—	—	—	—
97,971	29,889	23,602	16,773	7,652	5,538	—
8.8	2.7	2.1	1.5	.7	.5	—
2	—	—	—	—	—	—
189,080	47,268	43,220	15,553	29,253	12,948	1,967
12.7	3.2	2.9	1.0	2.0	.9	.1
3	—	—	—	—	—	—
122,691	43,830	43,775	15,633	19,634	12,790	2,412
9.2	3.3	3.3	1.2	1.5	1.0	.2
2	—	—	—	—	—	—
67,130	23,959	18,573	14,584	10,294	7,792	—
7.2	2.6	2.0	1.6	1.1	.8	—
1	—	—	—	—	—	—
23,064	7,025	10,357	2,239	4,504	6,931	9,290
10.2	3.1	4.6	1.0	2.0	3.1	4.1
—	—	—	—	—	—	—
2,236,141	1,239,492	1,135,546	557,025	480,122	392,419	227,064
6.1	3.4	3.1	1.5	1.3	1.1	.6
28	6	6	1	1	1	3
7	9	8	5	4	3	—·
35	15	14	6	5	4	3

26,748 PCI-PSI and associates; 24,091 Christian Democratic and associates; 20,234 Popular Democratic and associates; 2,198 MSI-DN; and 2,020 Radical.

Source: *Elezioni Politiche del 20 Giugno 1976 Risultati* (Rome: Ministero dell' Interno).

1976 ELECTION RESULTS, ITALIAN SENATE

Regions	Total	DC	PCI
Abruzzi			
Votes cast	674,409	305,757	229,862
% of vote	100	45.3	34.1
Seats	7	4	3
Basilicata			
Votes cast	302,057	130,685	99,161
% of vote	100	43.3	32.8
Seats	7	3	3
Calabria			
Votes cast	922,654	356,398	306,376
% of vote	100	38.6	33.2
Seats	11	5	4
Campania			
Votes cast	2,518,817	954,300	798,061
% of vote	100	37.9	31.7
Seats	29	12	10
Emilia — Romagna			
Votes cast	2,552,785	740,402	1,231,929
% of vote	100	29.0	48.3
Seats	22	7	12
Friuli — Venezia Giulia			
Votes cast	775,701	348,223	198,865
% of vote	100	44.9	25.6
Seats	7	4	2
Lazio			
Votes cast	2,774,705	1,007,153	979,426
% of vote	100	36.3	35.3
Seats	27	10	10
Liguria			
Votes cast	1,195,065	406,429	464,520
% of vote	100	34.0	38.9
Seats	10	4	4
Lombardia			
Votes cast	5,198,291	2,170,893	1,598,097
% of vote	100	41.8	30.7
Seats	48	21	16
Marche			
Votes cast	847,439	345,519	336,228
% of vote	100	40.8	39.7
Seats	8	4	4
Molise			
Votes cast	173,259	93,546	—
% of vote	100	54.0	—
Seats	2	1	—
Piemonte			
Votes cast	2,760,415	1,004,158	957,964
% of vote	100	36.4	34.7
Seats	25	10	9

PSI	MSI-DN	PSDI	PRI	PLI	Joint Lists & Other[a]
55,786	45,217	16,853	11,075	4,517	5,342
8.3	6.7	2.5	1.6	.7	.8
—	—	—	—	—	—
36,317	20,124	9,000	—	—	6,770
12.0	6.7	3.0	—	—	2.2
1	—	—	—	—	—
117,846	99,724	20,130	12,275	5,300	4,605
12.8	10.8	2.2	1.3	.6	.5
1	1	—	—	—	—
209,737	313,236	104,130	78,657	45,481	15,215
8.3	12.4	4.1	3.1	1.8	.6
2	3	1	1	—	—
234,469	80,241	102,583	114,276	26,152	22,733
9.2	3.1	4.0	4.5	1.0	.9
2	—	—	1	—	—
105,446	45,582	—	—	—	77,585
13.6	5.9	—	—	—	10.0
1	—	—	—	—	—
220,340	287,715	93,574	100,443	45,647	40,407
7.9	10.4	3.4	3.6	1.6	1.5
2	3	1	1	—	—
149,104	54,926	—	—	—	120,086
12.5	4.6	—	—	—	10.0
1	—	—	—	—	1
613,253	210,741	183,383	185,899	109,028	126,997
11.8	4.1	3.5	3.6	2.1	2.4
6	2	1	1	1	—
71,397	32,987	23,302	28,161	5,255	4,590
8.4	3.9	2.8	3.3	.6	.5
—	—	—	—	—	—
—	11,375	6,421	4,547	4,448	52,922
—	6.6	3.7	2.6	2.6	30.5
—	—	—	—	—	1
290,985	107,429	139,533	124,965	99,987	35,394
10.5	3.9	5.1	4.5	3.6	1.3
2	1	1	1	1	—

1976 SENATE RESULTS *(continued)*

Regions	Total	DC	PCI
Puglia			
Votes cast	1,853,027	761,576	582,217
% of vote	100	41.1	31.4
Seats	20	9	7
Sardegna			
Votes cast	761,851	313,673	262,457
% of vote	100	41.2	34.5
Seats	8	4	3
Sicilia			
Votes cast	2,356,432	939,926	643,815
% of vote	100	39.9	27.3
Seats	26	11	8
Toscana			
Votes cast	2,275,749	729,989	1,077,944
% of vote	100	32.1	47.4
Seats	20	7	10
Trentino — Alto Adige			
Votes cast	475,035	168,519	60,829
% of vote	100	35.5	12.8
Seats	7	3	1
Umbria			
Votes cast	503,587	158,828	237,600
% of vote	100	31.5	47.2
Seats	7	2	4
Valle D'Aosta			
Votes cast	65,095	—	—
% of vote	100	—	—
Seats	1	—	—
Veneto			
Votes cast	2,463,058	1,291,379	572,421
% of vote	100	52.4	23.2
Seats	23	14	6
ITALY			
Votes cast	31,449,431	12,227,353	10,637,772
% of vote	100	38.9	33.8
Total seats	315	135	116

a The "other" vote was as follows: 334,898, PLI-PRI-PSDI (2 elected); 265,947, Radical (none elected); 158,584, South Tyrol People's party (2 elected); 78,170, Proletarian Democratic (none elected); 52,922, PCI-PSI (one elected); 51,353, PLI-PRI (none

PSI	MSI-DN	PSDI	PRI	PLI	Joint Lists & Other[a]
177,862	208,056	66,792	—	—	56,524
9.6	11.2	3.6	—	—	3.1
2	2	—	—	—	—
81,718	68,028	—	—	—	35,975
10.7	8.9	—	—	—	4.7
1	—	—	—	—	—
229,653	289,826	88,265	92,882	53,496	18,569
9.8	12.3	3.8	3.9	2.3	.8
2	3	1	1	—	—
250,393	86,242	—	—	—	131,181
11.0	3.8	—	—	—	5.8
2	—	—	—	—	1
43,843	12,624	—	—	—	189,220
9.2	2.7	—	—	—	39.8
1	—	—	—	—	2
58,678	24,827	7,698	11,601	2,032	2,323
11.7	4.9	1.5	2.3	.4	.5
1	—	—	—	—	—
—	1,806	—	—	—	63,289
—	2.8	—	—	—	97.2
—	—	—	—	—	1
261,337	85,724	113,276	81,634	36,922	20,365
10.6	3.5	4.6	3.3	1.5	.8
2	—	1	—	—	—
3,208,164	2,086,430	974,940	846,415	438,265	1,030,092
10.2	6.6	3.1	2.7	1.4	3.3
29	15	6	6	2	6

elected); 22,917, DC-PRI and Associated Valle d'Aosta parties (one elected); 21,072, PCI-PSI-PDUP (none elected); 44,229, other lists (none elected).

Source: *Elezioni Politiche del 20 Giugno 1976 Risultati* (Rome: Ministero dell' Interno).

CONTRIBUTORS

SAMUEL H. BARNES is professor and chairman of the department of political science at the University of Michigan, where he is also program director of the Center for Political Studies of the Institute for Social Research. His publications on Italy include *Party Democracy* (1967), *Representation in Italy* (1977), and chapters in Robert Dahl, ed., *Political Oppositions in Western Democracies* (1966), and Richard Rose, ed., *Electoral Behavior: A Comparative Handbook* (1974). He is currently president of the Conference Group for Italian Politics and has taught at the Universities of Florence and Rome.

GIUSEPPE DI PALMA is professor of political science at the University of California, Berkeley, and the author of *Surviving without Governing: The Italian Parties in Parliament* (1977). He is currently working on regimes and regime changes in the Mediterranean area.

STEPHEN M. HELLMAN is associate professor of political science at York University in Ontario, Canada. He has written on the PCI and the Italian left for journals and books in the United States, Canada, and Britain. He is currently on leave in Turin, where he is studying PCI organization and elite recruitment.

JOSEPH LAPALOMBARA is Arnold Wolfers professor of political science and chairman of the department of political science at Yale University. His professional association with Italy dates from 1952. His most recent book on that country is *Multinational Corporations and National Elites*. In 1974 he was made a knight commander in the Order of Merit of the Italian Republic.

ROBERT LEONARDI is research investigator at the Institute of Public Policy Studies of the University of Michigan, Ann Arbor, and assistant professor of political science at the University of Detroit. He is currently engaged in research projects studying educational policy making in Europe, the role of parliaments in managing social conflict, the institutionalization of regional governments in Italy, American policy toward Italy in the postwar period, and urban decentralization in the United States and Europe.

GIANFRANCO PASQUINO is professor of political science at the University of Bologna and visiting professor of political science at the Bologna Center of the Johns Hopkins University. Managing editor of the *Rivista italiana di scienza politica*, he has written *Modernizzazione e sviluppo politico* (Modernization and political development, 1970) and contributions to several recent volumes on Italian politics. He was managing editor of the *Dizionario di Politica* (1976).

WILLIAM E. PORTER has been a freelance writer and has taught journalism at a number of universities including the Instituto di Pubbliccismo of the University of Rome. He is the author of *Assault on the Media, the Nixon Years* (1976) and has contributed to the *International Encyclopedia of the Social Sciences* and other scholarly publications. Now at the University of Michigan, he is preparing a study of the Italian journalist.

ROBERT D. PUTNAM is professor of political science at the Institute of Public Policy Studies of the University of Michigan. His published research, including *The Beliefs of Politicians: Ideology, Conflict, and Democracy in Britain and Italy* (1973) and *The Comparative Study of Political Elites* (1976), has focused on contemporary European political behavior.

GIACOMO SANI has taught at the Universities of Bologna and Florence and at Ohio State University, and his articles on the government and politics of Italy have appeared in books and journals in Italy and the United States. He received a Guggenheim Fellowship in 1976–1977 for work on Italy.

RICHARD M. SCAMMON, coauthor of *This U.S.A.* and *The Real Majority*, is director of the Elections Research Center in Washington, D.C. He has edited the biennial statistical series *America Votes* since 1956.

DOUGLAS WERTMAN has taught political science at the University of Missouri in St. Louis and The Bologna Center of The Johns Hopkins University School of Advanced International Studies. He is working on a book about the Italian Christian Democratic party.

INDEX

Abortion issue, party attitudes toward:
  DC: 24, 31, 136, 282, 343–44
  PCI: 16n, 181, 198
  PR: 86, 197–98, 246, 257
  PSI: 86, 197–98, 344
Absenteeism: 3–4
Abstentions, parliamentary: 151–52,
  181, 201, 222, 255, 329
Accame, Falco: 194
Acheson, Dean: 2
ACLI (Christian Association of Italian
  Workers): 71–73, 78, 140–41, 198n
Action party, 1943–46: 241
Africa: 13n, 324
Agnelli, Gianni: 54, 59, 143, 268–69,
  324
Agnelli, Umberto: 59–60, 143–44, 150,
  153, 193
Alberoni, Francesco: 32
Allende, Salvador: 301, 335
Alliances, international: 317–20
  see also European Economic Com-
  munity; North Atlantic Treaty
  Organization
Almirante, Giorgio: 234–38, 275–77,
  281–82
Amendola, Giorgio: 69, 70n, 73, 174n,
  294, 298
Andreotti, Giulio: 5n, 38–39, 60, 76,
  79, 147, 151–52, 280, 286, 329
  Andreotti government: 31, 222, 255
  Andreotti-Malagodi government:
  189n, 239
Angola: 13n
AO (Workers' Vanguard): 232, 248
Arab oil: 323
Arafat, Yasir: 323
Armed forces:
  compulsory service: 246
  reform proposals: 297n
Assassinations, political: 5, 281
Atlantic Alliance: see North Atlantic
  Treaty Organization (NATO)

Baffi, Paolo: 147
Balance-of-payments problem, 1976: 3,
  290, 334
Barca, Luciano: 294
Bari (city): 215–16
Barnes, Samuel H.: 114, 327–51
Bergamo (province): 27, 62–64
Berlinguer, Enrico: 31, 69, 133, 161–63,
  171–73, 275–77, 280, 286
  "historic compromise" proposal:
  13–16, 18, 165–67, 170, 178, 180,
  319
  re NATO: 297–301, 316, 320
  need for coalition government: 28–
  29, 146
Berlinguer, Giovanni: 178
Bersani, Giovanni: 62
Bisaglia, Antonio: 78n, 79
Blackmer, Donald L.: 315, 318
Bodrato, Guido: 60, 144
Bologna (province): 68, 74, 177n, 216
Bolzano (province): 85n
Bombardieri, Vincenzo: 63–64
Bombings: 5, 235, 281
Branca, Giuseppe: 27, 66
Brandt, Willy: 319, 325
Brezhnev, Leonid: 302
Bribery:
  in journalism: 260, 267
  Lockheed (see Lockheed scandal)

Broadcasting system: 261–66, 332, 346n
see also Radio; Television
Bucalossi, Pietro: 243
Bureaucracy, inefficiency of: 128, 131, 331–32, 343
Business interests, DC ties to: 126–28
Buzzi, Carlo: 62

Calabria (region): 6, 84, 213–14, 217
Campaigns, electoral: 98, 135–48
   for DC candidates: 76–79
   media in (1976): 273–83
   of PCI (1976): 171–82, 340
   of PSI (1976): 200–7
   use of radio: 265
Candidates, selection of: 51–75
   for Chamber of Deputies: 53–58, 65–71, 138–40
   in DC: 51–52, 54–56, 67, 138–41, 192–96
   in PCI: 51–52, 64n, 65–76, 79, 192–93, 195–96
   in PLI: 54, 64n, 143
   in PR: 52, 64n, 67
   in PRI: 54, 59, 143
   in PSDI: 54, 64n
   in PSI: 51–53, 64n, 192–96
   for Senate: 53–60, 65–71, 79, 138–39
   women: 52, 66, 71, 193–94
Capital, need for: 291
Capitalism: 310, 333
Carboni, Marino: 141
Carlassara, Giovanni: 73
Carli, Guido: 54, 143
Carrillo, Santiago: 317, 321
Carter, Jimmy: 335
Castelli, Angelo: 63
Catania (city): 215–16
Catholic Action: 78, 86n, 140, 331
Catholic trade unions: see ACLI; CISL
Catholicism:
   Concordat (1929): 86
   decline of: 121–22
   divorce referendum: 16–18
   role in 1976 elections: 26–27, 174
Catholicism and political parties: 103, 110–13, 116–19, 160–61, 263n, 343–44
   DC: 2, 7, 14, 26, 31, 73, 76, 78, 123–27, 134–37, 140–42; 175–76, 330–31
   MSI: 236
   PCI: 16n, 66, 71–73, 127, 141–42, 165–66, 192–93, 198, 246, 344
   PR: 246
   PSI: 196–98, 207, 211
Catholics, Dutch: 344

Cefis, Eugenio: 269, 271, 282
CEI (Italian Episcopal Conference): 141–42
Center, in Italian politics: 9, 28n, 85, 100–4
   see also DC; PRI; PSDI
Central Intelligence Agency (CIA): 314
Centro Studi di Politica Economica (CESPE): 73, 74n
Cervetti, Giovanni: 69
Ceschia, Luciano: 270
CGIL (General Confederation of Italian Labor): 112, 197
Chamber of Deputies:
   elections for: 10–11, 32–33, 36, 46–47, 85, 229–30
   electoral laws re: 44–48, 51
   PSI members in: 195
   selection of candidates for: 53–58, 65–71, 138–40
   voting for: 41, 74–79, 216–19
Chile: 13, 15, 133, 166–67, 301, 335
China: 13n, 273, 309, 333
Christian Association of Italian Workers (ACLI): 71–73, 78, 140–41, 198n
Christian Democratic party (DC):
   armed forces reform: 297n
   campaigning for preference votes: 76–79
   Catholic disaffection with: 73
   as centrist party: 9, 28n, 85, 100–4
   clientelistic practices: 75, 79, 128–30, 140, 143
   coalition problems: 144–48, 200, 234
   corruption in: 5–6, 31, 86, 105
   domestic issues: 17–18, 24, 31, 136–37, 169, 198, 239, 282, 311–12, 343–44
   election results, 1976: 10, 44, 174–77, 233, 250, 313, 341–45, 350–51
   elections, 1975: 19, 29
   Executive Committee of: 55–64
   factionalism in: 65, 76, 78, 124, 128–34, 160
   foreign policy issues: 287–89, 294, 309–10, 313, 324
   history of, 1948–76: 123–53, 160–61, 201
   lack of reform and renewal: 7–8, 153, 342–43
   and the mass media: 204, 261, 263, 270, 273, 275–77, 279–81, 286
   senatorial elections: 50–51
   social characteristics of: 110–11, 113-15, 121

use of patronage: 6–7, 135, 144, 332, 345
voter image of: 105–9, 137, 142–44
women deputies: 194
Christian Democratic party candidates:
campaigns for: 76–79
election of: 53n, 74–75
selection of: 51–52, 54–65, 67, 71, 113, 119, 138–41, 192–93, 195–96
Christian Democratic party relationships:
business interests: 126–28
Catholicism: 2, 14, 26, 71, 86n, 116–19, 123–27, 134–37, 140–42, 330–31
MSI: 235–37, 253–54, 350
NATO: 297
PCI: 11, 16, 135–37, 145–47, 152–56, 164–72, 177–82, 233, 336
PLI: 164, 189n, 234, 240, 349
PR: 247
PRI: 242–43
PSDI: 245
PSI: 21–24, 129–32, 135–36, 153, 159–60, 164, 182, 185, 189–91, 197, 202–3, 220–26, 233, 256, 331, 341, 346–48
trade unions: 4
Cicchitto, Fabrizio: 224
CISL (Italian Confederation of Workers' Unions):
71–73, 78, 140–41, 161, 197, 198n
Civil rights, party interest in:
PCI: 205–6
PLI: 255
PR: 11, 198, 205–6
PSI: 196–99, 205–8
Clientelistic politics: 6–7, 247
DC: 75, 79, 128–30, 140, 143
PCI: 254
PSI: 160, 191, 213, 346
Coalitions in government: 144–48, 170, 200, 223–26, 233–34, 239–40, 276, 315–17
Collective security: 295–302, 325
Colombo, Emilio: 79
Colombo, Furio: 274, 277
Colombo, Gino: 63
Common Market: see European Economic Community
Communism:
fear of: 1, 9–13
MSI-DN stance against: 236–37
see also Union of Soviet Socialist Republics

Communist parties, Western European: 157–58, 319, 339
Communist party, Italian (PCI): 2–4, 5n, 43, 81, 100–4, 116, 144
appeal to Catholics: 16n, 165–66, 198, 246, 344
campaign strategy, 1976: 171–82, 340
Catholic antagonism toward: 127
Catholic "independent" candidates: 66, 71–73, 141–42, 192–93
clientelism in: 254
commitment to democracy: 336–38
domestic issues: 16–18, 170, 181, 198, 205–6, 298, 300, 311–12, 335
election results, 1976: 10, 44–46, 53n, 62n, 85–97, 208–11, 214–17, 250, 255–56, 283–84, 327–41, 350–51
elections, 1972: 9–11; 1975: 19–22
European strategy: 318–20
Executive Committee: 67–70
foreign policy issues: 287–88, 294, 297–307, 310, 312–17, 323–26, 334–35
freedom from scandal: 6
growth of: 124–25, 129–30, 132–33, 148–51, 155–70, 183–84, 186
interest in regional governments: 331–33, 343
and the mass media: 271–72, 275–77, 279–80, 283, 286
participation in government: 155, 179, 344
proposed historic compromise: 14–16, 86, 133, 152, 156, 162–68, 172, 177–78, 180
selection of candidates: 27, 51–52, 64n, 65–76, 79, 174, 192–96
senatorial elections: 50–51
social characteristics of: 110–15, 121
and the trade unions: 165, 181, 306
and the U.S.: 297, 299–300, 305, 322–23
and the U.S.S.R.: 13, 15, 124, 157–58, 172–73, 297–302, 321–22, 339
voter image of: 105–9
women deputies: 194
youth vote for: 218–19
Communist party relationships:
DC: 11, 16, 135–37, 145–47, 152–56, 164–72, 177–82, 233, 336
DP: 248–49, 350
PLI: 224, 238–40

PR: 247
PRI: 242–43, 336
PSDI: 26, 243, 245, 298, 336
PSI: 107, 157, 172, 185, 189–91, 197, 200–3, 222–26, 336, 340, 345–49
Communist youth federation (FGCI): 161–62
Comunione e Liberazione: 78, 117, 140, 142, 150, 193, 343
Concordat (1929): 86
Confederation of Small Farmers: 57, 78
Conservative parties, European: 343–44
Constitution (1948): 331
Constitution of the Right (1976): 236–37, 253
Consumerism: 2, 129
Continuous Struggle (LC) faction: 232–248
Cooper, Richard N.: 293
Corruption, political: 132–33
  in DC: 5–6, 31, 86, 105
  oil scandal: 63, 139
  in PSDI: 25, 86, 345
Craxi, Bettino: 222, 226n
Crespi family: 268
Cuba: 13n, 321
Cuneo (district): 59–60, 62, 215
Czechoslovakia: 2, 161, 298, 301

DC: see Christian Democratic party
Debt, national: 3, 85
Defense planning: 323, 325
  see also Collective security
De Gasperi, Alcide: 124, 126–27, 151, 236–37, 287, 341n
De Marsanich, Augusto: 234–35
De Martino, Francesco: 22–23, 190, 200–2, 204, 220–21, 223, 275–77, 279–81
de Michieli-Vitturi, Ferruccio: 253–54
De Mita, Ciriaco: 79, 315
Democratic centralism: 338
Democratic Party of Proletarian Unity (PDUP): 110–11, 248–49
  Manifesto: 231–32
Democratic Socialist Party (PSDI): see Social Democratic party
Détente: 124, 297, 299–301, 307, 310, 326

d'Hondt formula: 30, 49–50
Di Palma, Giuseppi: 123
Divorce law:
  enactment of: 163
  as political issue: 11, 31, 169–70, 239, 343–44
  referendum re: 13, 16–18, 83, 125, 132, 207, 231
  sponsorship of: 197, 217
Dogan, Mattei: 36, 109n, 196n
Domestic issues:
  DC interest in: 17–18, 137, 198, 239, 311–12
  PCI interest in: 16–18, 170, 181, 198, 205–6, 298, 300, 311–12, 335
  see also Abortion issue; Divorce law
Donat Cattin, Carlo: 59–60, 136, 143–44
Dorotei faction: 132, 136, 146
Doxa Institute: 105, 108, 114
DP: see Proletarian Democracy party

Economic crisis (1976): 2–3, 85, 131–32, 147, 160, 182, 285
  balance-of-payments problem: 3, 290, 334
  DC allegations re: 137
  PCI use of: 157, 168, 335
  PRI proposals re: 242
Economic interdependence: 289–94
Economic miracle (1963): 159–60, 289
Economy, Italian: 333
  expansion of public sector: 127–31
  see also Economic crisis
Educational system: 4, 7, 119–21
EEC: see European Economic Community
Eisenhower, Dwight D.: 307
Election results (1976): 21–39, 85, 90–97, 135–51, 174–78, 229–57, 285, 327–51
  Catholic role in: 26–27, 174
  DC: 10, 44, 174–77, 233, 250, 313, 341–45, 350–51
  DP: 32–36, 96, 218–19, 229–33, 239n, 250–53, 257, 341
  geographical analysis of: 250–55
  MSI-DN: 64n, 88, 90–97, 145–49, 174–75, 229–33, 250–55, 328, 342
  PCI: 10, 44–46, 53n, 62n, 85–97,

208–11, 214–17, 250, 255–56, 283–84, 327–41, 350–51

PR: 30–35, 46–47, 85–90, 96–98, 214–17, 229–33, 246–53, 257, 328

PRI: 32–35, 46, 88–94, 229–33, 250–53, 256–57, 328, 349

PSDI: 29, 33–35, 46, 85, 88–95, 148, 175, 207–8, 213, 229–33, 250–53, 256, 328

PSI: 21–24, 27–35, 46, 85–98, 151, 207–22, 229, 328, 345–49

see also Chamber of Deputies, Senate

Elections: 1–39, 81–82, 132, 231

for Chamber of Deputies: 10–11, 32–33, 36, 46–47, 85, 229–30

polls preceding (1976): 29, 32, 87–89, 208–10, 283–84

role of mass media: 259–86

for Senate: 50–51, 85

setting for (1976): 2–13, 21–39, 82–89, 135–48

subnational: 19–21, 86–87

see also Election results (1976); Electoral process

Electoral commissions, provincial: 55–58, 62–64

Electoral process: 41–79

campaigns: 76–79, 98, 135–48, 171–82, 340

laws: 44–52, 83n, 327n

media in (1976): 265, 273–83

see also Elections

Electorate, in mid-1970s: 81–122

Elkan, Giovanni: 61

Emilia-Romagna (region): 59–62, 74, 139, 177n, 251–52, 256

Esso Italiana: 6

Eurocommunism: 319, 321, 338–39

European Economic Community (EEC): 13, 38, 287–88, 290–93, 302–7, 324–25, 333–34, 339

Eurovision (EVN): 262

Factionalism in political parties:

in DC: 65, 76, 78, 124, 128–34, 160

in PSI: 65, 190–92, 348

Family partisanship: 116, 122

Fanfani, Amintore: 17, 24, 59–60, 61n, 127, 129, 132–36, 138, 142, 145–48, 150–51, 171, 283

Fascism:

in Europe: 301

in Italy: 126, 128, 158, 164, 234–35, 238, 240, 255, 281

Federation of the Press: 260, 269–70

Feminist movement: see Women

FGCI (Communist youth federation): 161–62

Fiat: 143–44, 279, 291

Financing of political parties: 76–79, 191n

Floating vote: 99–100, 312

Florence (city): 59n, 133, 216, 256, 271, 279, 281

Foa, Vittorio: 248

Forcella, Enzo: 267

Foreign investment, in Italy: 334

Foreign policy:

emergent consensus: 287–326, 334–35

and international security: 295–302

and party alliances: 315–20

and public opinion: 302–15

Foreign trade: 289–91, 324

Forlani, Arnaldo: 134, 136, 151, 289

Forlì (province): 241, 256

Fortuna, Loris: 197, 217

France: 294, 307–8, 323–25

Communist party in: 157, 319, 339

Gaullism in: 143, 305

government of: 23

Italian trade with: 290

press in: 266, 272

Socialist party in: 11, 136n, 225, 340

voter participation in: 42

Free, Lloyd A.: 309

Friuli-Venezia Giulia (region): 217, 331

Galloni, Giovanni: 142

Gava, Silvio: 139

General Confederation of Italian Labor (CGIL): 112, 197

Genoa (city): 133, 215–16

Germany, East: 321

Germany, West: 42, 286, 290–95, 307–9, 319, 325, 335, 340, 344, 348

Giacchero, Enzo: 236

Giolitti, Antonio: 224, 260

Giustizia e Libertà (anti-Fascist group): 241

Great Britain: 3, 10, 307–8, 325n, 341n

BBC: 261, 264
elections in: 286
fear of communism: 294–95
Labour party: 319
newspapers in: 266–67
voter participation in: 42, 84
Greece: 301, 339
Greggi, Agostino: 236

Hassner, Pierre: 296, 326
Hellman, Stephen: 155, 159, 334–35, 339
Historic compromise: 22–23, 28, 38n, 86, 156, 172, 224, 226, 315, 329, 335
European version of: 318–19
PCI proposal: 13–16, 18, 133, 152, 165–68, 170, 177–80
PSI hostility: 18–19
"Hot autumn" (1969): 4, 163, 165, 230, 248
House of Deputies:
see Chamber of Deputies
Hungary: 298

Illiteracy: 2, 267, 274
Imperiali largest-remainder voting system: 45–46
Independents:
as DC candidates: 193
as PCI candidates: 27, 65–66, 68, 71, 174, 193
as PSI candidates: 193–95
Industrialists, as candidates: 143–44
Industrialization: 2–3, 119
Industry, nationalization of: 332
Inflation: 3, 85, 131
Institute for Industrial Reconstruction: 128
International Monetary Fund (IMF): 38, 291, 334
International security: 295–302, 325
Italian Confederation of Workers' Unions (CISL): 71–73, 78, 140–41, 161, 197
Italian Episcopal Conference (CEI): 141–42
Italian Social Movement-National Right (MSI-DN):
antidivorce position: 169, 239
appeal to Catholics: 236
in Chamber of Deputies: 33, 46
elections (1972): 132, 231; (1976):

64n, 88, 90–97, 145–49, 174–75, 229–33, 250–55, 328, 342
history of: 8–9, 52n, 234–38, 336
and the mass media: 275–76, 281–83
and the PLI: 236, 240
political violence: 133, 137–38, 146, 164, 327
position in Italian politics: 100–2, 329, 349–50
in Senate: 35
social characteristics of: 111, 121
trust of Americans and Russians: 310
voter image of: 105–6, 108
Italian Union of Labor (UIL): 197

Japan: 286, 339
John XXIII: 129
Journalism, in Italy: 259–61, 266–73, 275, 285
Federation of the Press: 260, 269–70

Kennedy, John F.: 307
Keohane, Robert O.: 293
Kissinger, Henry: 2, 13n, 254, 313, 326
Kogan, Norman: 287, 317

Labor situation: 131, 137, 181
absenteeism: 3–4
Workers Law (1969): 4
see also Trade Unions
Labriola, Silvano: 223
La Malfa, Ugo: 8, 22–25, 133, 232, 241–43, 275–76, 349
LaPalombara, Joseph: 1, 132, 329, 339
La Valle, Raniero: 27, 72–73
LC (Continuous Struggle) faction: 232, 248
Lebanon: 13n
Left, in Italian politics: 100–1
see also DP; PCI; PSI
Leftist majority, possibility of: 336
Lenin: 338
Leonardi, Robert: 229, 349
Levi, Arrigo: 262, 279, 292
Liberal party (PLI): 5n, 77n, 129, 310, 329n, 330n
decline of: 25–26, 348–49

election results (1976): 32–35, 46–47, 85, 88–97, 148–49, 175–76, 229–33, 250–53, 255, 328, 342
Europeanism of: 318
history of: 8, 123, 238–41
interest in civil rights: 255
on political continuum: 101
polls preceding 1976 election: 29
selection of candidates: 54, 64n, 143
social characteristics of: 111, 121
use of posters: 273
use of television: 263, 275–76
voters' image of: 105–6
Liberal party relationships:
DC: 164, 189n, 234, 240, 349
MSI: 236, 240
NATO: 297
PR: 247
PRI: 240
PSDI: 240, 245
PSI: 224, 238-39
Liguria (region): 50, 214
Lire, collapse of: 3, 136, 290–91
Lockheed scandal: 5, 25, 63, 78, 86, 136, 244–45, 277, 279, 283, 314
Lombardy (region): 21, 44, 59, 62–64, 139, 214, 216–18
Longo, Luigi: 16, 157–58, 298
Luxembourg: 296

Mafia: 5–6
Magazines: 272–73, 282–83, 285
Maghreb, states of the: 339
Magri, Lucio: 249, 257, 275
Malagodi, Giovanni: 239, 255
Mancini, Giacomo: 190, 213, 223, 280
Manifesto group: 162, 231, 248, 250, 338, 341
PDUP Manifesto: 231–32
Marchais, Georges: 317
Marchetti, Aristide: 63–64
Marradi, Alberto: 114
Mass media:
in Italian politics: 107, 122, 125, 203–4, 207, 247, 346
in 1976 elections: 259–86
see also Magazines; Newspapers; Radio; Television
Mattei, Enrico: 268, 324
Mazzini, Giuseppe: 241
McInnes, Neil: 318
Medici, Giuseppe: 61
Melandri, Leonardo: 61–62
Michelini, Arturo: 234

Middle East: 323–24, 339
Milan: 47, 133, 250
DC in: 63–64, 78, 150
newspapers in: 268, 271
PCI in: 21, 70, 74
PSI in: 214–16
radio in: 265–66
Military expenditures: 296, 298
Military service, compulsory: 246
see also Armed forces
Mitterand socialism: 220, 224–25, 317, 319
Monarchist party (PDIUM): 8, 28n, 235
Montavani, Cesare: 236
Morandi, Rodolfo: 186n, 199, 224–25
Moravia, Alberto: 266
Moro, Aldo: 22–24, 61–62, 76, 79, 132–37, 145–47, 151–52, 200–1, 237, 242–43, 275, 282–83
MSI-DN:
see Italian Social Movement-National Right
MUIS movement: 208
Mussolini, Benito: 234, 236, 281, 338

Naples: 6, 23, 28, 59n, 70n, 133, 216, 254, 256, 271
Napoleoni, Claudio: 27
National debt: 3, 85
National Right:
see Italian Social Movement-National Right
National security, and the PCI: 298, 300
Nationalization of industry: 332
Nenni, Pietro: 187, 190
Neo-Fascists: see Italian Social Movement-National Right
Neomercantilism: 324
Neutralism: 295
see also Foreign policy
Newspapers: 266–72, 279–82, 285
Nixon, Richard M.: 308
"Non-no-confidence" formula: 31, 152
North Atlantic Treaty Organization (NATO): 13, 287–88
Italian interest in: 295–302, 313, 317
PCI attitude toward: 27n, 172–74, 316, 320, 322, 334, 339
Nye, Joseph S.: 293

OECD (Organization for Economic Cooperation and Development): 3, 291

381

Oil:
crisis: 132, 290–91, 323–24
scandal: 63, 139
Olivetti: 291
OPEC (Organization of Petroleum Exporting Countries): 291

"Pacifist Atlanticism": 296
Pajetta, Giancarlo: 27n, 69, 71, 280
Pannella, Marco: 246–47, 275, 278
Pareto, Vilfredo: 123
Parisi, Arturo: 149–50, 153
Parliament, European: 288, 303, 305
Parliament, Italian: 44, 152, 194–95, 328n
    dissolution of (1972): 9, 131, 169; (1976): 171, 200, 202
    reform committees: 7
    small party representation in: 230–31
    see also Chamber of Deputies; Senate
Parri, Ferruccio: 241
Pasquino, Gianfranco: 149–50, 183–227, 345
Pasti, Nino: 66, 174, 301n
Patronage, political:
    DC use of: 6–7, 135, 144, 332, 345
    in PSI: 190–91, 346
Paul VI: 26, 141–42
PCI: see Communist party, Italian
PDIUM: see Monarchist party
PDUP (Democratic Party of Proletarian Unity): 110–11, 248–49
    PDUP Manifesto: 231–32
Pecchioli, Ugo: 69, 72
Peggio, Eugenio: 73–74
Pella, Giovanni: 235
Perrone family: 268
Petroleum products, Italian appetite for: 3
    see also Oil
Piedmont (region): 21, 59–60, 139, 144, 214
    Cuneo district: 59–60, 62, 215
Pius XII: 141, 331
PLI:
    see Liberal party
Pluralism, political: 12, 29, 66, 71, 107, 173
Political parties, Italian: 81, 285–86
    center (see DC; PRI; PSDI)

financing of: 76–79, 191n
left (see DP; PCI; PR; PSI)
right (see MSI-DN; PLI)
voter identification with: 98–109
"Political pluralism": 12, 29, 66, 71, 107, 173
Political reform:
    see Reform and renewal, political
Political traditions: 115–22
Political violence: 85–86, 137–38, 146, 238, 281, 327–28
    bombings: 5, 235, 281
    see also Terrorism
Politics in Italy: 1
    see also Political parties, Italian
Polls, pre-election (1976): 29, 32, 87–89, 208–10, 283–84
Porter, William E.: 259, 332
Portugal: 15, 301, 318n
Posters, political use of: 273–74
Pozzar, Vittorio: 63
PR: see Radical party
Preference votes: 48, 51, 57, 62n, 74–79, 346
Press, Federation of: 260, 269–70
Press:
    in France: 266, 272
    in Italy: 266–73
PRI: see Republican party
Proletarian Democracy party (DP): 30, 200, 275, 288
    Chamber of Deputies election: 46–47
    election results (1976): 32–36, 96, 218–19, 229–33, 239n, 250–53, 257, 341
    history of: 248–49
    and the PR: 247
    pre-election polls re: 88, 209
    role in Italian politics: 19, 184, 329n, 350
Proletarian Socialist party (PSIUP): 9, 11, 30, 184, 248, 310
    creation of: 8, 186, 196
    election results (1976): 33, 96, 229–31
    women deputies: 194
    youth vote for: 219
Proportional representation: 29–30, 44–45, 49
Provinces:
    Administration of: 17n
    electoral commissions: 55–58, 62–64

PSDI: *see* Social Democratic party
PSI: *see* Socialist party
PSIUP: *see* Proletarian Socialist party
Public opinion and foreign policy: 302–
15
Putnam, Robert D.: 287

Radical party (PR): 5n, 8, 25, 184, 203–
5, 211, 329n, 344, 350
   abortion issue: 86, 197–98, 246,
   257
   civil rights issue: 11, 198, 205–6
   election results (1976): 30–35, 46–
   47, 85–90, 96–98, 214–17, 229–
   33, 246–53, 257, 328
   and the mass media: 239n, 273,
   275, 278, 284
   pre-election polls: 209
   and the PSI: 193, 194n, 220, 232,
   246
   selection of candidates: 52, 64n, 67
   women deputies: 194
   youth vote for: 218–19
Radicalization: 4–5
   of trade unions: 4, 131, 137, 157,
   160–61, 163
Radio: 204, 264–66, 274, 278, 285, 346n
Radiotelevisione Italiana (RAI): 239n,
261, 274–75, 277–78, 283–85, 332
Rae, Douglas W.: 45
Ramella, Carlo: 73, 141
Ravenna (province): 241, 256
Referendum proposals, of PCI: 171n
   see also Divorce law
Reform and renewal, political: 163
   DC need for: 342–43
   failure of: 7–9, 127–31, 153, 160,
   195
   PLI attitude toward: 238–39
   as trade union strategy: 197
Regional governments, PCI interest in:
331–33, 343
   see also Provinces
Republican party (PRI): 8, 24–25, 129,
149, 202, 204, 310
   abstention by: 329n
   as centrist party: 100–1, 189n, 200,
   234, 236, 330n
   election results (1976): 32–35, 46,
   88–94, 229–33, 250–53, 256–57,
   328, 349
   Europeanism of: 318
   history of: 241–43
   on political continuum: 9, 28n, 85
   pre-election polls: 29

selection of candidates: 54, 59, 143
   social characteristics of: 111, 121
   use of television: 263, 275–76
   voter image of: 105–6
   women deputies: 194
Republican party relationships:
   NATO: 297
   PCI: 242–43, 336
   PLI: 240
   PR: 247
   PSDI: 245
   PSI: 224
Research and development: 291–92
Rhodesia: 13n
Right, in Italian politics: 100–1
   see also Italian Social Movement-
   National Right; Liberal party
Riva, Massimo: 144
Rizzoli, Angelo: 269, 271–72
Rome: 6, 46–47, 60, 133, 144, 150, 216,
250
   newspapers in: 268, 271, 279
   PCI in: 2, 71
   radio in: 266
   Treaty of: 303, 306
Rothschild, house of: 269
Rumor, Mariano: 78, 136, 280

Saccucci, Sandro: 137, 147, 237–38, 254
Salizzoni, Angelo: 61
Salò Republic: 234
Sani, Giacomo: 20, 36–37, 81–122, 149–
50, 217, 335, 342, 344–45
Saragat, Giuseppe: 244–45, 275–76, 298,
315–16, 349
Sardinia: 10, 17, 41n, 75, 139, 331
Sartori, Giovanni: 114, 128
Scaglia, Giovanbattista: 63
Scalfari, Eugenio: 204
Scalia, Vito: 141
Scandal, allegations of:
   see Corruption, political
Schmidt, Helmut: 293, 335
Secularization: 117–19, 121, 124–25,
129, 132, 143
Segni, Antonio: 235
Segre, Sergio: 228, 301n, 316
Senate: 30, 34–36
   candidate selection for: 53–60, 65–
   71, 79, 138–39
   elections for (1976): 50–51, 85
   electoral laws re: 44, 48–52
   PSI members in: 195–96
   voting for: 216–17

Sereno, Renzo: 309
Sforza, Carlo: 316-17
Sicily: 6, 10, 17, 19n, 41n, 75, 331, 342
Soares, Mario: 317, 319
Social characteristics and voting behavior: 109-15
Social Democratic parties, European: 319, 325, 340
Social Democratic party (PSDI):
    abstention by: 329n
    in centrist coalition: 9, 11, 28n, 100-2, 129, 189n, 200, 234, 236, 330n
    corruption charges: 25, 86, 345
    decline of: 184, 348-49
    election results (1976): 29, 33-35, 46, 85, 88-95, 148, 175, 207-8, 213, 229-33, 250-53, 256, 328
    Europeanism of: 318
    history of: 185, 243-46
    selection of candidates: 54, 64n
    social characteristics of: 111, 121
    trust of Americans and Russians: 310
    use of television: 275
    voter image of: 105-6
    working-class vote for: 196n
Social Democratic party relationships:
    NATO: 297
    PCI: 26, 243, 245, 298, 336
    PLI: 240, 245
    PR: 247
    PSI: 8, 186, 190, 224, 243-45, 256, 347
Social welfare laws: 2-3
    need for reform in: 86, 168, 197
Socialism:
    in France: 136n
    Italian road to: 15, 16n, 157-60, 173, 183-92, 338, 347-49
    tradition of: 116, 122
    see also Socialist party
Socialist parties:
    European: 318-19, 340
    French: 11, 136n, 225, 340
    Italian: 7-8, 10-11
    see also Socialist party
Socialist party (PSI): 9, 16n, 38, 121, 123, 133, 170, 183-227
    abortion issue: 86, 197-98, 344
    abstention by: 329n
    acceptance of NATO: 173
    armed forces reform: 297n
    campaign (1976): 200-7
    and the Catholic vote: 196-99, 207, 211

    in Chamber of Deputies: 195
    civil rights issues: 196-99, 205-8
    clientelism in: 160, 191, 213, 346
    DC view of (1976): 145-47
    decline of: 8, 179-80
    divorce issue: 17
    election results: (1975) 19; (1976) 21-24, 27-35, 46, 85-98, 151, 207-22, 229, 328, 345-49
    factionalism in: 65, 190-92, 348
    foreign policy issues: 298, 303-4, 310, 317
    hostility to historic compromise: 18-19
    inadequate organizational structure: 183, 199, 204
    leadership problems: 188, 204, 220
    and the mass media: 261, 263, 275-76, 280-84
    occupation of members: 187-88
    on political continuum: 11, 28n, 100-3
    selection of candidates: 51-53, 64n, 192-96
    Senate election (1976): 49-50, 195-96
    social characteristics of: 110-12, 114-15
    target groups: 196-200
    and trade unions: 137, 196-97
    use of patronage: 190-91, 346
    voter image of: 105-6, 108-9
    youth vote for: 215-19
Socialist party, relationships with:
    DC: 21-24, 129-32, 135-36, 153, 159-60, 164, 182, 185, 189-91, 197, 202-3, 220-26, 233, 256, 331, 341, 346-48
    DP: 248-49
    PCI: 107, 157, 172, 185, 189-91, 197, 200-3, 222-26, 336, 340, 345-49
    PLI: 224, 238-39
    PR: 193, 194n, 220, 232, 246
    PRI: 224
    PSDI: 8, 186, 190, 224, 243-45, 256, 347
Socialist Party of Proletarian Unity:
    see Proletarian Socialist party
Sondrio (province): 62-64
Soviet Union: see Union of Soviet Socialist Republics
Spain: 301, 319, 321, 339
Spaventa, Luigi: 27, 66, 193n
Spigaroli, Alberto: 62

Spinelli, Altiero: 27, 66, 70, 174, 193n, 301, 306–7, 310, 319
Spreafico, Alberto: 36
Stagflation: 3, 131, 144
Stalin: 2
Stalinism: 336
Storti, Bruno: 141
"Strategy of tension": 164, 167–70, 230, 235
Strikes: 3, 5, 280
Student movement: 4, 161–62, 194, 198–99, 257
see also Youth
Sturzo, Luigi: 236–37
Subsidies for the press: 271
Südtiroler Volkspartei (SVP): 77n, 85n, 329n
Sweden: 267, 296
Switzerland: 296, 309
Syria: 13n

Tambroni, Giuseppe: 235
Tanassi, Mario: 244–45
Tarabini, Eugenio: 63–64
Tax problems: 85
Television: 204, 239n, 261–63, 265, 273–77, 285–86
Tension, strategy of: 164, 167–70, 230, 235
Terracini, Umberto: 16
Terrorism: 4–5, 133, 136–38, 164
see also Political violence
Third World: 323–24
Italian trade with: 290–91
Togliatti, Palmiro: 14–15, 124, 157–58, 186
Tornabuoni, Lietta: 274
Trade, foreign: 289–91, 324
Trade union officials, as candidates: 52, 71, 141
Trade unions: 3, 15
Catholic: 71–73, 78, 140–41, 161, 197
for journalists: 260
and partisan politics: 103, 110–12, 193, 242
and the PCI: 165, 181, 306
PSI appeal to: 196–97
radicalization of: 4, 131, 137, 157, 160–61, 163
see also ACLI; CGIL; CISL
Trentino-Alto Adige (region): 85, 133, 211, 331
Treviglio (senatorial district): 63–64

Trieste dispute: 302
Turin (city): 21, 23, 27, 46–47, 59, 133, 143–44, 176, 214–16, 250
newspapers in: 268, 271
Tuscany (region): 217

Unemployment: 3, 85, 168
Unified Socialist party (PSU): 229
Union of Soviet Socialist Republics: 13n, 326
invasion of Czechoslovakia: 161, 186
Italian attitudes toward: 107, 245, 295, 309–10, 312–13
PCI attitudes toward: 13, 15, 124, 157–58, 172–73, 297–302, 321–22, 339
trade with Italy: 291
United Kingdom: see Great Britain
United States:
bribery investigations: 5
elections in: 286
Italian attitudes toward: 307–15
and Italian politics: 12, 123, 233, 254, 294, 335
loans to Italy: 291
mass media in: 266–68, 272, 278, 281–82
in NATO: 287, 295–96
PCI attitude toward: 297, 299–300, 305, 322–23
voter participation in: 42, 84
United States Information Agency (USIA): 307n, 315n, 325n

Valence issue, foreign policy as: 288, 294, 313
Valle d'Aosta (region): 45, 48, 91n, 331
Valsecchi, Athos: 63, 139
Varese (province): 27, 62–64
Venice: 27–28, 133, 215–16
Victor Emmanuel III: 234
Vietnam: 301, 308, 310, 314
Voters:
identification with political parties: 98–109
social characteristics of: 109–15
working-class: 176, 187–88, 196, 215, 252, 254, 340, 346
young (see Youth)
Votes:
floating: 99–100, 312

preference: 48, 51, 57, 62n, 74–79, 346
splitting of: 216–17
Voting:
electoral laws: 44–51, 83
participation level: 41–44, 83–84
see also Youth
subsidized travel for: 43, 83

Wage levels: 3, 168, 242n
Warsaw Pact: 172–73, 300
Wertman, Douglas A.: 41, 342
West Germany:
see Germany, West
Women:
in DC: 113, 119
feminist movement: 56, 103, 246, 264, 277
as political candidates: 52, 66, 71, 193–94
PSI appeal to: 196–98
Workers' Movement for Socialism (MSL): 232, 248
Workers' Political Movement (MPL): 184n

Workers' rights bill: 196
Worker's Vanguard (AO): 232, 248
Working-class vote: 176, 187–88, 196, 215, 252, 254, 340, 346

Yalta agreement: 299, 301, 321
Youth:
Comunione e Liberazione: 78, 117, 140, 142, 150, 193, 343
FGCI: 161–62
participation in voting: 19–21, 34–36, 82–83, 113–21, 138, 148n, 150, 215–19, 252
PR interest in: 248
Yugoslavia: 296, 298, 301–2

Zaccagnini, Benigno: 23–24, 59–61, 64, 76, 124–25, 133–40, 145–47, 151–53, 237, 275–77, 280
Zanone, Valerio: 25n, 238–40, 255, 275–76
Zeuch, Giuseppe: 78
Zoli, Adone: 235